# MADMAN

The Poet in Residence writes...

## KNIGHTHOOD

When you turned up at our meeting
The atmosphere was manic
We held it at the Concorde
But it felt like the Titanic!
The Albion ship was sinking
Our loyal crew was there
On the lookout for a captain
With a bit of cash to spare...

You sailed in to the gathering
With your trusty sidekick Mart
Promised us a new beginning
Showed the passion in your heart
So we headed up to London
(To the bloody CBI!)
And together took on Archer –
Looked the bastard in the eye.

And we beat him, sent down Hereford
And in exile simply said
'We're coming back to Brighton' –
Our opponents turned and fled,
No, it wasn't quite that simple
But we did it all the same
Then came glory under Micky –
And now Falmer was our aim...

So you became our Sisyphus
Our stadium was your boulder.
But each time it rolled down the hill
It went back on your shoulder.
The Nimbys, snobs and bat-spotters
Were done, not once, but twice –
You made our dream reality.
A shame about the price.

You gave your time, your guts, your love
(And, yes, a few quid too!)
And every single Albion fan
Knows what we owe to you.
So lead us out at Falmer, Dick.
We'll meet you at the gate.
The one and only millionaire
I'm proud to call a mate!

**John Baine –**
**Attila the Stockbroker**
**2009**

# MADMAN

## FROM THE GUTTER TO THE STARS

## THE AD MAN WHO SAVED BRIGHTON

**DICK KNIGHT**

**with**
**NICK SZCZEPANIK**
**& DAVID KNIGHT**

VSP

Vision Sports Publishing
19-23 High Street
Kingston upon Thames
Surrey
KT1 1LL

**www.visionsp.co.uk**

Published by Vision Sports Publishing in 2013

ISBN: 978-1-907637-58-2

Editor: Jim Drewett
Production editor: John Murray
Design: Doug Cheeseman
Front cover image: Artist Simon Dixon, commissioned by Alan Wares from an original photograph by Roz South

Typeset by Palimpsest Book Production Limited, Falkirk, Stirlingshire

Printed and bound in the UK by TJ International

A CIP Catalogue record for this book is available from the British Library

# CONTENTS

# AN INVITATION

I promised when I took over Brighton & Hove Albion from Bill Archer in 1997 that no one person would ever own and exercise complete control of the club again. Through a combination of economic *force majeure* and Tony Bloom's generosity, over 90 per cent of the club is now owned by one person.

My concern is that the ordinary fan should still have a voice at the club Annual General Meeting and be able to voice their concerns, if they have any. They would have the right to do this if they were shareholders.

I want to make sure that the club is always answerable to the fans, so I would like to make my shares available to you. These shares have a unique place in the Albion's history of course, being the ones that actually saved the club. I don't want to profit from them, so they would be priced at their face value, £1 per share, and you would be able to acquire as few – even just one – or as many (I've got over a million of them) as you like.

At the back of this book is an 'Expression of Interest' form for you to send back to me if you are interested in becoming an Albion shareholder. You will need to send this, along with the 'Dick Knight Invitation' token from the inside flap of the front cover of the book, to the address shown on the form.

The form invites you to tell me something about your history as an Albion fan – that great heritage we all share.

We started this journey together, and this legacy to you, the fans, would complete my dream for the club.

Share and share alike, I always say...

# ACKNOWLEDGEMENTS

I remember once, quite early in my time as Albion chairman, thinking "I should be keeping a diary about all this" as I was thrust into the public spotlight far more than I had ever been as an internationally successful ad man.

I never did. But it's remarkable how much we retain and how much came out as I opened up in discussions almost two years ago with my son David, and later Nick Szczepanik, Fleet Street football journalist and Albion fan, as my writing colleagues in this challenging task.

They were patient, persistent, memory-jogging, thought-provoking, deadline setting – all the things needed to get the best out of me.

They got immersed hearing a new perspective on subjects they thought they knew, and stories and experiences that even David didn't know – enough to even put up with my fastidious attention to detail which often drove them mad. Above all, they were faithful to my words. Thanks David for understanding and getting the whole thing started. And Nick, I can't thank you enough for helping me complete the story.

I also owe a huge debt to Tim Carder. However much of my story I remembered, I could always turn to Tim's *Albion Almanac*, his amazing daily chronicle of all things Albion, to check the detail. The Albion historian is the most dedicated football fan I have ever met, and I am grateful that his narrative recording of our club has included the whole period of my watch, as well as before and since.

To Bill and Jan Swallow, whose design and editorial input during my time at the club was of the highest quality. And Bill's wise counsel and advice has always been much appreciated.

Paul Samrah and John Baine were the unlikeliest leaders of the coalition of Albion fans – the accountant and the would-be anarchist – whose paths crossed for the worthiest of causes. Paul, the best chief executive I never had; John (aka Attila the Stockbroker), the poet in residence whose words had so much feeling.

To all the other fans who fought the good fight, who never gave up believing and who lent their weight where it was needed most: in the battle for people's minds and against mind-numbing red tape.

I couldn't have done what I did without my trusted lieutenants: Martin Perry and Bob Pinnock. Martin was always at my side when we went into battle – good cop, bad cop (our roles depended on the audience) – and, considering our strike-rate, we were a pretty good forward line. And Bob, who set up the same financial controls and reporting systems we had at my ad agency, and who ensured that everyone knew where they stood on their budgets. Usually, it was on tiptoe.

The other directors – Ray Bloom, Derek Chapman, Kevin Griffiths, Chris Kidger who helped me run the club; and to Norman Cook, Billy Brown and the other investors who helped us revive it. To the long-serving club staff – Derek Allan, Sally Townsend, Edward David and Ian Carpenter, who got their mojo back; and other mainstays like Ian Andrews, Matt Hicks and Kevin Keehan who did so much good work.

I thoroughly enjoyed working with Steve Ford and Alan Sanders, the people who made the Albion's community scheme the envy of other clubs. Thanks guys, your leadership gave AITC staff great inspiration for a worthwhile cause.

Liam Brady gave me the inspiration to get involved in the Albion in the first place. The football legend never too big to help save a football club. Liam, it's not just Arsenal fans who love you.

You all know how professional Des Lynam is as a broadcaster; well, he would deliver a voice-over of 18 pages of my script for a club video or DVD in less than an hour, with hardly a retake. Just the odd inflexion or emphasis change, usually at his suggestion. I've directed a lot of famous v/o's on commercials in my time, but no one beats Des for skill and perfect pitch. All for the Albion.

Film director on all those productions was Nick Apostolides, whose creative flair made the Albion highlights packages so watchable and solved many a Christmas present problem. Grateful thanks, Nick, especially for your film history of the club, a fascinating social record of the Albion through the decades with some rare early footage, which will be released on DVD soon and a must for Seagulls fans.

One ritual I always enjoyed was Withdean pre-match lunch at Topolinos with Des, Doug Hillman, Des's lifelong friend, and Mike Payne, cartoonist extraordinaire. Tracer bullets of wit and wisdom flew across the table, followed by our £1 score forecast bet on the game. We always let Des choose first. Great memories, great friends.

And finally, the person who stood alongside me throughout my Albion journey, my dear wife, Kerry. It was she who would listen patiently when I got home after a 0-0 draw away at Hartlepool, as I described every Albion near miss, while she had already seen on *Match of the Day* her idol, Thierry Henry, glide silkily through the entire opposition defence before gloriously slotting home. (Yep, she's a Gooner too!) She's got stamina, my girl. She's also got brains, and I can't tell you how many times her shrewd insights and reading of situations have helped me in the compilation of this book. Thank you darling, so much.

To the rest of my family. Enjoy. To Max, Sam, Emma, Louis, Natty and Daisy, never forget Brighton & Hove Albion is your club. You can tell *your* grandchildren about it.

**Dick Knight**
**October 2013**

# FOREWORD
## BY DES LYNAM

What makes a man give up his lucrative business with frequent trips to New York, Los Angeles, Milan and Rome to take on the responsibility of an outfit which seemed to be on a downward spiral with little hope of success and where his travelling would now more likely involve adventures at somewhat less glamorous places like Rochdale and Darlington? Well, the answer is love, actually; you know that old commodity that we are constantly told is blind.

Was some pulchritudinous siren with tempting ways too much for any man to resist, affecting his change of course? No, it was simply a football club very much down on its uppers with a distinct chance of going out of business.

Dick Knight and I had something in common. We were both fans of Brighton & Hove Albion since boyhood but we had never met. We had both stood on the terraces in different parts of the ground and watched as our favourites reached the dizzy heights of the old Second Division for the first time in the late '50s and followed their various ups and downs through all four divisions of the Football League.

Then years later, by which time I was watching the team only occasionally – little matters of *Grandstand* and *Match of the Day* were getting in the way – I received a phone call from an acquaintance concerned about the Albion. Could I meet with a group who might be able to save the club from probably going out of business? I turned up at a hotel in Park Lane and found one or two people I knew including the recent manager – the former star player, Liam Brady. One person there who I had never met before turned out to be Dick.

I knew the club was in a perilous situation, but I had been involved in trying to raise funds for them before and I was probably somewhat sceptical. However, there was something about Dick's manner I liked, probably without showing it.

Over the next few years, among other things, I found myself presenting a petition at 10 Downing Street, nearly catching pneumonia as I got soaked by fans with watering cans in a photo shoot to emphasise what it was like watching a team where almost everyone got drenched when it rained, and giving evidence in a court hearing as the case was heard for and against a new ground. Dick was a persuasive individual and, although he was not the only one who brought about the Albion's current healthy state, no one could possibly argue that he was not the driving force that made it all possible.

This is not just the story of one man and one football club; it is the heartening and uplifting tale of how an individual with courage and conviction and no little intelligence can win the day when the odds are firmly stacked against. When I saw what he was going through on occasions, I was amazed at his resilience and constant good humour. I would certainly have given up.

Dick's no longer the driving force of the club but he is its conscience and he has quite rightly been honoured with the position of Life President.

He still has the club's interest at heart and says what he thinks which doesn't always make him popular with everyone.

Wherever he goes in football, he is known as the man who saved a football club and, to my knowledge, the only club chairman who whenever he walked onto the pitch received standing ovations from the fans.

But as the title of this book might imply, to achieve all that he did, he certainly had to be just a little bit mad.

**Des Lynam**
**OBE**

# THE ROAD TO FALMER

On July 30 2011, the day of the official opening of the American Express Community Stadium, it took almost an hour to drive there from my house in Hove. That was about four times as long as usual, but I didn't mind putting up with an extra 45 minutes. In one sense, the journey had already taken 15 years.

Back in 1996 I had had a meeting in that same house which set me on the path that would eventually lead to this day. I had sat down with Liam Brady, a true football legend, to come up with a plan to rescue Brighton & Hove Albion, and ended up as chairman, and finally life president, of the club I had supported since I was a boy.

That July morning in 2011, I had helped the mayor of Brighton & Hove unveil the Goldstone Heritage Board in Hove Park, a memorial to the Goldstone Ground, the Albion's former home, paid for by our fans. In a short speech I said that the board was better located in the leafy park, across the road from where the ground had stood until 1997, than in the soulless retail development that had replaced it.

Now I was heading, with my wife Kerry, son David and grandchildren Sam, Emma and Natty, to the inaugural match at our new stadium, a friendly against Tottenham Hotspur. We were driving along the A27 Brighton bypass, a road that had symbolised the border of what was possible and impossible in the struggle to find that new home that I had waged as chairman of the Albion.

The road curls and swerves through the South Downs. Anywhere to the north was a no-go area for a football ground. So were most places to the south, but we had found one. Now, as we drove east down the long, sweeping left-hand bend towards Falmer – that one site – I felt an elation growing in me. I was looking for the view that would hit us as we came out of the cutting. I said: "Everyone, here it comes."

And as we came round the shoulder of the hill on our left, there it was, the first glimpse of the curve of the roof. As we slowly followed the road round, the traffic growing very heavy now, the whole of the stadium came into view in a gradual, thrilling reveal.

By this time the cars were almost nose-to-tail, and people in the crawling lines of traffic alongside us were waving to me. I kind of cut in across the queue onto the slip-road for the stadium, waving my thanks in regal fashion, and then had the cheek to go up the inside lane, which was clear because it was only for cars going to the University of Sussex. Again, when I got to the top I waved graciously as I went to turn right instead and everybody waved back and let me in.

From the road I could see threads of people weaving their way towards the Amex from every direction like lines of ants. The excitement was building up as I was waved up to the directors' car park at the University of Brighton above the stadium.

It was going to be a great day, with the Albion taking on Spurs in a friendly, with the prospect of something even better to come. Seven days later the stadium would host its first League game, when Doncaster Rovers would be the visitors. For me that would be the squaring of the circle, the perfect symmetry for my unusual journey with the Albion. Fourteen years before, we had played the very same opponents in the desperate drama of the last-ever game at the Goldstone Ground, which was also my first game as chairman-elect.

A lot of people want to become chairman of a football club because of ego, because they can afford it, because they work for companies that have bought a club and are parachuted in. In former times they were often businessmen made good, the local mill-owner, as isolated in their directors' boxes from the supporters on the terraces as they were in their oak-panelled offices from the factory floor. They never really had a dialogue with the fans.

At the first FA Cup final at the new Wembley, between Chelsea and Manchester United, I was in an otherwise-deserted gents having a pee when Harry Redknapp came in. He said: "Dick, I was talking about you the other day. You're one of the last of the old-time football club chairmen – a real football man who loves his club. I can't imagine you ever going to be chairman of another club."

And I said: "Absolutely right, Harry."

But there's love and love. If there are 50 shades of grey – or blue and white – then I was at the extreme end of self-flagellation. To volunteer for what I put myself through, you'd have to be a masochist. And it took me 18 months of titanic struggle even to become a chairman in the first place. Some people are eased gently into it by their chequebook or their company's. Mine was a somewhat different story.

I took over when the club was in a bad way, with no ground, impending exile 75 miles away, no realistic plans to return to Sussex, the team hanging on to its Football League place by its fingertips, and the fans having been in open revolt for two years. After the final whistle had sounded at that 1997 game, they dismantled the Goldstone around me, ripping out seats and chunks of the pitch. So in one way I was quite lucky – the only way was up.

Back then I had two idealistically simple objectives in my mind. Save the club, and deliver a wonderful, new permanent home for the Albion. You could argue about the date when objective number one was achieved – when my takeover was finally confirmed in September 1997 perhaps, or when the club came back to Brighton in 1999. But today was the day when objective number two was officially realised.

I wasn't a Jack Walker, let alone a Roman Abramovich or a Sheikh Mansour. I'd made a reasonable amount of money in advertising, but not enough to fund a Premier League title win or bankroll a bid for Europe. The title of this book comes, of course, from the American TV series *Mad Men,* about the ad business that has been half my life. And more than one person thought I was mad to get involved in football, where the only way to become a millionaire is to start out as a billionaire – unless you are a player. To say nothing of exchanging transatlantic flights to New York City's Madison Avenue for trips up the M1 to old York City's Bootham Crescent.

So it was just as well that I wasn't in it for the money, but rather to stand up against the people responsible for the calamitous position the Albion were in. And my main input was not eight-figure sums but the ingenuity that I had used to build up my own advertising agency, along with the determination not to let the club I loved sink beneath the waves.

Advertising is about persuasion, and I managed to persuade other people to help me, tapping into their talents and the love for the Albion that we all shared. Not that, as fans, they needed much persuasion to get behind the cause of saving their club and buy into my vision for the Albion's future. But we also had to persuade many who were uncommitted or downright antagonistic – civil servants, local councillors and MPs. Our campaign even took us to Downing Street itself.

A few years before the new stadium was due to be opened I'd talked to Andy Williamson, the operations director of the Football League, and asked whether there would be any chance of him having a word in someone's ear so that we could start the season with a home game when the new ground was finally ready. And a game that wouldn't be on television, so that we could kick off at 3pm on a Saturday. And it would be great if it could be against Doncaster.

I don't know if Andy remembered, but I think he may have done because now, 14 years after Doncaster had brought down the curtain at our old home, we were looking forward to playing the same opponents in the Albion's first league game at our gleaming new home.

To any Albion fan of a certain vintage, Brighton against Doncaster was a fixture with huge resonance. Like us, Doncaster had had their traumas (although unlike their former chairman, I never torched our old ground – my predecessor saw to its demise). Their difficulties started soon after ours, but they already had a new ground. Five other clubs left their old homes around the same time we left the Goldstone and all five celebrated 10 years at their new stadiums before we even had final permission to build our new home. What we had had to go through was mind-boggling.

Today's match against Spurs would be an exhibition, a test, known as a 'ramp-up' event, where we showed the fans around their new home for the first time. Doncaster would be the game where we brought the heart back, and proved wrong so many doom-mongers who had said it could never happen.

Back in 2007 I had been asked to write a piece for a book about my favourite Albion game. I said at the time that it hadn't happened yet. My favourite game would be the first real game at the Amex.

I had been chairman for 12 years, I'm told the longest tenure in the Albion's history. During that time, the team had won two league titles and another promotion, and also celebrated the centenary that, at one stage, we thought the club would never reach. But my time in the chair was dominated, perhaps defined, by the battle for the stadium, the state-of-the-art arena that would give our great club the chance to compete in the upper echelons of English football for the next 100 years.

I treasure a letter I received from Bill Kenwright, the Everton chairman, that week in 2011. He wrote: "This is just a short note, before you kick off the season in your wonderful new home, to say how very pleased I am for you. We undoubtedly work in a football world that is totally money-orientated, but it's your passion and vision that has got you to this place, and you should be proud of everything you have done. I salute the spirit in you."

But although I had been the chairman of the club, I was also only one fan among the thousands who played a part in the struggle to bring the club back to Brighton & Hove, first to a quirky temporary home at Withdean, and then to this magnificent permanent stadium.

In an era of football club debts, no club owed a greater debt than that owed by the Albion to their fans, because without them the club would not be alive. To an extent this is their story as much as it is mine.

The campaign was unique in the history of world football. The stadium was evidence of the power of football for good as fans all around the country supported our cause. But they would not have done so if the community of Brighton & Hove had not risen up first.

Football is a community thing. For more than 100 years sportsmen wearing blue and white have been heroes to Sussex people – from Charles Webb before the First World War to Bobby Zamora in the early years of the 21st century. For most of that time, the club was a vibrant part of the culture of Brighton & Hove, binding our local people together in a devotion few institutions can match. At its time of need, the fans, the community acted to support and save it. First we survived and then we thrived. And I aimed to repay that support with our award-winning community scheme and by delivering a community stadium the fans could be proud of. Today it would officially open its doors for the first time.

Although this is the story of how I became chairman of the Albion and led the fight to make that stadium vision a reality, nobody is born a chairman. First I was a fan.

# CHAPTER ONE

# EARNING MY STRIPES

My dad came back from the Second World War in 1946. He had had a hard time when he was in the Air Force and football had been far from his mind. But when he came home he told me one of the first things he wanted to do was go to the Goldstone Ground with his son, who by that time was eight years of age.

It was Saturday December 14. We played Mansfield Town, bottom of Division Three (South), who were to crop up on a couple of other occasions in my Albion life, but the most momentous was the first. Although to be honest, I wasn't really excited beforehand because I didn't know what to expect.

I remember walking up the banking behind the East Terrace and, as we got to the top, a feeling of shock as I saw this huge football ground. To my young eyes it looked enormous, but there were lots of empty spaces. The attendance was only 7,666, and it would be a few years before I experienced big crowds packing in there.

The terrace was uncovered, and it was a very cold, wintry day. It was windy and rainy, and the second half was played in semi-darkness because it was before the days of floodlights. It was kind of desolate, to be honest, not inviting.

I remember that there were kids down at the front standing on boxes, because the terrace went below pitch level. And of course there were the wooden rattles which made a loud clicking noise and then together an ear-splitting whirring sound that sporadically broke out when we scored or went close. You could buy them outside the ground, some painted blue and white. And everyone wore hats. You see pictures of northern crowds in those days when everyone is wearing a flat cap, but I remember most of the Goldstone crowd wore trilbies.

But once the game started, it was easy to fall in love with the Albion because we won 5-0. We were very much the better team and George Chapman scored a hat-trick, although I don't remember any particular player dazzling me with moments of skill. Ordinarily a father would be able to point out his favourite players, but these players in blue and white were all new because of the war so Dad didn't know any of them either.

My love affair with the Albion had begun, even though things went down-hill rapidly. That first game turned out to be the biggest home win of the season. We lost the next home game 6-1 to Exeter City, although I didn't go because it was on Christmas Day – and then we played *away* to Exeter on Boxing Day!

In fact, we had such a poor team that the following season we finished bottom of the league. In those days there was no automatic relegation into non-League football, teams applied for re-election to the League and it was usually a case of turkeys not voting for Christmas. All the Football League teams ganged up together and decided that they were going to retain the clubs that were in the League already and not bring in any outsiders. So Albion applied for re-election at the end of the 1947/48 season and were duly voted back in.

When you are young you form your relationship with your football club and if you are a true football fan you never lose that and, despite the Albion's poor form, I was hooked. I went to every game I could, even though the first sign of real quality for me at the Albion didn't appear until August 1948 when we signed Scottish inside-forward Johnny McNichol, who remains my all-time favourite Albion player, for a club record fee of £5,000 from First Division Newcastle United.

Johnny had been kept out of their team since the arrival of England inter-national Len Shackleton, the 'Clown Prince of Soccer', who had scored six goals on his debut for the Magpies. So, Albion fans like me had the privilege of watching a wonderful inside forward playing for the club. He was brilliant, mesmerising. He would show the ball to a defender, nutmeg him, go either way, and he was a goalscorer. Today he would be called an attacking midfield player because he created so many chances.

I think probably my all-time favourite performance from McNichol was in a midweek game against Newport County in April 1951. I went to Hove County Grammar School for Boys, about a mile away – now Blatchington Mill – and when the bell went I had to rush down Nevill Road to the Goldstone for a 4.30pm kick-off, because there were still no floodlights then. It was pouring with rain but McNichol absolutely turned it on. We won that game 9-1 with Johnny scoring four and making the other five.

By this time I'd left my dad behind with the other grown-ups to go and stand in the North Stand, behind the goal with my pals from school. The atmosphere was really intense in there compared to the open East Terrace. It was where the younger people went and where all the loudest shouting and cheering came from, so naturally I wanted to be part of that.

There wasn't the organised chanting or singing that came later – apart from

'Sussex by the Sea' when the Salvation Army brass band played it before every game; it was just 'Up the Albion' and the noise of the rattles, although that made for quite a racket with the low roof trapping the noise and creating metallic echoes off the corrugated iron.

The North Stand in those days felt very enclosed, and it was always packed – not only with youngsters but with the more vocal fans. There were very few women. I used to stand right behind the goal and when Frankie Howard cut inside from the left wing and shot you felt the ball was coming right at you. When we scored there would be an almighty surge forwards, resulting in an exhilarating crush down to the front.

You were close enough to the goal to see the goalkeeper fidgeting and hear him shouting to his defenders, and you saw the physical side of the game and felt the tension in the box at corner-kicks. One of the first games I saw from the North Stand was against Notts County who had Tommy Lawton, the England centre-forward, playing for them. I was close to the front when they got a corner. Lawton didn't just get head and shoulders above our defenders; he was trunk and head and shoulders above our guys. The ball rocketed off his forehead into the net.

I also remember luxuriating in the wonderful aroma of the North Stand. It was the smell of pipe tobacco although I never realised it until years later; to me it was all part of the atmosphere I soaked up as I was watching McNichol nutmeg a Coventry full-back or dummy a Norwich defender and stroll past him.

In the 1951/52 season I went to my first away game – at Gillingham, of all places. Most of the season we were neck-and-neck at the top of the league with Plymouth Argyle, and I decided to go with some pals to our crucial game at Priestfield on February 2.

At the age of 14 it seemed a long way away, a fact which was later confirmed to Albion fans who had to make the journey every other week. We went by train and it seemed to take about two days. My mum even made me some sandwiches for the journey and gave them to me in a red Oxo tin, which made it feel even more like an expedition.

Priestfield wasn't the most exciting ground to visit, but the thrill was in the fact that I was actually watching my team playing away from home. The crowd was around 15,000 including about 5,000 Albion fans – and don't forget that there was no crowd segregation in those days. I stood in front of the main stand with a great view as we won 3-2 and consolidated our second place. We never looked like losing.

On the way back through London we got the pink classified edition of the *Evening Standard* and I was able to read a report of the game that I'd just watched.

I remember thinking that I had a 100 per cent away record. I'd certainly got the taste for away games and after that I also went to see the Albion at Southampton, Reading and Crystal Palace and places like that, although I didn't do the long journeys north.

The biggest away game that season was at Plymouth. I didn't go, but in those days the reserves would play on Saturdays. So I went to the Goldstone to watch us play Arsenal reserves or someone and the tannoy told you how the first team were doing. We'd played well at Plymouth by all accounts and gone 2-0 up but ended up drawing, which summed up the campaign. That was the first year people really thought we could win promotion but we slipped away and finished fifth.

McNichol played for four years at the Albion, but in August 1952 he was sold to Chelsea for £12,000, which in those days was a lot of money. He went straight into the first team and with left-back Stan Willemse, another ex-Brighton player who was also a regular, they won the League title for the first time in 1954/55. I was devastated that McNichol had left, but I was also enjoying an experience that made me the envy of all my Albion-supporting school pals.

In that summer of 1952 two full-backs came to the club, and coincidentally into my life. One was Maurice McLafferty, a Scot who had played for Sheffield United and had been signed to replace left-back Jack Mansell who went to Cardiff (and he suffered by that comparison). The other was a young lad called Roy Jennings, who had been in the Swindon youth team and became a tremendous Albion player and a dominating centre-half.

I'd grown up in Foredown Drive in Portslade and then, in 1947, we moved to Fairway Crescent, which then had open downland at the end of the road, and the old West Hove golf course at the back. Joe Wilson, the Albion's trainer and the brother of Glen, our ironman wing-half, lived about 20 doors down and my mother was friendly with Joe's wife.

Joe's wife told my mother that the club needed to put these players up somewhere on a temporary basis, and before I knew it I was being moved out of my bedroom – but of course I didn't mind if it was for two Albion players.

At 14 and open to hero-worship, I had assumed that top footballers would be distant and aloof, but Maurice wasn't, even though he had played in the Second Division. I quickly got on speaking terms with him and wasn't in awe of him. Roy was different – a young lad who was just starting out, not much older than me, so he had less to say for himself. Years later when I was chairman I met Roy and asked him if he remembered his digs at Fairway Crescent and he said, "Yes, of course I do. How's your wife?" I said, "No, that was my mum – I was the kid hanging on your every word at mealtimes." I'd told him I was nervous in his presence and he said, "So was I. I'd never been away from home before."

But Maurice was much more grown-up, calm and thoughtful, and I would talk to him about the Albion's games. Mansell had been a hard act to follow, so I was slightly embarrassed to talk about Maurice's performances. If he misplaced a pass I was only too aware of it. So we spoke in general, non-specific terms about whether or not we'd deserved to win, and he told me about the banter that went on between players, which you didn't appreciate from the terraces. Most of it he didn't want to repeat exactly to spare my youthful ears, but he'd say things like, "The winger was telling me what he was going to do but his mouth was bigger than his feet."

So the first time I ever spoke to an Albion player was in my own house. It was only for a few months and they weren't there very much, but of course it was fantastic to be able to chat to them, even if it was just to ask them to pass the salt.

Maurice left the club in 1953 and was replaced by Jimmy Langley, who joined us from Leeds United as a left-winger. Manager Billy Lane quickly converted him into a defender and he became about the best left-back that ever played for Brighton – bar Wayne Bridge perhaps – and broke into the England team. He was a wonderful, buccaneering player – very speedy, as you'd expect from a former winger – and averaged about 12 goals a season from left-back.

Eventually Langley went to Fulham and played in the First Division, but also took part in England's humiliation by Hungary in Budapest. Hungary had beaten England 6-3 at Wembley in November 1953, the first time a foreign team had ever won at Wembley, and boy did they create a stir. It was a friendly, but Nandor Hidegkuti, Ferenc Puskas, Sandor Kocsis and company brought a new dimension of lightning attacking flair that completely dazzled England's leaden-footed rearguard.

Overnight, the Mighty Magyars became the heroes of our schoolboy kicka-bouts – most wanted to be the lethal Puskas, but I was always Hidegkuti, the playmaker. They were crucial to my football education. The following summer there was a return game, England got beaten 7-1 and Jimmy played in that team. He was up against these brilliant artists, and any defender would have been in trouble.

Billy Lane did in the end put together a team good enough to get that one elusive Third Division South promotion place in 1958. Albion had to win their final game of the season, at home to Watford on April 30 1958, my 20th birthday, to win their first ever title – but I couldn't be there to see it. I was doing National Service in the Air Force by then and I was based at RAF Coltishall, a fighter command station in Norfolk. It was a 6pm kick-off and around 31,000, just short of what was then the record crowd of 32,000, crammed into the Goldstone.

I had to wait until I could phone a pal who I knew had been to the game to find out the result. When he said, "We won 6-0" my reaction was, "What? How? Did Watford turn up?" But I was overjoyed. Then he added that 20-year-old local boy Adrian Thorne had scored five, including a hat-trick in four minutes. I couldn't believe it – I'd played against Thorne for Hove County Grammar when he was at Brighton, Hove & Sussex Grammar. He later became a teacher and, I believe, had no further involvement in football.

Years later, all sorts of allegations and rumours surfaced that Watford had not exactly tried their hardest that night, but for the Albion it was wonderful and we were in the Second Division for the first time ever. It was a great end to a season that had been clouded for everyone who loved football by the Munich air crash two months earlier, when so many of Manchester United's team were killed on the way back from a European Cup game in Belgrade.

Sadly, I had seen United beat Arsenal 5-4 at Highbury on the Saturday before, and I had also seen Duncan Edwards play for England twice. For me he probably remains the greatest ever British footballer. One of my pals in the Air Force was a big Arsenal fan and I'd gone to Highbury with him and another friend because we had a weekend off. At that time I hadn't seen many First Division games, because of course they weren't on television so actually going to matches was the only way to see big stars such as Edwards. He died in hospital several weeks after the crash, while killed outright were captain Roger Byrne, Tommy Taylor who'd scored two goals against Arsenal, and Eddie Colman and Mark Jones, both in the backline that day. It was a shock that the nation, let alone myself, didn't recover from for a long time.

I also saw the great Billy Wright when my dad took me to Fratton Park in the late '40s when Portsmouth won back-to-back First Division championships. One game we went to was at Easter against Wolves and we were close to the front of that old main stand – which was old even then – and I could hardly believe that I was watching Wright, the England captain. I'd only seen still pictures or black-and-white newsreel film of him. And here he was, a few yards away from me, leading out his team in the famous old gold and black. Then in the '50s we also went to see the Spurs 'Push-and-run' team play at Fratton Park, a fantastic side with Bill Nicholson at right-half and Alf Ramsey at right-back – players I'd only read about. They never passed it more than 10 yards, and the ball always stayed on the grass. I was 10 or so and I was in awe. It seemed to be a different world from the one the Albion inhabited. And there didn't seem to be any aspiration to change that until that season when we finally won promotion.

# CHAPTER TWO

# MIDDLESBROUGH AND MAYFAIR

Going into the 1958/59 season, the Albion's first ever in the Second Division, Billy Lane pledged to give the team that had won promotion their chance at the higher level, so we didn't really bring any new players in during the summer at all. The first game of the season was away at Middlesbrough and the only change was that Dave Hollins, a young Welsh goalkeeper, came in to replace Eric Gill, who was injured. And we lost 9-0.

It's a great pub quiz question: which Football League team played in two successive league games with a player scoring five goals in each? The answer is Brighton, the last game of the previous season when Adrian Thorne scored five and the first game of the next season when Brian Clough, a future Albion manager, did the same.

In fact, we conceded 17 goals without scoring once in losing the first three away matches in the Second Division, including a 5-0 hammering against Liverpool at Anfield, and we also lost the home game against Middlesbrough 6-4, Clough only scoring three this time. But amazingly we still finished up higher in the league than them. Billy Lane brought in a couple of decent players from Arsenal and we did all right, we finished 12th in the table.

It was hard for me to get to many games at this time, although I was able to play a good level of football if not watch as much as I'd have liked. I played for the RAF Coltishall team and one of my teammates, right-back Brian Thurlow, also played for Norwich City.

With Brian in our station team when he wasn't playing for Norwich, we were quite useful and I even had the privilege of playing at Carrow Road in the East Anglia Midweek League cup final against Lowestoft Town, as I later proudly told Delia Smith, the Norwich co-owner, who is now a good friend.

The game was played before Norwich's sixth-round FA Cup replay against Sheffield United, who were in the Second Division. As it happened, our station had a foot in both camps that evening. The United left-back, Graham Shaw, who was an England under-21 international, had been a National Serviceman at Coltishall, so we had two guys from our station who were playing in this game. Because Carrow Road had floodlights, their match was due to kick off at 7.45pm with ours starting at 5pm. When we kicked off there was a smattering of people in the ground but by the time our game ended, which I am glad to say we won, there were about 30,000 people in there. And of course we went on a lap of honour with our Midweek League trophy.

The FA Cup game featured the longest headed goal I have ever seen in football. Amazingly, Norwich went 3-0 ahead before United got a goal back and then threw absolutely everything at their opponents. Ken Nethercott, the Norwich goalkeeper, punched away a corner. He really got behind it and it soared way outside the area towards the halfway line where Gerry Summers, United's left-half, came surging forward, threw himself at the ball and headed it back at rocket pace. It sailed over all the players and into the back of the net. It was about a 50-yard header. Any older Canaries fan will agree that it was one of the strangest goals they have ever seen. City hung on and it stayed 3-2.

I enjoyed my football in the Air Force more than anywhere else. I played inside left – I was the Trevor Brooking of my time, well before Trevor Brooking himself actually played. And as well as Brian, I was lucky enough to play with one of the all-time Everton greats, Alex Young, as we were together during our training. Because people did two years of National Service and you couldn't get out of it whoever you were, you could suddenly find yourself bumping into a really well-known footballer.

Of course, I wasn't in the Air Force to play football. I was in the very last National Service intake to the RAF in March 1957, and most of the other entrants at that time were university graduates; I wasn't because I had taken myself overseas backpacking instead. It was unusual at that time but I'd wanted to go abroad and learn a bit about life. The idea of travelling really excited me.

I'd gone with my friend Paul, also from Hove Grammar School. We'd got down to Spain after a few weeks, and went to Barcelona because we wanted to watch their team, who were pretty good even in those days. They played in the Camp de les Corts stadium (the Nou Camp wasn't built until 1957). When we were in the queue to get in we saw two guys busking who'd been a couple of years ahead of us at school. They'd done the same rites-of-passage type of trip and hadn't gone back.

That was Franco's Spain, but after that we went to the south of France, which was completely different. This was the beginning of the Brigitte Bardot/Roger Vadim era of promiscuity and French coolness. The whole region was incredibly relaxed and a guy we met in Marseilles said, "You need to go to this village called St Tropez, just along the coast." It was just becoming known and we ended up working on a farm nearby with a lot of other student types. I remember being at a party with Manou Bardot, Brigitte's sister, although I never got to ask her to dance.

My father had been a bit annoyed that I'd waived the chance to go to university to go on this trip and then my call-up papers for National Service arrived and I wasn't around. I was in contact with my parents from time to time – usually to get them to send 10 quid or something – so they told me that I had to go back.

I was 19 when I went into the Air Force and they wanted me to take up a flying commission, but that meant signing up for three years rather than two and I wasn't having any of that. Three years seemed an eternity, and my father had seen some terrible things in the war because he would never talk about it, so I was not interested and rejected the offer. So they made me a medic instead, like many others in that final draft who were only serving the basic two years.

The medical training took place up in Wharton near Blackpool, which at that time was the sin city of the North. We had a great time, as you do when you are young and good-looking! In those days a lot of towns and cities in the North had Wakes weeks, when whole cities would come to Blackpool for their designated holiday period. I remember being in the Tower Ballroom one Saturday night with my pals from the RAF station. I looked across the room and saw a girl that I could have sworn was Elizabeth Taylor, the raven-haired beauty who at that time was the number one Hollywood film star, standing at the side of the dance floor. So, after plucking up courage, full of southern bravado, I sauntered over to 'Liz Taylor' and said, "Would you like to dance?" She looked me up and down and replied in a broad guttural Glaswegian accent, "Ask ma friend, I'm sweating."

The RAF gave us an intensive 12-week nursing course and immediately after that I became a flying squadron medic. It was a job that I really came to enjoy and it made me grow up fast. Having come from a nice middle-class family where my parents looked after me, it was a big change to have responsibilities and people relying on me. I was thrown in at the deep end. At times, frankly, we were first at the scene of plane crashes and I saw a lot of things which, at that age, toughened me up.

Once, when I was stationed at Middle Wallop in Hampshire, there was a nationwide Asian flu epidemic. Plenty of people in the camp got ill and some were dying of high temperatures which we just couldn't get down. I remember one particular night in the middle of winter with snow everywhere, we had to drive one desperately ill airman across Salisbury Plain in an ambulance to an army hospital in Tidworth, where he got intensive care and survived. Years later when I was in the advertising business, a guy was selling advertising space to me and I found out that he'd been at Wallop when I was. It turned out he was a mate of the chap we had driven through the snow. Small world.

As my time in the Air Force was coming to an end in 1959, I was thinking about becoming a doctor. I really felt that I could do the job. I was interested in it. I had even been given the task of running of the station sick quarters' morning surgeries. In my white coat and horn-rimmed specs I must have looked the part, but at 19 I was hardly the person to be giving the airmen's wives advice on their marital problems! But the doctors had confidence in me, and I'd been forced to use my brain and act responsibly. It was the first time I had any real sense of what I might be good at. But it would take several years to qualify and I wanted to get out in the world after being in the RAF.

At the same time, one of my Air Force pals was in advertising. He worked in a London agency and because I had always known that I could write reasonably well, I thought that this could be the direction I might go in. My friend had talked about the sort of money you could earn, but it was the idea that you had to use your brain to be creative that intrigued me.

It so happened that the father of my then girlfriend, Margie, knew someone who worked at J Walter Thompson, the top London advertising agency. So I got an interview when I was still finishing in the Air Force at their offices in Berkeley Square, Mayfair. I turned up to do the copy test and was interviewed by the personnel officer, a Polish countess who looked like something out of *The Addams Family*. She was dressed in a long, flowing black dress and had mauve fingernails.

She was very dramatic but must have taken a liking to me. I went for two or three interviews and eventually they hired me, along with Richard Lindley, who later became a top BBC foreign correspondent and presented *Panorama*, and Peter German, who became one of the top men at Colgate-Palmolive. I had managed to get a traineeship at J Walter Thompson which was then effectively the University of Advertising. Today it is still one of the world's best agencies. And I married Margie that year, 1959, on July 4, Independence Day. How ironic.

Margie and I made our home in Hove, which meant commuting, but I didn't mind. It made it easier to see the Albion at weekends. While travelling I learned a lot about people, not least by playing cards for money. I played brag every day with more or less the same group of guys and our game had a defined end – when we arrived at either Victoria or Brighton. I was younger than most of them, not earning much, so I became quite a canny player. I must go up against Tony Bloom some time – I was gambling on cards before he was born!

Once I was dealt an amazing hand – three jacks – just as we passed Gatwick on a Friday night. We were still playing out the hand when we arrived at

Brighton. We always sat at the front of the train and after we'd arrived at Brighton station some of the passengers who'd got off and walked past our window stopped to watch because they could see all the money on the table and three of us betting on. There was a guy called Nat, who was a very hard-nosed player, and Terry, who wasn't so good and at the end of every week would produce an envelope full of 10 shilling notes to settle his debts – which was a condition of being allowed to play. I eventually won with that hand by bluffing Nat who had an even better hand into stacking his cards. So in one memorable game I must have picked up more than £300, and we bought a suite of G-Plan furniture with the proceeds.

In between these morning and evening games, I began learning copywriting as a trainee in the JWT television department which meant writing scripts as opposed to press and magazine ads. We weren't talking Hollywood, though. Television commercials in those days were usually simple pack shots filmed in close-up, with maybe a shot of a delighted housewife about to get down on her hands and knees and scrub the floor.

Commercial television in Britain had only started a few years before, and although the ad business was changing – otherwise they wouldn't have let someone like me in – at JWT it was still run by a lot of toffs and public-school types. One of the account handlers, the people who look after the client's business in the agency, was a chap called Robin Douglas-Home, later to have a well-publicised fling with Princess Margaret, and whose uncle Sir Alec became Prime Minister.

And I got to rub shoulders with some interesting people. Once I was going to a meeting about a new TV ad for Horlicks. I was contributing a bit of the script, doing the captions, although at that time they didn't allow me to write a whole commercial. I got into a lift in Berkeley Square and there was Robin, who brusquely dismissed me with a "Hello Knight". Then a beautiful Swedish-looking blonde lady got in. We all went up to the fourth floor together and it was obvious that we were all going to the same meeting. I thought, "She's kind of vaguely familiar", and when we all sat down she was introduced as Mai Zetterling, a famous Scandinavian film star of the time who was also a TV director/producer at JWT between movies – this time on my commercial!

My first secretary was Pamela Vandenberg, an heiress to the Unilever millions. Like every other secretary in that agency in those days she was a debutante. She was supposed to work for a few of us, but rarely did anything as mundane as typing. One of the only tasks she had all day was to go down to the other end of Berkeley Square every morning, pop into an extremely expensive flower shop, and buy a green carnation for the boss, who wore it on his lapel every day. It was his trademark and that was the sort of world I was entering.

After a while I began going into the TV media department, which was concerned with buying advertising airtime, a completely new science at that time. I kept asking why the ads that I'd helped to write were always shown at the same times every evening. There were ratings books that showed what percentage of the TV audience was watching at any one time, broken down by regions – and don't forget that there was only one BBC and one ITV channel in those days. So *Coronation Street*, which was big even then, and other top shows got ratings of over 80 per cent. I was conscious that you could get better value by buying slots earlier or later in the evening, not at prime time. The TV companies charged much less at different times. Between 6pm and 7pm and after 10.30pm, the price was a third of what it would be at 8.50pm.

The big blue ratings books, called TAM (Television Audience Measurement) books, came out every week and showed graphs of the audiences across the day from the time programmes started – lunchtime in those days through to midnight. I would look at them and say, "Hang on, the viewing figures are as high at 6.30pm as at 8.50pm, why don't we have some spots there?" I was so inquisitive about this that they asked if I'd like to switch to that department, so I said yes. It was another part of the learning curve.

Then in 1961 I was approached by a rival agency, Foote, Cone & Belding, an American company whose headquarters were in Chicago. They offered me more money to work for them as a TV time buyer in London because I was becoming a bit of an expert in this new field. I joined and we pioneered TV audience research computer programmes to evaluate buying airtime for different product markets at different slots in the day.

While I was at FCB I managed to buy the highest-rated spot ever in British television, during one of the first broadcasts of the Royal Variety Command Performance, an audience of more than 30 million people. Frank Sinatra was on it, Sammy Davis Jr stole the show. The BBC didn't have a prayer against the top ITV shows, and the highest-rating ITV region was always the Tyne Tees area. One of our clients was Kleenex, and I bought into the first commercial break in the show on Tyne Tees. The break started out with a rating of 93, and the first slot was for Kleenex tissues. The ratings fell off after the start of the break as people went to the loo or put the kettle on. I was quite proud of that and kept the page from the TAM book.

But while my career was on the up, the Albion were heading in the opposite direction. We'd done okay in the Second Division after that inauspicious start. We fought back and on December 27, while on leave, I saw us beat Fulham, who were promoted that season and had Jimmy Langley playing for them, 3-0, in front of the biggest-ever Goldstone crowd. When they told us the attendance, 36,747, which was a record, I remember thinking, my feet not touching the ground in the North Stand, that it was a bit of a squeeze and they'd surely never cram that many in again.

In the second season, after I had left the Air Force and become a Goldstone regular again, we had a good FA Cup run, reaching the fifth round, where we lost to Preston North End. Roy Jennings came into his own in that season, but he later told me that he had marked the great Tom Finney at Deepdale and hadn't got anywhere near him.

Billy Lane resigned as manager at the end of the 1960/61 season, disappointed that the team had only just avoided relegation. He was replaced by George Curtis, who had been a guest player for the Albion during the war years and was a highly-respected coach who had worked at Sunderland and with the England youth team. His whole vision was about youth. He put a team of inexperienced youngsters in the Second Division and they got annihilated, going down twice in as many seasons to the newly-formed Fourth Division.

Nevertheless in May 1964, the club made one of its best ever moves, in terms of publicity, signing Bobby Smith from Tottenham Hotspur, who had been playing centre-forward for England at Wembley only six months earlier. I was amazed and tremendously excited that Smith was coming to the Albion. He had been a member of the fabulous Spurs side of the early '60s, and played in the best football match I ever saw, against Burnley in December 1960, the season Tottenham won the Double, in front of 58,000 at White Hart Lane. Something told me this game might be special. Spurs were top and Burnley second, so I wanted to be there.

Spurs went 4-0 up in the first 30 minutes and everyone expected a landslide but Burnley were made of better stuff and in the end the score was 4-4. It could have been 9-9. The whole match was played at high pace, much faster than football was usually played at that time, even though it was pouring with rain and on a quagmire of a pitch. Desmond Hackett of the *Daily Express*, who was then the top football writer in the country, called it the 'Game of the Century'.

There was a huge anticipation that the England centre-forward was coming to play for us. There were six gates of over 20,000 – in the Fourth Division – and we won the league with a total of 102 goals. Smith scored 19 and the two wingers got 30 between them – Wally Gould scoring 20 from the right, Johnny Goodchild 10 from the left. Jimmy Collins, the captain, scored 17, and so did Jack Smith – there were goals across the board.

In January 1965 Barrie Rees, in my opinion one of Brighton's classiest-ever players, came from Everton. An attacking midfield player and a wonderful passer of the ball, you immediately sensed he was something special. At 22, he had a big future ahead of him.

We beat Southport 3-1 at the Goldstone on a Friday night in March, and the players were given the weekend off. Barrie decided to go home to Wales and, tragically, was killed in a car crash. It took a long time for the club, players and fans to get over it. He'd only played 12 games but everyone who saw Barrie Rees play knew that we had lost an outstanding young talent.

But the team's attacking style had captured the public's imagination. The biggest attendance at the Goldstone was the last game of the season when 31,423 packed in for a Fourth Division match, which remained a record crowd for years in that league.

All through these years the Albion had that core support of big crowds and I always knew in subsequent years that it was there. The club was on the up, we had some excellent players and no one would have thought that it would be another 36 years before the club won any more silverware – by which time I would be chairman.

# CHAPTER THREE

# BILL SHANKLY'S PYJAMAS

**M**y football education and love of a passing style that I later encouraged as Brighton chairman developed in the late '50s and early '60s when I started going to watch West Ham.

My brother-in-law, John, was a big fan of the Hammers so I often went to Upton Park when Brighton were playing away. In 1958 I saw Bobby Moore make his debut, as well as Martin Peters and Geoff Hurst coming into the team a year later. West Ham were always in with a chance in the cups and although they weren't consistent enough to win the league, they played with an open, cavalier style. At the same time they had some real deep thinkers: Ron Greenwood, the manager, and players like Dave Sexton who subsequently came and played at Brighton, and Malcolm Allison.

Sexton and Allison were the leaders of a group of players who all became managers, including Noel Cantwell, John Bond, Ken Brown and Frank O'Farrell. They would talk football after training at Cassettari's Cafe near Upton Park, and go to Italy to watch games after the English season had ended. Football in Italy was much stronger defensively but with defenders who could attack, everyone with a good first touch, tactics that were totally different based on the catenaccio system which included a sweeper behind a back four.

The Hammers learned and were ahead of their time. They also embraced Italian dress-sense, becoming the first team in England to show their thighs by wearing very short shorts! I loved the way they played – fast, flowing football with the full-backs, John Bond and Noel Cantwell, joining in and scoring goals. They weren't too bothered about defending. But they were playing football that the Albion at that time were just nowhere near.

Of course, the 1966 World Cup was also a wonderful time for me as a big football fan, although before the tournament there actually wasn't a huge expectation that England would do well. There were plenty of tickets floating around the London advertising scene, so I was able to get to all the games at Wembley except the first one, the 0-0 against Uruguay.

The only England players who I sensed were really world-class were Moore, Bobby Charlton and Gordon Banks. I also liked Hurst and Peters because they came from the club I knew more about than any club other than the Albion. I knew they deserved their places because they could play.

It was Portugal in the semi-final which, for me, was the best game of all, because they were a terrific side. Brazil had been literally kicked out of the competition by Hungary, who proved nothing like the team of the 1950s. Portugal were their heirs, and they had Eusebio who at that time was the best player in the world.

It was the first game where the atmosphere really caught fire. It was played on a balmy summer evening in front of 100,000 people, including me and my friend John Hewson from the agency, in the main stand a little below the Royal Box. There was a carnival atmosphere. Banks kept England in the game after flashes of Eusebio brilliance and in the end it was two goals by Bobby Charlton that won it, the second an absolute screamer.

For the final, I was behind the goal at the tunnel end where the teams came out and the end where Hurst scored the third 'goal'. It was impossible to tell whether it had crossed the line at normal speed and from our angle, although my first thought was that it hadn't gone in. The reaction afterwards was unbe-lievable – the tube trains were full of people singing their heads off, and even the German fans didn't seem to mind. I think they thought they'd been quite lucky to get to the final.

The 1960s were not only a great time for me as a football fan – even though my first love, the Albion, were in a bit of a rut after the Bobby Smith season – but also in career terms. In London advertising I was working in an amazing atmosphere. Everyone knew that they were in a business that was electric. And in 1967, these two areas of my life crossed over and led me into a venture of my own that took me inside the world of professional football for the first time.

The whole thing actually grew out of something I had witnessed in 1963 on one of my 'afternoons off' from the Albion at West Ham, and it was one of the first examples of football hooliganism. West Ham got a disputed penalty near the end of a fifth-round FA Cup tie against Everton and an Evertonian kid ran on from behind the other goal. He had a banner that he brandished like a spear and ran the length of the pitch towards the referee, naked to the waist. Eventually the stewards and police caught him and he went off to the cheers of the Everton fans, and next day his picture was all over the Sunday papers, effectively glorifying him. Other kids started to copy him, the media reported it, and the whole thing became the catalyst for hooliganism, which began to spread like wildfire over the next two or three years.

This got me thinking. On the one hand there was this growing undercurrent of hooliganism, and on the other a total absence of dialogue between clubs and their supporters, which was anathema to someone in the communication business. I began to think that we needed to engage with supporters, including the people who might be likely to cause trouble, with something directly related to the game.

I came up with the idea of a 'Men of the Match' competition, in which spectators could judge the players they were watching, giving people at matches a greater incentive to concentrate on the game and get actively involved both during and after. My idea was that people would select their five men of the match in descending order, and would win if their selection matched that of an expert panel. And this would happen at every league ground. It would be a national competition, so you would need considerable prize money, £1,000 each week, which was big money in 1968: the equivalent of more than £25,000 today. It was all based on what people did naturally at matches anyway – talk about the game and talk about the players. I was tapping into what I knew as a football fan.

Through my work, which by now had taken me to Ogilvy & Mather, another big London ad agency, I had connections with a magazine called the *Football League Review*, which was an insert in League club programmes. Harry Brown, the magazine's editor, had been looking for some advertising from Player's cigarettes, whose advertising account I handled. (Yes, in 1968 it seemed like a good idea for a cigarette brand, especially one called Player's, to be associated with sport.)

I saw the *Football League Review* as the perfect platform for my new competition, because it was already in the programme of virtually every League club and had a circulation of 330,000 per week – and it was read exclusively by football fans. Arsenal didn't have advertising anywhere in their programme or at their ground, but apart from Highbury, one Men of the Match ad with an entry coupon in the *Football League Review* could run in every Football League ground in the country.

I devised the basic format. You'd pay a fee of a shilling (5p) per entry for up to seven entries and try to put the top five players in the match in the correct order, as judged by the independent panel. The panel would be the match reporters from the local papers covering each team, together with a nominee from each of the two teams' supporters' clubs, so four in total. The first prize each week would be £750, with £250 for the runners-up. If more than one person agreed exactly with the five selections of the judges at their game, the prize would be shared. Ditto the runners-up prize for anyone who got the first four right. It would be a chance to pit your judgement against that of the experts.

Then I put the idea to Harry as a way of combating hooliganism by giving fans something to think about other than fighting, and getting them to focus on the skills in each game.

Of course, I needed the support of the 92 clubs, which would also persuade the local papers to get involved, so I asked Harry to arrange a meeting with Alan Hardaker, the secretary of the Football League. He was the top dog in English football, the all-powerful boss of the organisation that ran the professional game – this was long before the days of the Premier League, of course. "Give this young bloke a bit of your time," Harry said to Hardaker. "We need the Player's advertising."

Nowadays, of course, cigarette advertising and football seem an impossible combination. Something told me that smoking was unhealthy, but I didn't have a moral stance on it; no one did. There were no health warnings on the packs. The only sporting negative we encountered was the death of the popular motor racing driver Jim Clark in a Player's-sponsored car in 1968. In the TV pictures of the wreckage of his fatal crash at Hockenheim, all you could make out was a Player's logo.

Men of the Match was more of an editorial concept than an advertising one, and it didn't conflict with my work for Ogilvy & Mather, so I decided to set up my own company called Sports Marketing – two words that had seldom been seen together in those days. I rented a small office in Regent Street in the West End.

Harry set up a meeting at the League offices. These were not in London but in Lytham St Anne's, near Blackpool, because that was where Hardaker lived – which gives you an idea of how influential he was. What he said went. He didn't have advisors or consultants. He preserved the status quo. He was a dictator, although he believed he was a benign one who was doing it all for the good of football and his 92 clubs.

The meeting was arranged for 10am. I couldn't afford an overnight hotel stay so I had to get a ridiculously early train from London. At 11am, I was still waiting for Hardaker to deign to call me into his office. After almost two hours, I was eventually summoned into an enormous oak-panelled Victorian-style room that seemed almost Dickensian to a person used to the glitzy world of the London advertising scene.

Hardaker sat there in all his pomp – you felt he should have been wearing a starched collar – no doubt thinking, "Why am I spending valuable time talking to this young upstart from London?" But Harry had obviously done a good job in persuading him, and when I started talking, his attitude changed. I said, "You are the leader of English football. I want the Football League to be the patron of this competition, it has to be a League initiative."

When he realised the potential benefits of what I was proposing, he got interested and said, "How will it work? What do you need me to do?" I said, "If you endorse it, then all the clubs will get behind it."

What he later told me was intended to be a very short meeting ended up as lunch, then another long session in his office. I eventually left at 5pm. He said the League would be patrons and he would send letters to the managers of all the top clubs, including Matt Busby of Manchester United – not yet Sir Matt, of course – Bill Shankly of Liverpool, Bill Nicholson of Spurs, Don Revie of Leeds, and everyone else in the League, telling them to support the new competition. Their clubs would be contacted by Mr Dick Knight, from Sports Marketing of Regent Street.

The result was that I got official club letters from Busby, Shankly and the rest that I could take to every local paper in the land, saying they thought it was a great idea. Just imagine the power of a letter on Manchester United-headed note paper, reading, "Dear Dick, our club will fully support your competition, et cetera, et cetera. Signed, Matt Busby."

It is hard to believe now, but this was one of the first pieces of marketing that had been applied to football, using an understanding of the game to address a problem and get people involved. And Hardaker was brilliant. I would phone him up and say, "Alan, Manchester City aren't getting behind it as much as Manchester United – can you give them a call and gee them up?" The business plan needed 8,000 entrants a week to break even, but I was soon able to revise my expectations. The local newspapers bought into the scheme and it didn't cost me a penny to use their reporters as judges – often they also gave the competition a mention. And Hardaker had not asked for any Football League royalty in exchange for using his games. They gave me free whole-page advertising in the *Football League Review*, but also plugged the competition on their main editorial page, describing it as "the first competition ever devised for testing the skill of football supporters themselves . . . we welcome its inception". And there were announcements over the public address systems before, at half-time and after at all grounds, from scripts I had written. "Don't forget, keep your programme, choose your men of the match, £1,000 to be won every week." All this for nothing.

To cap it all, on the Saturday the scheme launched, in March 1968, Kenneth Wolstenholme mentioned the new Men of the Match competition on *Match of the Day* at the beginning of his commentary – so I was even getting free publicity on the BBC.

In the week before the launch, Harry Brown tipped me off that two of the big football pools companies, who also advertised with him, were so scared of the potential of the competition that they might try to buy me out and kill it.

My brother-in-law, Michael Keehan, said, "Hold out for £100,000 from the pools companies."

I replied, "I'm not selling. It's too good an idea."

These days, of course, it could all be done online or via text, almost instantly. But in 1968, during the week after the launch, three large sacks of mail containing thousands of entry forms and postal orders arrived at my house in Hove, forwarded by Royal Mail from the office in Regent Street. In preparation, I'd hired a couple of students who were good at maths to handle all the admin side – dealing with the entries and the returns from the four judges at each match.

In that first week we had about 15,000 entry forms. I was actually disappointed because I thought there would be nearer 20,000. However, it all worked out because I'd estimated that the average form would have three entries, but it actually turned out to be nearer six, and eventually the numbers did go up to 20,000.

When I was confronted with all this on a weekly basis, it actually began to become quite a burden – I thought I might have to give up my day job to deal with it all, and I didn't want to do that. It was an exciting time to be involved in the advertising business, my career was on the up and I was getting back into the creative side. Eventually, after several of my student helpers had left and it was becoming a pain to keep replacing them, I decided I couldn't keep on with it and the competition stopped at the end of the 1968/69 season. I'd made some money, but before the arrival of the internet it was just too labour-intensive.

Harry was distraught, because he saw it as a circulation-booster for his magazine, but I retained the copyright and I never abandoned the idea or thought about selling it. I felt it was waiting for live television to happen, as has been proved today with invitations to text in your man-of-the-match vote on live games. And when England were drawn against West Germany in a two-legged European Championship tie in April 1972, I saw a perfect opportunity to capitalise.

The format of the 1972 Euros meant that there would be a two-legged quarter-final round between the qualifying competition and the semi-finals, and the first leg at Wembley on Saturday April 29 was going to be shown live, a rare TV treat. For a big European tie against the old enemy, millions of people would be watching.

The *Football League Review* was no longer relevant because this wasn't a

League fixture, so I'd have to put the Men of the Match ads with entry forms in the national press on the day of the match. I called in a few favours from advertising pals in Fleet Street and was able to get some amazingly cheap deals. But to get the public's attention the prize had to go up to £5,000, and I had to get some really big-name judges so that the public would feel they were matching their judgements against the very best.

I thought about the people who had been very helpful to the League scheme. I called Hardaker and got the phone numbers of Bill Shankly and Joe Mercer. Joe had taken Manchester City to the League title and cup success at home and in Europe. They were not only great football men but also enthusiasts for the game who loved talking about it. Hardaker prepared the ground by calling them in advance and reminding them who I was.

I phoned Shankly on his private number. Nessie, his wife, answered.

"Oh yes, Bill's expecting your call, I'll just get him."

He said in that sharp Scottish voice that was so familiar: "Hello there Dick, we're playing in London on Saturday so come and see me on Friday evening at the Russell Square Hotel at 7pm. The lounge will be full of reporters, so go to the concierge and ask for 'Mr Scott' and they'll direct you to my room."

Liverpool were always a big story so he was right about the reporters, several of whom I recognised from their newspaper byline photos, although none of them knew who I was – or so I thought. Peter Lorenzo of the *Daily Mail* did know me vaguely and came up to me.

"What on earth are you doing here?" he asked.

I replied, "Er, I've got a meeting with a client" – which was true, although 7pm on a Friday night was a pretty strange time.

I went to the concierge and said, "Dick Knight, to see Mr Scott."

He said, "Go to the sixth floor, room 615."

So I went up there and knocked on the door of Shankly's suite.

"Hang on, hang on."

He opened the door and couldn't have been friendlier. "Hello young man, come in, sit down. What would you like to drink?"

He was only offering soft drinks so I had an orange juice, and explained I had a file of stuff to show him. He knew the general idea but wanted me to talk him through what he had to do and when. He was enthusiastic about it.

"It's a great idea. I'm honoured for you to ask me as a Scot to make a judgement on England players."

I told him, "Well, you were so supportive of the competition when I was doing it for League games a few years ago."

He said: "It's on live television and I'm the judge – so you'll get a huge response."

"Don't forget there's Joe as well . . ."

"Oh yes, Joe. Good man, Joe. Played for Everton, but never mind."

We talked about football and I mentioned that I liked Trevor Brooking of West Ham, Liverpool's opponents at Upton Park the following day.

"Why d'you like him?" Shankly asked.

I explained that I watched West Ham a bit and I liked their way of playing.

"Yes," he said, "but they're not tough enough."

We talked football for about an hour. Eventually I needed to go to the bathroom and he said it was off the other room of the suite, through the bedroom. I went into the bedroom and couldn't believe the sight that greeted me.

Laid out on the bed was this pair of silk pyjamas in bright red – the colour of course of the Liverpool strip. And on the left breast was the club crest – the Liver Bird. I must have been transfixed because after a while he called out and said, "Are you all right?"

I said, "I'm just looking at your pyjamas."

He came in. "Don't you like them?" Then he picked up the top, turned it round and said, "Look."

On the back was a white No.4 – his number when he'd been a player. There was no name above it because shirts then only had numbers.

He laid it back down. "Aren't they great? You're the only person who knows about these pyjamas apart from my lady wife Nessie and me."

I said, "Bill, I swear I'll never tell anyone as long as you live." Which I never did.

The following day I went to meet Joe Mercer, who was then general manager of Manchester City. They were playing at Coventry, so Joe invited me to meet him at Highfield Road.

I went up with my son David and Joe couldn't have been nicer – very avuncular and self-effacing. So much so, in fact, that it was hard to imagine him motivating a team until you realised that he and Malcolm Allison had won almost everything with City by playing good cop, bad cop.

There was none of Shankly's spikiness, none of the aphorisms – just a calm, quiet intelligence that seemed to wash over you. He immediately saw what was required and he was only too happy to help. He appreciated the reason for the competition.

After the game was played they got their nominations in straight away. Shankly just gave me the five names, while Joe explained his choices in detail. And we got 36,000 entries, more than enough to make a good profit.

By the way, neither asked me for a penny. They were both happy to help someone trying to do something helpful to football. Even if you had told them then the fee they could have earned now – negotiated on their behalf by an agent – they probably wouldn't have cared. They felt lucky to be in key positions in football and never asked, "What's in it for me?" There are very few people like that in football today.

As well as bringing me into contact with these legends of football, my experiences with the Men of the Match competition gave me some insight into the way the game worked, and in some cases didn't work, at the top level. The more I saw of the way football was run at the top level, the more I realised how naive it was. The administration of an incredibly popular sport was based on old institutional principles that hadn't really changed since the Football League was formed in 1888. Harry Brown was the PR man, magazine editor, advertising manager – everything. Football was being run almost like a corner shop.

I was bringing them new thinking and their willing acceptance reflected the fact that the game was being run by people who had no idea of football's commercial or social potential. When I became chairman of the Albion almost 30 years later, I found that things hadn't moved on quite as rapidly as I might have expected.

As for the results of the 1972 Men of the Match competition, the best player was never in doubt. Günter Netzer, the long-haired Borussia Mönchengladbach midfield player, was majestic for West Germany that evening and scored one of the goals in their 3-1 win. He strolled around, had time on the ball, stroked it here, pinged it there. They completed the job against England with a 0-0 draw in the second leg in Berlin, and went on to win the tournament easily. Sir Alf Ramsey's tactics were looking threadbare. Perhaps England needed someone like the brash but talented manager at Derby County.

# CHAPTER FOUR

# CLOUGH COMES TO TOWN

I n 1973, Brian Clough was one of the most skilled managers in the game, but also the most outspoken. He had proved his ability by taking Derby County into the first division in 1969 and then winning the League Championship only three seasons later.

But Clough had fallen out with the chairman at Derby, Sam Longson. Clough was then doing an awful lot of television and was becoming too big for his boots in Longson's eyes. Because he'd won the League title for Derby, Clough thought that he could do what he liked, but Longson decided enough was enough and sacked him.

The chairman of the Albion at this time was Mike Bamber, ably assisted by Harry Bloom, the vice-chairman, and Keith Wickenden, who was Bamber's right-hand man and finance director. They made a very good combination. Bamber and Wickenden brought a new kind of vision to the Albion because they were moving with the times and could see that it was possible to use property development as a means to fund a football club. But nobody really grasped the scale of Bamber's ambition for the club until he announced that Clough would be the new manager of Brighton.

People were even more dumbfounded by this than they had been when Bobby Smith had arrived a decade earlier, and so was I – totally amazed. It was an astonishing coup for Bamber, but also a statement of intent. It showed he wanted our club to go somewhere. Not only did he hire Clough but also Peter Taylor, his right-hand man and a great talent-spotter. The Albion were the talk of football and on the back pages of all the papers.

My first thought was that it was fantastic. But I soon began to have misgivings. The fans were hypnotised by the idea of having Clough as the manager, but anyone expecting the team's performances to improve to Derby County levels was to be disappointed. They hardly improved at all.

Even when Clough was pictured sitting in the Goldstone dugout with his son Nigel, I never thought he seemed genuine. Through my contacts in television, I was hearing stories about his huge ego and arrogance that began to worry me. I assumed that he wouldn't have come to Brighton unless he was being paid big money, and I later learned that he also took liberties with Bamber's goodwill.

If you talk, as I have done subsequently, to some of the Albion players who played for him, they really didn't have much time for him because his attitude was: if you are not good enough, then I'm not going to bother with you at all. He was now dealing with Third Division players but he expected the same from them as he had done from First Division players.

The thing is, many of those players had played in a team that had got promotion to the Second Division only two seasons before, in 1972, under Pat Saward – a terrific, entertaining team. Ever since I've supported the Albion, we've tended to be an attacking team, slightly cavalier, and Saward's team took it to extremes.

We scored a lot of goals and one of my favourite strikers was Alan Duffy, even if he was quite tubby: he loved a pint or two. Once we stood on the East Terrace level with the penalty area and we were right in line with Duffy when Peter O'Sullivan slipped him into space between two defenders and he slotted the ball home. The linesman, right in front of us, put his flag up for offside and there was this stunned silence before the crowd started booing. In that split-second my mate, Don, shouted out, "Hey linesman, Duffy wasn't offside – his stomach was."

Going into our final game that season, we had just needed a draw at home to Rochdale to secure promotion. It was an evening match in front of 34,766 and once again I missed out on seeing the Albion promoted. I'd been working in London and the train was late getting into Hove. I knew then that I had no real chance of getting in. When I walked along Newtown Road from the station I could see huge queues, and when I turned the corner by the church, from which you could see down into the ground, it was obvious that it was already packed. The North Stand was a sea of humanity.

Even the front gardens along Goldstone Lane, where people used to go to get a free view over the back of the East Terrace, were so packed you couldn't get in. I went over into Hove Park and followed what was going on from the roar of the crowd, but that was frustrating, so I went home and listened to it on the radio. We scored early on through John Templeman and it finished 1-1 so were promoted for the first time since 1965, behind Aston Villa, who were champions.

Sadly, Saward's team were out of their depth in the Second Division. The players just lost heart and went on a run of 12 successive league defeats from November through to February. The team finished at the bottom of the league, quite a bit adrift from everyone else, so it was back to the Third Division. And when the next season didn't start much better, Saward was sacked by Bamber, who had become chairman the previous Christmas, having been a director since 1970. Then Bamber made his big move.

But players like Ken Beamish had proved they deserved better than their treatment by Clough. Later, when we were preparing a DVD history of the club, Brian Powney, the goalkeeper, told a story about Beamish getting injured in one game. Clough told him, "You're all right, just put your boot on and go back on." And then the trainer said, "He's damaged his ankle," but Clough said, "I don't care, get him out there." It turned out he had badly damaged his ankle ligaments and Beamish never played for the Albion again. He left and joined Blackburn and helped them get promoted.

I remember seeing a wonderful picture of Bamber, Bloom and Clough on the terraces at the Goldstone, signed by all three of them – but both Bamber and Bloom look as if they are thinking, "What's he going to say next?" They looked a bit in awe of him.

There was one incredible week when we played at Walton & Hersham in an FA Cup first-round tie and drew 0-0. The replay at the Goldstone was a few days later. It was an afternoon kick-off, at 2.30pm, and that was the day I realised for myself what was going on.

My work stopped me going to the game, but I was going in late to the office because I'd been to the dentist. My train got into Victoria at about 1.20pm and it was due to go back to Hove at about 1.45pm. As I was walking towards the barrier at Victoria, who should be strolling down the platform the other way but Clough, on his own with a paper, looking like he didn't have a care in the world.

I thought, "What the hell? Why aren't you down in Brighton by now? This train is not going to get in to Hove until half-time." That was what Clough did. Albion lost 4-0 at home, to a non-League team. And if that wasn't bad enough, three days later we played Bristol Rovers in the league at home. Rovers were not a bad side, but we were a rabble and they whacked us 8-2. To this day that is the biggest home defeat the Albion ever had. The humiliation was made even worse by it being the featured game on *Match of the Day* that evening.

And so in the space of half a week, Clough's team conceded 12 goals at home. The fans were seeing right through Clough and it wasn't too long after that that he left to go to Leeds.

But for Brighton, that Bamber era put the club in the headlines in a way it had never been before. Clough said later that Bamber was the best chairman he had ever had at a football club. Perhaps that was because Bamber let him get away with whatever he wanted. But getting Clough definitely gave the club a higher profile and it was the prelude of course to the start of much better things. Taylor declined to go with Clough to Leeds because he wanted to have a crack at managership on his own, and he put together a very good Brighton team.

One of the key players was Peter O'Sullivan, an excellent wide player who came from Manchester United because a winger called George Best was keeping him out of the team. Taylor encouraged him as a playmaker and 'Sully' became a lynchpin in the side for over a decade.

Taylor's strength in his partnership with Clough had always been his ability to spot a player, and he carried that on with the Albion. His two best signings, who both made their debuts in March 1976, were Brian Horton from Port Vale, a hard-tackling box-to-box midfielder who was also a great leader, captain (and later manager), and one of the all-time Albion heroes, Peter Ward.

After Taylor left to join up with Clough again at Nottingham Forest in July 1976, Bamber replaced him with Alan Mullery, which was a very, very good move. Mullery added drive and motivation to the very good squad he inherited from Taylor and got us promoted in 1976/77, the first year he was in charge.

It was a tremendous season, very exciting. Mullery's team were near the top the whole season and had a fantastic run in the League Cup. In the third round, I remember driving up to West Bromwich Albion from my office in London with a couple of mates, one an Albion fan and one a Baggies fan, a client in the record business. It was a foul night and the traffic on the M1 was awful so we got into the game 15 minutes after the start by which time Brighton were winning 2-0, both goals courtesy of Ward. He was absolutely dazzling that night and the game could have finished 5-0 to Brighton instead of 2-0. Third Division Albion absolutely outplayed the First Division Albion and Brighton fans knew that they had a very special team.

There was also a truly memorable game at the Goldstone against Walsall in October on another foul night, when the half-time score was 0-0. Final result: Brighton 7 Walsall 0, the goalscorers Ward 4, Ian Mellor 3, all seven goals coming in 28 minutes. Those of us who were there will never forget that game. Ward got 36 goals that season, 32 in the league and four in the League Cup – a club record that stands to this day, although Bobby Zamora got close a couple of times.

The question was whether we could do better than we had the last time we went up to the Second Division, when we finished bottom and came straight down again. The answer was yes, and part of the reason had been glimpsed in February 1977 when we played Preston at the Goldstone.

I remember standing on the East Terrace and saying to my son David, "That centre-half is exceptional." I was admiring this youngster's reading of the game and couldn't believe how good he was. Anyway, to my delight, after we'd clinched promotion, we signed Mark Lawrenson.

I used to say to my advertising colleagues in London, who always had a laugh with me because my team was Brighton rather than Spurs or Arsenal or Manchester United, "We've got a player who's as good as Franz Beckenbauer." They all said, "Oh yeah, and pigs will fly, and Brighton will get to the cup final."

The fact is that he was as good or almost as good as Beckenbauer, the legendary German sweeper. Lawrenson was 20 and had already played international football for the Republic of Ireland. Eventually, when he was at Liverpool, he was so good he would have walked into the England team. Even with us he was outstanding, arguably the finest player ever to play for Brighton.

We finished the 1977/78 season in fourth place in the Second Division, level on 56 points with Spurs, who went up in third place. As Brighton played their last game at home against Blackpool in front of over 33,000 people, Spurs and Southampton were playing at The Dell. It suited them just fine to draw 0-0 so that they'd both be promoted, meaning we would miss out, even if we won – which we did. Sure enough the result was 0-0 after Spurs and Southampton basically passed it to each other in the centre circle and every now and then back to their keepers.

After another great season in 1978/79 we had to win our last game, away to Newcastle, to seal promotion to the First Division for the first time in the club's history. I went up with Bob Pinnock, one of my business partners. Bob and I had known each other since we were kids together at Hove County Grammar School back in the 1950s – he was a speedy winger in the house team running onto my probing wing-half passes – and Bob had been an Albion fan for just about as long as me.

While I had gone into advertising, Bob had become a chartered accountant, and we lost touch for a few years. But then the Albion brought us back together. From the 1970s onwards, we had watched hundreds of games in tandem – mostly from the East Terrace at the Goldstone. And then Bob got involved in my business: in 1977 he became the financial director at my ad agency, Holmes Knight Ritchie, and later would join my consortium and then become the financial director of the Albion.

So Bob and I went up to Newcastle and stood in the Leazes End, which was packed by 1.30pm for the 3pm kick-off. There must have been 9,000 or 10,000 Albion fans there. The thing I remember, apart from the game which was a done deal at half-time with us 3-0 up, was something aptly bizarre. When Argentina hosted the World Cup in 1978, whenever they ran out onto the pitch, a waterfall of paper always cascaded down from those near-vertical terraces. The team, the pitch and everything ended up covered in confetti and strips of paper.

The Albion fans had decided to do the same thing when Horton led the team out at St James' Park. While we'd been waiting, Bob had been passing the time reading the *Financial Times*. So when the Albion emerged from the tunnel, a huge mass of blue-and-white paper was hurled into the air and then fluttered down, except where we were standing where the paper was pink. I don't think the FT has ever been torn up at a football match before and used to shower the gladiators.

One of our young fans standing in front of us shouted, "Oi mate, don't tear up the share prices page yet, I want to check my investments." Brilliant.

Reaching the top flight for the first time in 78 years was the pinnacle of the club's achievements. For many of us, it was a dream that was hardly believable. You felt as if you were going to wake up any moment. To put it in perspective, in the 12 years we were at Withdean, from 1999 to 2011, we won four promotions. But I'd had 12 years to wait watching Albion from when I first went before we won one. Then there was 1965 and 1972, but they were short-lived successes; nothing like this had ever happened.

In a way you could say it was overdue. Even at the worst times, always for me there was this incredible kind of spirit around the Goldstone. Loyalty to the Albion was really more based on a love of the club, which all genuine fans have, than results or status.

Part of this feeling was because we were the only League club in Sussex, or we were until recently. It's no coincidence that 'Sussex by the Sea' is our rallying cry. People all across the county have a special affection for the Albion. But I believe it also goes back to the pre-war years. I used to hear my grandfather speak about the club's cup exploits in those days. They were always a Third Division team until 1958 but could usually be counted on to put up a fight in the FA Cup. They beat First Division Everton, Chelsea, Sheffield United and Oldham, and also won the Charity Shield in 1910, against the league champions Aston Villa. Huge crowds would pack into the Goldstone for big cup ties, which showed how many people were out there waiting, wanting to come.

We were almost permanent underdogs in those days, fighting against the odds, but from time to time there were also special players: Tommy Cook, who came up through the ranks in the 20s and played centre-forward for England, Johnny McNichol, Barrie Rees, Peter Ward; and managers like Billy Lane and Alan Mullery, whose teams played thrilling football. So there was always a glimpse of what could be, a hint of something waiting to be realised, both on and off the pitch.

# CHAPTER FIVE

# HELLO BOYS

D uring the decade Bamber was on the Brighton board, I had set up my own advertising agency, Knight Keeley, and its trajectory had been steadily upward, in parallel with the Albion's.

I had been earmarked for future promotion to the board at Ogilvy & Mather and had become an account handler, which was at the suit end of the business, working on some pretty big accounts – Rowntree's, Gillette and Cunard.

It was working with the cruise ship line Cunard that first took me to New York. They were beginning to look more to the Caribbean for their cruises and were concentrating their business in the United States, so I had to work closely with our office in Madison Avenue, going there regularly in 1969. David Ogilvy, our legendary boss, was the first British ad man to make an impact in America, and I got to talk to (and sometimes disagree with) him about what makes good advertising.

There was an incredible buzz about Manhattan and the ad business in America in the '60s, as the hit TV series *Mad Men* showed. If you were any good you got recognised. Promotion was not by rote or age or according to what school you went to. You worked long hours, you smoked and drank, but it was a meritocracy. You could see why they talk about the 'American Dream'. And the entrepreneurial spirit in me was beginning to take hold again. I began thinking about starting a London agency of my own. Although I was earning a decent salary, I knew that I was bringing in much more revenue for my employer.

The time to make my big decision came in 1971. I used to travel up to London with a friend called Don Baldey, who was an ad visualiser. One day somebody we knew who was doing some technical work for a new plumbing/ drain unblocking company called Dyno-Rod approached us and said they needed some marketing help. I met the boss, Jim Zockoll, a self-made American and an absolute character. His day job was flying Pan Am jets across the Atlantic. That company was to figure large in my future, but meanwhile Jim had borrowed the unique 'flying wing' lettering style from their logo for his new drain-clearing venture.

He wanted Dyno-Rod to spread out round the country but had only a minute budget, so I said they should advertise on the London Underground because so many people going from city to city have to cross London by tube.

Before long I'd become Dyno-Rod's freelance marketing guru in addition to my full-time job with Ogilvy & Mather. They were expanding quickly on the back of one of our ads – 'Dyno-Rod guarantees complete satisfaction, or your blockage back' – and wanted me to take the account into O&M. But it wasn't quite as prestigious as Cunard, so I gave it to Don, who was a freelancer, although I said I'd help with the writing. However, Dyno-Rod wanted more service and promised me the account if I opened my own agency. When I confided in Cunard and sweets manufacturer Rowntree's, they as good as promised me they would give me some business as well.

I talked to a creative colleague at the agency called Jim Vakeel, a real gentleman of the world. His father had owned and then sold the harbour rights in Bombay, now Mumbai, to P&O so he was fairly well-off. Jim went to Marlborough College where he got expelled and then Oxford, where the same thing happened – he was 'sent down' as they call it there – but he was an elegant writer who had some interesting connections. His mother was a couturier with salons in Sloane Street, on Rodeo Drive in Beverley Hills, and in Paris. She dressed Sophia Loren, Liz Taylor and the wife of the Aga Khan.

Jim was up for joining me, and so was Don, a production guy, Graham, and my secretary Shirley, from the agency. The 'Keeley' part of the company name was a combination of 'Vakeel' and 'Baldey'. In the end we didn't get Rowntree's or Cunard – they probably thought it was too risky – but we pitched for the Air India account and then the Indian Government tourist office account and won both, so we'd got started. And if Dyno-Rod wasn't a glamorous start, things improved pretty quickly on that front.

We began in the basement of Jim's house in The Boltons in Chelsea – you couldn't get a more exclusive address. Within a couple of months we got a top Swiss watch account, Jaeger-LeCoultre – very upmarket watches and timepieces. They had produced a range of limited-edition beautiful silver clocks and we said they should have special presentation cases.

Jim's mother was friends with the great Paolo Gucci, founder of the dynasty, and arranged for us to meet him in his original shop in Florence, where he was based. This kindly old gentleman in a pullover, master of Italian design, accepted my agency's first-ever packaging brief. He designed six different beautiful cases in blue-grey pigskin lined in dark blue velvet, and I used my Cunard connection to arrange to hold the launch on the QE2 in mid-Atlantic.

We were pretty good at what we did, and we weren't afraid to innovate. I'm pretty sure my agency was the first to use television to advertise records. My brother-in-law, John Coletta, who had also been in advertising, and a friend had decided to take a punt on the music business and, as managers, had launched Deep Purple. The band soon became huge in the States but John wanted to make the same impact in the UK. I approached Larry Krieger, the owner of the Harlequin record shops in London, and we launched a joint TV campaign with them for Purple's new album, *Machine Head*, taking advantage of much cheaper local advertising rates.

We filmed a live gig of theirs at the Hollywood Speedway and used the footage to make the ad. One of the cameramen got a bit too close to Ritchie Blackmore during one of his solos so he smashed his guitar into the camera. We kept that shot in the commercial – and in March 1972 *Machine Head* went straight into the UK charts at number one. People in the music business took notice of this and Polydor Records approached us to do the same for one of their albums – a compilation of music from *The Strauss Family* TV programme. It began a long client association with record companies.

But I was always keen on radio advertising, which was very powerful in America and a medium I knew was very involving. It was theatre of the mind because people used their imaginations to create pictures for themselves. I wanted to use new voices and had the idea of using Malcolm Macdonald, the Newcastle and England star, who was quite a personality, to do the voiceover for some commercials.

I got his number from Harry Brown. Malcolm was keen and I went up to see him at St James' Park at an evening game against Leeds United. We were going to do the recording locally the next day. He was friendly with Duncan McKenzie, the Leeds forward, who stayed on after the game. We all met up in the players' lounge afterwards and went out to a nightclub.

On our way out through the car park, we passed a big Jaguar with a black-and-white mascot hanging in the back window. Malcolm said, "See that mascot? When the car turns left, its right foot kicks. When the car turns right, the left foot kicks. Whose car do you think it is?"

"I haven't a clue, Malcolm."

"It's the manager's, Gordon Lee."

Later Malcolm told me a story about Lee and a young Newcastle player called Aiden McCaffrey. After one game, Lee told McCaffrey, "Aiden, you've been playing so well that I've recommended you to Ireland."

McCaffrey said, "But gaffer, I'm not Irish."

"With a name like Aiden McCaffrey? You must be."

"No boss, I'm English."

Then Tommy Cassidy, who was a real character, chipped in, "Your name's Lee, boss – did you play for China?"

I liked Malcolm a lot. He was his own man and he enjoyed the limelight, but he was very intelligent. He had opinions and could talk about anything. He went from Tonbridge to Fulham as a left-back before Bobby Robson, the manager, tried him out at centre-forward, and he never looked back.

Well, almost never. In one of his first games up front he got in the way of a goal-bound shot by Johnny Haynes and tried to score himself. As they were going off at Craven Cottage at half-time, Haynes caught up and said, "Don't ever do that again or you'll never get another pass from me as long as you're here." Malcolm moved on to Luton within a year.

The agency kept developing. Art director David Holmes joined as creative chief in the mid-'70s – the quintessential English gentleman, a brilliant illustrator and watercolour artist, and a great influence on me and the agency in the years to come. So the name changed to Holmes Knight Keeley, then later Holmes Knight Ritchie because Vakeel left, deciding he wanted to live in Geneva, where we had an office.

Alasdair Ritchie became our new partner, a Scot from the right side of the tracks – his father had been chairman of Bowater-Scott, a huge conglomerate. Alasdair could play golf off scratch, which always comes in useful in advertising. Our backgrounds were like chalk and cheese but we hit it off and in a new business pitch we instinctively knew which of us would suit that client best.

The next step was to go international. In 1985, I sold 40 per cent of the company to Wells Rich Greene, a New York agency who wanted a European presence. They were owned by Mary Wells, the first female chief executive of a company listed on the New York stock exchange, and the first woman ever on the cover of *Time* magazine. She had married a client, Harding Lawrence, the boss of Braniff Airways, and their address was 1 Park Avenue. They invited me to dinner where they had an elevator that went directly from the entrance hall straight into their lounge.

While keeping control of the company, we got access to the American market and picked up our biggest client yet, Pan Am. On the first trip I ended up having breakfast with Boris Becker, who had just won his first Wimbledon title, and Mats Wilander, both staying at my hotel while playing in the US Open. One morning the only free seats were on my table. I'd nodded to both of them in the lift and so we got talking. "Who are you playing today?"

Our link with Wells Rich Greene meant that I might have spent two or three days in New York or Milan but always made sure that I'd arrive back at Heathrow on the 'red-eye' flight on a Saturday morning, so that I could get off the plane and come down to Hove, get into my house, have a quick shower and change and then go over to the Goldstone. The glamour and pzazz of Madison Avenue or the Piazza del Duomo was followed immediately by a reality check at the Albion.

By now I'd moved from the North Stand back to the East Terrace. I never went as far as the West Stand because I didn't like the idea of sitting down. I wasn't the prawn sandwich type of fan. I stood in the open air and quite often had long chats with Bob Pinnock.

For years Bob and I would catch up on the previous working week while watching the game. For 100 or so minutes our conversation would bounce between what was going on down on the pitch and what was going on in the agency. I often wondered what the regulars nearby on the East Terrace made of this bloke always arriving five minutes after kick-off, then spending the rest of the game prattling on about some brilliant ad campaign he'd sold or deal he'd done in New York, interspersed with the occasional shout of "In the channel, Sully" or "Nice one, Lawro" as Lawrenson exploded from the back on one of his audacious forward runs. Wardy was dazzling the opposition and I was telling Bob about the dazzling I'd been doing in New York.

It was my escape valve, a perfect way of relaxing. I never consciously felt under any pressure in the advertising business, because I wouldn't have been able to be successful at it if the pressure had got to me. But maybe the Albion helped to make sure that stress never built up, even if I'd been in America twice that week, New York and back in a day. I still had the passion for it, the annoyance when we got hammered − all the things that real football fans share.

I worked in London, I worked in New York, I worked in Milan, wherever − I could have supported the Arsenal, Chelsea, Spurs but I didn't, I supported the Albion, because they were my team. But at that time I never had any inclination whatsoever to get involved in the club.

In 1990 I had got out of our relationship with Wells Rich Greene and joined up with another American agency, TBWA, who had a better-established European network. The 'T' was William Tragos from the USA, 'B' was Claude Bonnange from France, 'W' was Uli Wiesendanger, a German, and 'A' was Paolo Ajroldi, an Italian.

They invited us to be their London arm, and I sold them the 40 per cent I'd got back from Wells Rich Greene for another few million. We immediately became the lead agency for their European operation and, with our own organic growth, won the accounts of some top clients: Absolut Vodka, Evian, Mercedes, Nikon, Grolsch, Sheraton and later Nissan Cars, who became our biggest client. And we still had Dyno-Rod.

We did brave, sometimes startling, often award-winning stuff. For the launch of the Nissan Micra we created the first ever all-cartoon campaign for a car known as 'The Shape'; we hired the special effects expert from the movie *Poltergeist* for our 'You can't top a Grolsch' campaign featuring its special cap, to recreate the house destruction scenes when the spirit gets mad because he can't open a bottle in the fridge. For the launch of a new European business airline that had a brand new fleet from a famous plane manufacturer, we had huge 96-sheet posters in major cities with headlines, "It's all business class on this Fokker" and "It's a Fokker to get to Paris". At the time when American football was all the rage on British TV, one of the ads I did promoting the frequency of Pan-Am's 747s to the Big Apple, on the front page of *The Sunday Times*, announced, "More New York Giant Jets." For The Macallan Malt Whisky we did arguably the least ad-like ad of all time: no brand name, no packshot, no copy, no visual – alongside *The Times* crossword there was this blank ad space with one extra clue: Down. 1 (3,8). (Come on, you can figure it out.)

And we worked for small brands too, helping them to get off the ground with some groundbreaking stuff. A cinema commercial showing sepia shots of old couples, captioned 'Mr and Mrs Hitler, parents of Adolf', 'Mr and Mrs Stalin, parents of Josef', etc., finished with the voiceover, "If only they'd used Jiffi Condoms." That sort of work certainly made people sit up and take notice.

But the campaign that became best-known, and which was most often mentioned when I launched the battle to take over the Albion, was Wonderbra. The brand was owned by Playtex, but they had licensed it out to Berlei. Neither really knew what to do with it, and when we were asked to take the account in 1992, because by that time we could pick and choose, we wanted to do it on our terms.

Nearly 60 per cent of our staff were women, so we got them to try out the Wonderbra, and the reaction was universally positive. Then we looked at all the other bra advertising by the competitors. It was either based on the construction of the bra itself, or on pure sexism. 'Cross your heart', comparing it to the aerodynamics of a 747 – or showing a woman in a bra lying in hay, Jane Russell-style.

We decided to do it a different way, with wit, and to make the woman the dominant figure in the advertising, the person controlling the situation. She would be delivering the line. A simple, bold line. Somebody suggested, "Say goodbye to your feet." In the end "Hello boys" was the one we went with first, and the one everyone remembers. It was English advertising at its best: intelligent, using language, using humour, not treating the consumer as a moron.

The budget was only £150,000, so we decided to launch with a small number of very large poster ads, 96-sheet posters, in prime 'fender-bender' sites in a few British cities, meaning cars bumping into each other because the drivers were so transfixed, and where a maximum number of people would see them

We wanted a model who had never been seen before, so we concentrated our search on central and eastern Europe, where we had offices. So in Munich, Warsaw, Prague, Budapest, they had a sort of photographic talent contest. In the end we brought half a dozen young ladies to our offices at Battle Bridge Basin, overlooking the Regent's Canal – an old Guinness bottling plant superbly converted by a firm of architects based on the ground floor. We had open-plan loft-style offices, bare brickwork, plenty of glass, full of light, and when it rained you could still smell the hops. Most meetings take place at clients' offices, but it was amazing how many clients wanted to have their meetings at our offices while our Wonderbra photo tests were going on.

Eva Herzigova, from Prague, was the obvious choice. The camera loved her and she looked fantastic. But this wasn't a glam shoot; it was about real women, their personalities coming through. She's a bright character, had a devilish smile, and she was absolutely fresh. And she had a look on camera that said, "I'm in charge here."

As soon as the campaign launched, we had protests from women's groups who claimed that women were being exploited. It was the opposite. The ads were sexy but not sexist. The woman, Eva, was making the statements. She made you laugh and think at the same time.

The campaign got us millions of pounds' worth of publicity around the world based on those few posters that began running in London, Birmingham, Liverpool, Manchester and Sheffield.

Every year my agency made a bigger profit than the year before, and every year we won creative awards. By June 1994, the London company's turnover was over £100 million a year, and employed a couple of hundred people, with 3,000 in the group worldwide.

# CHAPTER SIX

# DOWNHILL FROM WEMBLEY

S adly, while my advertising business went from strength to strength, the Albion had begun to go in the opposite direction. After falling out with Mullery, Bamber replaced him with Mike Bailey, who'd been doing well at Charlton.

The average crowds leading up to our promotion to the old First Division had been around 28,000. We were in the top flight for four years and the highest average, over the first season, was only 24,795. Under Bailey that dropped to 14,676 and one home game attracted only 9,845.

It was partly down to the style of play, mean and defensive unlike Mullery's teams, partly down to the fences that were being put up around the terraces, and partly the fact that the old North Stand roof had been demolished on safety grounds and not replaced which badly hurt the Goldstone's atmosphere.

Bailey changed his cautious style, but the consequence was that we started losing too many matches. Jimmy Melia, the chief scout, took over and brought back the attacking emphasis, which took us on an improbable run to the 1983 FA Cup final, but at the same time the cup games ruined our focus on the League and Albion were relegated back to the Second Division a fortnight before the final at Wembley.

I went to every game in the cup run except the third-round replay away to Newcastle. I couldn't be there because we'd arranged to go away on a family holiday, a Caribbean cruise on the QEII, taking advantage of my old Cunard contacts. I knew the captain and, instead of having lunch in the Pacific Restaurant, I arranged to go to the radio room to listen to the commentary from St James' Park on the BBC World Service, wondering how we were going to hold onto our 1-0 lead as Newcastle threw everything at us.

Reaching the FA Cup final for me was all about the utter amazement that we'd got there. For me growing up, football meant watching a Division Three (South) team. How could we ever be playing in the cup final?

Although the club had reached the First Division, the cup final meant something really special in those days and here we were playing Manchester United in the biggest single game of the season, watched by millions around the world.

I was never an Albion season ticket holder except in the first season in the First Division when it was erroneously imagined that every game would be a sell-out, so I joined the queues for cup final tickets in Newtown Road outside the main stand.

I went to the game with my friend John Gold and my son and his friend Barry and we stayed overnight in the flat I'd bought after I started my own agency, just off the Edgware Road, near Marble Arch. We were on the tube by 11am, walking up and down Wembley Way within the hour, just taking it all in. So this is what actually being in the cup final is like!

Standing behind the goal at the Tunnel End at Wembley, it was hard to believe that we were really there – even though we'd had weeks to prepare for it. In this land of make-believe, was Brighton's name already on the trophy? We had a decent team and United under Ron Atkinson weren't that great – certainly not the monolith they are now.

It was into the goal at our end that Gordon Smith guided his header to open the scoring for Albion. Frank Stapleton levelled, also in front of us, and then Ray Wilkins scored a good goal to put United ahead – possibly the only time he sent the ball forward all season. Gary Stevens equalised with a thumping shot near the end of normal time.

The fact that we came so close to winning it in the last seconds of extra time when Smith had his shot saved by Gary Bailey, the United goalkeeper, and that our chance had gone – as the replay proved – was almost irrelevant compared to the occasion and the thrill of seeing Albion in the final after 37 years of following them. I was determined to enjoy that whole day. I remember saying to David, "Make the most of this because it may never happen again."

In 1993, I met Bailey in Johannesburg where my agency had an office and he worked as a football presenter on South African TV. When I told him I was from Brighton he said, "Sorry mate, if Gordon hadn't hesitated for a split-second I would never have saved it."

After Wembley, I began to get disillusioned with football, and to go to fewer games. I could see that the club was going downhill fast. They lost Wickenden, who was killed when his private plane crashed at Shoreham Airport only a couple of months after the final. His death took away the financial nous and left a great hole alongside Bamber.

The rot set in very quickly after relegation. The club lost its way and went on a downward spiral. They were living the dream in reverse, the spirit of the club ebbing away fast. Bamber suffered a heart attack in March 1984 and resigned in July "as a result of major and mutual disagreements on policy" with the rest of the board. All that excitement had dissipated and it didn't look as if it would return.

The exception was the run to the 1991 Second Division play-offs on a surge late in the season. I was at that 1991 Wembley final which was best remembered, or forgotten, for our awful raspberry ripple kit with matching shirts and shorts. The home strip the next season also had matching shirts and shorts – blue-and-white stripes all the way down, which made us look like Tesco bags. How could anyone expect a team to play well wearing that?

We were distinctly average against Notts County in the final and never really looked likely to get back on terms when we went behind. Their manager was Neil Warnock and whenever I met him later he always said the same thing to me, "I've always wanted to manage your club, Dick – what great supporters." I agreed with him on the last part.

That play-off run was a brief halting of the downward spiral. The club was living on borrowed time. It was like being airlifted off the Titanic and onto the Hindenburg. It was actually a pretty dramatic crash. The year after being 90 minutes from the top tier in the play-off final, we were relegated again, and back to where we'd started – the Third Division.

The increasing shabbiness of the Goldstone Ground was a reflection of the club. I remember, during the first public inquiry into the Falmer Stadium, the QC for Lewes District Council was trying to get to why the club had sold the Goldstone Ground and said, "You must have wonderful memories of the Goldstone," wanting me to eulogise about it so that he could then say, "So why did you sell it?" – ignoring the fact that it hadn't been me who had sold it.

I replied, "Yes, I've got great memories of games there, but the Goldstone itself was a disgrace. The terraces were crumbling and more sections of them were closed off every season. The catering was awful. They used to put sausage rolls into the hot, dirty kiosks at the start of the season in August and leave them until the last one was sold in April. And don't even get me on the toilets."

By the early '90s a creeping virus of depression was gripping the club. In 1992 I was approached by Ray Bloom, one of Harry's sons, who was a director at that time. He wanted me to join the board and help in running the club.

I had known Ray for some years because he had a lot of dealings with John Keehan, my brother-in-law, when they were involved in local football. So he was aware of me and he knew that my business was doing well, and that I was a genuine fan.

He said the club needed my expertise in business and marketing and my enthusiasm for the Albion. He never overtly mentioned money, but I knew there would be a price in return for joining the board – the club had been subject to more than one winding-up order and had to sell Mark Beeney, a good goalkeeper, to Leeds in 1993 to stave off bankruptcy. Ray assumed that I would have money to put in as the major owner of a hot ad agency.

When I pointed out that I would be too busy to attend club board meetings in Hove during the week, he said that they could be held in London.

Had I agreed to join, I would have encountered Bill Archer and Greg Stanley, both directors of the Albion by then but yet to take over the club or to appoint former Liberal Democrat MP David Bellotti as chief executive – although I was to have plenty of dealings with them soon enough.

Why didn't I? I knew that I couldn't go at the Albion problem half-heartedly. I knew I would have to tackle it with a completely fresh approach. I couldn't continue with any of the people who were fully or even partly responsible for getting the club in the state it was in.

And the time wasn't right. My business was my life. I spent a lot of time in America and elsewhere, so I was hardly available. Even when I was in the UK I worked at least 12 hours a day and slept four hours – eight at weekends. I was lucky to be living that life and I was good at my job, but my kids David and Amanda and wife Margie suffered enough with me being so occupied that there was no extra space for a full commitment to the Albion in there. If I was going to do it I had to do it properly.

Ray understood, but soon after he called me again, this time for an entirely different reason. He asked if I could give some advice to his teenage nephew, Tony Bloom, who was about to go to university. Tony was a mathematics whizz-kid and also very interested in gambling, and he had devised a very clever and entirely legal system for improving your odds on the tables that he wanted to try out and market in Las Vegas.

I told Ray to get Tony to phone me, and arranged to meet him in my office at Battle Bridge Basin one evening the following week. Tony duly arrived and was very willing to take in what I had to say. I talked to him for a couple of hours and even sketched out a possible ad for him, and suggested that he put it in some of the free newspapers and magazines that were given away in hotels and motels in Vegas. He asked a lot of questions and thanked me for my advice and help.

Ray later told me that Tony's venture in Vegas had gone well, so it seems that in one small way I helped to set my successor as Albion chairman on the route to his considerable business success. And perhaps, albeit unknowingly, even before saving the Albion I helped to secure the long-term financial future of the club.

But getting directly involved wasn't for me at that time. Nevertheless, I said to Ray, "I love the Albion and maybe one day I will." In the back of my mind

I thought that it was a possibility when I retired, because the club needed someone with my leadership and drive, and I had an understanding of how football worked. I felt that one day I could bring some of my enthusiasm to the Albion.

But I always knew that if I was going to do it, I'd have to do it my way, and full-time. I was used to being the chairman of my company, and I made it clear to Ray that if I did become involved in the Albion, it would have to be as chairman.

There was no set timetable in my mind, but events took a hand. First I was to suffer a personal tragedy and then, in April 1996, came a phone call that was to change the direction of my life.

# CHAPTER SEVEN

# THE PHONE CALL THAT CHANGED MY LIFE

To be perfectly honest, when Liam Brady first called me on April 23 1996 I wasn't very engaged in what was happening at the Albion. For the first time in my life, I had been facing a personal crisis that made it hard to get through the day, let alone do something about the worsening situation at the club.

And it had been a tumultuous 12 months for the Albion. In July 1995 Bill Archer and Greg Stanley, who had taken control of the club in late 1993, had sold the Goldstone Ground for £7.4 million to property developers Chartwell, part of the huge Kingfisher retail group, with only illusory plans to build a new 30,000-seater stadium. Claims that the new ground would be built at Waterhall, north of the Brighton bypass and in an area protected from development, funded by a retail development at nearby Patcham Court Farm, were soon revealed to be completely false – plans for the project had been rejected by Brighton Council two weeks before the Goldstone sale.

News leaked out that the Albion would play their home games the following season, 1996/97, at Fratton Park. The club didn't announce it, probably because it was the refuge of fierce local rivals Portsmouth – not the friendliest place to pitch their temporary tent. Albion fans were up in arms. The same month Archer, the major shareholder, had replaced Stanley as Albion chairman.

In August 1995 the local *Evening Argus* (now *The Argus*), with help from Paul Samrah, an accountant and Albion fan, had revealed that the 'no profit' clause had been removed from the club's original Articles of Association – the crucial founding legal principles behind the club dating from 1904. The clause had stated that, should the club fold, any residual funds would go to another

Sussex sporting institution rather than to individuals, such as club shareholders or directors.

Removal of the clause was a breach of FA rules and effectively permitted the club's owners to profit from the sale of the Goldstone if the club was wound up. The club claimed that this was just an 'administrative oversight' that had occurred when Albion had been taken over in November 1993 by a new holding company, Foray 585, set up by Archer and Stanley with share capital of just £100, Archer's personal investment being £56.25. (I should mention here that the dictionary definition of the word 'foray' is 'raid'.)

Archer reluctantly reinstated the clause and got away with a light rap on the knuckles from the FA, but the Albion fans were not convinced. From the start of the 1995/96 season, they had been demonstrating week after week, home and away, with increasing fury and desperation against the actions of the owners. The response from the club towards the fans was disdain and contempt – personified by the behaviour of David Bellotti, the Albion's chief executive.

Bellotti, a former Liberal Democrat MP, saw his job as defending the dealings of his master, Archer. He had reacted to the original *Argus* story of the sale of the Goldstone by telling fans to "stop whining". Later, after *Argus* reporter Paul Bracchi had turned up at Archer's house in Lancashire and offered to buy his shareholding for the original £56.25 he had paid, Bellotti banned *The Argus* and all its employees from the Goldstone. Supporters' club vice-chairman Liz Costa, a person with the club's best interests unquestionably at heart if ever there was one, was another loyal fan he banned.

Nor was Bellotti consistent in what he told the media. He had said in a press statement that the club needed to sell the Goldstone in order to cover debts of £4.7 million. Then, a month later, he wrote in the official club programme that the debts were £6 million.

Mindful that promises of the new ground were his 'get out of jail' card, Archer had then switched his attention to Hove, shrewdly exploiting the fact that Brighton and Hove Councils – separate entities at that time – rarely confided in each other and harboured decades-long grudges when it came to the Albion: Hove, because although the town was officially part of the club's name, the national media always called the team Brighton; Brighton, because the ground was actually in Hove.

So Archer had initially been able to continue discussions with Hove Council about the necessity to sell the Goldstone on the spurious promise that Brighton Council were taking care of the other business: they were going to build the new stadium. With the Waterhall rejection now public, he started to bring pressure to bear on Hove to give the go-ahead for an alternative replacement for the Goldstone.

Just before Christmas 1995, Archer and Bellotti announced new plans for a stadium located within a retail complex – at Toads Hole Valley, on greenbelt land on the outskirts of Hove. This had been greeted with a hail of local criticism, both for environmental reasons and lack of credibility. The club did not own the land, road access would be a nightmare, and numerous previous attempts to develop it for retail use had failed.

The Archer regime then received a third blow. The Football League had withheld its permission for the Albion to play at Portsmouth, until the club could prove it had planning permission in place for a new ground in the Brighton area – and it threatened expulsion from the Football League if the club moved to Portsmouth with no plans to return.

The team itself had been in freefall. By early April 1996 they were about to be relegated to the bottom tier of English football, after a season playing in front of the lowest gates in the history of the Albion as a Football League club – an average of only 5,256, with the nadir an attendance of 3,629 for the visit of Chesterfield on December 22. The season had begun with Liam Brady as the Albion's manager, but he had resigned in November, to be replaced by Albion old boy Jimmy Case. The Albion dropped into the relegation zone and stayed there for the rest of the season.

As the end of the 1995/96 season approached, it was no exaggeration to say that the future of the club was in the balance. Relegation was likely, the club would be homeless in a matter of weeks, and, with no replacement on the horizon, expulsion from the Football League was a possibility.

There seemed one chance for a stay of execution. With planning permission assured to convert the Goldstone into a retail park of anonymous sheds housing carpet warehouses and a Toys'R'Us, Chartwell 'generously' offered the club one more season at the ground before the bulldozers moved in, albeit at a sky-high rent of £480,000 for the year.

Bellotti attempted to get the price down even though the club's negotiating position was diabolical. It would give the club a year to find a site for a new ground in Brighton & Hove and satisfy the Football League – but he stalled on signing the deal. The Albion were facing oblivion. The clamour among the fans for the removal of the board reached fever pitch.

I was aware of all this, of course. Like every Albion fan I had reacted with outrage and disbelief at the news of the club having sold the Goldstone Ground, with no plans for a new home in place. I knew that Brighton & Hove Albion – by which I mean the players, the decent people who worked for the club, and most of all its supporters – were living through a sort of nightmare and heading towards catastrophe. But I had gone through an experience that put even the huge problems of the Albion into a different perspective.

In early 1994 my wife Margie was diagnosed with bowel cancer, and for nearly two years she bravely fought the disease. Because her cancer had progressed to other parts of her body, it was already a very grave situation. After several months of responding very well to treatment, she became increasingly ill from the turn of the year onwards.

Margie died in October 1995. She was just 58 years old.

The months following Margie's death were for grieving, and reflection. I had spent much of the previous two years helping to look after her. In the meantime, things had moved on at the ad agency I'd built. It was not going to be possible to turn the clock back to how things were.

It would have felt wrong if I had simply picked up the reins again and plunged straight back into my 'hands-on' 12-hours-a-day business style. It would have been as if nothing had happened. I was at a crossroads, because it seemed my life in advertising was coming to an end.

I started watching football again. I remember going with my son David and his Geordie friend Paul to a tremendous Premiership game at Loftus Road between QPR, with Les Ferdinand in his pomp, and Newcastle United, with David Ginola weaving his wide magic, which ended 3–2 to the Magpies. But it didn't feel right.

And then, on April 23 1996, the day Albion's relegation to the League's basement was confirmed by defeat at Notts County, another event took place that was also to influence the club's destiny. I took what turned out to be a very important phone call from Liam Brady. For me, a life-changing one.

It wasn't completely out of the blue. My brother-in-law John Keehan – Margie's older brother – had given me advance warning that Liam was going to call me. Hotelier John, a well-known figure in local football in Sussex, had become friends with Liam over the previous couple of years, following his appointment as Albion manager in December 1993.

Back then, there had been a lot of optimism that the arrival of this genuine footballing legend at the Goldstone would inspire a revival in the club's fortunes. But it soon became clear that Liam was working in almost impossible circumstances, with virtually no money for either team-strengthening or building the club's youth development set-up.

Convinced by the Arsenal and Republic of Ireland hero's passion for the game, and his desire to turn the Albion schoolboy and youth scheme into one of the best in the country, my brother-in-law had become chief fundraiser for the Brighton & Hove Albion youth development project. Pop concerts, greyhound nights and other events which John organised and promoted helped keep the Brady dream alive. But starved of funds by the Archer regime, the scheme struggled. When Liam announced at a supporters' club meeting that the club had refused to pay the insurance on the youth team minibus, it was the supporters themselves who stumped up the money, presenting Liam with a cheque for the required sum.

Despite the obvious need for the club to nurture its own young prospects with real potential – 13-year-olds Gareth Barry and my great-nephew Michael Standing (later to become England's most-capped schoolboy) were with Albion at the time – Bellotti refused to offer any explanation. Fans justifiably feared for the Albion's footballing future if the youth set-up was being neglected.

When Brady resigned as Albion manager in November 1995, the Goldstone had been sold behind his back and the Seagulls were lurching towards a slow and painful death.

By this point, Liam had long since recognised Archer's modus operandi, and knew what lay ahead for the club if his regime went unchallenged.

Of course, someone of Liam's stature within football could have easily walked away from the whole situation, and forgotten all about the imminent disaster at Brighton & Hove Albion. It says everything about the man that he wanted to do something about it. He was determined to get rid of Archer and Bellotti.

So what could he do? Liam decided to seek help in putting together a takeover consortium.

But where were the serious players? The enormous publicity given to the fans' uprising against the club owners had failed to reveal anyone with the steel and financial clout to go head to head with the people responsible for the Albion's downfall.

John was certain there was someone out there. He had mentioned my name to Liam some time before. He said to Liam, "You should speak to my brother-in-law Dick now. He has the things you want and need – a love of football, he's a big Albion fan, and he's got some money."

John probably also added that the time was right for me to get involved. There had actually been some rumours six months earlier, following his resignation, about Liam going up against Archer, and there had been a suggestion that he should talk to me then. There was no way that I could even contemplate it at that point. But by April 1996 things were a little different. In a sense, I was ready when Liam phoned me.

It was a Tuesday morning, and I was in my house in Islington. The phone rang, and a voice said, "Hello Dick, Liam Brady here . . ."

There was a split-second of me thinking, "My God, here am I talking to this world-famous player" and "It's actually happening." But then after a few pleasantries, Liam came out with it, no messing about.

He said, "Dick, I know you're a proper Albion fan. Are we going to do something about the club? I mean try to get rid of Archer, Stanley and Bellotti – otherwise it's going to go under. We really need you now."

"Liam, someone certainly has to take them on," I replied. "Have you spoken to anyone else?"

"No."

"Not to any of the old guard – the directors during the Archer takeover?"

"No, they took their money and ran."

"Good. I wouldn't want to work with any of them now anyway."

At that moment, my mind was racing. I sensed that I was Liam's first, and probably only, resort. It was instantly exciting – and scary. What would I be letting myself in for? How much money would I have to put in? Richer friends of mine would often say, "Don't worry about the noughts, just the commas." I'd seen enough of how football clubs were run to want to do it better. But given the terrible state the club was in, could anyone actually save it, let alone remove Archer and company?

While my primary concern was Margie, the whole Albion business had been nagging away in the background, occasionally breaking through even what was naturally occupying most of my attention. Since she had passed away, the club's troubles had just become more ominous and were occupying more of my thoughts. But I was still an observer, looking in, and slightly detached from the situation, hearing reports in the media and from friends. Now, when Liam asked me that question, it brought everything to the fore.

I already shared the feelings of my fellow Albion fans – their pain and outrage at what was happening. The way that the club had built up an antagonism – a hatred – from its own supporters was almost without precedent. To be honest, I found it deeply depressing. But it was also motivating. Someone had to confront Archer head on. Liam was the instrument to get me thinking seriously about it, but I also knew that he couldn't do it alone. He needed someone working with him, to show some leadership to get a significant and effective group of people together, who could take on the odious current regime.

So after Liam asked me that question, a lot of things went through my mind. After what probably seemed to him like an age while I collected my thoughts, I said, "Yes, of course, I'll be with you Liam."

I was up for it. My mind was half-made up even before he called, because I knew the call was coming. I'd also realised that I might be the only person who would be able to do something about it. I had the money, but I also had the love and the understanding of the football club. There were few other people, if any, with that combination of attributes. I felt I was capable of leading the battle against Archer and I was ready.

My feeling was, "This is a challenge. Let's get on with it." I didn't assume I was going to win, but I had no fear of failure. Obviously I never realised how long it would take, and I knew Archer would be a tough nut to crack – all his behaviour up to then made it clear that he thought he was untouchable, and would be able to force the council to give him permission for the development at Toads Hole Valley. The criticism of the fans just bounced off him.

But Liam had inside information about what had been going on, what they intended to do and their motivation, which was why he had resigned. We agreed to meet as soon as possible. I drove down to Hove and Liam came to my house the next day.

We immediately got on very well – it felt as if we knew each other already. I was more likely to be in awe of Liam than some rock musician or film star – because I'd met plenty of them – but I wasn't, although when I met him I thought he was absolutely outstanding. I just liked his personality and his obvious commitment.

He was completely down-to-earth and nothing like what I assumed a former star footballer to be. He wasn't arrogant or full of himself. On the contrary, he was more interested in what I could bring to the table. Even though nothing was sealed until later, he understood straight away that I was instinctively drawn to the project.

We were on the same wavelength, right from the off. He had that dry Irish humour, was very intelligent and a real man of the football world. When he had played in Italy for Juventus, Sampdoria and Internazionale, he had endeared himself to fans over there by learning the language. And not just the fans. A few years later Liam took me to the San Daniele restaurant near Highbury one evening after an Arsenal Champions League game and introduced me to two friends – Roberto Bettega, the great former player, and Giovanni Trapattoni, a management legend, both of whom had been with Liam at Juventus, as team-mate and manager. The respect and affection that these two huge figures of Italian football had for him was obvious.

Liam and I quickly agreed at that first meeting at my house that our first step would be to sound out Greg Stanley, the one man in the present set-up likely to be open to change, the man responsible for bringing Archer into the club.

Stanley, a wealthy man thanks to his family's DIY business, had originally come in as a potential saviour who was going to restore the club's fortunes. He spoke at fans' meetings and described himself as one of them, albeit a richer version, but he had also brought in Archer, his mentor and managing director at Focus DIY. Stanley had become nominal club chairman when they took over in 1993 but Archer was in charge because of his majority shareholding and became chairman in July 1995.

Stanley had originally put £600,000 into the club, then later another £200,000. But this £800,000 was not equity, it was loans, on the condition that he could give six months' notice of withdrawal, after which interest would kick in if the club didn't pay back his money at that point.

Well, of course the club couldn't afford to do that and so interest started accruing. On top of that – how the auditors ever allowed this I will never understand – a £250,000 penalty clause which had been inserted into the loan agreements was now triggered because the loans continued not to be paid back. So by the time I got involved with Liam, Albion owed Stanley, its one-time 'saviour', the astonishing sum of £1.4 million. Now he was coming under pressure from the fans and didn't like it one little bit.

Liam had no problem arranging a meeting at Stanley's house in Arundel, West Sussex the following day to talk about a possible takeover. Stanley was clearly rattled and looking for a way out. He became very emotional during the meeting, almost tearful at one point, and said he really regretted the whole situation.

He said, "I don't deserve all this flak. What has happened isn't my fault."

During the conversation he tried to distance himself from Archer. He was clearly very wary of him. But it was also obvious that Stanley was never going to be able to influence Archer. He offered us nothing but indecision on that score.

He said, "I think it would be good if you do take over. But I can't make it happen.

"Archer is in charge. It's out of my hands."

Liam and I left that inconclusive meeting in absolutely no doubt as to who was calling the shots on the Albion board.

Within 48 hours, events in the Albion saga took a rapid turn for the worse, culminating in one of the most shameful episodes in the club's history.

On Saturday April 27, already-relegated Albion were playing their last home match of a depressing season against York City, a fixture that most Albion supporters believed was going to be the last ever game at the Goldstone.

The outcome was hardly surprising. Incensed by the situation, more than 3,000 fans invaded the pitch within the first 20 minutes, broke the crossbars and caused the match to be abandoned – all under the watching eyes of the nation's press and TV. Although that behaviour went way too far, the root cause of this huge PR disaster for the club was David Bellotti's attempts to hold out for a last-minute deal with Chartwell that had apparently failed.

I was driving down from London to Hove after a meeting when news of the abandonment of the York game came through on the car radio. I immediately phoned Liam and we quickly agreed that we had to do something. This was not the time to stay silent. We had to give the fans some hope.

I said: "You must be the spokesman right now, Liam, and we need to make a serious statement of intent. Archer has to know that this is a group of supporters, a consortium that is not going to stand by and let him treat the club and its fans with complete contempt."

I knew I had to make Archer sit up and take notice. "We must try and delay the process of digging up the Goldstone. Liam, to guarantee we stay there for at least another year, offer to pay the £40,000 deposit Chartwell require to start the lease-back. I'll bankroll it.

"And to provoke a reaction, we should politely ask Archer and his cronies to leave the club."

That evening, in the eye of the coming storm, Liam called a press conference for the following morning, to be held across the road from the Goldstone in Hove Park. We decided that he should go alone. Everyone knew Liam, while nobody knew who I was. In my view, it was far too soon to be forced by events fully to go public on our embryonic opposition group before anything had been agreed. "We have to finalise the make-up of the consortium," I told Liam. "We need other expertise."

Some Sunday newspapers reported the previous day's events as a riot. The question was whether it could have been averted if the club hadn't delayed sorting out the ground issue so long. The answer was almost certainly yes.

In front of a large gathering of fans and journalists, Liam condemned the violence – even though privately we both knew the pitch invasion was an act of utter frustration, and a desperate plea for help from the fans.

Then Liam told the crowd he was in discussions with a consortium that was very serious about taking on Archer and co. "There are people with me who have money and are willing to invest in the club, but they are adamant the owners must go. Leave us to pick up the pieces."

No names were mentioned. Then Liam offered to pay the £40,000 deposit Chartwell wanted for the Goldstone lease-back deal.

The club's reaction was predictable. Bellotti treated the proposition with disdain. "The offer is totally irrelevant," he said. And within a few hours, Archer – well aware of the meeting we'd had with Stanley a few days earlier – turned the offer down flat, and rejected any interference from Liam and the consortium.

But Liam's timely appearance in Hove Park did mark the beginning of the struggle as far as the consortium was concerned. It was clear that if Liam Brady was prepared to be the spokesman for this new group, it meant something. At a desperate moment for the club, it gave the fans something to cling on to.

Here was a guy who was world-famous, but who was prepared to stand up and be counted for a lower division football club that he had managed for a relatively short period of time. And when the situation was at its bleakest, he did so.

And it did force the hated regime into a humbling climb-down. Forty-eight hours later, as the clock ticked on deadline day, April 30, Bellotti finally signed the lease-back deal that would allow Albion to play one more year at the Goldstone, at Chartwell's full asking price of £480,000 – over £20,000 for each home game.

The club's future was on a mortgage. And a short-term one at that. I wanted to get to Chartwell to see if negotiations were possible to delay the timing of its redevelopment plans. A slim chance. After that, there was nowhere to go. No ground, no plans, not Portsmouth, nothing.

The mismanagement that had brought the Albion to this pathetic state was by now making my blood boil. My mind was made up. The fans' plea for help was not going unanswered. Archer and Bellotti had to be stopped, in the only way I knew how: by sheer cussedness, brains and organisation.

The need to get the consortium up and running was now urgent. Liam couldn't do it all on his own, and that's where I came in. Later that week he and I met away from public gaze at the Edwardian Hotel at Heathrow Airport, to discuss tactics and potential other members of the group. I had mentioned Bob Pinnock would be interested, and I now confirmed that Bob was on board.

Bob had been the first person I had called following my initial conversation with Liam. It was the obvious and logical thing to do – a no-brainer. He was someone I knew and could trust. During most of the '80s and early '90s, while our agency had prospered, Bob and I had witnessed the Albion's steady decline from the crumbling terraces. Often the oranges and satsumas that we brought to eat at half-time were tastier than the football – and the beloved Goldstone gradually disintegrated around us. So it was natural that Bob was joining me.

We decided that the three of us would be it for the 'investor' part of the consortium for the moment, but we needed to get together as soon as possible with the other interested parties who could form an effective fighting group.

Liam organised that first gathering for the following week, at his house in Hove on a Saturday morning, May 11 1996 – a meeting that was really about bringing together a group of people I was determined would form a task-force in the fight against Archer and Bellotti. A day earlier, at my suggestion, he had called Archer to tell him the meeting was taking place and that he should start to take the consortium seriously. Archer had sworn and put the phone down.

The meeting was attended by six people: Liam, myself, Bob, Ivor Caplin, the

Labour leader of Hove Council, and two other people I'd never met before – Richard Baldwin and Martin Perry. They were both directors of Alfred McAlpine, the construction firm responsible for building two of the most impressive new stadia in England: Bolton Wanderers' Reebok Stadium and – not surprisingly – Huddersfield Town's McAlpine Stadium.

I had met Ivor for the first time a few days earlier with Liam at the Gatwick Hilton for a background briefing that went well. Ivor was a seasoned local politician and an Albion season ticket holder. He'd had various run-ins with the club at this point, particularly with Bellotti. He was a vocal opponent of the club's ownership and its plans to move to Toads Hole Valley.

He was now leader of the council that in June 1993 had given the club planning permission for a retail warehouse development on the Goldstone, a scheme that Ivor – then a councillor – actually backed, believing the argument that the ground needed to be sold to clear the club's debts and that it would increase its borrowing power until a new ground could be found. Archer hadn't taken over at the time, but his influence as a director alongside his chum Stanley was growing.

Hove Council had eventually given planning permission on legal advice that they would lose an appeal if they didn't approve it. And once Archer gained control of the club a few months later, it was that permission that he planned to fully capitalise on – which he did in the summer of 1995.

Did Archer have to sell the Goldstone? I very much doubt it. For a start, the quoted amount of the Albion's debts varied by millions depending on whom he or Bellotti were talking to. Also, the club had a mortgage on the ground – the means by which Archer took control of the Albion in 1993 when he introduced an £880,000 loan from the Co-operative Bank, secured against the Goldstone. It's unlikely Archer would have been under any pressure from that source to foreclose on the mortgage. Especially as government planning law at the time had turned against out-of-town retail development and favoured urban regeneration, such as on a site like the Goldstone. It was a much more valuable piece of real estate.

Archer exploited that development opportunity, ostensibly to save the club. Selling the Goldstone was an important business deal which, crucially, would involve him with retail developers – and that might come in very handy for his future plans for his own business, Focus DIY. So would his original pursuit of Patcham Court Farm and then Toads Hole Valley, where his scheme envisaged a large retail development with a football stadium in the corner.

Whatever his motives, the situation he had contrived was that the football club didn't have a ground to go to, and Archer was relying on that unpleasant reality to force Hove Council into giving him planning permission for his Toads Hole complex.

Ivor struck me as someone very anxious to encourage the setting up of a meaningful group to challenge the Archer regime. I'd wanted Ivor to understand quickly what I was about, confirm his 'anti' position on Toads Hole Valley and get his input on the one extra aspect I knew the consortium would need: stadium know-how. I was sure he would have been in contact with Huddersfield's Labour council, part-owners of their new stadium.

It was Ivor who invited the men from McAlpine to that Saturday meeting. Richard and Martin were there because of their stadium-building expertise – and they had come to the meeting because they clearly saw a potential new business opportunity. Having sold the Goldstone, the Albion needed a new stadium. I never did find out if they had been approached by Archer or Bellotti as well.

Richard was McAlpine's managing director, while Martin had been in charge of the company's Huddersfield stadium project.

That first consortium meeting was very much a 'getting to know you' affair. We all knew why we were there. The meeting ended with handshakes and a commitment to meet again shortly. It had really been a preliminary get-together, to see if this could actually work – whether our personalities were compatible enough to do what was needed. I liked Martin. He seemed to know what he was talking about. I could work with him.

After the meeting, things began to move fast. A few days later Ivor, who'd had contact with senior Chartwell people during the Goldstone sale, attempted to arrange for me to get together with them to discuss the Goldstone situation. My tactic would be to see if there was any chance of delaying their redevelopment beyond the one year's grace for which they were charging the club £480,000, but at a more reasonable rent. I needed time to find a location for the new ground.

They weren't interested even in meeting. As far as Chartwell were concerned, they had done a very good deal with the chairman of the ground's owners – Archer – and the deal was going ahead. Business was business. They weren't remotely concerned with the problems of the football club. It wasn't their problem. I suppose I was a fool to think Chartwell's attitude would be anything different. But here was stark proof of the size of the task I was about to take on, and the realisation began to sink in.

Also early that following week, I met up with Martin at the Grafton Hotel in London to hear more about the Huddersfield stadium. He told me about a potential investor in the Albion, named Alan Corbett, with whom McAlpine had previously had dealings.

Although he was not a local Sussex man, I was interested in what Mr Corbett might bring to the consortium – he had been the owner of Oxford United after the Robert Maxwell family. Martin arranged for us to get together with him and his adviser, Stuart Petch, at the Royal Garden Hotel a few days later on May 17.

That meeting was promising, but no more. They asked some sensible questions and apparently had money, but I needed more time to suss them out. I invited Stuart to the next meeting of the consortium.

I quickly brought the group together again. The second meeting – the one that formalised the consortium and cemented my decision to go up against Archer – took place on the morning of May 22, in a suite at the Intercontinental Hotel, Park Lane in London.

Everyone from the first meeting was there – myself, Liam, Bob, Ivor, Richard and Martin – with a few additions: Desmond Lynam, Ray Bloom and Stuart.

Des needs little introduction, of course. A hugely experienced sports broadcaster and TV presenter, Des was the anchor of the BBC's *Match of the Day* at the time and, of course, a lifelong Brighton & Hove Albion fan. He had not, at that point, expressed any views publicly about Archer, Bellotti or Stanley. Being the consummate BBC man that he was, he no doubt felt he should be seen to be neutral or objective. But being an Albion fan he was also deeply concerned about where the club was heading. He was keen to help the club, and was at the meeting to see if the consortium was going to offer genuine opposition to Archer.

This was the first time I had met Des (although I suppose, like every other viewer who watched *Match of the Day* on a Saturday night, I felt I already knew him quite well). I've since discovered that Des is even more witty and urbane off-screen than he is on it, but in our first meeting he came across as slightly more prickly than his TV persona. He was distinctly cool with me. That's probably not so surprising. He wasn't putting himself forward to take on this battle himself, but he wanted to see the cut of my jib, what I was made of. He was both curious and slightly wary about this new consortium. He knew Liam, of course, but at that point he didn't know me.

Des was thinking, "Who is this guy? Can I trust him – bearing in mind what most football club chairmen are like? And that he made his money in advertising?" So I think he assumed I would be brash, a self-made man who was probably a bit above himself. He mellowed a bit when we discovered that one of my big business competitors, Mike Greenleas, boss of another ad agency, had shared a London flat with Des in their young, hedonistic days. Apparently they were like 'The Odd Couple' – Greenleas as fussy Felix, Des as laid-back Oscar. When he found out I'd often tangled with Felix, I was getting to be okay in Des's eyes.

Perhaps more surprising was the attendance at the meeting of Ray who was, after all, an existing director of the Albion – the only director who was still involved apart from Archer, Bellotti and Stanley. In fact, Ray actually hosted the meeting, hiring the suite at the Intercontinental for the purpose.

It may seem strange that a director of the Albion under Archer was involved in the meeting that set the ball rolling for the battle against Archer – but it's true. The fact is, the consortium was going to meet again anyway, and on hearing through the grapevine about the first meeting at Liam's house, Ray was ready to facilitate this next one quickly and quietly. As far as I was concerned this was okay. I knew Ray, and I knew that he wasn't the enemy. He had the interests of the club at heart and wanted to see the club through this terrible time. And whilst he never threw in his lot with the consortium, he wanted to see if it was genuine opposition to Archer.

Nevertheless, mainly because of Ray's involvement, I was eerily conscious of Archer's presence at that meeting. Ray wasn't necessarily siding with him, but I think that he did want to convey to Archer whether we presented a proper and serious level of opposition to him. And there would definitely be something important to report.

At the beginning of that meeting there was a lot of discussion about the club's seemingly irreconcilable relationship with the fans. Of one thing I was certain: at the Albion the natural bond between a football club and its supporters had been totally destroyed. Nothing would change while Archer and Bellotti remained in charge. We moved on to the issue of the level of the club's debts and what the consortium might have to invest in the Albion once the true financial position was known. I already knew in my heart that, to give the club a fighting chance of survival, in my case the sum would be a seven-figure one. I was prepared for that.

There, in the lush surroundings of the five-star London hotel, with Des, Ivor and the rest munching on expensive biscuits while I chain-smoked (yes, it really was that long ago), the consortium was finalised, interrogated, challenged and put through a barrage of 'what ifs' before the three-hour meeting ended, with the big decision agreed. To save the club, we would attempt to open negotiations with Archer to take over the Albion. Our plan, in theory, was straightforward: a) get access to the club's books b) ask Archer and co to leave. My feeling as I left the Intercontinental? I couldn't wait to get on with it.

The takeover consortium was comprised of Liam, Bob and myself, as leader. Corbett and Petch still had to make up their minds, and to be honest I wasn't sure I wanted them in anyway. Martin wasn't an investor, but he would be our stadium adviser on behalf of McAlpine. Richard Baldwin and Ivor Caplin wouldn't be involved, although Ivor would continue his support at local government level. Des was not part of it, but he obviously felt we were made of the right stuff because he offered his tacit support for our cause.

Meanwhile, following Liam's announcement in Hove Park, there had been a lot of public speculation about the 'mystery' investors making up the consortium. The name Milan Mandaric had come up, a man who had made a lot of money in Silicon Valley, California, and who apparently wanted to invest in an English football club. Later to achieve that with Portsmouth, Leicester City and Sheffield Wednesday, Milan was never on my radar at that time. I was eventually to get to know him well, of course, chairman to chairman, and I asked him recently if there was any truth in the rumour that he'd been in direct contact with the Albion during that period. He confirmed that in fact he had, and had been shown plans for a new stadium (presumably by Archer and Bellotti for Toads Hole Valley) but when he learned there was no planning permission, it was all very vague and the fans were against them, he decided that Brighton was not for him.

No, there were no mystery investors, just the three of us. Mystery money? A bit. I'd sounded out my ad agency partner, Alasdair Ritchie, and he'd given me £180,000 to invest because everything we did turned to gold – and he was keen on the idea of the new stadium. But even before I'd finished dealing with Archer, I'd paid back Alasdair's £180,000 because he was too impatient. Within weeks of lending me the money, he'd phoned me and asked why the stadium hadn't been approved yet!

We also had no contact with Albion supporters whatsoever at that point. I wanted to keep our identities under wraps until we'd opened negotiations with Archer and had something tangible to tell the fans. There were rumours that the main investor was 'from the London advertising scene' and a long-term Albion fan, but we only became known to the public when our first attempts to take over the club faltered, in early July. But the fight had begun.

Looking back now, I'm pretty sure that if Liam hadn't called me I would still have got involved. The feeling that I had to do something to help the club would have grown stronger until it was impossible to ignore. I knew I had this dual asset of having senior-level business experience and loving the club. Those two things would have driven me to get involved with the supporters, or make contact with Ray to facilitate taking Archer on – and then meet Archer to try to make him see sense.

But actually I'm not sure if Bill Archer ever did see sense. In the coming months, we would have to fight for everything we got out of him, every step of the way. To save the Albion, we would have to do it the hard way.

# CHAPTER EIGHT

# FACE TO FACE
# WITH ARCHER

In building my advertising agency I'd locked horns with tough, sharp New York lawyers. Mary Wells lined up seven of them when I sold part of the company to her and I dealt with her sharp, Brooks Brothers-clad henchmen pretty well. I'd also sold campaigns and clinched deals with bosses of global companies on numerous occasions. In short, I knew how to deal with people in this kind of situation. But in all my experience in business, I'd never met anyone quite like Bill Archer.

Archer wasn't that clever – because his motives were obvious. You knew what he was up to. But he was street smart, and he was cocksure. I soon realised I was dealing with someone who had a very clear idea as to how far he could go, and I think he was certain he could see me off. I was battle-hardened in knowing how to handle tough business people, but I was about to encounter a level of armour-plating that I'd never had to deal with before.

From the start, he used every trick he could to avoid meeting with me and the consortium. After the meeting at the Intercontinental Hotel which Ray Bloom had attended as a kind of observer for the club board, Ray attempted to set up the first meeting with Archer.

But my target wasn't going to play ball that easily. Archer started as he meant to go on; he would always be a very tricky customer to deal with. He was, of course, aware of the 'hard man' public profile his Brighton activities had gained him. I think he thrived on it and relished the fact that his growing notoriety would do his business reputation no harm.

Certainly, however much thousands of Albion fans and I might have craved it, he was never going to give up the football club immediately, admit he had got it wrong and walk away. His ego would never allow it.

Throughout the acrimonious, frustrating and endless negotiations that would be needed to prise Archer's hands off the club, he would never let every sticky finger be completely removed all at once. Instead he embarked on a double-handed game. First, to mollify the supporters, he acknowledged the existence of the consortium and told the world he would meet with us, provided we were able to meet certain financial and stadium criteria beforehand. It was a good way of stalling the talks. Second, he intended to get valuable information that way from the consortium, while he privately continued to pursue his holy grail of Toads Hole Valley with Hove Council.

Archer spelt out his terms: we had to show what sort of expertise we had to build a new stadium; what funds were there to build it with; and how we would 'deliver the future'. He even told the fans and the media, "If they can do that, I will step aside."

With the bait of opening the club's books to the consortium, he was trying to find out as much as he could about what our finances were, where we would build a new stadium, and what the local councils had promised us – information he could of course then use against us while he maintained the façade of being an accommodating football club chairman.

The Football Association by this time was aware of the existence of the consortium and in mid-June summoned us to its headquarters at Lancaster Gate for discussions.

The severe, oak-panelled room and plastic cups of coffee didn't dampen our spirits, as the meeting which Liam, Bob and I had with chief FA lawyer Nic Coward on June 19 was constructive and encouraging. We outlined our intentions and Nic gave us a fair hearing. The Brighton blip on the FA's radar was coming under closer scrutiny at last. But when I raised the subject Coward stopped short of promising FA action against Archer for bringing the game into disrepute.

I suspect that knowing Archer's intransigent, hard-man reputation, they feared a repeat of the humiliation heaped on them two years earlier, when a certain Mr Alan Sugar, then chairman of Tottenham Hotspur, had successfully overturned in the High Court draconian measures imposed by the FA on Spurs – a 12-point deduction and expulsion from the FA Cup as punishment for financial irregularities. The media coverage of the case meant they wanted to stop the football governing body's authority again being challenged in a public court of law.

Within the hour, I was about to have my own foundations rocked.

We were in a London cab, following that FA meeting, when Liam dropped the bombshell that he was thinking of leaving the consortium. He had been offered the job of director of youth development at Arsenal. He said he hadn't made up his mind and there was a lot to consider, but I knew in my heart straight away that he wanted to take it.

And why not? After all, Liam genuinely is an Arsenal legend and was being offered a fantastic opportunity, developing the youth side at the Gunners at a time when Arsene Wenger's influence was just starting to take shape.

David Dein, the Arsenal vice-chairman who was in charge of the club's footballing affairs, had made the approach to Liam. David told me later that they had been desperate to get him. When Liam told me, it was obviously a huge knockback because he gave the consortium immediate credibility. Yet I could hardly stand in his way.

I was hugely disappointed at the prospect of losing him, but I didn't throw a tantrum and accuse him of getting me into something and then quitting. I knew Liam didn't deserve that; I was already grateful to him for involving me.

Although it would take a little time for Liam to make his decision, be interviewed and tie up his deal with the Arsenal board – and we agreed there would be no statements until it was done and dusted – I never really tried to talk him out of it because I knew that the Gunners were in his blood and he was tailor-made for the job. Clearly, Liam was torn as he had a very high regard for the Albion. He wouldn't have stuck his head above the parapet the way he had those months earlier if he didn't. That had been the trigger for me getting involved. It may have happened anyway, as I saw my club being destroyed, but Liam was the catalyst that got me into it. In the nick of time, as it turned out. Liam had done his job. He had made the first meaningful rebel yell against the odious dictatorship. And he wasn't deserting a lost cause.

Liam was not bowing out because he had lost confidence in the Albion project or had lost faith in me. By that point we had established a real bond. He was as sure that we would eventually wrest control from Archer as I was. And he assumed, quite rightly, that I would continue the fight.

The frustrations mounted. Archer told supporters that he'd meet the consortium but we hadn't yet satisfied his conditions. One of these was for us to answer the impossibly vague question: how we would 'deliver the future'. When we supplied him with relevant information – without revealing all our hand – he then kept changing the goalposts. (In fact, he changed the goalposts enough times to have qualified for the job as groundsman at the Albion – assuming of course that we had a ground.)

But still we were no closer to examining the books.

Up to that point, confidentiality had been an aspect of the negotiations until we made some sort of breakthrough. But Archer digging in and the complete absence of progress of any kind demanded another tactic. I decided to go public on his shenanigans, to force him into the media spotlight and under closer attention. And with Liam's departure imminent, it was time for Bob's and my role in the Albion takeover bid – still regarded as 'Liam Brady's consortium' – to be revealed publicly for the first time.

I called Andy Naylor, chief sports writer of *The Argus*, announced myself as the main backer of the consortium and revealed that our talks with Archer, which took place mainly through lawyers and via Ray Bloom, had collapsed. I offered him the exclusive story to ensure maximum coverage (my knowledge of the media would come in useful in football) and we agreed to meet later that day, Wednesday July 3, at Liam's house. (It was still a month before the news broke that Liam was leaving.) When Naylor arrived I gave him the evidence regarding our financial resources that we'd already given Archer.

The following day *The Argus* splashed the story on the front page under the headline 'Is This Albion's Knight In Shining Armour?' They reported that we were long-term supporters, a group of backers ready to invest in the club and clear the debts, who wanted to instil a new sense of optimism – but were being prevented from inspecting the books, so couldn't make a realistic offer to buy out the current owners.

"New leadership is required," I told the paper. "The local community feels that those in charge are responsible for the present predicament. We are offering the owners a sensible option." This calm, measured approach may have come as a surprise, but I needed to convey a sense of dignity in contrast to the Archer regime's behaviour. I also made the strong point that, with the co-operation of the local authorities, the consortium was confident that a new stadium could be viably developed. I was reminding the politicians that, even with new owners, the stadium problem wasn't going away.

The national press who had been following the Brighton saga as a potential headline-grabber picked up on the story. The consortium was now in the public eye. The battle against Archer would be fought with both local and national media ringside – if only I could get him into the ring. The pressure was going to be on me in particular as leader, but that didn't worry me. I was used to being in pressure situations; they seemed to bring out the best in me.

But now Archer was under pressure too; he showed it by launching a charm offensive on key supporters such as Paul Samrah, John Baine and others who were leading the fan opposition. He called them to a meeting where he told them he was going to be more open and that I was a scallywag. His argument was that they didn't need me because he had plans for a retail development with a football ground in it, and they didn't need "this chancer", as he called me to my face later. He tried to blacken my name with them and make them believe that everything was going to be all right.

Presumably he hoped that the supporters would be taken in and see the error of their ways, and I would be forced to give up. They weren't taken in and I wasn't giving up – from that point I had taken on responsibility for the hopes of all Albion fans.

Almost from the moment Liam had called me, the Albion's future had become my total preoccupation. The scale of what I was getting into hit me very quickly but, while it was challenging, it wasn't frightening. I'm quite tough when it comes to battling things out, and I'd grown up in a tough negotiating environment in the advertising world and knew my way around a balance sheet.

I felt I could bring fresh thinking to it. I was so confident that I had a new blueprint for football clubs in the way they dealt with supporters, marketed themselves and became part of their community. I had this vision of community from the very beginning.

Throughout all my time as a fan, the club had never spoken to its supporters. There was no dialogue. The club knew we would turn up and buy a programme full of local ads with no real information in it, and didn't feel a need to do any more. I saw it differently. I saw the power that clubs could have to help their communities, although they didn't realise it then or have a clue how to do it.

On August 1, Liam publicly announced that he had accepted Arsenal's offer to head up their youth development and reluctantly would be leaving the consortium, hitting out at the actions of the Archer/Bellotti regime in the press. The news was seen as a blow but not a fatal one – the consortium and I personally had gained a lot of credibility and support following the story in *The Argus*, and no one questioned Liam's right to follow his heart.

Archer continued his delaying tactics. He made a ludicrous demand for a blind offer for the club from the consortium (without us seeing the books), which I dismissed out of hand. He was doing his utmost to frustrate us, but he couldn't avoid us forever.

Finally, after mounting media and fan pressure and, I believe, his own curiosity to go head to head with these troublemakers, Archer agreed to meet us. Bob and I came face to face with Archer for the first time on Thursday August 22 1996 on neutral territory at the City offices of the lawyers, Wilde Sapte.

Martin Perry and Stuart Petch were with us, too. Archer was on his own and was already waiting for us when we arrived. He obviously felt that he needed no assistance from his friend Greg Stanley or his chief executive Bellotti to deal with the likes of us – whom he had already publicly described as the "half-baked" consortium. Ray Bloom was in attendance, presumably because he was still a director of the club, but he took no real part in proceedings.

The meeting took place in a very austere, modern, minimalist meeting room. It was a cold place. The setting seemed entirely appropriate for the mood of a distinctly icy encounter.

Archer was every inch the northern English, working-class man-made-good.

Fairly short, bespectacled, overweight, white-haired – although only in his early fifties – and supremely self-confident. It was as if he wanted to show these soft southern bastards how tough he was. Obviously I already knew what he was capable of, but meeting him was different. I saw him as someone who had no business being involved in Brighton & Hove Albion but I sensed straight away that I had to be very careful with him.

There were basic handshakes, few pleasantries, and no small talk. In fact, you could cut the tension with a knife as the meeting got under way. I think both of us were out to impose ourselves on the other. There was a lot of meta-phorical antler-locking. He wanted to show me he was a tough guy and wasn't going to roll over. At the same time I was determined to show him that I wasn't going to be shaken off. And it immediately felt very personal between me and him, even though I had the others with me.

Our position was straightforward: stand down and let us – people who care about this football club – take over and save Brighton & Hove Albion. I made a direct appeal to Archer to resign his chairmanship and quit the Albion board. "Stand down. You have gone too far and we have to save this football club, not worry about building a retail park in Hove."

I asked why he was so reluctant to open the books to us, when his public statements indicated otherwise. His response was essentially to treat me as if I was some kind of upstart, as if the consortium were an inconvenience to him. He was very dismissive of us and kept referring to me as a 'chancer' – "You're not one of these chancers, are you?" – his description of an opportunist with no money.

It was his way of trying to intimidate me. Perhaps that sort of talk played well in Crewe, where he was getting Focus DIY under way, but it didn't cut any ice with me.

"I wouldn't have come this far if I didn't have the funds to back up my position," I replied. "I'm not in the business of wasting my own and other people's time, or giving the fans false hope."

Archer then proceeded to lecture us about his plans for the club, all linked to the proposed development in Toads Hole Valley. According to him, it was going to generate huge sums of money for the Albion – he mentioned a figure of £11 million a year.

He ignored the fact that local politicians had been lining up to criticise the Toads Hole Valley scheme from the moment it had been announced the previous December. Indeed, earlier that month, Hove Council had voted unanimously to reject the plans after receiving virtually no information.

But listening to him, my sense was that Archer believed he could eventu-ally force Hove Council into giving him planning permission for the scheme.

After all, he had gained its permission to sell the Goldstone Ground, and he was gambling on the fact that the council wouldn't be able to resist his big business proposition. Oh, and it would provide Albion with the ground they needed.

To me, as with a few other interested observers, Archer's Toads Hole Valley scheme was less about the Albion's future and more about him using the football club to facilitate a huge retail property deal. And this was why he thought he didn't need to stand down. He thought he could win.

"Why would I need you?" he asked. "Why do you need to get involved? I'm the one doing this for the club." He managed to say this with a straight face. Maybe he did actually believe it.

There was no doubt Archer was testing me out. Because I believe that something else had occurred to him. The mounting opposition of the fans – and the level of anger aimed directly at him – was clearly becoming a serious problem. I suspect he was entertaining the idea of going into partnership with someone, in order to solve that problem. That would be someone who could invest some money into his project – and who could also act as a new frontman.

I think that was likely the real reason he agreed to meet us in the first place. He probably imagined that if I fitted the bill he might be able to manipulate me into being a better form of Bellotti. If so, he was quickly put right on that score. I made it very clear to him that I was going up against him in a major way and he needed to consider his position very seriously.

"I'm not interested in any form of partnership with you. The consortium are not prepared to buy anything less than 100 per cent."

"I'm not prepared to sell all my shareholding," Archer replied.

"Your position is untenable at Brighton," I said. "And I'm not concerned about whether we can build a retail park. It's nothing to do with that. First and foremost my job is to save the football club. And I can only save it if you walk away from it."

I reminded him that the consortium had reasonably demonstrated its ability to meet his takeover criteria. "Now honour your side of the bargain."

It certainly wasn't the most friendly or affable meeting I've ever had. Most meetings in my experience, even with top-level business people, were all directed at finding consensus. There were discussions, but I always knew the aspect they would be concerned about, so I would have done my homework beforehand. I would be ahead of it and mostly they would finish with mutual understanding, and I have always been able to defuse any tension with humour.

This was very different. There was no search for compromise. Archer seemed to think that he could beat me down. I never tried humour with him because

I knew it would fall on deaf ears. I could tell he would not appreciate it. He would think I was some soft, nancy boy whizz-kid from the advertising world – and why would Archer give into him?

So there was an underlying tension, but it didn't quite degenerate into a slanging match. And even though Archer had no intention of selling because he still believed he could force his retail plans through and I'd dismissed the 'chancer' slight, he still had to ask one important question: what kind of funds did we have at our disposal to put into the club? He wanted to see the colour of our money.

My response was to ask again to see the club's books. As with the purchase and takeover of any business, we couldn't make an offer without having full knowledge of the club accounts and its financial health (or otherwise). And, after a moment's hesitation, Archer agreed to my request.

So it did look as if we had, in fact, made some real progress with that first meeting – getting Archer's permission at last for us to begin the process of due diligence. But as Bob said to me a few minutes after leaving the meeting, "We've got to be careful here, Dick. I don't trust this guy one bit." It was no coincidence that I was feeling exactly the same myself.

Sure enough, two days later, with Archer having got a better press because he had agreed to meet us, that all changed. He announced that we hadn't demonstrated to his liking that we had sufficient funds, nor had we shown any signs of being able to 'deliver the future' – that vague phrase again. As a result, he had decided we weren't going to see the books after all, unless we could meet one more condition: namely, that proof be provided that we had identified a site for a new ground to which the local councils would give approval. His latest requirement was impossible for us to meet at that time and Archer knew it, but he was probing for his own purposes.

And that was how it was with Archer. He would use this kind of tactic again and again in our negotiations over the coming months – firstly agreeing to something, and then finding some excuse not to do it. This would be his strategy, which he continued to employ for more than a year.

It had quickly become a personal duel for him. When he realised I was much more of a direct threat to him than he originally imagined, he then gave the impression that he was prepared to talk to me again. But his main reason for doing so was simply to buy time. Also, he calculated that he could buy some much-improved media coverage, along the lines of "at least Archer is now sitting down with this new consortium" – but, of course, without ever intending to give up control.

He thought he could see me off by making it difficult for me to proceed. That's why at first he said, "Yes, you can see the books" and then stopped it.

By putting up all these barriers, he thought that I would eventually just go away. And he did that all the way down the line.

It was a case of digging in and a having great deal of determination. He was bloody-minded. We had to be bloody-minded right back at him.

# CHAPTER NINE

# THE FA GET
# INVOLVED

The 1996/97 season had begun later than usual in mid–August, due to the Euro '96 tournament held in England that summer. But in Brighton there was none of the optimism normally associated with a new campaign. Albion were now in Division Three, the lowest tier of English League football, and beginning what would definitely be their final year at the Goldstone Ground – now renting from the new owners, for the absolutely extortionate rent of £480,000 for the year – with no home to go to at the end of the season.

The fans were in revolt, the anger being generated among its own supporters by the Albion regime probably unprecedented in English football, and the start of the new season saw another setback. On August 16, the club was found guilty of 'failing to control a crowd' over the York City pitch invasion and received a suspended three-point deduction from the Football League.

On September 9, Bill Archer wrote to contractors McAlpine, now revealed as members of the consortium, asking if they were interested in a separate deal with the club to build the new stadium. Of course, whoever won the battle for control of the club, the Albion would need a new stadium and someone would have to build it. He was dangling the carrot in the event of me failing, assuming that they were just in it for the business. I think McAlpine ignored it; certainly my group remained united.

There were a lot of things going on away from the Goldstone to highlight the resistance to the Archer regime. The efforts of councillors Steve Bassam and Ivor Caplin, respectively leaders of Brighton and Hove Councils, at a meeting at the FA attempting to provoke action, were rebuffed by the promise that the governing body would meet the club's owners soon, if there was a "pressing need".

Various letters from the fans to the FA met with equally feeble responses. A demonstration against Albion chief executive David Bellotti, still an active Liberal

Democrat party member, was held outside their conference in Brighton. The media paid more attention to the demo than to the politics, but there was little understanding of the fans' grievances.

In the wider world the reputation of Brighton & Hove Albion as a football club was going through the floor.

It was a terrible situation – and our dealings with Archer had become a war of words. In the early days of September he released to the media a letter which he had written to me, telling me he was continuing a dialogue with the supporters, and making a number of controversial claims, raising implied criticism about certain members of the consortium, designed to show his concerns for the club. By putting it into the public domain, he had quickly broken the confidentiality agreement we had both signed at our first meeting a week or so earlier.

My reply reminded him that for four months we had been trying to get him round the table for some serious talking. We had demonstrated that the consortium had the resources, business expertise in marketing, finance and stadium development and, above all, the commitment to resolve the Albion's current problems.

I wrote: "But our patience is running out. We have met all of your conditions. I now expect you to respond in the manner agreed at our meeting, by providing the club's financial information so that we can take things forward.

"I am informing you that unless I receive the agreed information by Friday next, September 13, the consortium will withdraw from any further dealings with you."

Since Archer had made his letter to me public, I decided to follow the precedent he had set and make key supporters aware of what I had written back to him. They responded by agreeing to pull out of any discussions with him.

Believe it or not, his next ploy was to demand that I demonstrate I had the total amount of money to build a new stadium at my immediate disposal. This was the justification he came up with, as to why my consortium wasn't a fit and proper group to take over the football club. "Where's the £30 million to build a new stadium?" he asked. Which was a ridiculous question, of course. As if he had that kind of money ready to hand.

Instead, we provided Archer with further substantiation of our funding resources, which were quite sufficient for a takeover and to get the club back on its feet.

As far as I was concerned, we had done enough. On September 13, following his failure to meet that day's deadline, I announced that the consortium was pulling out of talks with Archer because of his refusal to provide the agreed information.

It had come to the point that the football authorities could no longer ignore what was happening at Brighton.

However, the Football League continued to stand by and do absolutely nothing about the situation. But it had now undoubtedly become a national issue. At last, after months of taking no decisive action, the FA (the guardians and governing body of English football), which hadn't reckoned on the growing public furore over Archer's failure to keep his word and show us the club's books, felt it finally had to intervene.

On September 20, FA chief executive Graham Kelly called the club board and the consortium to a meeting at Park Court Hotel in Lancaster Gate – just around the corner from its then-headquarters – on September 30, to try and thrash out a solution to Brighton & Hove Albion's problems.

I did a couple of media interviews that week, on BBC Radio 5 Live and with Paul Hayward in the *Daily Telegraph*, vowing to continue the fight to save the club from what Hayward described as, "A parable for modern football: a story about right and wrong".

We went into that meeting with high hopes that we could get Archer to agree to stand down. That was the whole purpose of the meeting as far as we were concerned. And our hopes were obviously matched by the fans, a group of whom had travelled up from Sussex and gathered outside the hotel awaiting a decision.

The national press were there in force. They had carried stories that morning and the previous day, discussing this summit called by the FA, the hopes of the fans, the Albion's trauma and the wider implications for football. Everyone was expecting some kind of resolution at the meeting.

The local councils had been invited to brief the FA on the prospects for a new ground, where they would explain why Toads Hole Valley was a non-starter, but they took no part in the main proceedings – they were the opening act in the grand theatre that was a formal FA meeting. It took place in a large meeting room on the first floor of the hotel. To avoid detection by the fan and media scrum, Archer and Bellotti arrived late and sneaked in through the back entrance of the hotel, and they would leave by the same route.

Bob Pinnock, Martin Perry and I sat on one side of the room while Archer, Bellotti and, somewhat surprisingly, Ray Bloom – also representing the current board of the club – sat on the other.

In fact, it almost felt like a show trial. Between our table and Archer's table, on a level looking down on us, was the top table occupied by various FA bigwigs, including head of corporate affairs David Davies, director of communications Steve Double, about half-a-dozen blazers and Kelly – who was chairing the meeting. The chief executive seemed to me to be more interested in the publicity aspect of it: that the FA was seen to be doing something. I remember that he left the meeting at least once to deal with other business.

Once the meeting got underway, Archer was up to his old tricks. When he wasn't attempting to justify his position and stating he was not prepared to give up his major shareholding, he was putting up various objections to the proceedings – as if he was trying to score points. Bellotti said virtually nothing, apparently following his boss's recent directive that "his profile in future will be zero".

Bob and I made it clear that the consortium wanted to acquire 100 per cent of the club; no partnership would be countenanced due to the breakdown of trust in Archer. The blazers asked me some questions that were only marginally relevant, for example, if we had complied with statute so-and-so of the FA regulations, usually to do with controlling our fans – nothing remotely vital to the subject in hand. They weren't addressing the issues.

It showed a deep absence of any grasp of the real point. The FA kept wanting to threaten the club with some form of retribution if there were more crowd misdemeanours, rather than realising that there soon might not be a club to threaten. The FA treated both sides the same: in a totally condescending way. It was as if we were being court-martialled, but without the searching interrogation.

I wanted to jump up and shake them out of their complacency, even if it set off a few pacemakers. I sensed that Messrs Davies and Double were embarrassed by their colleagues' lack of understanding, but it seemed that their own lack of significant contribution was perhaps because they were acting under orders – restrained by the FA's fear of possible legal repercussions from Archer in the public arena.

So the whole thing was unproductive. Archer was not being called to account at all, to answer for all the actions that had put the club in jeopardy and so riled its supporters. In the end, it all really came to nothing – a huge disappointment for us, and all Albion fans, particularly those who were waiting outside. I remember Kelly standing on the steps of the hotel and giving an interview, talking in that ponderous, monotone way of his, as if he was announcing the election of a new Pope. "Both sides want complete control, their positions are irreconcilable. This is not a football issue, it's a business issue." He then asked the supporters to stay calm. But actually he had done nothing to make Archer account for his actions, face a disrepute charge, come back to the table or, in fact, do anything.

The Brighton story had descended into pathos.

And the next evening, we had a home game against Lincoln City. I was staying away from games at that time, which seemed to me the best thing to do. But because the day that had begun in hope had ended in total frustration, some members of the supporters' club, fearing a repeat of the York troubles, asked the club to postpone the game. The plea was ignored

Before kick-off Archer inflamed the situation further by issuing a statement rejecting the consortium's approach; he said the club would persevere with the Toads Hole Valley plans and share Fratton Park in 1997/98. That night a group of fans vented their frustration and disappointment by invading the Goldstone pitch during the game, causing several stoppages. The Football League put its decision whether to penalise the club with another points deduction on hold, ducking the issue.

What we were seeing, disgracefully, was the absolute unwillingness of the football authorities to do anything of any consequence. The Football League had basically washed its hands of it completely. They saw Brighton & Hove Albion football club as an embarrassment to their organisation, and were more than happy to pass the buck to the FA.

And as for the FA – what I saw at that meeting was their chief executive Graham Kelly paying lip service to the problem, but not really wanting to get their hands dirty, even though it was of national significance. Kelly seemed more interested in the England team than sorting out grassroots problems like ours.

Problems that were getting worse. Just two weeks after Archer's statement about Fratton Park, Portsmouth announced that Brighton couldn't play there the following season. The obvious alternative was a groundshare in London, but Bellotti revealed a plan to play at Gillingham, much further from Brighton. Strange.

A two-year deal with the Kent club was duly confirmed, condemning Albion fans to the furthest groundshare in the history of the Football League (a 150-mile round trip). Bizarrely, some of our away matches – in London – would be closer to Brighton than our home games.

It was time to talk to the fans, to let them see what I was about – and explain to them fully what I was trying to do.

On October 28, I stood up in front of an assembled gathering of Albion fans for the first time. It was at Hove Town Hall, and it was a huge meeting with about 1,600 people in attendance. The number of people didn't surprise me at all; I've always understood the level of support that the Albion has. And the fact that only around 4,000 were turning up at the Goldstone was no reflection of the true fanbase of the club.

I was a little nervous going into that meeting. I was used to giving presentations to client companies in my advertising career, but normally that would be to 50-100 people. But this was 1,600 people, who mostly didn't know me from Adam, all trying to suss me out.

And instead of speaking as an ad agency boss, I would be speaking as someone who wanted to become the head of a football club that meant so much to everyone in that hall. I was electioneering in a sense, even though they had shown they were supportive of me by turning up in those numbers. Any political candidate would have envied that size of audience at a first public meeting.

But I was prepared. What I wanted to do was present myself in a way that told the fans that I was not a hothead, that I was not just someone who felt very emotional about the whole situation but had no plan. So I gave them a presentation about what my aims were. I tried to give an order, a strategy, about what I was intending to do. I had to put over that I was coming at it from a very objective point of view as well as the fans' point of view. There was clinical thinking behind what we had to do.

But firstly I made it clear that I was a long-term (very long-term) supporter of the club and that my favourite Albion player to that day – and to this – was Johnny McNichol, our magical inside-forward in the early '50s. Our heroes as kids are always the ones that stay with us.

I wanted them to understand my credentials as a supporter, that I was genuinely a fan of the Albion, that I wasn't there for a business reason. But secondly that, in a way, I *was* there for a business reason: to get rid of Archer and run the club in a proper business-like way. That had to be done. We were in the Football League, we were a business, we had to be run like one.

Archer wouldn't have expected that kind of calm approach. He was used to a very emotive reaction from the fans and he thought that, to get them onside, I would use that fervour against him.

Not that I didn't speak from the heart. I told the audience that I was horrified that the club and the fans were at each other's throats – and the shame was all on the club. The people running Brighton & Hove Albion had treated the institution in a shameful way. "My clear objective is to overthrow Archer and get him and his cronies out of it, but also to create a proper relationship between the club and its supporters – that means involving you and making you aware of what we are doing all the time.

"We are hopefully going to usher in a new era for the club. We will always talk to the fans – and by doing so we will avoid the massive problems that exist now."

Martin outlined the new stadium issues confronting the club from the McAlpine perspective. There were limited options and the planning process was complicated to say the least. But the confident way in which he presented showed the fans that the consortium had been put together with some thought.

I remember one of the questions from the floor. "We're in dire straits. What if we get relegated out of the League? Will you, Dick Knight, still be interested in taking over?"

"If the team is relegated it won't alter one bit my absolute determination to take over the club and bring it back into the League," I replied.

And this was a real cause for concern, because Albion getting relegated from the Football League for the first time ever was already looking more than a distinct possibility. The team was in freefall. From the start of September to the middle of October, they lost nine games out of 11 and defeat at Wigan in early October sent the club to the very bottom of the Football League.

But a genuine feeling of optimism was generated at that first public meeting. At long last this was a properly organised, formidable opposition to Archer. I thought the meeting went well. The local media reported it impartially but, on fans' phone-ins, early internet chatrooms and in the pubs, a wave of support was building.

I was hugely encouraged by the reaction. I felt that I was giving people hope where previously there had been none, and that I'd reassured them I wasn't just another Archer in disguise – I had to be a genuine Albion fan because of what I knew about the club and how I spoke about it.

They seemed to have confidence in me. I don't remember there being a single dissenting voice (I do remember there being one weird question, asking about where the badge was going to be on the following year's shirt if I took over – about as relevant as some of the questions the FA blazers had asked a month earlier).

But I'd constructed my arguments and prepared my presentation. I don't think they'd ever seen a presentation from the club before – just a lot of bullshit. I systematically went through what Archer had claimed and how we'd answered that. I undermined his case by being forensic about it. I gave them a reason for believing, "This guy knows what he's talking about, knows what he's doing, he's got some organisation, and some guts – and a love of the Albion."

I think after that they believed I could be their leader, finally someone to rally behind, who had a plan and the resolve to go head to head with Archer to the wire. I was enthused because the meeting had been so positive. I came out of it feeling that we were really on the road. We were going to win this battle because I had all those supporters behind me.

And actually something positive did come out of that FA meeting on September 30. David Davies, who had sat next to Kelly on the FA's table, was the only individual from the FA who genuinely had shown an interest in trying to resolve this issue. He was acutely aware the FA had stopped short of enforcing its own rules, but understood that it could not sit idly by while Brighton & Hove Albion was being destroyed. He had realised how important this was, not just for Brighton, but for football as a whole.

It was David's idea that we sought to resolve the issue through mediation – and for the FA to pay for it. That would prove to be the crucial breakthrough.

# CHAPTER TEN

# MEDIATION

Would Bill Archer have finally crumbled against the force of the supporters' opposition, anger and protests alone? My take on it is that he would never have done anything unless he was absolutely forced to. And it's questionable whether the fans themselves, on their own, could have mustered that kind of power. The other thing was that Archer seemed to enjoy riling the supporters – his brazen approach suggested so.

I must admit that there was actually a point – after the breakdown in negotiations with Archer and the failure of the FA meeting on September 30 – when I seriously considered that I might have to start a new club again with the supporters: a 'Brighton & Hove City' as it would have been known after the award of city status in 2000.

I was so frustrated with the lack of progress, with Archer's prevarications and ludicrous demands, that I even made enquiries, through a third party, with the FA as to how far down the pyramid a new Brighton & Hove club would have to start. It was very discouraging, because they were talking about the ninth level, which was where AFC Wimbledon would begin in 2002. But there was a moment when the Albion were being run so badly into the ground, and possibly could be thrown out of the League, that this might have been the better option.

So the intervention of David Davies, the FA's Director of Public Affairs, could not have been more welcome. It was into November when he phoned me. He said: "Dick, I think the way to take this forward is through mediation, and to have the issue resolved by a third party. The people we would go to are professionals who specialise in this work from the Centre for Dispute Resolution [CEDR] – it's part of the CBI. And the FA would be prepared to pay for it."

David and I had kicked around ideas of possible ways forward, and for the first time in weeks I saw a chink of light. Although the FA was wary of acting against clubs for fear of setting a precedent after the Tottenham case, David had eventually persuaded Graham Kelly that the FA couldn't afford *not* to move to solve the long-running saga of Brighton & Hove Albion.

The fact that the FA put its weight behind mediation was absolutely crucial. Although legally it could do nothing to change the ownership of the club, Archer, as chairman, would be forced to attend these meetings to resolve this issue and the deadlock would have to be broken. If this didn't work, they might as well send in the UN peacekeepers.

The mediation momentum all came from David Davies. He made the FA finally act as it should: as the guardian of the game. I can't thank him enough, and neither can any Albion fan, for that matter.

"Brighton's plight filled me with despair," he said later. "I know the FA are not a police force and cannot just go into a club simply because they don't like the look of someone, but we had to get involved. I talked to Bill Marsh of CEDR and said, 'I need you to broker a deal so Archer can leave and Dick Knight can run the club'."

But whatever David's intention, there was no guarantee that mediation would deliver the result that he and the fans wanted. In fact, I was also being asked to make an important commitment – to get a resolution, whatever that resolution might be. Both parties had to agree that the result of this mediation was binding. If it ended up with Archer still in control of the club, it would be all over for our side.

I'm convinced that Archer went into the mediation thinking that the outcome was by no means certain, and that the process afforded him a chance of hanging on in some way. I believe he never intended to give up his entire shareholding, although he probably sensed that retaining overall control was unlikely. But the word 'mediation' suggests compromise, and I think he always had the thought in the back of his mind that Martin Perry and McAlpine might switch sides if it was going his way.

However, there really was no other, or better, route forward, and ultimately I was confident that we would win. Because while Archer probably thought he could fend me off, I was certain in my own mind that the momentum was with us. I can be pretty determined. I have been involved in some pretty tough negotiations in my business life and nearly always ended up on top. But this was much more than a business issue. I felt I had a moral justification above and beyond the norm. I was absolutely determined to overthrow him and to ensure that, in a new era for the club, no one person would ever again have overall control and manipulate the Albion as they liked.

The story was now attracting further national attention. The battle for Brighton had become a sort of parable for football in the modern era. Here was a money man in control of a football club, exploiting its financial potential and seemingly not caring about its ultimate fate. And on Monday December 9 our story made both the BBC and the front page of *The Times*.

That morning I was invited to appear on BBC2's *Newsnight*, along with Chris Wright, the then chairman of QPR. It was highly unusual for football to feature on the BBC2's flagship current affairs programme.

Peter Snow anchored the discussion, most of which was about the huge sponsorship deal that the Premier League had just done that meant even more money was going to its clubs compared to poor clubs like the Albion. In the green room beforehand Chris, who I knew as the boss of the Chrysalis media group, sympathised with our ownership predicament.

But the programme only used the Albion's struggles to highlight the differences between top and bottom. They showed clips of the crowd trouble at the Goldstone, but mainly to show what a struggling club we were rather than reflect our specific problems.

However, I emphasised in one exchange with Snow that even at Brighton the problems were caused by an intention to exploit the real-estate potential of the club regardless of its sporting future, and that many other smaller clubs could be lost this way. Wright and I bounced off each other well and it was a good discussion that brought our case to a wider audience – the general public rather than just football fans.

The front page of that morning's *Times* addressed our problem more directly. It carried the story that Des Lynam had called up the BBC Radio 5 Live 606 phone-in during a discussion on the Brighton problem two days before and said, "I'll get Archer and Knight into a room and knock their heads together." I thought, "Bloody cheek." But six months had gone by since the Intercontinental meeting and as far as the outside world was concerned nothing had happened.

On December 19 the mediation process finally began at the offices of CEDR, in a lane alongside St Katherine's Dock, just east of Tower Bridge – at a time when things were really as bad as they could get for the Albion both off and on the pitch. By now the team were bottom of Division Three, 92nd and last in the League ladder – bottom of everything. And not only that, we were effectively being cut adrift.

Jimmy Case was replaced as manager by Steve Gritt in December, with the team 11 points below the side in 91st place – which represented safety. Finishing bottom would mean relegation to the non-League Vauxhall Conference as it was then known. And in Brighton's position as a soon-to-be-homeless club, how could we possibly survive that relegation?

So it was not an especially auspicious moment to embark on what we expected to be a few weeks of negotiations in the offices of CEDR. There was no fixed end date; we would be there until we got a resolution, and in fact it took four months to get one. They were difficult talks and initially quite strange, because I was not speaking directly to Archer. That was the whole point. CEDR appointed each side its own mediator, and my mediator, Bill Marsh, would talk to me while Archer's mediator, David Richbell, would talk to him. Then they would talk to each other. Archer and I never talked on our own. We were never in the same room.

Basically they would address a subject and get your perspective on it. And then they would take that perspective and talk to their colleague who was representing the other person, who would then share that with the other person – in other words, Archer. It was very protracted, but it was designed to give the mediators full understanding of the issues while also keeping Archer and me apart.

Marsh and Richbell were both very level-headed, as you would expect. They had both recently been involved in a successful mediation between parties in the Gaza Strip, which showed their level of competence.

The whole process was extremely long and drawn-out because the mediators had a whole series of subjects they wanted to cover regarding the governance of the football club – how a club worked day-to-day, how it integrated into the League, the fact that football was governed less by the laws of the land than by its own rules, which had been formulated by the FA.

They weren't interested in the emotional side of things. They were forensic in their approach because they had to be, but I made it very clear to them that the fans were the lifeblood of any football club, and they quickly grasped that. They met a group of Albion fans, because it was important that they heard their side, and how Archer related to them. He joined the meeting later. It didn't go well because the fans saw through his attempts to offer them an olive branch or two.

The mediation was a long and difficult process aimed at getting significant movement from both sides, to a point where there was some synergy on an issue. We often had two sessions a week, and sometimes would go on long into the night, because there was a lot of wrangling.

The media wanted to know what was going on, and so did the fans, but we couldn't tell them because it was a confidential process. One dark night it was pouring with rain, and around midnight I opened a window to let some cigarette smoke out. I heard a rustling of leaves in a tree outside and then a thump, and I saw a dishevelled, rain-sodden figure that turned out to be Andy Naylor of *The Argus* who had been up the tree trying to earwig the proceedings inside CEDR.

On our side, it was myself and sometimes also Bob Pinnock and Martin Perry. I was bringing Martin into more of the discussions, mainly to get his perspective on the stadium aspect. I knew he had an expertise which would be invaluable – his know-how about planning and dealing with local authorities.

From the sidelines, McAlpine were retaining a very strong interest in how the discussions were progressing. They were of course hoping that the eventual result would involve a new stadium, built by McAlpine. But I made it very clear to Martin that, although he could join my team in terms of discussions, there were no guarantees from me whatsoever that if I was successful it would mean McAlpine would automatically get the building of the stadium.

Because Archer routinely underestimated the fans, I can't begin to imagine his reaction to the events of Saturday February 8, when the Goldstone was crammed for an amazing show of supporter fraternity at the Fans United match. Football fans from all over the UK and overseas came to show solidarity with the struggle of Albion fans – making a statement of what football is really about: the people's game.

The whole thing was the brainchild of a young Plymouth Argyle fan called Richard Vaughan, whose suggestion, spread around football internet chatrooms, inspired Albion supporters to launch Fans United for the visit of Hartlepool.

In the run-up to the Fans United game – and indeed after that game – I didn't go to matches at the Goldstone. I was in the middle of complex nego-tiations for the future of the club and it just didn't feel right going there.

In fact, I admit that I had actually found it painful to go to the Goldstone during the previous couple of seasons. Of course, there was a lot of vitriol flying around – understandably from the fans' point of view. Now, while negotiations with Archer were continuing, I decided it wouldn't be very clever of me to attend matches and potentially wind up the crowd even more.

But the Fans United game was something different. Of course I had to be there. I wouldn't have missed it for the world. I wanted to witness this expres-sion of fan power at first hand and, apart from anything else, I realised that it could be the last time I would ever stand on the East Terrace.

On the day of the game the Goldstone was shrouded by a thick sea mist, which somehow increased the sense of occasion. Part of the East Terrace had been closed since the start of the season, so I couldn't actually stand in my usual spot, in line with the 18-yard box at the North Stand end. The attendance was more than 8,000, the highest in the division so far that season, and it marked the start of a steady increase in crowds for the rest of the campaign as Albion supporters realised that the club really was in danger of oblivion as well as relegation.

Bob and I found a place nearer the south goal. As supporters began to realise who I was, there was reassuring disbelief that I was standing there, as opposed to sitting in the West Stand. But I was among my own on the East Terrace where I had been all my adult life. People began to come up to me and shake me by the hand and wish me success in my battle. That was very encouraging – the first of many moving moments. But they realised that I couldn't talk about CEDR; I was there to enjoy the game and the incredible show of support from the wider world of football.

There was more than a glimmer of hope at the Fans United game. For a start, the atmosphere was fantastic. You could see scarves and flags being held aloft from clubs all over Britain, plus banners from Real Madrid and Munich 1860 and other European clubs. The greyness of the weather contrasted with the riot of club colours everywhere.

One group of fans, walking along Old Shoreham Road behind the North Stand before the game, summed the whole thing up for me. They were three guys – a Newcastle fan, a Sunderland fan and a Middlesbrough fan, wearing their club shirts, arms around each other's shoulders. That said it all about how people around the country had responded to the plight of Albion fans. They were rising up and understanding what this meant, what was going on here. Brighton today, our club tomorrow. Club rivalries were not as important as this. This was the first genuine fans' revolt against financial opportunists who were getting control of football clubs.

Fans United also produced a dream result: we beat Hartlepool 5-0. That not only meant three valuable points, but a big improvement in our goal difference and that would ultimately prove crucial at the end of the season.

We had already started winning home games (while continuing to lose away games), which I believe was primarily because of the growing crowds at the Goldstone. However much they despised the board, with relegation looming they realised the team needed their support.

But if Fans United brought hope, the very next day provided a reminder of the obstacles still to be overcome and the trickiness of Archer. Meridian – the ITV broadcaster in the South of England – had scheduled a programme, *Goodbye Goldstone*, to go out live on the Sunday afternoon, February 9, featuring a studio discussion about the problems of the Albion. Not surprisingly, they wanted Archer and myself to appear – and I turned it down flat.

My reasoning was that the CEDR negotiations had reached a critical stage. By this point, we were making progress, but discussions weren't finished by any means. The last thing we needed was to air issues in public when nothing had been finalised.

On the Friday before the programme I said to Archer at CEDR before our session started, "We shouldn't go on. We've come this far, we can't spoil things now." He was non-committal – almost certainly weighing up what kind of opportunity this TV discussion presented to him. So then I got Marsh and Richbell involved.

"We need to have an agreement that Bill Archer and I are not going on this programme – absolutely not," I said, in a specially arranged meeting between the four of us. "We should not be washing this sort of linen in public. It's all very well for the fans, they can have their programme. But we must keep this private until we have something concrete to talk about." Marsh and Richbell both agreed – and so did Archer. He and I signed a piece of paper saying that we wouldn't go on.

When the programme started that Sunday afternoon it was announced in the TV studio that, "Dick Knight, the leader of the consortium, has declined to appear". And in the studio instead was . . . the Gillingham chairman, Paul Scally! Although the groundshare at Gillingham was still to be ratified by the League, Scally was being presented on this programme as a benefactor of the Albion – and also someone who had club connections. It was announced that his then-wife's father was a "Brighton legend" – Peter Donnelly, who played a not-very-legendary total of 59 games for the Albion, mainly in the 1962/63 season in which we were relegated into the Fourth Division.

But then, the Meridian presenter, Geoff Clark, announced, "Live from our studio in Liverpool, we welcome the Brighton chairman Bill Archer." And there he was – despite what he had promised the mediators two days earlier!

Bizarrely, he was sporting an eye-patch. He hadn't been wearing it on the Friday and I can't remember if it was explained why he was wearing it, but I wondered whether it was a ploy to garner sympathy from the TV audience. Arguably it just made him look more villainous in supporters' eyes than he already was, if that was possible.

While Clark largely ignored an invited audience of the club's fans, including some who were to play a major part in the coming struggles, Archer was allowed to attempt to justify his position, and mostly belittled the fans' concerns at the way the club was being run. Whatever he hoped to achieve he actually did himself an awful lot of damage with the mediators, because he had completely disregarded his pledge to them.

But the CEDR negotiations dragged on during the early months of 1997. Throughout the process, Archer was looking for every opportunity he could to disrupt it. I remember he got a couple of meetings cancelled at short notice because he suddenly wasn't available. By now I think he was beginning to realise that the writing was on the wall, but he wasn't going to hand complete victory to me.

It was Martin who became the key to the eventual resolution. It was clear that he was an outside party who could, in theory, have served either my consortium or the existing owners – and that's what we used in the negotiations as a bargaining tool with Archer.

Intensive discussions with the mediators produced a structure where my consortium and Archer would take equal shares in the club – 49.5 per cent each – with Martin holding the remaining one per cent on behalf of McAlpine. In effect Martin, independent of both of us, would have the casting vote.

That gave Archer a route out of the situation that would save face. Because although he was letting me in, the possibility remained that he could still control the club if he could persuade Martin to vote with him. So he agreed to the plan.

But what would 49.5 per cent of the club actually mean, in financial terms? My absolute stipulation in the agreement was that if Archer and the consortium were to have an equal shareholding, we must also have an equal financial stake in the club. Clearly that would not be the paltry £56.25 that he had put in so far. It would be the just under £1.5 million (£1,487,500) that Greg Stanley nominally had in the club.

That was the debt the club had accumulated from the original £600,000, and later another £200,000, that Stanley had put into the club, as loans rather than equity. He only ever put £800,000 into the club in total, but the debt had almost doubled thanks to interest payments and the £250,000 penalty clause activated when the interest wasn't paid.

At our meeting at CEDR on March 12 1997 where agreement in principle was finally reached, I said to Archer: "You are the mentor of Greg Stanley, you have looked after his interests in the Albion all the time you've been involved in the club. And the football club owes Greg Stanley £1.5 million. So the deal is this: you will convert that money into your personal financial stake in the football club. It's up to you how you agree that with Stanley, but the football club is not going to be paying Stanley back £1.5 million.

"Also, the £1.5m that the club owes him – the figure stops here. It's not going to accrue any more interest, and that will be your stake in the football club. The consortium will match that (myself £1,367,5000 and Bob £120,000) – and the total will equal 99 per cent of the shares of the football club." Martin would be paying a minute sum (£130) for his one per cent, so the club would initially be valued at £3 million, although the consortium's £1.5 million would be the only significant new money going in.

And Archer eventually agreed to this – with one condition: he didn't want to convert his stake (Stanley's loans) in the Albion into shares. And the reason he wanted to keep his money in the club as loans was so that he could give notice to take it out at a future date. And, six months after that, interest would start accruing – the same arrangement Stanley had had.

It wasn't a perfect deal from my or the mediators' point of view, but after months of negotiations with him it was a concession I was prepared to make in order to reach an agreement. Because as far as I was concerned, I would get rid of Archer as soon as possible. Obviously I didn't want him involved at all. And I privately vowed to myself that not only would I get him out of the club, I would make sure he would never get more than £800,000 – the amount originally put in by Stanley. Forget about the £1.5 million that the club 'owed' them, due to interest and the outrageous £250,000 penalty clause. There was no way I was ever going to let him benefit from that clause, or indeed any of the interest that had been accruing.

Equally as important as the financial structure, the other condition was that Archer must relinquish his position as chairman and that I would take over. I would not accept him keeping that title in any way, shape or form, and the mediators also said that it was non-negotiable. There had to be a significant shift in the ownership of the club for it to be meaningful as far as the public were concerned, and that meant him standing down.

Marsh said to me early on, "So that I know: would you consider Archer staying on as chairman?"

I replied, "Absolutely not. The fans would just think that the whole thing had been a waste of time, because nothing had changed."

I knew it would be hard enough for me to convince them that the deal we had was any sort of result at all, with Archer and the consortium having 49.5 per cent each. The key thing was that he'd lost control, but Albion fans would still consider any outcome that left Archer staying on as chairman unacceptable.

Archer didn't like it but he grudgingly accepted the case that the mediators and I made and agreed to step down. Of course, he could still retain his control even without the title, if he could get Martin Perry to vote with him.

Following that meeting on March 12, seven weeks before the end of the season, CEDR announced to the public that there had been a breakthrough, but they did not say that a deal had been done, because every detail still had to be final-ised by each side's lawyers. This should not have been a particularly difficult or time-consuming process. But true to form, Archer continued to delay, prevaricate and time-waste – pretty much do anything possible to move the goalposts still.

During the next meeting at CEDR, he invited Martin up to his offices in Crewe. He said, "If the three of us are going to work together, we need to exchange information, particularly about the new stadium. I've had a lot of research done that I can share with Martin." What he really meant was, "I want to find out exactly where the consortium is on the stadium, how much money they have got, and how much clout." And of course, because I had told Martin that I could not guarantee McAlpine the contract to build our new stadium, Archer could try to get Martin on his side by saying that he would be very inclined to use them.

Days, and then weeks passed, and not surprisingly Albion's long-suffering supporters became increasingly frustrated. They wanted to know why nothing had apparently changed. Why was there a delay in the takeover by the consortium? Why were Archer and Bellotti still in charge? I was hugely frustrated myself – and angry. I began to think there was something behind Archer's brinkmanship.

The trouble was that, because of the confidentiality clause in the CEDR mediation, I couldn't reveal any details of the agreement. I couldn't tell the supporters that I was levering Archer away from having 100 per cent control of the club. I also couldn't talk about what he had been getting up to since March 12. If I went public on any of this, it would give Archer the excuse to say to the CEDR people, "Knight has broken the agreement, I'm not doing the deal."

But by early April, I felt I had to make some kind of statement to allay the fans' anxiety, and tell them that the final legalities were just being ironed out. On April 7, there was a meeting of fans organised by the Brighton Independent Supporters' Association (BISA) at the Concorde bar on Brighton seafront. That was the obvious opportunity, and I invited David Davies and Richbell to join us; Bob and Martin would also be there.

When I phoned David, I explained about the fans' meeting, and how important it was. "I need you there, David," I told him. "We need to make it clear to the fans that we're pressing on with this deal, and we have the support of the FA."

David was only too happy to do what he could – but he was also understandably nervous, thinking he was about to enter the lion's den. I quickly moved to reassure him. "David, the fans are frustrated and angry – but not with you," I said. "It'll be quite rough, but they'll certainly listen to what you have to say."

Having Davies and Richbell at the meeting was to demonstrate first of all that they were totally in support of the CEDR agreement, and secondly, that the consortium was honouring its side of the deal. They wouldn't be at the meeting if we weren't.

On the platform with us were BISA officials Paul Samrah and John Baine, and Ivor Caplin, and the place was absolutely packed. We were facing hundreds of the Albion's most vociferous and vocal supporters, all desperate to hear some good news. Some were still queuing outside as we started, unable to get in. You could have cut the atmosphere with a knife.

It was not an easy meeting. Having said I would never work with Archer I had to explain to the fans that the mediation was a process of compromises – on both sides. I told them, "You've got to trust me on this. We will get there, but not necessarily initially with the perfect outcome."

While most of the audience accepted that this was an inevitable consequence of weeks of hard-fought negotiations with Archer, that news went down like a lead balloon with some of the audience.

David was superb. There were boos and a lot of chanting of "The FA have done fuck all" when he was introduced and again when he started to speak, but he won over any doubters and made it clear by the end that the club had an ally inside the FA. "I will fight for Brighton," he said. "Unless the break-through deal is ratified before the final game at the Goldstone, the FA will take decisive action."

After a couple of hours of intensely-expressed emotions, my fellow panellists and I emerged from the Concorde feeling that we'd done all we could to allay the fans' fears – they'd got some reassurance that we would not be denied, and that we'd move heaven and earth to ensure that Archer would be held to his side of the unsigned deal. Afterwards, over a late spaghetti, David said to me, "My God, now I really understand what Brighton means to these fans."

I flew out to the United States the next day for a travel industry conference in Nashville, during which I got talking one evening to a top local official about our stadium issue, which he'd heard about even in distant Tennessee.

He told me that the Nashville local authority had pledged to fund the building of a new 16,000-seat arena if they managed to land an NHL ice hockey franchise, and he wanted to know, "Why doesn't your local authority just build it for you?" I had to tell him things just didn't work that way back in the UK.

When the conference was over, I left the USA, where a 'can-do' attitude prevails, to return to the land of 'over my dead body' legislators. I did later put forward the idea at a Brighton City Forum meeting of the local movers and shakers that people could opt to have £1 a week added to their council tax to pay for schemes like the stadium, to the agreement of quite a few of the audience, but the horror of the council officials present.

The truth was that Archer was not coming under any real pressure from CEDR to sign the final agreement. The end of the season drew closer. And the end of the Goldstone – but surprisingly, perhaps, not our League status.

Remarkable things were happening on the pitch. The Albion were still bottom of Division Three, but the gap between us and the sides above had narrowed considerably as a result of our near-perfect record at the Goldstone since the turn of the year. In fact, with our away form remaining as bad under Steve Gritt as it had been under Jimmy Case, our amazing run of results at home was the only reason why we hadn't already been relegated from the Football League by the beginning of April.

It was an extraordinary turnaround. From August to early December we won only two matches at home in the league, losing five and drawing the rest. But from January to April we took virtually maximum points at the Goldstone, winning all but one drawn game. Steve had made a real difference.

But I believe that the biggest reason for the team's revival from the start of 1997 onwards was the fans. They knew that the team desperately needed them and were now turning up at the Goldstone in ever-increasing numbers.

On April 12, in our penultimate match at the Goldstone, we beat Wigan Athletic 1-0, an absolutely crucial win. Paul Rogers, who was to become a hugely important player for the Albion at Withdean and is now our commercial manager, was playing for Wigan in that game.

Then, on April 19, I saw my first Albion match since Fans United – away at Cambridge United. I stood behind the goal with my son David, Bob and the rest of the Albion fans and watched us battle to a 1-1 draw. We played well and should have won, but we had at least gained our first away point since February 1. We were still bottom, with two games of the season to play – three points behind Hereford United, who were now 23rd, having been leapfrogged that day by Hartlepool.

Most importantly, I went to that game at Cambridge knowing that we were finally moving towards the settlement with Archer.

We had been summoned to FA headquarters at Lancaster Gate by chief executive Graham Kelly for a meeting on Friday April 18, and I arranged with Archer for Martin and me to have dinner with him the night before at Green's Restaurant in Mayfair. His behaviour throughout the evening was strangely amicable, if a little nervous, and I was happy not to change the mood because the real reason for Archer's new-found bonhomie was clear.

The FA's patience had finally run out. Kelly had eventually realised – with the prodding of David Davies – that Archer was never going to sign an agreement without being forced to do so by an authority he couldn't ignore or defy. Kelly was rightly concerned that, without an announcement of ownership change beforehand, the final match at the Goldstone the following week, against Doncaster Rovers, could become very ugly indeed.

It certainly focused Archer's mind, because that FA meeting was decisive. In a matter of hours their lawyers drafted a Memorandum of Understanding that detailed the restructuring of the club, which would be formally announced at a press conference in London a few days later.

I left the meeting at the FA and made a statement to the press waiting in the street outside, "After the long process of mediation talks, at last we have a resolution that I'm happy with. And because I'm happy with the deal, I believe Albion fans will be happy with it too, because Bill Archer no longer has control of the club."

And so, on Tuesday April 22 – 20 weeks after we had begun mediation at

CEDR, and just four days before the Albion's final game at the Goldstone Ground, we gathered at the London Metropole Hotel in Edgware Road to announce the new structure of the Albion.

That day even Brian Clough, whose links with Brighton were marked by that short blip in his distinguished managerial career, was moved to tell the world: "I'm always sad to hear about any football club being in a mess, so you can imagine how I feel when it concerns one that has employed me. Somewhere along the line the club's demise must be on one or two people's conscience and my only hope is that out of all the trouble and trauma they have experienced, Brighton will re-emerge as a footballing force once more. I'm keeping my fingers crossed."

CEDR issued a press release that set out the main points of the Memorandum of Understanding between the existing owners and the consortium, which Archer and I would sign that day, in front of the TV cameras and journalists packed into the hotel conference suite. The most important elements were the new share ownership, and the fact that I would become chairman of Brighton & Hove Albion FC.

The composition of the board would be myself, Bob, Martin and Archer. At the suggestion of the mediators, two independent non-executive directors would also be appointed: Sir John Smith, former deputy commissioner of the Metropolitan Police (who had chaired the FA's football bungs enquiry that had snared then-Arsenal manager George Graham), and Richard Faulkner, vice-chairman of the Football Trust.

In my view, having Sir John and Richard (later Lord) Faulkner on the board – both highly experienced men who could watch over the club and in particular, keep an eye on Archer, who eventually agreed to their appointments – was a bonus. Sir John in particular would become a hugely valued friend to the club, and to me personally, in the next few years.

Other parts of the Memorandum were aims that were never fulfilled rather than statements of fact – for example, that there would be a supporters' representative on the board. A few days later I met a group of key supporters at my house in Hove to honour that pledge, but they declined the offer, saying they were comfortable with the board structure as Archer was no longer the majority shareholder, I was in charge, and provided we kept them in the loop on developments as before, which I was happy to confirm.

The statement announcing the deal also said that "all parties agree that playing locally next season is a priority" and noted that the club had yet to be given approval for groundsharing at Gillingham.

CEDR further announced that "a planning application will be made for a permanent stadium in the Brighton and Hove area within the next three months.

The scheme will include a 15,000-seat capacity initially, with plans to extend up to a 25,000-seat capacity in the future". This timescale proved to be hopelessly optimistic.

The CEDR statement concluded with the observation that: "This has been a long and difficult mediation and has involved significant movement on all sides. It should be recorded that the official purpose of the mediation laid down by the Football Association was that professional football should continue to be played in Brighton and Hove and that the future of this historic club should be assured. We believe that aim has been achieved. The parties have confirmed that this settlement is firm and will not be affected if Brighton are relegated . . ."

The start of the press conference was delayed because Archer arrived late, even the assembled press corps seeming to tense up as he walked into the hotel foyer. When it got under way, Kelly and Davies had their say and then I spoke.

"After all that's happened, I can't help thinking about my dad, who would never have believed it possible, and would have been so proud that I had become Albion chairman." I also tried to convey what it meant to me, saying it was an honour for a long-term fan like me to be in charge, but that the real job was just beginning.

Archer made his own statement – everyone on the platform shifting uncomfortably in their seats when he started talking – and did something quite extraordinary. He apologised to the fans for the all the pain he'd caused. Then, in answer to a question from Paul Hayward, who wanted to know how he could justify his actions, he described the club's travails as "a price worth paying to get us into a position where we can build a brand new stadium". I sat through that hypocritical claim – Archer taking credit for, and being part of, the salvation of the club – with an unconcealed grimace.

And at one point Archer also made a memorable faux pas, describing the Albion as "Brighton & Hove DIY" – a Freudian slip if ever there was one! Finally he confirmed, to widespread relief, that he would not be attending the Doncaster game.

Afterwards, we spoke to the assembled media and the few Albion supporters who had sneaked into the press conference. I told Nick Szczepanik of *The Times*: "I want to thank all Albion fans for their resilience and patience over the last months. I'm looking forward to being chairman. The past year has been a fantastic show of the emotional ties that bind supporters and clubs. We must all get on with rebuilding the Albion to prove that every single person's effort has been worthwhile."

He began his piece in the following day's paper, "After a year of pitch invasions, demonstrations and boycotts, supporters of Brighton & Hove Albion finally got the result they wanted yesterday." And ultimately I was satisfied that it was the best deal that could have been done.

In an ideal world we would have got rid of Archer instantly. But I'd made a secret commitment to myself to get rid of him as soon as I possibly could. I never thought he would play an active role in the new structure. We both knew that it was a smokescreen for him to exit without the ignominy of being booted straight out. This gave him a more dignified way out.

I was pretty certain he intended to take that route – although Archer being Archer, it was never going to be that straightforward. The whole ownership issue would still drag on for several months more. But at that point I didn't want to think about Archer any more. It was all about what happened on Saturday.

# CHAPTER ELEVEN

# THE BEGINNING AND THE END

From the moment the FA announcement of the club's restructuring was made on April 22, I became chairman-elect of the Albion. But even though the legalities were still to be settled it was agreed by the FA, the mediators, myself and, reluctantly, Bill Archer that I would be regarded as chairman from that point on.

The day after the press conference in London I issued a statement, via *The Argus*, which summed up my feelings. "I step into the role of Albion chairman with some humility, knowing what the club means to thousands of fans like me." I spoke about my plan to rebuild the club, and I also made the point that, in the circumstances, I was satisfied with the outcome of the negotiations, as were the FA, CEDR and my co-directors – and the fans should be too. The crucial outcome was that Archer no longer had control.

In many ways it was a prompt call to 'move on' from the Archer and Bellotti years, to put them behind us in order to focus completely on the future and on one of the most important football matches in the club's history, happening in just three days' time. Until the legals were completed, Bellotti was officially still chief executive, but I wanted him gone straight after that.

"The time for turmoil and confrontation must now be over," I wrote. "We must all now get on with rebuilding the Albion. The new board will work together to achieve the following key objectives: i) an injection of new finance into the club; ii) rigorously pursue all our options to ensure Albion will be playing their home matches as close to Brighton as possible next season; iii) making real progress in the plans for our permanent stadium."

And then I wrote about that final game at the Goldstone, against Doncaster, and I ended with a promise. "On Saturday . . . I'm sure the team will rise to the occasion. There won't be a dry eye in the place, whatever the result. But I pledge that this board will bring brighter days back to the Albion." I was praying that brighter days would be starting sooner rather than later.

I did a couple of interviews, on BBC Radio 5 Live and local radio, on the Thursday. The media pressure was building around the club after the strange mediation process and the realisation that it was facing the abyss if relegated. But after the months of hand-to-hand combat with Archer, nothing was going to faze me, and I felt relieved to be able to concentrate on football for once. I was calm and confident and I hope I conveyed that to the listeners.

On the Friday, the day before the game, I went to the training ground at the University of Sussex in Falmer to meet the players for the first time. I arrived there late morning, met up with Steve Gritt, and went over to speak to them in the peaceful surroundings of the distant pitch where they were training to escape the attentions of media and fans.

You would think I would have been prepared for that moment. But as I approached the players and coaches, gathered on the pitch, I was strangely tongue-tied – a most unusual occurrence for me. I was used to speaking to an audience, of course, and I usually ad-libbed from knowledge of what I was talking about, but this was different. I didn't know these guys, only from afar. Were they expecting some brilliant, inspirational speech from me? I felt inadequate being confronted by a squad of professional footballers for the first time, waiting, seemingly thinking, "Well, come on then."

They formed a circle round me and I started off underwhelmingly, by introducing myself and explaining to them (in case they didn't already know) that I was an Albion fan. And I told them that things were going to change. Then, as if this is what I meant by 'change', I blurted out, perhaps subconsciously comparing myself to Archer, "I am never going to be an absent chairman; I will be at every match, home and away."

The players treated this earth-shattering news with a polite respect, and even though I could have been seen as a distraction from the task at hand, I began to feel that they appreciated that I had come to see them. The chairman visiting the training ground was completely unheard of.

Warming to the task, I made the point that Albion fans had already rallied around the team, had come back to the Goldstone in droves, and the team had responded brilliantly. Now they had the chance of making the great escape from relegation. The players obviously knew how important the game was from a football point of view – but they also understood the historic nature of this game. They were up for it.

Ross Johnson, the local lad who played centre-half, said, "I know what this means, Mr Chairman. My family have always supported the club." Ian Baird, the centre-forward and captain, and the team's most seasoned pro, came over as understanding what the club meant to its community. "Don't worry, Mr Chairman," he said. "We won't let the fans down. We'll be giving it our best shot." It was the first time I realised that I was going to have to get used to the traditional football title of 'Mr Chairman' rather than just 'Dick' or 'Mr Knight'.

I didn't quiz Steve about his tactics. It was too late for that. He had obviously got the squad up to a fine pitch. They had the bit between their teeth. I wished him, "Good luck tomorrow" and came away from the training ground reassured by the mood among the players. They knew that there was going to be as big a crowd as there possibly could be the next day for the game against Doncaster – it would be one of the most important games of their lives.

Saturday April 26 1997. Every Brighton & Hove Albion fan who was there, for the final match at the Goldstone, will have memories of that day. I don't believe that anyone could forget it.

My home is very close to the Goldstone Ground – a five-minute walk across the park. For many years I had left the house about 2.50pm, trudged over Hove Recreation Ground, into Old Shoreham Road, down into Goldstone Lane, paid my money at the turnstiles and would usually be standing on the East Terrace, in line with the north penalty area, by kick-off. Or maybe 3.05pm. As people who know me will attest, timekeeping is perhaps not my most impressive attribute (in fact, it's not an attribute at all). But those days were coming to an end, along with the East Terrace itself. No – they had already ended.

I had become chairman-elect just as Brighton & Hove Albion were to play their last-ever game at the Goldstone Ground, their cherished home for the past 95 years. A game that would also determine the fate of the club. Our survival in the Football League, arguably our survival as a football club, almost certainly depended on us winning the match with Doncaster Rovers that April afternoon. We were three points behind second-bottom Hereford with two games remaining. Anything but victory would be all but fatal.

The circumstances of this game were so momentous, the stakes were so high. It was incredible, almost surreal. The fact it was me – Dick Knight, who had watched the Albion from the terraces since I was eight, perhaps 1,000 games, and had never before watched them play sitting in the main West Stand, let alone in the directors' box – who had become chairman on this day. And that, at this dark hour, my elevation represented a ray of hope for the club.

It was almost too difficult to reflect on the enormous significance of taking over at this moment. And for all the huge tension and the very real sense of solemnity that existed in the hours leading up to the game, I couldn't help thinking, "Is this every fan's dream come true? Or will it be a nightmare?" Maybe that was the best way of dealing with it.

In 51 years as a fan, I had never expected to become the chairman of the Albion, nor ever aspired to that position. Although I hadn't watched the team from the West Stand I had sat there for one game, an England under-21 international against Norway in 1977, when Peter Ward played and scored a hat-trick in a 6-0 win. I'd been invited by a friend for that game and didn't particularly enjoy sitting. I preferred standing in my spot on the East Terrace.

But on this day, the final ever match at the Goldstone, I would watch the Albion from the West Stand for the very first time – and from the director's box. As chairman! And then, if that wasn't unreal enough, after the match, the whole place would be pulled to pieces . . .

It was raining on the morning of the match. I did an interview with BBC local radio at 11am, suddenly a main player in the drama about to unfold. And then I went to the Goldstone, a few hours earlier than I would normally arrive for a game. John Surie, my daughter Amanda's boyfriend and soon to be my son-in-law, dropped me off at the 'directors' entrance' in Newtown Road for the first and only time. I went in, noticed there was no one to greet me, met Bob and went up to the boardroom at the Goldstone for the first time. And what a bleak place that was.

Cracked and peeling, faded eggshell-blue walls, virtually no furniture apart from a few chairs, no trophy cabinet, a couple of grime-stained honours boards on the stairs leading up listing Albion players who had won international caps – the last name, I think, was Steve Penney for Northern Ireland – and some very basic catering, comprising tea, coffee and a few biscuits. Bellotti and Archer, neither of whom was there, had done the occasion proud.

Then I went out onto the pitch. It was about 12.30pm – two and a half hours before kick-off – and fans were already arriving. There was already a palpable sense of tension, and reverence. In the south-west corner of the pitch, a lady bagpipe player appeared and started rehearsing *The Last Post*, which she was to perform just before kick-off. There was a feeling of history being made. I had been asked to do a live interview on the pitch for the pre-match *Football Focus* programme on BBC *Grandstand*, with Steve Gritt. He came out from the tunnel in the main stand and onto the pitch, looking composed and very serious.

Steve and I shook hands and exchanged a few words before the interview started with us talking to the presenter in the studio, so looking directly into the TV camera that was positioned near the north stand, with lots of fans standing around. This was also a strange experience – certainly for me and probably for anyone else who'd been to the Goldstone in recent years. We weren't used to having TV cameras there – apart from when they were filming crowd trouble – and here were the new chairman and the manager standing there talking to the nation in a civilised fashion.

I was asked a few questions, but I only remember one. That was when the presenter said, "How does it feel to be taking over for the last-ever Brighton game at the Goldstone?" I replied, "Very sad. But nothing compared to the way I will feel if this turns out to be the last-ever Brighton game played anywhere in our home towns, full stop. I intend to make sure it isn't."

I often think, as I look out today over the 30,000 spectators enjoying our magnificent new home, the Amex – my vision – that more than half of them are completely unaware of just how close the club came to oblivion a few years earlier.

After the interview I returned to the boardroom. Bob's wife Jenny and daughter Jane had arrived. So had Martin. My son David and daughter Amanda joined me. Sir John Smith and Richard Faulkner came in soon after. That was it – no guests, no sponsors. The new board rattled around that depressing place. There was not a sign of a Doncaster director all afternoon.

I thought about Margie. Before she died, she had told our kids, "Dad should get involved in trying to save the Albion, he needs a new challenge." It was a real pang of sadness, something that put football into some kind of perspective. Even on that day.

But you couldn't get away from the magnitude of it, and the emotion. It was close to kick-off, from inside the boardroom you could hear the noise of the crowd outside. It was time to join them. I was pointed towards the directors' box, and came out.

The Goldstone was packed, of course. By that time the capacity was under 12,000 – and tickets for the game had sold out weeks before. As I stood in the directors' box with my children, and with Bob and his family and Martin just behind, taking it in, the crowd started applauding. For a moment I thought, "What are they applauding?" – and then I realised it was me.

In retrospect, I probably should have been more formally dressed to reflect the sense of occasion. I'm not particularly keen on wearing suits and ties, but for some reason I had made no special effort whatsoever with my appearance that day: I was wearing a black T-shirt under my blue-and-white checked shirt, so I looked like a slightly scruffy French fisherman standing there, accepting the applause of the crowd, waving back. And this was a huge moment. The crowd's reaction was basically an outburst of relief that we had finally clinched the deal and, of course, finally broken Archer's hold on the club. This was a victory that the crowd could actually see and believe in. I looked at my kids and they smiled, probably thinking of what their mum had said. I did feel a sense of pride that we'd actually done it. But it was all about what happened out on the pitch now.

Just before kick-off two Doncaster substitutes left the bench and started moving up the touchline, as if they were warming up. But they were carrying a banner and they continued on round the pitch, the applause rising. The banner read: "Rover players salute Brighton fans." A wonderful gesture.

The game got under way, and it was pretty ugly stuff early on. Very ugly in fact. Baird got into a 'handbags' scuffle with the Doncaster centre-half, Darren Moore, and they were both sent off. But the incident was made even worse by the fact that bananas were disgracefully thrown on the pitch, aimed at Moore, from a moron on the West Terrace North. I saw that, and I vowed to myself that that sort of despicable racist behaviour would never be allowed to happen at a Brighton match again.

The game went on with 10 men on each side and with Rovers creating more of the few goalscoring chances in the first half. The atmosphere in the ground was unbelievably tense. The teams went in at half-time at 0-0. We returned to the desolate Albion boardroom and had a cup of stewed tea. I remember saying to Bob, "Normally we'd be over there on the East Terrace at this point, enjoying our satsumas instead of this excuse for a cuppa."

It was just a way of breaking the tension a bit. Because no one in our team was playing particularly well. But I was quietly confident that we would do it. I always thought we'd win that game, and I still believed. I was actually quite calm. Maybe what I'd been through with Archer made it seem like a relatively small matter to win a game of football. But I felt that the momentum from the fans behind the team was so strong that they would almost will the ball into the Doncaster net. And that's pretty much how it happened.

As the second half got under way, the Albion, kicking into the south goal, started to take more control of the game. Robbie Reinelt came on at half-time, and Albion winger Stuart Storer, moved infield when Baird was sent off, went wide right again and the Doncaster defence were finding him a handful. We created a couple of chances and then on 68 minutes we won a corner on the right. Every Albion fan knows what happened next – even the ones (like my grandchildren) who hadn't been born yet.

Jeff Minton took the corner and Storer headed the ball towards the goal where, surrounded by defenders, the Doncaster goalie punched it up a few feet in the air towards Albion defender Mark Morris who, jumping, won the scramble but, from about three yards, headed it against the bar. And then Storer, running in, volleyed the rebound into the top right-hand corner of the net.

The ground erupted. Pandemonium, unrestrained joy, massive relief. As the ball hit the net, I leapt about three feet in the air, arms outstretched in triumph, then sat down again straight away, realising that chairmen don't behave that way. Then, with an instinctive "Why the hell not?" I was up again, cheering madly, thinking, somewhat selfishly, "Yeeesss, that'll do – the first Albion goal of my reign."

Although I don't remember Doncaster really threatening us seriously, there were 22 minutes plus three minutes' time added on of nail-biting tension before the final whistle as we held on, by the skin of our teeth, to win 1-0.

There was euphoria. We had done it. Three precious points. We had survived – at least until the final day of the season.

The players had shown a determination in that game that proved unbeatable. They had given us a chance – and then the news came through that Hereford had lost at Leyton Orient. Brighton & Hove Albion were no longer the bottom club in the Football League.

The second the final whistle was blown, the fans poured onto the pitch – and the players ran off down the tunnel – and then reappeared with us in the directors' box, to take the acclaim of the crowd. They were naturally ecstatic – Reinelt, in his stockinged feet, attempting to stand on the arms of the chairs to raise himself higher and milk the applause of the crowd, almost slipping and shooting off into the massed crowd below. Luckily he didn't! We would definitely need Robbie at Hereford, who – as fate would have it – we were playing in the final game the following week.

It was a moment where players, fans and the new boss could bond. I remember joking to someone that I was the only Albion chairman with a 100 per cent winning record. But it was a brief moment. Joy was not the only emotion felt by the fans – it was mixed with sadness, even anger. The supporters hadn't only poured on the pitch to celebrate with the players (I don't think it was even the main reason); they came on the pitch to take souvenirs of the Goldstone away with them.

When we went back to that depressing, inhospitable boardroom, we stood and listened to the incredible, even frightening, sounds above our heads. There were loud bangs and creaks as fans prised away their mementos of the old ground – sometimes even the wood and metal seats from where they'd watched the Albion play. At least, that's how it sounded – as if the West Stand was being torn asunder around us. And they were taking the pitch away with them as well – strips of the hallowed turf, penalty spots, goallines, being carefully cut out and lovingly carted off to be meticulously nurtured in gardens across Sussex in the years to come. The police never intervened. Why should they?

And then we left the Goldstone for the last time. I felt bitterly sad, obviously. But I was also looking forward. We could look back at the history of the Albion, and would always appreciate the importance of the Goldstone Ground. But after the Doncaster match I remember feeling almost an element of relief that the awful saga of the last few years of the Goldstone was finally over.

The truth is that, for me, the Goldstone had already died as a ground, even before we had got to the last match. Like many other Albion fans, all my good memories of the place were wrapped up in things that had happened many years before, when we'd seen great matches graced by wonderful players like McNichol, Langley, Ward, Lawrenson, and many more. That was when it was a great football ground – contained, compact, and usually generating a fantastic atmosphere.

Despite the fact that in the previous six months virtually every game at the Goldstone had been a mini-cup final, it didn't alter the reality that what had happened in the last couple of seasons was terrible. An atmosphere of doom hung over the place. Years of neglect, regulation, hooliganism and gross misman-agement had all conspired to turn the Goldstone into a bit of a hellhole.

It could all have been different, of course. During the game, as I looked out over our crumbling mausoleum, playing out its final act, I kept thinking that if I had been custodian of the club a few years sooner, the last game at the Goldstone would have been a joyous affair, preceding the first game at our shiny new home just three months later at the start of the next season. There would have been none of the sadness, rancour, and fear for the future that now came with the badge of being an Albion supporter.

I would have planned, consulted, negotiated and implemented a seamless move to a brand new stadium as normal clubs such as Bolton, Derby, Stoke and Sunderland were all doing that summer. But the club I had inherited had long ceased to be a normal club. Courtesy of Archer & Co, we were about to start playing all our home games further away from Brighton than some of our away games. Just how dysfunctional a club was that? We were going into distant exile, the most far-flung groundshare in Football League history, and I was taking on a monumental task to get the Albion back into a 21st-century stadium in our own city via that tortuous route.

And not even a Hollywood fantasy scriptwriter would have come up with the idea that it would take 14 years to do it.

# CHAPTER TWELVE

# THE GREAT ESCAPE

And if the Doncaster game wasn't momentous enough, then it all came down to the Hereford match.

My second game as Albion chairman (or, strictly speaking, chairman-elect) was even more important than my first. Quite simply, it was the most important game in the club's history.

In an excruciating twist provided by the fixture computer, our fate was now wrapped up in a game between the two bottom teams in the Third Division. This match – away at Hereford United, on Saturday May 3 1997 – was a sort of anti-cup final. The prize for the winner was survival, and the loser would be relegated from the Football League. Never before, since the League was founded in 1888, had two teams played each other for such a prize on the last day of the season.

Our victory over Doncaster had given us a slight edge, in that Hereford were now below us and a draw would be good enough to keep the Albion up. But if we lost at Edgar Street, 77 years of active service in the Football League would be over.

At that time, only one team was relegated into the Football Conference each season and it was considered a disastrous fate for any club to lose its League status. But for it to happen to a club like Brighton & Hove Albion would have been unprecedented. Dropping into the nether-world of non-League football opened up the possibility that you would never return, condemned to be an also-ran that might occasionally cause an upset in the early rounds of the FA Cup.

And my lurking fear was that if we went ahead and played our home games – League or non-League – the following season at Gillingham, as we were contracted to do, it could be a death sentence.

In short, following the last game at the Goldstone, my first away game as Brighton chairman was the most historic and portentous day for the club. And the most nerve-shredding game any Albion fan was ever likely to witness.

The week between the Doncaster and Hereford games is now a barely-remembered blur. Nothing happened, even my birthday, that was remotely as important or memorable as the two football matches that flanked it. Apart from the fact that the national media, who had already given the last Goldstone game a lot of coverage, then had a field day with the scenario developing for the final day of the season.

Oh yes, and there was also the small matter of a General Election, in which on the night of Thursday May 1 and morning of Friday May 2 Labour won a landslide victory and Tony Blair became Prime Minister. Following a huge swing against his Tory predecessor, Ivor Caplin became the first-ever Labour MP for Hove – the result that told Blair it was a walkover – and without question Brighton & Hove Albion's biggest fan in the House of Commons.

I stayed up late on the Thursday night, watching the election results come in and realising that Labour were coming back into power for the first time since the 1970s. It provided something of a diversion from thinking about the Hereford match, but then I had to bring a football analogy into it – it was the equivalent of a 5-0 thrashing.

Although it was a very tense week, I was essentially optimistic about our chances. We only had to draw this game to stay up, and I knew there were going to be as many Albion fans at Edgar Street, Hereford's ground, as home fans. Also, we'd been in the relegation zone virtually all season and were battle-hardened. Our fans had rallied around the team as the season progressed.

Hereford, by contrast, had got into this dreadful slump. They were drained of confidence and now they were rock-bottom, for the first time since September. They had to win. But there was one important cause for concern, which I tried not to think about: Brighton's dreadful away record. We had only won one game on the road all season, drawn just three and lost 18 matches . . .

I received a lot of well-wishing messages beforehand – mainly coming from Albion fans, and from my friends in London in the advertising business. I spoke to Liam Brady, of course. He obviously wouldn't be at the match but told me, "This is your second big test, Dick. Enjoy it."

"I will, Liam," I replied. "It's what I signed up for." I knew deep down that, for all of the troubles, it was the love of my club and the game that drove me to get involved.

There were messages from the CEDR people, from David Davies – but nothing from Bill Archer. Another example of him showing his true colours. But at least he wasn't going to show up. David Bellotti was also informed by Hereford that he wouldn't be welcome, but he turned up at Edgar Street all the same.

On the morning of the game I faced some gloom-laden questions in a couple of radio interviews, where I hope I lifted spirits, before setting off for Hereford by car with my daughter Amanda and her fiancé John. Amazingly, my son David, as big an Albion fan as me, had taken himself off to Scotland for a university reunion and wasn't going to the match. The journey all the way to Hereford was like a travelling convoy of Albion fans, with blue-and-white scarves and banners resplendent in the backs of cars and coaches.

I had the feeling that, at this critical moment, the natural support of the club was coming to the fore – and were showing their colours again. And I could see, from the number of people who were waving at me, growing evidence that after years of torment, the supporters had received a genuine boost with news of the takeover.

We arrived at Edgar Street a good two hours before the 3pm kick-off. Again there were plenty of fans of both sides already there and the atmosphere and the tension were already building. But from the Brighton point of view it was a bit different from the previous week. Albion fans were almost in a party mood – most likely because of our win over Doncaster and also, perhaps, a teeny bit because they had a new chairman.

For my part I had to negotiate the fact that I was entering the boardroom of another club and officially representing Brighton & Hove Albion at an away game for the first time. This was a proud moment and I was determined not to appear nervous or ashamed to be there. I knew that from that day we had to start changing the image of the Albion. And fortunately I remembered to wear a tie.

I met up with Bob Pinnock, who had driven down with his family and, together with Sir John Smith, we entered the small, cosy Hereford boardroom. The Hereford chairman, Peter Hill, and his board were welcoming and friendly – whilst privately no doubt wishing that they were going to beat us 6-0. It was what I would come to recognise as the unwritten code of the boardroom on match-days – a layer of respectability and cordiality to the visiting team that masks a deep-seated desire to thrash the pants off them.

Bellotti was there, sitting apprehensively in a corner, and was ignored by almost everyone – certainly by us. There were two nice ladies serving – hot food, sandwiches, pies, cakes – and I thought, "Wow, you get all this thrown in." There had certainly not been any of that at the Goldstone Ground the previous week. Going into the Hereford boardroom felt a bit like going to a country fair.

But having entered the boardrooms of most of the clubs of the Football League since then, I can say that the Hereford boardroom is also quite unusual, because it was situated really close to the pitch – just off the players' tunnel leading out onto the playing surface in fact. And right across from the board-room were the teams' dressing rooms. That would actually prove to be quite significant later on.

To say that Edgar Street is a compact ground is something of an understate-ment. It's so tight you can virtually reach out from the directors' box and touch a player as he runs down the wing. And then there was the Hereford mascot – like our own beloved seagull in a way, a symbol of the club's surroundings. It was a huge Hereford-bred bull, which was paraded out on the pitch in front of the main stand before the game. It took up virtually the whole of the entrance of the tunnel, bumping against the dugouts on either side. By this time, about an hour before kick-off, I was being interviewed on the pitch for TV and radio, again with Steve Gritt.

I have to say that Steve put a lot of pressure on himself that day. He was doing interviews before the match, looking calm and collected as usual, but inwardly probably as anxious as the rest of us. I must have wished him good luck half-a-dozen times.

The atmosphere inside the ground before the game became more and more muted as kick-off approached. Everyone knew what was at stake.

And then the game started, and it was probably the worst game that I or anyone else had ever watched. There was so much riding on it that I don't think anyone really expected anything different. The pressure on the players was absolutely huge, and what's more the weather was sunny but windy, and the pitch was rock-hard. And, of course, these were two pretty poor teams. But people weren't there for the quality of the football; what was at stake was far more important than that.

Twenty minutes of nervous non-football crept by, and neither team remotely looked like scoring. That was fine by us, of course. But in the 21st minute, Hereford's Tony Agana won an aerial challenge on the left, then poked a weak cross into the goalmouth past Mark Ormerod. Racing back in an attempt to clear, Kerry Mayo turned the ball into his own net. 1-0 to Hereford.

Kerry held his head in his hands, the massed Albion fans fell silent and I had this horrible feeling in the pit of my stomach. And the players' heads seemed to drop. Hereford came at us again and again and at times it was desperate stuff. But the defence held out until half-time.

As the players trudged off, I could see the despair on Kerry's face. He was one of the youngest players in the team, if not *the* youngest, and our least experienced player. He was also one of the few local lads in the team, and he had actually been one of our better players on the day, before disaster had struck. I felt desperate, for him and my team. So I did something at half-time in that match that I've never ever done since.

# THE GREAT ESCAPE

The proximity of the team's dressing room to the Hereford boardroom gave me the chance. Before the end of the half-time interval I was able to leave the boardroom, and within a few steps I was outside our dressing room. Immediately I could hear Steve talking inside, urging our players on. But I didn't go in; I waited outside. I waited for the door to open.

I think the first player to come out was the right-back John Humphrey who registered this look of surprise, seeing me standing there. Then they all filed past me, most of them not even conscious I was there, their thoughts fixed on something more crucial. But I was waiting for Kerry, who was still in the changing room – the last one to leave. He looked awful, shoulders slumped. And Steve was still sitting in the dressing room, looking worried.

Kerry came out and starting walking the few yards across towards the players' tunnel. And I walked with him, and started talking to him, as quickly as possible. "Kerry, the game's not over," I said. "Forget what happened – you're playing well. Put it out of your mind. We are not out of this game by any means. We can get back in the game, absolutely no problem."

By this point I think I had my arm around him and was squeezing him, in my attempt to give him as much encouragement as possible. And finally I said, "Come on – you're a Brighton boy. We're not going to go down today. We're not going to get relegated!" By this point we were at the side of the pitch. Kerry mumbled a "Thank you Mr Chairman" and ran out onto that rock-hard, grassless Edgar Street surface.

The second half began. Immediately we were more positive, putting pressure on the fairly fragile Hereford defence, who sat further and further back and encouraged us to come forward. And the Albion fans roared them on. Hereford had a centre-forward, Adrian Foster, who was quite useful. They left him up front virtually on his own, but he was dangerous, Ross Johnson almost conceding a penalty for one tackle on him. The tension was unbelievable.

And then, in the 63rd minute, we scored: Craig Maskell collected a weak clearance, took the ball on his knee and hit a left-foot volley past the keeper, Andy De Bont, which came back from his left-hand post across the goal. And Robbie Reinelt – only just on as substitute – went for the rebound. I just had that instant feeling, when he was sprinting forward, that he was going to win the race with the defenders to the ball and bury it. And he did.

Four thousand Albion fans including me, Bob and Sir John in the directors' box – all showing a distinct lack of decorum – erupted. An explosion of euphoria and, after their celebrations, when the players trotted back to start the game again, I saw Kerry looking over to where I was sitting and giving me a thumbs-up.

For the next heart-stopping 27 minutes plus four excruciating minutes of stoppage time, we clung on for the 1-1 draw that ensured Brighton & Hove Albion's continued status in the Football League.

Robbie Reinelt became the hero for getting the goal that kept us there – but I think our goalie Mark Ormerod deserves at least as much credit. Bradley Sandeman, the Hereford midfielder, bulleted a shot towards the bottom corner and Mark made this wonderful one-handed save down low to his left and put the ball around the post – a brilliant stop because it was definitely going in. Then a minute into added time, Foster broke clear and was through on goal, but Ormerod stood his ground and the striker lifted the ball straight into his arms.

When the whistle finally went, the elated Albion fans at one end of the ground went crazy, while the other end was in complete despair. Police came onto the pitch and took up positions along the halfway line to prevent any trouble. For a moment it looked like there might be some, but it quickly passed. The Hereford fans were in a state of collective shock, scarcely able to believe what had happened.

And then the Hereford chairman was shaking my hand, and graciously congratulating me. I thanked him, meaninglessly apologising. I'll never forget the look on his face – he was ashen. What an awful way to be relegated. As with Kerry an hour earlier I felt sorry for him, but this time it was tempered with other emotions – complete joy and total relief.

I went on the pitch, where the players and Steve Gritt were being engulfed by Albion fans. Steve was quite rightly inundated with people congratulating him. There were interviews. A gorilla in a blue-and-white scarf came up and hugged me.

We'd done it. We'd actually saved ourselves. And I was an unbeaten League chairman. Two games, four points – easy!

Years later I discovered that one of my all-time favourite sports writers, the great Frank Keating of *The Guardian*, was a big Hereford fan, and the day Brighton cost them their Football League place, he said, was one of the worst of his life. Apparently Frank took up growing roses to help him get over it. Although it didn't stop the flow of witty, perceptive articles in the following years, and his way with words never failed him, it was only when Hereford regained their League place in 2006 – after a period of wilderness years I'd feared for the Albion – that all was well again. Frank died in early 2013; he'd given me so much pleasure and my regret was that I never got to say sorry to him.

Escaping relegation hadn't been easy. But it was certainly historic. To have two games of such magnitude when you take over as chairman is unusual. Maybe it's actually unique and unprecedented. But it did in a way set the standard of what was to follow. Little was I to realise that there would be plenty more days like that in the years to come.

Okay, maybe nothing quite as momentous as that day at Hereford. But it was the start of the rollercoaster. And hardly ever a dull moment in 12 years.

# CHAPTER THIRTEEN

# THE WORLD AGAINST US

So there had been the unbelievable drama, tension, fleeting euphoria, and sadness of the last game at the Goldstone – followed by the unbelievable drama, tension and eventual euphoria and relief of the 'Great Escape' at Hereford. And for a couple of days I could savour those feelings like every other Albion fan. But then I came crashing back down to earth. The scale of the task ahead was daunting.

First of all I still wasn't officially the chairman yet. I was only chairman-elect – and that wasn't quite settled either. It should have been quite straightforward to implement the deal, a sale and purchase agreement of shares, and for us to go through due diligence – as you must when you take over an existing organisation – even though in this case we were going to reorganise it, close down Foray 585 and call it Brighton & Hove Albion Holdings Limited.

However, Bill Archer seemed in in no hurry to complete the transfer of power. I met him with Martin Perry and Bob Pinnock at McAlpine's offices in London on the Friday after the Hereford game and he talked about working towards the eventual handover, but he was more interested in finding out about the consortium's plans for a stadium.

That feeling I'd had in the run-up to the FA press conference that Archer had something up his sleeve came back to me, and my instincts were soon confirmed by a meeting I had with Chris Griffin, a senior administrator at the Football League, at the Mountbatten Hotel in London the following week, on May 15.

As far as I was concerned, I was meeting him to bring him up to speed on the club's situation. But instead I learned far more from him. He told me that the Football League were holding a board meeting that same day to discuss the Brighton situation. And that, unknown to me – and the mediators – Archer had been continuing to meet and correspond with the League as Albion chairman.

In fact, the very day after Archer had agreed in principle to give up control and step down as chairman on March 12 at CEDR, he had met the League board and David Dent, the League's secretary, in London. He wanted agreement to his Gillingham groundshare and to persuade the League that his board was pressing ahead with plans for a permanent stadium.

What was more, in a letter he wrote to Dent on April 8, he announced that "the club have chosen Chartwell Land PLC, major developers, to build the new stadium".

Chartwell, of course, had already appeared in recent Albion history. They were the developers to whom he had sold the Goldstone. The letter was signed 'W E Archer, Chairman'.

So although Archer knew that the FA-backed CEDR deal had effectively removed him from the chairmanship of the club, he had continued to deal with the Football League as if he still had total control, and the League was dealing with him on the same basis. And neither I, CEDR or the FA had been told anything about it. All this came out at the meeting with Griffin, along with the news that the club had neglected to reply to League requests for further information on more than one occasion. I confirmed to Griffin that the consortium had had absolutely no dealings whatsoever with Chartwell Land regarding any new stadium.

I was now more convinced than ever that Archer hoped to ally himself with Martin on the promise that Chartwell would give McAlpine the stadium building contract. With Martin's casting vote, Archer would still have majority control and render me a chairman in name only – a respectable figurehead whose credibility could be used to make his plans acceptable to the fans and Brighton & Hove Council.

If I hoped that my meeting with Griffin would lead to a reasonable response from the League and the beginning of a constructive dialogue aimed at taking matters forward in a positive way, I was soon disappointed. On May 16, the day after my meeting with Griffin and the League board meeting, I was sent a letter by Edge & Ellison, the League's solicitors, reiterating demands they had earlier sent to Archer, and taking no account of the pending change of regime.

Crucially, this was the first I'd heard of a list of stringent requirements that the League intended to impose before they'd permit the club to groundshare at Gillingham or anywhere else. They wanted agreement in place for a return to a specified site in the Brighton area, including planning applications, assurances that the funding for a new ground was in place, and – a massive sting in the tail – a £500,000 'performance bond', a guarantee that we would fulfil our fixtures while playing away from Brighton, and return to 'an approved site' in our local area within three years. And they wanted all that by May 31 – a fortnight away.

With all the hardships the club and the fans were facing, this was the Football League's way of 'helping' Brighton & Hove Albion, a club desperately in need of money: to grab half a million pounds in cash, a sizeable chunk of our liquid assets, and stick it in the League's bank account. If we missed a single game in the three years at Gillingham (the only permitted exception being a match postponed for bad weather), or if we failed to take the club back to the Brighton area within three years, we would forfeit that total sum.

But then, the Football League was not interested in helping Brighton. We were considered pariahs, and in my view they would have been quite happy to see the back of the club. In fact, having done nothing and passed the buck to the FA, as a dire situation at the Albion worsened week by week under Archer – making that bastion of the football establishment look like go-getting visionaries in comparison – the League suddenly prepared to deal a potentially fatal blow. If it felt like things couldn't get any worse, they then did. The solicitors' letter contained one other bombshell. The League board intended to include a resolution in its AGM to expel Brighton & Hove Albion from the League if the necessary assurances were not received.

They had sent a copy of the letter to Archer, but he claimed not to have seen it until I forwarded one to him. He wrote back to Edge & Ellison, stressing that he was still chairman and saying that it wasn't possible to meet all the League's conditions in the brief period since the signing of the CEDR agreement on April 22. That was true. But he also claimed that "three sites had been identified as suitable for a new stadium". This was pure flim-flam, because we were only considering one site, Waterhall, at that time (to meet the League's immediate planning application requirement).

I decided to inform the FA. I told David Davies about the League letter and wrote to Graham Kelly. "Given the well-publicised and hugely optimistic response to the outcome of the mediation talks . . . this letter threatening expulsion from the League came as a complete surprise to the new board of the club," I said. "The new shareholders, including myself, were completely unaware of the previous correspondence between Archer and the League referred to in the solicitors' letter until my meeting with Chris Griffin."

The League, it seemed, was content to deal with Archer and not complicate its view of the club by including the consortium in its considerations. The only way for me to change that was to implement the CEDR agreement and complete the takeover, but Archer continued to put obstacles in the way.

There were delays in answering our many questions over the due diligence that we had to do on the club's books, which David Bellotti had been forced to make available to us. There was a dispute over the performance bond. I insisted that, if Archer was going to retain 49.5 per cent of the club, then he had to come up with half the £500,000 that the League wanted lodged with them. Even when he eventually accepted, there were disputes about the wording of the agreement. The result was that we missed more than one deadline for the delivery of the money, which didn't help our credibility with the League members who might be asked to consider voting us out.

Through all this Bellotti was, limpet-like, still ensconced in the Albion offices, which were now on the fourth floor of a nondescript building in Queens Road, very cramped and reached by a very slow and rickety lift. The 'official' demolition of the Goldstone had begun early in June, so the club had to relocate. But neither I nor any other member of the consortium had an office or any sort of permanent presence there during that summer of 1997. The old regime carried on as though nothing had happened.

The one bright spot during that period had been the wedding of my daughter, Amanda, to John Surie, in June. I felt very proud as she swept gorgeously down the aisle on my arm that beautiful sunny afternoon (and as far as Amanda was concerned, that was the only sweeping she'd be doing from then on).

Meanwhile, I had work to do. There were a series of briefing meetings, for example with Brighton & Hove Council, who had become a single unitary authority on April 1 1997. Then there was the matter of the team. We had survived relegation from the Football League but that didn't alter the fact that the squad was weak. We had only just avoided the drop on the strength of our record at the now-defunct Goldstone. And from a financial point of view there was little chance of serious strengthening.

For a start, it became clear that the club really had no assets. Despite the delays, Bob's examination of the club books indicated that most of the £7.4 million that had come in from the sale of the Goldstone had gone straight out again to clear the club's debts.

There was virtually no money left. In fact, the club was heading for a loss in that 1996/97 year of over £1.4 million – coincidentally, the amount that had been owed to Stanley. I said to Bob, "Thank God we converted it into Archer's shareholding. At least it wipes out the loss."

But it meant that most of the money that I had just put into the club would now be immediately swallowed up. And the reason for that was the problem that dwarfed all the others.

We were now a football club without a home. And not only that, thanks to Archer and Bellotti, we were now tied into a disastrous contract to play at a football ground more than 70 miles from Brighton. The Albion was committed to spending £300,000 over two years on the most distant groundshare in the history of English League football – something like a 200-mile round trip for any supporter who happened to live a few miles west of Brighton. And this to watch a team that had had the threat of relegation hanging over it all the previous season, with little chance of being much better.

The financial implications of this were horrendous. We were looking at a perfect storm of generating minimal gate receipts from much smaller crowds, combined with paying high landlord's fees to Gillingham FC.

Clearly my biggest priority by far was to try and get out of the contract with Gillingham and find a more suitable groundshare for the Albion than the expensive and potentially fatal move to Kent. It was never going to be easy, but I had to try. But even I was surprised at how difficult it turned out to be. It was an eye-opener to discover just how low the reputation of the club had fallen within the world of football, and beyond.

Not surprisingly, we had begun looking at alternatives to Gillingham long before the mediation was completed, starting our search in Brighton and Hove itself. And the obvious choice was only a stone's throw from the Goldstone. Unfortunately it almost immediately turned out to be a non-starter.

Coral's Brighton & Hove Greyhound Stadium is about 400 yards away from the site of the Goldstone. And in theory, it could have worked. Other grounds have doubled as football and greyhound tracks in the past – like Wembley, for instance. But Wembley held its greyhound meetings on Friday nights, whereas Hove's big night was Saturday. They told us straight away that staging matches at the traditional 3pm Saturday kick-off time would therefore be a problem. As a short-term solution, that ruled it out.

And there was another problem. Although the club had played at the nearby Goldstone for all those years – and obviously transport arrangements were no problem for Albion fans then – suddenly there were parking and traffic objections to us moving to the Greyhound Stadium.

It was fairly astonishing, but what this reflected was how the Albion had alienated everyone. Most of the community was fed up to the back teeth with how rotten the club appeared to be. They now always thought the worst of the Albion, and justifiably so because of the way the club had conducted itself.

Meanwhile, when Gillingham chairman Paul Scally heard about our Greyhound Stadium enquiries, he was very quick to comment that he would hold the Albion to the deal he'd struck with Archer, and make the club pay the full £300,000 rent at Gillingham for the two years whatever happened.

But I felt that I had to ignore those threats. There was no question about it: Albion did have a contract with Gillingham, but the Football League had yet to approve it. If we could find a more suitable groundshare, I was prepared to tackle the League and Scally on the issue.

So I approached Crawley Town. Outside of Brighton itself, it was clearly the best option for the Albion. Crawley were in the Dr Martens League Premier

Division at that point, one level below the Conference, playing at the new 4,800-capacity Broadfield Stadium, just over 20 miles from Brighton. Our plan was to bring the capacity of their stadium up to 10,000 and we would pay for it.

I spoke to John Maggs, the Crawley chairman, and his reaction was, not surprisingly, very positive about the idea of us improving their stadium. But the club didn't own the ground; Crawley Borough Council did. So I wrote a letter to the chief executive of the council, Michael Sander, expressing my wish to discuss a groundshare/stadium enhancement plan for Broadfield, and how we would more than double the capacity and add extra facilities, all at no cost to them. Then I waited for a response.

Steve Bassam, leader of Brighton & Hove Council, wrote a letter of support and when Sander replied it was to Steve, not me. He produced a list of reasons why Crawley Borough Council couldn't possibly consider it. The Albion had 6,000 season ticket holders (they had made that up, and anyway we were offering to increase their capacity). They were worried about overloading the newly-laid pitch. The stadium bordered a housing estate and councillors had given assurances about car parking, usage and noise.

Steve tried to broker a meeting with Sander so that I could explain everything to him and go into our proposals in more detail. But we got a short, sharp reply that curtly rebuffed my proposal. It said, "We see no purpose in meeting Brighton's new owners."

I was dumbstruck by this but figured that maybe I was caught up in some kind of political rivalry I had nothing to do with, between the New Labour movement that had romped to victory in the General Election in May and 'old Labour', who had run Crawley Borough Council for years. Maybe they were resentful of the Blairite types that had taken over everywhere else.

I think the Crawley decision turned out to be hugely significant for both clubs. Had the Albion gone to Broadfield in 1997, and improved Crawley's ground to Football League standard (by building a new stand down one side of the pitch, as we planned), the chances are we would have stayed there until we had built a new stadium back in Brighton. We would have played in front of larger crowds than we ever did at Withdean, starting two seasons earlier. And it would have greatly benefited Crawley Town. They would have been playing at a League-standard ground long before they became the second Sussex club to reach that level, in 2011.

Could I have pursued it further? I think there are times when you realise there is no way in, no chink of light, and this was one of those times. Crawley – the town rather than the club – had shut the door on us.

There was nothing for it but to look outside Sussex, although not as far as

Gillingham, and I started thinking seriously about my second choice, Millwall. I had discussed this possibility with Bob and Martin and they had both raised their eyebrows, Bob exclaiming, in his customary way, "Dear oh dear, Millwall?" – obviously influenced by trips he had made to their forbidding old ground, The Den. But they both soon realised that the London club's new ground had potential.

In my view Millwall, after Crawley, was by far the best option for a groundshare for the Albion. It wasn't the closest Football League ground to Brighton, but there were very good reasons not to attempt to groundshare with the one that was – Crystal Palace. Never mind the rivalry between Albion and Palace (although that would probably have been enough to kill the idea), Palace were already sharing Selhurst Park with another club, Wimbledon.

As for Portsmouth – the next-closest Football League ground – our rivalry with them at the time was almost as great as with Palace, and the suggested move there following the sale of the Goldstone had been vociferously opposed by Albion fans less than two years earlier.

Millwall fitted the bill as far as I was concerned. It was just an hour by train from Brighton – and they had fairly recently moved into a brand new stadium, also called The Den, but referred to by all and sundry as The New Den. And Millwall also had a new owner and chairman: a young(ish), bright, successful businessman called Theo Paphitis.

Theo had become Millwall chairman only a few months previously, with an agenda to modernise the club and improve its reputation. He appeared in a TV programme, *Back to the Floor*, in which he worked behind the scenes at a food counter in the new ground's away end and got to know the inner workings of the club.

This was some years before he achieved star status on *Dragons' Den*. I remember him, years later, interrupting some of us chairmen at a Football League conference while we were discussing financial governance or something, by telling us about his new TV career, "I'm going on this TV show *Dragons' Den* and I'm going to be a star," he said. "I'm going to give some of my children's inheritance money away to people with good business ideas. Now that I'm on it, the show's going to be an absolute smash, a real winner. We've already filmed some of them. And I'm brilliant."

We all hooted with laughter. But you thought, Theo being Theo, that he would make a success of it. He's always got something interesting to say. He has a lot of brass neck, and nothing intimidates him.

Within days of the Crawley plan falling through I got his number, called him and outlined my idea. He wanted to hear more, and we arranged to meet on the afternoon of Wednesday June 11 at the Tower Bridge Hotel, very close to CEDR's headquarters.

We met in the lounge and hit it off straight away. In many ways we were very alike. It was clear that he knew about business and he knew about people, how to read them and to get on with them. I saw Theo as a very shrewd operator, but he's a very likeable guy and he has a humanity. He showed that in his time on *Dragons' Den* where he went for people as much as the ideas. If he thought he could work with somebody he was more likely to buy into the proposition that they were asking him to consider.

Over coffee, I came straight to the point. "Theo, Brighton needs to find a groundshare, probably for the next couple of years – and Millwall makes a hell of a lot more sense to me than going to Gillingham. But we need to do it very quickly before the League sets the Gillingham deal in stone."

Looking back on it, I guess it was a little bit like making a *Dragons' Den* pitch – and one that grabbed Theo's attention straight away. He couldn't believe the problems I was facing. He could see it was ludicrous for our fans to travel 75 miles to north Kent rather than 43 miles to The Den.

He could also spot a decent business opportunity for his club, and he was completely receptive to the idea. It helped that there had been a certain rivalry between Millwall and Gillingham. He was in, but with certain reservations.

"I'd love to do it," he said. "When I first took over, one of the things I wanted to know was why our new ground was empty most of the time. But let me go and talk to my safety officer first. I'll do it today."

Obviously there was an important issue to address, namely the Millwall fans who still had a fairly fearsome reputation. But even at Millwall, great strides had been made, thanks largely to their excellent safety officer, Ken Chapman. Formerly the senior police officer for the area, he is a highly competent guy whose experience and methods of handling matches at the Millwall ground had virtually eliminated crowd trouble.

So Theo went to Ken, who by the next morning had spoken to Millwall fans' representatives, and also to Mike Humphreys, who had succeeded him as the local police chief for the area. We met again at The Den later that day to sit down with Ken, discuss all the implications, look round the stadium, see where our fans would sit and other details.

We took it very far very quickly and Ken was confident they could make it work. He said that the local police had raised no objection and Millwall fans were supportive because they were backing the Brighton fans' cause and it would bring money to their club. Theo and I quickly came to a financial agreement that was more beneficial to us – £100,000 per season rather than the £150,000 agreed with Scally. We had a letter of agreement signed within a week of our first meeting.

Theo and Ken felt it was a win-win for everyone. The deal made sound business sense, and as well as helping out Brighton fans, it represented a hand of friendship between clubs and between two rookie chairmen who wanted to do things a different way. All being well, we would be able to cut the distance, time and cost of our fans' round trip to 'home' matches by a considerable margin. Plus The Den would also give them a flavour of the sort of new stadium we would be playing in, in what I thought would be the reasonably near future.

But it didn't happen. We were invited to a Football League hearing in London at which both clubs presented their proposals and reasons for the groundshare. But when the police spoke, Humphreys's attitude had changed. Now he was against the plan. I think Ken believes that there had been influence from someone more senior, who was under pressure on crime figures.

The reasons Humphreys gave were that the local force didn't want to divert manpower to football that could be used to improve efficiency on reducing crime statistics. He also said that some Millwall fans would prefer to hang around The Den to confront Brighton fans instead of following their team away from home, which understandably annoyed Ken and Theo.

So when the police strongly recommended to the Football League that they didn't allow the groundshare, the League did not have to think twice about hiding behind the police stance, and rejected it. I was bitterly disappointed, and Theo was also frustrated. If it had been up to us, we'd have done a good deal for both clubs, and very quickly. "Idiots" was his reaction. "Neanderthals. They live in the Stone Age. They don't understand business."

"And they don't care about football fans," I replied.

I was disappointed but not surprised by the League's decision. As far as they were concerned, they were making a huge concession to Brighton to allow us to play at Gillingham. In fact this had only happened officially at the League's AGM on Monday June 16, attended by Archer and Bellotti, who were officially still in charge of the club. Permission to play at Gillingham was granted provided the £500,000 performance bond was lodged with the League by Friday June 20.

But Archer had either not heard the bit about lodging the performance bond, or not taken it seriously for some reason. He continued to procrastinate over the wording of the bond agreement, and the bond was not delivered on time. The League ran out of patience. A week later it announced that the resolution to expel the Albion from the Football League mentioned in the solicitor's letter sent to me in May was to be put before the other 71 clubs at a specially-arranged Extraordinary General Meeting (EGM) on July 24.

There had only been four previous EGMs called to expel a member club in the history of the League – all for financial reasons. But this was different. We had not gone out of business – not yet anyway. The single motion on the agenda was to throw Brighton out of the League for bringing the game into disrepute. If anything showed how far the reputation of the club had fallen, this was it.

The League was naturally concerned about the failure of the club to sort out the ownership issue once and for all. The fact that Archer was stalling over the delivery of the performance bond also gave the League board no confidence that the club intended to honour the bond's conditions.

The decision to call the EGM was unnecessary in my view, but you could understand it. What I couldn't understand or believe was that, as far as the League was concerned, Archer and Bellotti were still in charge. I'd even been up to Lytham St Anne's to see David Dent at the League's offices to make it plain to him that I was the chairman-elect and that he should deal with me now, but it had clearly had no effect.

I had spent the summer fully occupied with the groundshare situation, and also trying to progress the full transfer of power at the club, and being frustrated at every turn. Now I read the riot act to Archer at a meeting of the board members at Cameron McKenna, our lawyers, on July 16, near the Barbican in London. "It is ludicrous that we are in this situation, and all because of your prevarications. For God's sake, we've got to move this on."

Two days later, the bond was finally lodged with the League. But that was too late to stop the EGM, which was held at the Radisson Portman Square Hotel in London. I was invited to attend, but not allowed to speak. Archer was representing the club, and Bellotti was in the audience, but I made sure I didn't sit near him.

Not all the 72 Football League clubs were present at the meeting – eight were abstaining and didn't attend. The circus that followed was a succession of football club chairmen arguing why Brighton & Hove Albion should be ejected from the league. Ian Stott, chairman of Oldham Athletic, was especially passionate in his view that the Albion should be expelled with immediate effect, criticising the way the club had been run, and also hammering the fans. And this attack was repeated time and again, by club after club.

To be fair, a lot of the vitriol was aimed fairly and squarely at Archer and Bellotti. It was clear that the assembled chairmen knew that they were the main architects of this situation. But there was also a lot of sniping aimed at the fans. They were part of the problem as far as most delegates were concerned. There was very little understanding and appreciation of the feelings of outrage and helplessness felt by Albion supporters that had resulted in pitch invasions and demonstrations.

Archer then had a chance to defend the club himself – and gave a pathetically weak and badly-argued case. As I looked on in helpless frustration and impotence, Archer attempted to justify himself and defend his actions. He tried to make out that he had done everything for the good of the club and in order to get a new stadium built. He had been forced to sell the Goldstone. He was going for the sympathy vote.

What was entirely lacking in Archer's performance was any passion for the club or any feeling for what it would mean to the fans and the community of Sussex if the Football League banished them after 77 years' membership. Archer probably didn't even know the history of the club well enough to be able to make a decent case based on our traditions, culture and values. He came over as a businessman rather than someone passionate about a football club.

I wanted to get up from my seat and shout out that they were talking about a wonderful institution, an important part of the fabric of its own city and community, and of the League itself. That it had been brought low by its owners, aided and abetted by the inaction of the football authorities. The members of the League might not have liked that, but they would have seen that the man who was going to be in charge in future had a genuine and deep-seated love for the club and the game.

Significantly, the only voice in support of the Albion – and quite a passionate voice – came from Dan McCauley, the chairman of Plymouth Argyle. He had been brought up in Sussex, and he spoke about how he had regularly been taken to the Goldstone by his dad and stood behind the north goal. "This motion is invalid because we should not be charging the club," Dan told the meeting. "Brighton & Hove Albion is a fine club. The problem is the people who are running it."

In a very articulate manner, Dan (who ended up falling out with his own fans) stood up for the Albion and made the case for keeping us in the League – and I loved him for it. It occurred to me that we had possibly rubbed shoulders in the North Stand when we were kids, and on that day he showed that he was still, in a sense, an Albion supporter.

Later, I went up to him and said, "Dan, thank you so much for that. I think you were our only friend in that room. I won't forget what you said."

He replied, "I was only telling the truth. I spoke for Brighton because I feel for it and know something about its history."

What worried me was that I hadn't noticed any nods of assent or heard any murmurs of agreement while Dan was speaking. And when the chairman of the meeting asked if anyone else wanted to speak against the motion to throw us out, there was silence. It was if the other clubs just wanted to get it over with.

But perhaps Dan's voice had swayed enough neutrals, because at the end of the meeting the motion to expel Brighton from the Football League failed. Forty-seven clubs voted to keep us in and 17 voted for the motion to throw us out, so it wasn't carried and we survived the day.

But the fact was that 17 clubs wanted to throw the Albion out of the Football League. Plus eight clubs had abstained, so those clubs were sufficiently in a mood to censure us rather than reject the motion outright. That meant that 25 of the other 71 Football League clubs were prepared to condemn Brighton – 17 of them with the ultimate sanction of expulsion.

What did that tell me about how Brighton & Hove Albion were regarded? Without a doubt, it was another striking message about how low the reputation of the club had fallen. Yes, we survived the motion at the EGM, but I knew I had a huge task of re-establishing the club within the football world. And just getting rid of Archer wasn't going to be enough. We had to rebuild and restore the good name of the club.

And by now, the new season was fast approaching. With great reluctance, we committed ourselves to starting the season playing our home games at Gillingham. I would make one more attempt to move somewhere closer to Brighton, but that also came to nothing. We were locked in.

During that summer I resolved that we would get that £500,000 performance bond money back from the Football League, in full. I vowed to myself that we would never miss a game at Gillingham for any reason, and I would bring the club back to Brighton – not in three years, but in two. I was determined that we weren't going to stay in Gillingham for any longer than we absolutely had to.

# CHAPTER**FOURTEEN**

# IN EXILE

W hile I searched in vain for a better groundshare for the Albion, and watched helplessly as the Football League deprived us of half a million quid of much-needed funds with its 'performance bond', the day-to-day business of the club had to go on as best it could.

But the whole club was in a state of turmoil as we prepared to take over. The staff were completely demoralised. Some people had been fired by David Bellotti as he reduced the club's commercial and marketing activities to virtually zero – anything he didn't understand, he closed down. Others resigned or had their jobs changed – office manager Sally Townsend was delegated to run the club shop during its limited opening hours.

Bellotti was of course a hate figure among Albion fans. But the problem was that as the opening of the 1997/98 season drew closer he was still there, as chief executive of Brighton & Hove Albion FC. I must admit that by now I had dismissed Bellotti as something of an irrelevance. After all, my dealings towards the takeover of the club had been entirely with Archer and then with the mediators. Archer never allowed Bellotti to be involved which, to me, said everything about the chief executive's competence. But a few things about him had got under my skin.

Bellotti had barred a whole range of people from the Goldstone Ground on match-days – including leading supporters like Liz Costa and Paul Samrah, who had incurred his bully-boy wrath through perceived misdemeanours on their part, such as Liz selling supporters club lottery tickets in the ground.

But the one that really outraged me was his treatment of Fred Oliver, *The Argus* seller. Fred, who was over 80 years old, had been selling the newspaper at the Goldstone on match-days for decades – as far as I could remember since I was a boy. Fred, walking around the cinder track in front of the stands in his white coat shouting "*Argus*" was part of the milieu of match-days at the Goldstone – and Bellotti barred him from the ground because he didn't like what *The Argus* was writing about him. What a shabby thing to do.

So it was not surprising to learn that Bellotti wasn't any more popular with the people who worked with him. During the close season, when we still hadn't signed off on the club's new structure and Archer was up to his tricks to delay it, I gave Bellotti a wide berth. But I'd had an early indication of just how he was regarded by the staff soon after the April 22 takeover announcement, when we were starting the due diligence on the club's books.

I arranged a meeting with Bellotti and Derek Allan, the club secretary, and asked them to come to my house in Hove one morning to discuss some papers. They arrived, I showed them into the living room, gestured for them to sit down on a wide chaise longue, and went off to make coffee. When I returned I virtually dropped the tray of coffee because at one end was Bellotti sitting po-faced, bolt upright. And, with loads of empty space between, there at the other end of the chaise longue was Derek — sitting as far away from Bellotti as possible. His body even curved away over the arm, seemingly in an attempt to get ever further away from him. They call it body language.

Not long after that meeting Derek resigned. But I already knew enough about him to realise that he was one of the football club's most important backroom staff. As club secretary Derek was responsible for all the administration needed for the Albion to operate as a Football League club — any issues surrounding fixtures, dealing with other clubs, the signing and transferring of players, players' contracts, and more besides. And even during the bad times it was clear that Derek was doing a great job — one of the people, in fact, who was actually keeping the club going. When I heard the news that he'd quit, I phoned him and told him, "Derek, if I ever win this battle, I want you to come back."

Derek replied, "I'd love to come back and work for you, but not if he [Bellotti] is involved."

I said, "I can assure you, Derek, he won't be involved with Brighton & Hove Albion in the future in any capacity whatsoever. Not even as tea boy."

I was true to my word, and it was one of the best decisions I made as chairman of Brighton & Hove Albion. Although a bit of a dour Lancastrian sometimes, Derek is a brilliant administrator and there isn't anything he doesn't know about football regulations. And he is widely respected in football.

Derek and I made a great double-act when dealing with players' agents. I'd negotiate a complex deal with an agent and phone all the terms over to Derek, who would immediately translate them into a detailed contract. The agent would later be amazed to find out what he had agreed to.

But before I could bring Derek back, I had to get rid of Bellotti. And as the new season loomed, we couldn't actually do that. As a chief executive, Bellotti was now a lame duck. But while the final takeover was still unsigned, he remained in his job.

The issue dragged on through the summer amid fears that Archer was reneging. As Tony Banks, the Minister for Sport, joined the FA in calling for a resolution, I said to Archer in a meeting where again he was pumping Martin Perry for information, "This has got to end. You just keep your word, and get on with it."

"I will," he replied. I briefed our lawyers to put his under even more pressure.

With the setback of the Football League 'performance bond' coming on top of our other money worries, I calculated my first 'playing budget' – the money I could afford to give Steve Gritt to maintain and strengthen the playing squad for the coming season. It was a small increase, less than £200,000 above the previous season. So Steve would mainly be working with the squad that had survived the drop on the last day at Hereford.

Steve told me he was okay with that. "I can do something with this squad, I've got their confidence." And maybe, fired up by what he'd achieved, he did think that he could carry on the momentum that he'd built up with those players. I must admit that this set alarm bells ringing. This was a struggling team which had just survived relegation by the skin of its teeth – and the team no longer had the advantage of the Goldstone as its home ground. But I was in no position to ring the changes.

Our first match at Priestfield was a pre-season friendly against old rivals Crystal Palace. I didn't go as I was still only chairman-elect and wasn't actually invited. Then the 1997/98 season got under way on August 9 with a trip to Swansea City. I was always going to be at that game.

I drove to Swansea with Sir John Smith, who said that week, "I think I'll come along and give you moral support. Brighton should have more than one director at the game." I was very glad to have him with me. Bob Pinnock would have come, of course, but he was still on holiday, so Sir John and I met up at Reading services on the M4 and went on in one car.

I had been very much in favour of Sir John and Richard Faulkner coming on the club board because it gave notice to Archer that no misdeeds would be tolerated, but it was also salutory for me in that it showed the FA wasn't 100 per cent sure of the outcome. Sir John was more involved, not just at board meetings. I found him steady as a rock. Avuncular, with a ready smile – more village policeman than *The Sweeney* – he had somehow made his way up from being a bobby on the beat to the top of the police force. He was extremely well-respected and obviously had the confidence of the FA to oversee the Brighton transition.

He came to all the home matches and made himself very visible at key moments. For example, when I decided to invite Ray Bloom back on the board in late 1998, after he'd served a period of 'penance', there was opposition from many fans who saw Ray as part of the Archer regime. But he was an Albion fan through and through and had kept his money in the club (£90,000) when the other directors took theirs out after Archer had arranged the Co-op Bank loan.

But before he could return, I had to win the fans over. I called a public meeting at Southwick FC's ground in Old Barn Way, and so many people came – around 1,500 – that some spilled out of the clubhouse onto the pitch and the proceedings had to be broadcast to them over the ground's PA system. Bob and Sir John were there, but Ray himself wasn't. After I explained to the crowd that the time was right to give Ray another chance, several people spoke against him being brought back, and the mood turned a little ugly. Sir John then made a very clear and dispassionate statement to the meeting. "Dick has explained to me that Ray Bloom's family have a background involvement with the club, and I believe that if the chairman feels it is right, you should back him on this one." He was unassuming but convincing. He came over as a voice of calm and good sense. People listened to him and felt that he was very much a safe pair of hands.

The sum Ray had to pay to come back into the club was the same I'd set for any new director – £500,000 (I'd decided the club could no longer hand out directorships in return for much smaller sums, as it had in the past). That meant he had to give the club £410,000. When he handed me the cheque, he said, "This represents to some extent an investment for my family. In years to come, my nephews may want to become involved in the club."

Sir John lived in Horsham, and although he wasn't an Albion fan, he was aware of the club and took being a director very seriously. We were mainly looking forward to a football match, the first of a new era, on a beautiful August Saturday. The journey was the first chance I'd had to ask him about the FA bungs inquiry he'd headed, but he was very discreet, as you'd expect. His view was that football needed to get its act together on governance after what he'd learned during his inquiry.

When we got to Swansea's ground – still the Vetch Field in those days – we made our way to the boardroom. I was expecting to have to take on a formal role as the Albion's representative but we discovered that Bellotti had arrived there before us.

This was an unpleasant surprise – and we soon got another one. News that our takeover was going through can't have reached south Wales, because the Swansea directors and their wives effectively cold-shouldered Sir John and myself, while continuing to act perfectly sociably with Bellotti. We weren't even allowed into the boardroom and had to go into a guest room, one level below the boardroom as it were, very cramped and with a low ceiling.

We were, of course, still not officially in charge of the Albion while Bellotti was legally an officer of the club. It was an uncomfortable situation, and Sir John and I soon left to make our way to the stands to watch the match (which we lost 1-0 to a goal 10 minutes from time). At half-time and full-time we again suffered the cold-shoulder treatment. I think we were lucky to get a cup of tea.

It was strange behaviour but I found out the reason a few months later. The Swansea chairman at the time was Steve Hamer, who would become a good friend of mine, from our encounters at various matches, Football League AGMs and League meetings down the years. At the first club meeting I attended officially, Steve said, "Dick, I need to apologise for what happened in our boardroom at that match. You remember that David Bellotti was at that game, and arrived before you did?"

"Of course," I replied.

"Well, before you got there, Bellotti was telling everyone who would listen that you had no right to be there. He had briefed our owners that we had to ignore you. My instinct was that it was wrong but unfortunately they took his advice."

Now it all made sense. So the Swansea board ignored the new regime at the Albion and continued as if the old regime was still in charge, which is exactly what Bellotti wanted them to believe. He was still clinging on to the last vestiges of power. He also ignored us as if we were totally irrelevant.

I always regarded him as a sideshow to the main event. Plenty of Albion fans will no doubt disagree with my assessment, but Bellotti is not even my biggest hate figure among Liberal Democrat MPs from Sussex. That is unquestionably the member for Lewes, but the behaviour of Norman Baker – until recently Transport Minister in the Coalition Government – in the Albion story will have to wait for now.

And talking about transport, on the way back from that game at Swansea, Bellotti got himself ejected at Bridgend from a train heading back to London. Apparently he was creating a disturbance simply through his presence, to which Albion fans on the same train objected.

One of those fans, Roy Chuter, a great campaigner against the Archer regime, got off at the next stop in order to get on the following train carrying Bellotti, to exchange a few more pleasantries with him. Roy, with a first-class honours degree in English, was great with words and enjoyed jousting with Bellotti. He had already gained an instant place in Albion folklore by returning a letter Bellotti's lawyers had sent him, pointing out the 27 grammatical errors in it. Roy tragically died in 2013, but that sort of campaigning style and wit will never be forgotten.

Sir John was massively unimpressed by the Swansea directors' behaviour. He said, "My God, have you got a job to do in restoring the image of the club! The fans are with you, that's clear. But when other clubs treat you like that . . ."

Four days later I made my debut at Gillingham as chairman-elect for our first competitive 'home' game of the season at the Priestfield Stadium, against Leyton Orient in the League Cup. I was still living mainly in Islington, so I took the A102 through Hackney to the Blackwall Tunnel, out through those grey south-east London suburbs and down the motorway to Gillingham, which is pretty grey and depressing itself. The whole experience felt very alien and I made the journey with a heavy heart. Here I was, almost in charge of the Albion, and driving to north Kent for a home game.

I hadn't gone there in advance, even once. The whole deal had been done between Archer, Bellotti and Paul Scally, none of whom were present. Scally always went to away games with Gillingham, Archer never turned up, but Bellotti had the gall to appear in the directors' box twice later in the season, where he wisely kept a safe distance from me.

I never got to Gillingham more than an hour before kick-off. I felt that the less time I spent there, the better. Having said that, I can't say enough about the staff at the Priestfield, who looked after our home games. They were perfectly nice people and very friendly. There was a lovely chap called Edward who served in the very small boardroom. This was before they built a new stand and Scally created a new boardroom heavily influenced by the Spearmint Rhino school of design. (Sorry, Paul. But it's still friendly.)

But I felt we had been stitched up, forbidden by the League to play at Millwall and forced to accept a groundshare that neither I nor our fans wanted. David Dent, the Football League secretary, never did us any favours. They put us under huge pressure with the 'performance bond'. Their attitude was very obviously, "Your club was lucky not to be thrown out of the league. Just behave yourselves." But we did. We were from Brighton and should have been playing there, or at least closer to there, not at Gillingham.

The match was a low-key occasion which Barry Hearn, the Orient chairman, later to become a good friend, didn't attend. It finished in a 1-1 draw, and we were abysmally poor, which pretty much set the tone for another dire season of struggle. In a crowd of 1,037 only 800 or so Albion fans had turned up. I say 'only' – God bless each and every one of them.

It was the same story on the Saturday for our first 'home' league game, against Macclesfield Town, who had just been promoted from the Vauxhall Conference – replacing Hereford, of course. Alan Cash, the Macclesfield chairman, and his directors were thrilled by the whole occasion, plus they got a point from their first away game in the Football League. But for us it was a huge anti-climax.

The drab surroundings were to be the backdrop for far too many losing and drawn games at Priestfield that season. We only managed three home wins all season and our away record was no better and just as bad as it had been in the previous campaign. Arguably the most important of our three away wins was at Doncaster, the only team that finished below us, on October 4. If it hadn't been for them, we would have been relegated for certain because we got 13 points fewer that season than we did in 1996/97.

That day in Yorkshire was quite a memorable one for another reason. After our 3-1 victory, I got back to Doncaster station and grabbed a spare seat in first class to find myself sitting opposite Joanna Lumley, who it turned out was heading down to London from Edinburgh.

As Albion fans made their way up and down the packed train, quite a few of them spotted me and said hello or shook my hand, and there were chants of 'Dicky Knight's blue-and-white army'. Several even asked me for my autograph, completely ignoring the legendary actress sitting opposite me, although some did realise who it was. It certainly didn't do my reputation any harm that Albion fans thought I was pally with Joanna Lumley.

The attention I was getting piqued Joanna's interest. "You seem to be very popular, what do you do?" she asked me. "It's wonderful, all these people seem to love you."

"Well, I'm in football," I replied.

"You play? You're a bit old, aren't you?" she said.

She had no idea about football so we had a conversation and I explained what I did and how I had managed to attract such adulation. We had a most pleasant journey and it was definitely the highlight of the season – a rare away win and talking to Joanna Lumley afterwards.

Predictably, our home gates were terrible. From an average of 6,000 at the Goldstone, we basically lost two thirds of our revenue overnight. We had 2,336 for the Macclesfield match, 2,285 for the following match, against Leyton Orient in the League – and then the crowds got steadily worse. The club laid on buses from Brighton, charging under a fiver for the 150-mile round trip, but it only worked to a limited extent. Albion fans refused to go to Gillingham for all sorts of reasons: the distance, the expense, the team – and out of principle. And you could hardly blame them for not coming.

We were really scraping the bottom of the barrel at Gillingham. So in late August I made another attempt to move the club, to Woking in Surrey – not much closer to Brighton but certainly easier to get to. Woking, in the Conference, were helpful, but it was never really going to work out. Their ground only held around 5,000, and once again we would have faced battles with the Football League and the Gillingham chairman.

So we finally conceded defeat over Gillingham. From that point, we would just have to grit our teeth, rely on some smart housekeeping to keep the club afloat, and get on with it – and absolutely make sure we didn't stay there any longer than two seasons.

Thankfully, there was one good thing that did happen. On Tuesday September 2 1997, the deal that changed the club's ownership was finally signed. Archer's shareholding of the club was reduced to 49.5 per cent. His control over Brighton & Hove Albion was officially over. We'd done it.

At the club board meeting that day to ratify the takeover, there was one final, symbolic gesture that had to be made. I wrote out two cheques from my personal account – one to Archer for £56.25, and one to Greg Stanley for £43.75, to formally buy them out of Foray 585, and took some pleasure in handing them to Archer. He reluctantly accepted them, and I just about resisted the temptation to add, "Now fuck off."

Stanley cashed his cheque a few days later, but Archer never did.

The following evening we had a league game against Peterborough at Priestfield. It was a cold and rainy night, and another forgettable match that we managed to draw 2-2. It was all rather ironic. The first game when people had called me 'Chairman' – when I was actually only chairman-elect – had been the last game at the Goldstone and one of the most important matches in the club's history. But the first game when I became chairman for real passed by pretty much unnoticed, in front of only 1,215.

There was no sense of occasion, there were no speeches, only a brief PA announcement followed by a smattering of faint applause and a small 'Stop Press' item in the programme. For me, and probably for the few fans there, it felt like a complete anti-climax.

My main emotion – and, I suspect, theirs – was anger that the takeover had taken so long. It should have been finalised soon after the Hereford game, exactly four months earlier. But Archer had continued to behave as if he could disregard any authority, and stonewall his way out of the situation. By the way he carried on dealing with the League behind our backs, he had treated the FA and CEDR – an international mediation body – with total disrespect.

I never felt like a chairman when we were at Gillingham. It was like a charade. I was more formally treated as a chairman at away matches. The staff at the Priestfield were very polite and deferential, but they weren't our staff. We didn't really have any.

Until the final agreement had been confirmed we couldn't move forward, get on with doing the job. But at last, we were properly in charge. It was more a question of steeling ourselves than raising a glass of champagne, either at Priestfield that night or the next morning in the club offices in Queens Road, which we were now able to occupy. There was relief but also an awareness of the scale of the task ahead. I said to Bob, "The first time we can celebrate will be when we get back to Brighton. The second time will be when we are in the new stadium a couple of years after that." If only we knew . . .

What we did already know was that, with the huge challenges ahead, there was little room for financial manoeuvre. We had scant resources to improve the playing squad, we were stuck at Gillingham with its minimal gate receipts – and we were about to incur serious legal and consultancy costs as our task of finding a new home back in Brighton got under way. The remaining cash in the company coffers would quickly be drained once we began the planning application processes for both temporary and permanent homes.

There wasn't much we could do about those problems in the short term, but one thing I knew I had to address straight away, now the Archer era had finally ended, was to restore the club's reputation within football and in the wider world. We also had to rebuild morale and pride within the club, among its loyal staff.

My first step was to ensure that they knew they were working for an organisation that was worthwhile. That would begin by immediately sacking Bellotti, the lamentable chief executive. He may have been Archer's stooge, creating more problems for the absent chairman than he solved, but for me he could never deflect the flak from the real culprit.

No doubt quite a few Albion fans wished that Bellotti's departure could have been conducted by a group of soldiers, lined up with rifles, or by building a bonfire, as suggested by the song and then the book of the same name. Or at least with an Alan Sugar-style 'You're fired' pointed finger. But it wasn't quite like that.

For one thing, I didn't even want to see him. So I got our lawyer to draft a letter of dismissal and I 'Dick'd' it a bit, and then it went to him, on some new club-headed paper I'd had designed by Dean Bigelow, from my office in London. We'd been running down stocks of the old paper, with Archer's name on it as chairman, never suspecting that we would have to make it last for months.

Bellotti was paid through to the end of his notice period, which was three months, and he was 'terminated'. He wrote back saying that he reserved the right to seek compensation but we never heard anything more.

Bellotti's final departure saw the first glimmer of improvement in staff morale. It meant that I could coax Derek Allan back to become the club secretary once more. He had taken a job as a schoolteacher, which he was qualified to do. I phoned him and asked him if he would come back and he said, "Bloody hell, you've done it then?" He knew all about the deviousness of Archer and Bellotti, but he didn't know me well enough then to understand how bloody-minded I was, how determined to make things better. All the same, he was prepared to give me a chance.

Other issues could also be addressed. When we went through the club's accounts as part of the due diligence process during the takeover, Bob and I had been astonished to discover that the club had virtually no revenue from merchandising or commercial activities at all. Whereas it was normal for clubs to have around only 40 per cent of their revenue from gate receipts, with the Albion, 75 per cent of revenue was gate income (and under five per cent from merchandising and commercial). Then we realised it was just another way the fans had protested against Archer and Bellotti. They had hated the regime, so they didn't buy their replica shirts or become sponsors. The marketing side of the club didn't so much need reviving as to be completely reinvented.

Bellotti didn't want fans going to the ground in case they had a go at him, so he opened the club shop only on two afternoons and for limited hours. Ironically, just about the only useful thing that Bellotti ever did as Albion chief executive was move the shop into the town centre of Brighton. That was actually a sensible move. Obviously we were leaving the Goldstone, so we had to have a shop somewhere, and it was now situated near the club offices just down Queens Road and nearer the Clock Tower, slap bang in the middle of Brighton. This at least gave us a base from which to develop the merchandising side of the club, and gain some much-needed income. And we also managed to squeeze the ticket sales operation into those premises as there was no ground to sell them from.

A little while later, Paul Samrah phoned me up and asked if he could come over for a coffee. I said, "Okay, sure." Paul came round to my house and we sat in the garden. I said, "What's on your mind?" He told me he wanted to be the new chief executive, and laid out a compelling case.

I had actually decided not to have a post with that title, because it had been tainted by association with Bellotti, but we definitely needed someone. I had already put out a few feelers in the marketing industry, because I wanted to get a person with that type of experience into the club quickly. Even the shirt sponsors, Sandtex, about the only commercial contract we had, had given notice that they would not be renewing at the end of the season.

Of course, I took Paul's offer very seriously. His devotion to the club was not in question and he had proved – and would prove again – that he was a very capable motivator and organiser. A qualified accountant, he impressed me in that he was prepared to give up a likely partnership in the top London firm he worked for to come and work for the Albion. He relished the challenge and we got on very well.

But I already had Bob as financial director and I knew he would take care of that side of the club, and I had a very strong sense that Derek and Sally Townsend – now restored to her rightful job – could handle most things administration-wise. I felt that Samrah was uniquely suited to make a contribution that would be even more important.

I said: "Paul, I understand why you want the job, but I honestly think your talents would be more valuable to us outside the club. You are the natural leader of the supporters, you are a superb spokesman for them and we will need their help enormously in the months and years to come. The council, the football authorities, everyone we deal with needs to know that the fans are with us. That we're working together in a unique football partnership. You can help me deliver that."

Paul was very disappointed but hid it well, because I'm sure he recognised that there was a huge job to be done outside the club. But I always felt that I was being very selfish at the time, because I have absolutely no doubt that in another period of the club's history he would have made an excellent chief executive.

Instead I advertised for a general manager in *Marketing Week* magazine in October and made up a shortlist of six candidates. I appointed Nick Rowe, who had been a marketing director in the music business. I was aware of his name already, and it was easy for me to check him out. He understood what was required. It was a difficult marketing job, for a product that wasn't on sale in its own city, but I had a vision for the club and I knew that there was more to be done in marketing football than had been done up to that point.

Nick bought into that vision and we built up a new marketing structure and set up the club website. We were one of the first clubs to do so and soon we were getting 300,000 hits a month. Paul Camillin, a young fanzine writer I took on, who was to become the club's head of media, began there as well as part-editing the programme. Our website became successful quickly thanks to some special user-friendly features we devised – such as proper pub guides to away grounds and statistical analysis of our next opponents – while I got used to hearing people at other clubs saying, "How did you do that?" or "We can't get our website to work."

But of course by far our biggest priority was getting the Albion back home as soon as possible. For a start we had this condition set by the Football League to return in three years, otherwise we'd lose the £500,000 'performance bond' we'd been forced to lodge with them. But I knew I had to get the club back in two years. Beyond that, it was quite likely that so many fans would lose interest in the club, with the grind of the long haul to Gillingham every other week, that the fibre of the club would be lost forever.

So after our initial efforts before we reached Gillingham, now the search for a new home began in earnest. But because we now knew that it was going to be impossible for us to build a new permanent stadium in two years, finding a suitable temporary home was actually our immediate priority. So the search was twofold, and we had two processes going on at the same time. We had to find a temporary home in the Brighton area – a stop-gap venue – and we needed to make sure we chose absolutely the best site for our permanent home.

Back in November 1995, Brighton and Hove Councils – the latter perhaps with some conscience about giving Archer retail planning permission for the Goldstone – had jointly commissioned a survey of all potential sites for a new home for the Albion in and around the Brighton area. This was effectively the start of the club's very long, very complicated, very arduous, very expensive, extraordinary journey through the British planning system, which finally led, 16 years later, to the American Express Community Stadium being opened.

What the survey did was identify a total of 16 sites and evaluate whether or not they were suitable locations for the new stadium. And the criteria for evaluating their suitability included traffic impact and access, environmental issues, cost, economic benefit and planning implications. Some of these sites lay outside the boundaries of Brighton & Hove – an area in Newhaven, some land near Shoreham Airport, Shoreham Harbour West and Beeding Cement Works, but they were still evaluated.

Within Brighton & Hove the list included Hove Greyhound Stadium, Waterhall, Stanmer Park, Sheepcote Valley and land at Brighton Station. Surprisingly, Withdean Stadium was not included. I even jokingly suggested buying a war-surplus US Navy aircraft carrier, putting artificial grass on the flight deck and mooring it off the Palace Pier for home games.

When we finally took control, Martin and I immediately met with Glynn Jones, chief executive of the by now single Local Authority of Brighton & Hove, to discuss the survey. All but Shoreham Harbour of the sites outside Brighton were now ruled out, because they fell outside the eight-mile limit for our permanent home imposed by the Football League 'performance bond'.

And in terms of a temporary home back in Brighton, most could be ruled out immediately for time and cost reasons, or were simply inadequate.

Hove Greyhound Stadium had been found to be unworkable. We considered Stanmer Park, and you could have put up temporary stands on the flat part closest to the A27, but the traffic management would have been very difficult and there would have been high environmental impact. We looked at Whitehawk's Enclosed Ground at the bottom of Sheepcote Valley, but the slope of the pitch was impossible for League football. The Sussex cricket ground was also mentioned, but they didn't want to host football and it was never a serious contender.

But there was one other option, not previously considered. Withdean Stadium was the home of three local athletics clubs, with a 400m track cut into the natural bowl of the valley, surrounded by trees, and a pitch in the middle that already had football played on it. With a small stand along the finishing straight, the capacity was 1,200, but there was plenty of space on the other three sides. I knew that 12,000 had once packed in to see the Brighton B52s American football team play San Francisco City College. As a venue for athletics it was used mostly in the summer, and it was owned by Brighton & Hove Council. We spoke to Steve Bassam about it and he had been thinking along the same lines. He fully supported the idea.

By November 1997 Withdean was the preferred choice for our temporary home. In our opinion it was the only viable option. We still needed the permission of the council – and also to deal with opposition that, as we were to discover, were dead set against us coming to Withdean, or even returning to Brighton at all. It would provide the first opportunity for the club and the fans to work together towards a common goal (almost certainly for the first time ever). It would set the standard for further struggles down the years.

The battle for Withdean was, in effect, a rehearsal for the longer battle for Falmer and the Amex.

# CHAPTER FIFTEEN

# BRING HOME
# THE ALBION

Shortly after we had agreed that Withdean Stadium was the ideal site for the temporary home, a group of Albion fans – led by Adrian Newnham, of the official Supporters' Club, and encouraged by the board – launched the Bring Home The Albion campaign. We all knew that we would have to build some popular pressure behind our bid to return home, and be able to show that there was backing from more than the 2,000 or so hardcore fans who were travelling to Gillingham.

It was a crucial move, one that began a process of the club and the supporters working closely together to achieve their objectives, in the face of what would be near-constant opposition. From that point, a month or so after I'd properly taken over, a pattern was set that would continue pretty much throughout the time I was chairman of the Albion – fans and club working for the same goal, and doing it with a style and sense of humour that the opposition couldn't match. The campaign's first move was to decorate the town with blue-and-white ribbons – lamposts, even the Steve Ovett statue in Preston Park. They got *The Argus* behind them too.

On November 11 Martin Perry and I had an important meeting with Glynn Jones and his senior officers at the council. We needed them to embrace our plans for Withdean because he had to give his planning officers the brief to make it happen. "We have to bring the club home," I told him.

That evening I held a meeting of key fans at the home of Tony Foster, the chairman of the Supporters' Club, and told them our plans. From the start of the season we had already had several meetings with Albion fans – supporters' groups had declined my offer of a place on the board in favour of regular and open consultations with the club.

The next morning I went on the Danny Pike breakfast show on local radio and revealed that we were on our way home and that Withdean was our choice for the temporary stadium. The news lit up the studio's phone lines with happy callers straight away. At last we were making people feel good about the Albion again.

On December 15, Martin and I made a 'stadium vision' presentation about our Withdean plans at a packed public meeting at Hove Town Hall. As we explained to the audience of 1,500, it was by far the best option for bringing the club home, and we intended to upgrade the existing stadium into one that measured up to Football League requirements – with a capacity for 6,000 people.

I also warned that we would have to work together to make it happen and address probable opposition from local residents. Most of the people present were fans and were with us. We needed them, because the Bring Home The Albion campaign would be intense in the coming months.

Vitally, we needed to get planning permission from Brighton & Hove Council to convert Withdean Stadium so that it was fit for the purpose of playing League football. We estimated that the planning process would take a few months, probably stretching into the following season. And although we made our decision in November 1997, we didn't submit our planning application until the following March. The main reason was the conditions set by the council.

Sheila Holden, the senior council planning officer, made it clear that we would be subject to much stricter rules regarding the transport of fans and ticketing of matches at Withdean than were ever in force at the Goldstone Ground. "In order to allow you to play there, the council will insist on a very stringent transport scheme that protects the Withdean area," she said. So before the application went in, we had to work out a complete travel policy and an advance ticket sales system so that casual fans did not turn up on the off-chance of getting in, causing crowd chaos in the quiet suburb.

As expected, opposition to our move to Withdean soon emerged, mostly from residents who lived near the stadium, who didn't want the Albion 'in their back yard'. The same month that we submitted the Withdean Stadium application to the council, they formed SWEAT (Save Withdean Environmental Action Team) and became active in the area – distributing leaflets and encouraging other residents to send in their objections during the consultation period before the council considered the application at a planning meeting in June.

By early April, SWEAT had gathered 850 letters against the Albion going to Withdean. And because our fans were initially slow to react in terms of the letter writing, there were only about 130 in favour. And *The Argus* was only too happy to print that there were people against it – it was a good news story. They also ran a readers' poll whose results suggested that most people didn't want the Albion playing at Withdean.

To some extent, I could understand the locals being wary about the Albion coming to play there, what with the club's reputation over the previous few years. The game itself was still tainted in some people's eyes by the epidemic of hooliganism of the 1970s and '80s. Withdean was situated in one of the more affluent parts of Brighton and Hove, where a certain amount of Nimbyism (Not In My Back Yard) would be expected. But the 'environmental action' promise in the SWEAT name didn't wash with me. We always intended to do everything possible to minimise any effect on the local environment, whether it was protecting badgers in the adjacent nature reserve, keeping fans out of there or picking up any litter after every game. And we kept our promises.

One of the few complaints ever made against us came years later with the so-called 'Rocket Man,' a mystery character who let off fireworks somewhere among the trees above the south side of the stadium every time we scored – and that was pretty often. At first police thought he was in the nature reserve, but he turned out to be a resident of one of those £1 million houses in the area, setting off fireworks from his garden.

From the beginning, SWEAT waged a fairly dirty campaign against the Albion's Withdean plans. They painted the club and its fans in the worst possible terms and they used scare tactics, with the idea that there would be football hooligans urinating and rampaging through gardens a prominent feature of their campaign literature.

One of their leaflets sank even lower, claiming that there was another Hillsborough disaster in the making. It was an unfounded warning about over-crowding when people were leaving Preston Park train station (the closest to Withdean) which, they said, would lead to a crush of people. It was simply outrageous scaremongering. And the SWEAT people rarely showed their faces, they just issued statements and leaflets.

We ran a full-page ad in *The Argus*, headlined 'The Facts', answering all their points one by one. But I must admit that I was surprised by the vehemence of this opposition. There was a total lack of appreciation of the circumstances in which Albion fans – not 'football hooligans' of common media parlance – had occupied the pitch at matches at the Goldstone. It was upsetting and frustrating that some residents of Brighton and Hove didn't seem to want their football club back.

What's more a lot of my time, and Martin's, was now being spent in various meetings with council officers. And what we encountered from some of them was an attitude of arrogance, bordering on contempt, for what we were trying to achieve. The politicians, with a feel for public opinion, might have appreciated that the club was changing for the better. Their officers often didn't.

At a review meeting before we submitted our planning application, in the council offices in Grand Avenue, Hove, in early February, a senior council officer was very patronising and began lecturing us, "You don't have any divine right to come back to Brighton and play here," she said. "Whatever you get from the council you should be grateful for."

What we were seeing was an inherent dislike of football and distrust of the club, which was very apparent in our early dealings with the council. "We have every right to be here," I said. "Don't condescend to me or the football club. I have a right to fight to get the best for the football club and our supporters." She didn't like me answering back.

Not everyone was like this. Some council officers recognised what we were trying to do. But I was learning that representing the football club meant dealing with the consequences of how the Albion (and not just Archer) had treated the local councils in the past. I think some of the hostility towards us went all the way back to the time of Mike Bamber, Albion chairman in the glory years of the 1970s and '80s.

In the early 1980s, Bamber had effectively demanded that Brighton Council build the club a new home, to help the Albion maintain their top-flight status, in return for the publicity the club brought the town. Bamber had selected Waterhall, the valley on the edge of the Downs, as the site for a new stadium. The council didn't like being told what to do, and refused. Although Brighton and Hove were now merged into one local authority, I don't think the relationship between council and club had ever really recovered.

Now we had to convince the planning officers to recommend approval for the redevelopment of Withdean as our temporary home. These officers would make a recommendation to the councillors – the ones voted in by the people – to approve or reject our application.

Little did we know it but the planning process, in all its complexity, would become a constant in all our lives for the next 10 years – for the leaders of the club, and also the fans.

I decided it was time to employ some of my advertising experience, to get the message across that the Albion needed to come home, and that Withdean was the only place for it. I came up with a poster after calculating the number of hours we would actually spend at the ground against the total number of hours in a year. The result? One per cent of the year.

The poster design showed '1%' repeated 100 times, with just one highlighted in red. I used my contacts in the poster industry to get us some cheap sites locally, while we also took a full-page ad in *The Argus* at well below normal cost. I showed the poster at a public meeting and it was well-received, although one or two SWEAT supporters were there, and one shouted out, "One per cent is one per cent too much."

SWEAT, though, soon found that they could not claim to speak for all the residents of their area. A body of people in Withdean itself, led by long-time fan Paul Whelch, who were quite happy for the Albion to come and play there, formed a group called WISH (Withdean Invites the Seagulls Home).

Martin, our growing team of consultants and I had a lot of meetings thrashing out the detail of the planning application with Sheila Holden. After her initial wariness about us, she became one of the more helpful people we encountered. Not because she was pally, but because she was a stickler for rules and procedure, which guided us in the right direction, and she would advise us where the planning application needed to be changed so that it would have the best chance to gain approval. There was a process of getting the application to a point where they were prepared to receive it, knowing it would stand up to robust scrutiny. And the protests that SWEAT were making meant that everyone was being even more careful.

But at the same time as the project to secure planning permission for Withdean was running – and we were spending a lot of money on that – we were also progressing on the first steps of the project for the permanent stadium. Withdean was never in the running for that – the site was too small, you could never move 20,000 people safely in and out of there, and it was in the middle of a residential suburb.

By April 1998, the council's survey, started 30 months earlier, had evaluated 16 possible sites for the permanent stadium, and had eliminated 11 of them. Only the five remaining sites had any potential whatsoever: Waterhall, Hove Greyhound Stadium, Brighton Station, Shoreham Harbour and Village Way, Falmer.

None of them was perfect, but on our narrow strip of land, surrounded by sea and hills, no such site existed. I already knew that, but I also knew that we had to make one of these work. We had to investigate each site against all the criteria of government planning requirements, a mammoth task. The process began with a Sequential Site Analysis, starting from that closest to the Goldstone – which meant the greyhound stadium, still a possible contender.

The complex and vastly expensive project, involving teams of lawyers, independent consultants and specialist experts, was under way. We had narrowed the field to five, and I was totally committed to finding the best and seeing it all the way through to its ultimate, glorious conclusion, whatever obstacles were put in our way.

Meanwhile, there was the reason why we were doing all this – the football team. And in that respect, as the 1997/98 season wore on, the situation became increasingly dire. It was like a horror movie that wouldn't end.

The terrible gates for our matches at Gillingham were really hurting. At the Barnet game in November, we recorded our lowest-ever attendance for a home match: 1,025.

I went on my own to an Auto Windscreens Shield game at Walsall on a foggy and rainy night early in January when we lost 5-0, and I knew that we were out of the game at 2-0. It could have been 10. We played without spirit, without organisation, we were awful. It was really only down to luck that we didn't get relegated that season, due to the fact that Doncaster Rovers were even worse than us.

The home game against Doncaster, on February 14 1998, was the second Fans United day – and gave us the biggest crowd we ever had at Gillingham. More than 6,300 people turned up – fans from clubs all around the country to again support the cause. And if it didn't quite have the same impact as the previous year, it was still a great statement by football fans.

That Fans United game was also notable for another reason – we launched the club's mobile shop. Fans could now buy Albion merchandise on match-days at Gillingham, a simple but important step in demonstrating that the Albion were now functioning properly as a business.

The only thing that spoilt the day was the football match. It was possibly the worst game between two professional teams that anyone had ever witnessed (even worse than the Hereford match). It not only finished 0-0, but I don't think either team managed a shot on goal.

It was around this time that I came to the decision that we had to have a change of manager. I'd thought about it after that 5-0 drubbing at Walsall, but instead tried to gee up Steve Gritt and Gary Hobson, the captain, in long chats separately with them over coffee in the following days. It obviously hadn't worked.

By now the die was cast in terms of the team. They were just not performing – results were poor, and morale in the dressing room was virtually non-existent. We lost the next game, 2-0 at Rochdale, and on Tuesday February 24 I watched us go down 2-1 at Exeter, where we again played badly. It was our 10th game without a win, eight of them lost. I knew that I had to do something about changing things. We needed someone to lift the team and lift the club, and at that point I decided that I had to sack Steve Gritt.

Obviously this was not an easy decision. Steve was the man who had saved the team the previous season, and that gave him a certain amount of football capital. Now, years later, it may look callous that less than 12 months on from those heroics I would fire him. But we were dreadful that season, and there was no sign of things improving. Quite the opposite in fact. I saw Steve getting demoralised and it was affecting the team.

It certainly didn't help that Steve and I had a slightly strained relationship in those months when I was chairman and he was manager. Of course, he had been Archer and Bellotti's appointment, and I don't know if he felt some kind of residual loyalty to them, but he seemed to be a bit wary of me and quite distant, perhaps because a new chairman often spells trouble for a manager. That didn't help us develop any sort of personal chemistry, although I met him regularly and took him out of the normal club environment, for example to Bertorelli's off Tottenham Court Road, one of my favourite restaurants.

Unfortunately Steve and I were never close enough to discuss things openly, as I would have liked. And the most important relationship in a football club is the one between the chairman of the club and the manager of the team. What you don't want is any kind of 'yes-man' mentality either way. You need a frank, honest relationship to get the best out of each other, for the good of the club.

I knew what the parameters of my job were, regarding the football side of things – I think I had a good sense of this long before I became chairman of the Albion. I knew it wasn't my place to tell Steve, or anyone else who happened to be managing the team, how to do their job. Of course, I had my views about the way the team played, the tactics, and how it was being coached – and I shared them with the manager – but I never interfered in the running of the team.

I never told Steve who he should pick (not that there was much of a choice, to be honest!) but as a fan I had become increasingly frustrated by the fact that the team never seemed to try to play good football, on the deck, passing it. Our match on Boxing Day against Colchester, when we fought back from three goals down at half-time to draw 4-4, was probably the only decent and exciting game all season. In terms of football, there were only a few crumbs on the table.

The whole playing side of the club needed an overhaul. We needed new blood and fresh thinking about the way the team was prepared. And ultimately the chairman is there to make the big decisions, those big calls that affect the direction of the football club. Hopefully those decisions are good ones and you make them at the right time – and in my view it was definitely time for a change.

The day after the defeat at Exeter, I called Steve in for a meeting in the offices and he probably knew what to expect. I'd sacked people before so I wasn't unfamiliar with the process and I wasn't nervous, although of course it was significant because it was my first sacking as a football club chairman – something of a rite of passage, I suppose. Even though I hadn't issued the traditional vote of confidence beforehand.

"We're going to have to part company, Steve," I said. "I've got to make a change. We can't be sure that Doncaster won't revive, and the way things are going, I can't see you being able to re-motivate the squad. We are not in a position to bring in a load of new players, so I've got to bring in a new manager to rejuvenate them."

"You must do what you've got to do," Steve replied. His face was gaunt, but he took it like a man. I showed him a statement for release to the media that fully recognised and respected his contribution to the club. We shook hands.

After my first blooding, I suppose I should have felt more like a real chairman, but I just felt sad to have to do this to a guy who had given his all and been so lauded after we had beaten Hereford. But ultimately, results speak for themselves. I had to act.

I already had someone in mind, so that evening I contacted him. It was Brian Horton. He was, as every Brighton fan of a certain vintage will know, an Albion legend. He was the captain of the great team of the late 1970s, who had gone from Division Three to Division One in three seasons. He was a great leader on the pitch, and had gone on to become a successful manager.

Brian wasn't working, but until quite recently he had been manager of Huddersfield Town. And not long before that, manager of Manchester City, where he had suffered through not being the big name that City felt they deserved, but had done a good job. My call came out of the blue, but it hardly surprised me that he was very interested.

Although he was part of that great Albion team of the late '70s – and a team very well known for their sociability in the heart of Brighton nightlife – I'd never actually met Brian before. But I'd heard him interviewed many times and knew he had a big personality as well as managerial pedigree, and that was what we needed now, to lift the fans as well as the team. For me, he was the ideal candidate for the job. I arranged to meet him the next day, at the Mottram Hall Hotel near Manchester.

So, after my first sacking, my first appointment – I hoped. I did pinch myself, thinking, "Here am I, who stood and cheered Brian Horton on from the East Terrace, about to discuss with him the Albion manager's job." And when we met in the hotel lounge, I said I'd been a fan. He replied, "Yes, but you're chairman now and that's how I'm treating you now, not as a fan."

He'd done his homework on me and knew about the battle I had fought and was continuing to fight. It was obvious that Brian still had a strong affection for the club. And it was also obvious that he was more streetwise about the football industry than Steve, who was more of an idealist.

Brian and I just hit it off straight away. We spent a few hours at the hotel talking about football in general, and the Albion in particular. We agreed on a lot of things – like the football philosophy of getting the ball down on the floor and passing it, as much as was possible on the bottom rung of the League.

Our long conversation merely confirmed to me that Brian was the ideal man for the job, so I offered it to him there and then. With his feelings for the Albion it was probably an easier sell than it might otherwise have been. But I still had to make sure he believed that we wouldn't be groundsharing for ever.

"Brian, we aren't going to be staying at Gillingham for very long, you can be absolutely certain about that," I told him. "We'll be back in Brighton the season after next."

So Brian accepted the job, on a two-and-a-half-year contract, taking him into the first year back in Brighton – as long as our planning application for Withdean went through. Jeff Wood, Steve's versatile assistant, would be invited to stay on. I knew Brian's would be a popular appointment, although I would get criticism for sacking Gritt, the saviour at Hereford. I was right on both counts. But as chairman those were the sort of decisions I had to make.

Brian would go on to oversee what was, in all honesty, only a marginal improvement in the team's performances and results in the final two months of the 1997/98 season. But we won his first game in charge, and even managed to pick up the odd point on the road, including a creditable 0-0 draw away to Cardiff City on March 28.

That was a trip that was intended to provide a romantic weekend away but began in chaos and ended in farce. I had planned to drive down to Cardiff from London with my girlfriend, Kerry, but as we headed for the M4 we found ourselves stuck in traffic heading for the Boat Race, which was taking place that afternoon.

It meant that we crawled through west London before we could get to the motorway and by 1.45pm we were still only at Reading. I remember seeing a sign that read 'Cardiff 107 miles' and said to Kerry, "Strap yourself in tightly and hang on." We were in my Porsche 911 and I put my foot down. We pulled into that small car park behind the main stand at Ninian Park at 3.02pm.

Kerry's face was still pale when we took our seats. Anyway, we got a point, and I was in a good mood in the boardroom after this rare success, chatting with Samesh Kumar, the Cardiff chairman, and Neil Kinnock, the former Labour party leader and a big Cardiff fan. Kerry and I were going on to stay in a beautiful country manor hotel in Somerset before driving back to London on Sunday to watch the League Cup final between Chelsea and Middlesbrough. However, just as we were leaving, someone came into the boardroom and said, "Your team coach has left but the skip full of your dirty kit is still in the dressing room. The kit man has forgotten it."

I said, "Well, I'm in a Porsche, and it's not over-endowed with luggage space." But anyway, I stuffed the boot – which is at the front of a 911 – absolutely full of shirts, shorts, socks and even jockstraps. The skip would have to wait. Then off we went. When we got to the very swish hotel, I called Jock Riddell, the kit man, who was still on the team coach, nearing Brighton. I said, "Jock, what the hell happened? You forgot the kit and I've got it in my car."

"Thank goodness for tha', Mr Chairman, tha's great," Jock replied in his broad Scottish brogue. "Just drop it off at ma' house. Or shall I come over and pick it up?" he added cordially.

"No, I'm having a go at you, Jock. And I'm now in Somerset, and I'm going to Wembley tomorrow. I won't be in Brighton until Monday. You come to my house and get it then."

So we went on from this beautiful country hotel to the old Wembley Stadium the next day, had lunch in the main lounge at a table with Kevin Keegan and Mick McCarthy, and watched the game. And all the while, my Porsche 911 was full of putrefying Albion playing kit. The car almost made it back to Brighton without me switching on the engine.

There weren't many other laughs during our first season at Gillingham and my first season as chairman, but both were coming to an end with the promise of better things to come.

The serious work of our Withdean Stadium planning application was coming to fruition. We had done our work in the planning process, submitted the application, generated more than 8,000 letters of support to the council, and put the case for Withdean on billboards and elsewhere – and through the Bring Home The Albion campaign we had started to engage with the real support that existed for the club throughout the county of Sussex.

Also, lifelong fan and Albion historian Tim Carder organised a petition which, in only seven weeks, collected more than 32,000 names supporting the Albion's cause of coming back to Brighton at Withdean. In May, he and Adrian Newnham handed the petition to Steve (now Lord) Bassam, leader of Brighton & Hove Council. He struggled to carry the 16 volumes of names, including more than 1,300 from the Withdean area, into the Town Hall.

If Steve ever had doubts about the passion for the club among his constituents, this would have removed them. And I told him: "If you think this is impressive, wait till you see what else I can conjure up to make your people understand that this is an important part of the culture of these towns."

And then in early June, we got our planning permission. Brighton & Hove Council Planning Committee voted 10-2 in favour of our application for Withdean, giving us permission to develop the stadium, and to play there – initially for two years. Football was coming home! As I'd promised to myself, the Albion would be returning well inside the three years stipulated by the Football League.

But it still wasn't over. In a sort of prelude to every planning obstacle that would follow in the years to come, before we could draw up the agreement for how the Withdean approval would be implemented (known as the 106 Agreement), SWEAT appealed. They wanted it reviewed in the High Court. So we weren't free to go ahead quite yet.

Our go-ahead finally arrived in August when SWEAT, probably advised that they had very little chance of their judicial review succeeding, withdrew their appeal.

We had won – but SWEAT's tactics had delayed us for more months. We planned to have Withdean operational by October, but their stalling was followed by a series of contractual wrangles and delays with Ecovert, the stadium's managers, eventually making any chance of occupying Withdean during the following season impossible. And the noise SWEAT had made meant that the council were going to impose very tight restrictions on our use of Withdean – much more stringent terms than the Albion ever had at the Goldstone.

Martin and I were now involved in negotiating the 106 Agreement with the council, who confirmed the worst with a whole set of regulations. This included a three-pronged transport policy designed to keep fans from driving to Withdean, and using public transport instead. All paid for by the club, it involved a free park-and-ride scheme from two locations, subsidised public transport on buses and trains, and thirdly, a parking exclusion zone involving 80-odd stewards controlling the Withdean area. You wouldn't be able to park within a mile of the ground if you tried.

On top of that, the council insisted that no tickets could be purchased at Withdean on matchdays, or any other day of the week, and there could be no pay-at-the-turnstile admission on the day.

We were restricted to 15 minutes' music over the PA before games, and we were initially only allowed to play 'Sussex By The Sea'. We agreed to set up a monthly residents' liaison meeting to hear any complaints, and a telephone hotline during games. We provided post-match litter patrols and once we started playing there the Withdean area was tidier than ever before.

Well before the move, we gave our supporters all the information they needed about Withdean – travel, ticketing, behaving responsibly – through leaflets, website, press coverage and briefing meetings, and as I expected, they responded magnificently. I was so proud of the rapport and understanding that had already built up between fans and club. We were in this together.

Peter Drury in *The Independent*, covering an early game, summed up the "extraordinarily 'different' match-day ambience" of the leafy suburb. "Fans walking to the game are required to behave as if they were passing by the headmaster's study. Conversation among the match-bound fans is of the hushed, reverential sort normally encountered in the vicinity of the British Museum."

We had a lot of rules to abide by, just to play football in our own town. Our fans' impeccable behaviour would not only prove SWEAT's threats puerile, but also show what can be achieved when club and supporters are on the same wavelength. And in fact our transport policy was groundbreaking in its environmental approach. That was obviously no bad thing. But once again it was an immense financial burden on us, consuming half our gate receipts, which no other club in the country had to face.

As well as the granting of planning permission by the council, another good thing happened in June. Bill Archer wrote to me on June 17, nine months after the takeover, resigning from the board of the club and citing health reasons. He had attended two board meetings in London in that time, but was very passive, almost chummy by then.

After that, he never met with the board again. He'd finally given up. He'd decided that he wasn't going to get anything out of this, his Toads Hole Valley dream was over. The 'chancer' had won. He could concentrate fully on his fast-growing Focus DIY chain.

I immediately made it clear that I wasn't allowing him to take his loan money out of the club then. He told me he had no intention of pressuring the club to repay, and he didn't – at least not for some months.

But if he imagined he would ever be able to get all his money back, he had another think coming . . .

Our meticulous work continued on evaluating the possible sites for the new stadium, and to many people there was one stand-out location: Waterhall.

It was easy to see what made this greenfield site the favourite. It was a natural bowl on the northern edge of Brighton; there were no problems with neighbours, the nearest houses were hundreds of yards away; it was already used for football and rugby, with a dozen or so pitches there; it was next to a major road and the London–Brighton railway line; and it was owned by the local council, so land costs would be minimal.

We even put in a planning application for a stadium there, but in fact that was simply to keep the Football League happy, to show them that we were actively pursuing a permanent return to Brighton. But the more we looked into it, the less feasible it became.

For one thing, it was north of the A27 Brighton bypass, in an area that was designated to be part of the new South Downs National Park. Steve Bassam had already pledged publicly that his council would never allow any building on land north of the bypass.

The bypass itself, far from being a transport plus, was a problem. The only road access to Waterhall was via one tunnel under the bypass, and that tunnel was reachable only through a narrow railway bridge to the east or a long, winding, steep uphill road to the west. To change that would have involved major road reconstruction or an access road from the top of the valley, winding down like something in the Swiss Alps.

The railway would also not be an asset. In most people's minds, it would be a simple matter to build a new Waterhall Parkway Station to be used on match-days, but in fact there was no chance of that happening. The site was close to a tunnel, and new rail regulations prohibited the building of new stations within certain distances of a tunnel, even though there were plenty of existing stations which contravened that rule. In addition, the London-Brighton line is one of the busiest in the country, working at full capacity on most weekdays and a station that stretched it even further during the evening rush-hour – as it would have done for midweek games – was impractical.

So Waterhall was out. We revisited Hove Greyhound Stadium but that, too, had to be ruled out. I had learned in 1997 that owners Coral considered sharing would be a non-starter, and when we looked at trying to buy the site outright, the additional ownership by the Alliance & Leicester building society of the land on the east side, where a stand would have to be built, proved an insuperable problem. The combined costs of buying the existing stadium and the strip of building society land put it way out of our range. And the problem of parking would have reared its head again.

Prohibitive cost also eliminated the land adjacent to Brighton Station from our evaluation – although traffic gridlock alone might have ruled it out. British Rail, the owners, required £22 million for the purchase of the site, and some bean-counter decided it was non-negotiable. They thought a supermarket would cough up, which it did. We never could have.

Shoreham Harbour was a brownfield site, which was a plus, and there was plenty of room, but if we thought that would make it cheaper, it proved to be hugely expensive – because of the infrastructure costs. Access would have been a real problem – there was only one narrow road in, by Hove Lagoon. The only recognisable solution would have been to dig a tunnel under Portslade. The cost of that alone would have been at least £50 million, which would have grown to more like £300 million for the whole project by the time it got built.

But we still had to have meetings with people such as the chief executive of the Shoreham Harbour Authority, to hear exactly what was feasible. We had to demonstrate that we had fully investigated every option. There was no possibility of short-changing on this. It was time-consuming and costly. We sometimes went to meetings with three experts, all charging us £500 per day, but we had to go through that process. It was a thankless task.

That left Falmer.

The site, adjacent to Village Way North, a quiet road leading into the University of Brighton, was owned by Brighton & Hove Council. It was a ploughed field, separated from Falmer village by a B road, and bordered on the other two sides by the A27 trunk road alongside the railway line to Lewes, and the northern edge of the university campus.

Although our architects attempted to fit the stadium footprint into that plot of land, it became clear that we would need to encroach a little into a corner of the campus, which made for complications later. And it was close to the Downs, which would almost guarantee opposition from the green lobby.

But Falmer was our only choice, the best available site. It had good transport links, including a railway station on the doorstep. It was within Brighton & Hove, if only just – but then any major development in a city confined by a narrow, developed strip of land would face the same geographical strait-jacket.

It would never score 100 per cent. It wasn't even a 92 per cent. More like a 63 out of 100. But the next best site got no more than five out of 100. Falmer was the least-worst option. And it was on home ground.

I still remember standing on one corner of that very chalky field at Falmer, turning through a full 360 degrees and seeing, in my mind's eye, a stadium – and one not very different from the one that stands there now. A stadium with sweeping curves that blended into the surrounding hills.

The landscape wasn't a sea of green waving corn, but it was still my *Field of Dreams* moment. The only thing missing was a ghostly voice saying, "If you build it, people will come."

That was okay. I knew they would.

# CHAPTER SIXTEEN

# BRIGHTON'S PERRY MASON

*John Gregory said, "Dick Knight wouldn't recognise Gareth Barry if he stood on Brighton beach in an Albion shirt with a football under his arm and a seagull on his head" – but who had the last laugh?*

Gareth Barry had gone to Aston Villa before I took over the club, along with Michael Standing, my great-nephew. I discovered that Villa had offered a paltry sum in compensation, only £3,000 for each player, the mandatory minimum. I refused to accept it, and insisted it should go to the Football League Appeals Tribunal, rare in those days for youth players. We'd had both these boys since before they were 10 – for six years – so I maintained that we were entitled to a considerably larger amount of compensation.

Neither Gareth nor Michael had ever played in the Albion's first team, or even the reserves, but we could obviously see their potential and had offered them both professional contracts at 16, as soon as we were allowed to. They had both turned the offers down, become free agents and gone to Villa in early 1997, who'd been watching them for some time, because, as far as they could see, the Albion was on its last legs. Who knows if they would have gone if I'd taken over earlier?

But even if the club was in ruins, the youth side was still operating. Even under severely restricted financial circumstances, we kept the two centres of excellence. Because of the wide reach of the Albion across Sussex there were two centres – in West Sussex at Worthing, and in East Sussex at Seaford. Gareth came from Hastings and was with the East Sussex centre for six years.

The interesting thing at the time was that midfielder Michael Standing was the better prospect. He'd played 18 times for England schoolboys (to this day a record) and it was obvious that, at first, Villa saw Gareth as promising and – as they were best friends – a handy companion for Michael far from home. But to us, his reading of the game, positional sense and range of passing was already showing a maturity beyond his years.

We had been trying to get a tribunal to sort out compensation and it kept being delayed. The Football League took its own time in calling these youth tribunals and eventually arranged it for October 21 1998 at the Premier League's palatial headquarters near Marble Arch, the delays playing into our hands to some extent. Gareth had got into the Villa first team at the back end of the 1997/98 season and by this point was an ever-present in the Premier League side.

A three-man independent panel headed by Sir John Wood, and also including Nottingham Forest stalwart Frank Clark, was to decide compensation for Gareth, Michael and Jlloyd Samuel, all young players that Aston Villa had taken. Jlloyd had come from Charlton, so Peter Varney, the managing director of Charlton, was there too.

Each case was handled separately and Gareth's was first. Villa were represented by their youth team head, Kevin MacDonald, and their club chief executive, Steve Stride. And during the proceedings, John Gregory, their manager and a former Albion player, strutted in, chest puffed up, having just come back from winning a UEFA cup tie at Celta Vigo. At that time Villa were near the top of the league as well, so John was very full of himself.

I had with me our manager, Brian Horton, and the late Les Rogers, who had been the coach of the two boys through our centres of excellence. In those days the same coach took them through from under-10s to under-16s, so Les had been working with these boys for years. He was able to talk about them with great knowledge and passion. He was superb in that meeting. It was a wonderful occasion for him because he'd never been exposed to that level of football and here he was convincing the panel of his professionalism and integrity.

We made the case that Albion had seen Gareth as a player of real potential from the early days and had given him and Michael top-quality coaching. Gareth regularly appeared in our youth teams both as a back-four player and a left-sided midfield player. He had played left-sided central defence and left-back as he had come through various years of the Brighton centres of excellence.

Gregory claimed that it was his inspirational management that had made Gareth a left-sided central defender, but I challenged him – supported by Les – and we emphasised the fact that Gareth had played in that position in our youth squad. Gregory didn't like that.

I sensed the case we were making was seen to be a solid one. At one point I remember Brian nudged me under the table and whispered, "You're the Perry Mason of Brighton & Hove Albion," referring to the famous TV lawyer. And I was quietly confident that the outcome would be positive for us. The tribunal also interviewed Gareth – although we were not present – and clearly this boy had broken into the Villa's first team in a position that wasn't unfamiliar to him. He had apparently told Gregory, "I can play there" when he was on the bench and Ugo Ehiogu had got injured.

There was a lot of media attention because he was from Brighton, who were in dire straits at the very bottom of the league, and here was one of our former players who'd broken into Villa's first team at the age of 17, and was already a regular. So the possibility of significant compensation, because the powers that be had agreed to a youth tribunal, interested the media.

I hadn't suggested a figure – although I had a startling sum in mind – I just made it clear that we had developed Gareth to a point where Villa were keen to take him, and they had contributed only a relatively small amount to his coaching as he had only been with them for a few months. Whatever this boy had become – he was already being talked about as a future England player – was 95 per cent down to the football education he'd received from Brighton. And when the panel called us back in it was obvious they agreed.

They went through a list of the benefits that we were to be paid for Gareth: an immediate payment of £150,000 and then tranches totalling £650,000 for every 20 first-team games he played up to 60. It included incremental payments if he played for England – the full team and the Under-21s. The whole package added up to £1,025,000, and there was a sell-on clause that gave us 15 per cent of any future fee if Villa sold him.

This was easily the most Brighton had ever received for a player, beating the £900,000 we got for Mark Lawrenson in 1981 – and we got that when Lawrenson was an established international. Over a million pounds was an amazing result. It was what I had hoped for, although I hadn't necessarily expected the tribunal to deliver it. Villa certainly hadn't; Gregory was furious and stormed out of the building. Perhaps he should never have boasted to the press when Barry was establishing himself, "We stole him from Brighton."

When I was interviewed outside Premier League HQ by the national press, they just couldn't believe the figure, because nothing like it had ever been paid for a young player. It was regarded as quite a coup – especially for a club like Brighton, in our situation. We gained a lot of prestige, firstly for producing these very good players, but also for the way we had negotiated, having showed that we knew how to stand up for ourselves.

It was seen as a test case that struck a major blow for smaller clubs, by establishing the principle that big clubs must pay adequate compensation when enticing promising young footballers away from the clubs who have nurtured them. Had Albion failed, then the youth schemes of smaller clubs might as well have been scrapped. I told the *Daily Telegraph*, "What would be the point in wasting all our time, effort and money when Premier League clubs can just cherry-pick the best? The lure of joining them is so irresistible that we have to be properly compensated."

With Michael, the tribunal asked us to make a submission on his behalf and then unbelievably delayed their ruling for a year due to 'registration technicalities'. I'm sure that held him back at Villa. They finally came up with a decision on Michael which was based on the same principles as Gareth but on a lower scale and gave us about £200,000. The same tribunal had awarded Charlton £150,000 for Jlloyd Samuel, so there's no doubt that they were influenced by the fact that Gareth had played in the Premiership. Samuel and Standing had yet to do so.

However, our battle with Aston Villa was not over. They sent us the first payment of £150,000 but in January, when we sent them an invoice for £200,000 after Barry had played 20 games in Villa's first team, they refused to pay it – despite having agreed to abide by the findings of the tribunal in October.

That created another storm. The Premier League intervened, as did Gordon Taylor, the PFA chief, basically in total support of our position. Anything else would have reaffirmed the right of the top clubs to poach the best players from lower clubs without paying proper compensation.

Trying to justify the non-payment, Gregory came out with his widely-reported cheeky-chappie comment that, "Dick Knight wouldn't recognise Gareth Barry if he stood on Brighton beach in an Albion shirt with a football under his arm and a seagull on his head" – a nice soundbite, but total nonsense of course, because I'd seen Gareth play many times alongside Michael in the youth side.

The Premier League demanded to know why Villa weren't paying up – they had to abide by the tribunal otherwise there would be anarchy. Villa explained that they had written to Sir John Wood asking him to justify the decision and had received no reply. But there had been no right of appeal, so why should Sir John write back to them justifying the tribunal's decision?

On top of his comment about me not recognising Gareth, Gregory also said that Villa had been made to bail out a club that was so badly run that it almost went to the wall, and asked why Villa would have spent £1 million on an untried teenager. My response was that if he only valued Gareth at £150,000, we would buy him back for that amount. Of course they didn't have any answer to that.

For a former Albion player, Gregory surprisingly seemed to take it as a personal affront. His position was patronising and the behaviour of Aston Villa scandalous. The previous year they had been competing for the signature of Juninho, the Brazil midfield player. They were quite happy to pay £12 million for him, but didn't want to have to pay more than £150,000 for a key defender – and in fact offered £3,000 for a player who went on to pass the 500 Premier

League games mark in September 2013, an achievement which deservedly puts him in football's hall of fame.

My retort to Gregory in the press was, "You've got a Premier League star in the making for a million pounds. How is that a bad deal for you? And it allows Brighton to get some compensation for their important role in his career development."

Eventually Villa were forced to pay by the Premier League, who deducted the £200,000 from their television payments. They were prepared to make us wait – all because my club had challenged them with the facts.

This was a landmark case because this was a player who was always capable of going on to play for England, and that needed to be reflected in the value of the compensation we received, indeed he went on to make his full international debut only two years later. I thought long and hard before I went into that tribunal. Obviously it was the first time for me, and the first time for the Albion to be in that situation, but we were setting a benchmark for smaller clubs.

In the end I did a deal with 'Deadly' Doug Ellis, the Villa chairman, in 2000 that basically kept us afloat, negotiating £500,000 in lieu of the remainder of the instalments at a time when our club really needed it. I said, "Doug, if you were to make me an offer for a decent sum of money, then we might be able to resolve this once and for all. I know you resent having to keep paying tranches of money to Brighton for Gareth, who will be a very good servant for you for years to come, and who you got for an absolute snip."

Doug replied, "All right, young man [although I'm only about 10 years younger than him], I suppose I should thank you for not driving a harder bargain at the tribunal."

So we got £850,000 instead of the entire £1,025,000, and we missed out on a further £1.8 million when Gareth was sold on to Manchester City in 2009 – which would have ultimately made him our first £2 million-plus player. Why did we accept less? Well, we knew Villa would procrastinate over paying the next tranche. All of a sudden he disappeared from the first team when he was close to the next 20 appearances, and I didn't have the luxury of being able to wait.

We had never been in any danger of relegation out of the Football League in 1998 because Doncaster only got 20 points all season. We were poor, but they were worse. It was clear to me that the squad was hugely in need of rebuilding and revitalising. We were living on borrowed time – the second season in exile in Kent just couldn't be as bad as the first, while I was fighting to get the club back to Brighton. I had to give the fans something to believe in on the pitch instead of being demoralised.

By the time the 1998/99 season started, I'd been able to give Brian some money to strengthen the squad. We also had a marvellous contribution from the supporters through the 'Buy A Player Appeal', which produced a sum of £25,000 to help us sign Rod Thomas, a tricky left-winger from Chester City, towards the end of the previous season, when Brian had also brought in Richie Barker up front.

Brian was a very good motivator, and was tactically aware. He got the team playing in a basic 4-4-2 system, but with a midfield playmaker in Jeff Minton and a useful holding midfielder called Andy Arnott. Then Paul Armstrong came into the team, a young Irish player who added some good creative attacking midfield play, and Rod played wide and was very exciting. He had that darting acceleration that took him past defenders and he scored goals – not many, but good ones. He quickly became a favourite of the fans, so their spirits began to lift.

In the autumn we put together a very good run of away results – winning five away league games on the trot up to the end of November, an Albion record. We got to January 1999 and were just outside the play-off places – and then Port Vale sacked John Rudge, their long-serving manager.

Brian was immediately identified as the prime candidate to replace Rudge in the local press up there. Initially I had no formal approach from Port Vale, but I was sure Brian would feel a strong pull. He comes from that area, and had played for Vale before he came to Brighton. When they asked permission, I decided that I would have to let him speak to them, because he wanted to.

At the time when this happened, Port Vale were in Division One, now the Championship. He met with them, and when he came back from Burslem he told me he wanted to go. I did everything to persuade him to stay, and pointed out that although Vale were in Division One and we were in Division Three, there was no end to the potential at the Albion when we got the new stadium, whereas Vale were always going to be the second club in the Potteries behind Stoke City. Knowing our club's past history as he did, I hoped he would stay and help me deliver a new vision of the Albion, but maybe he thought it just wasn't possible.

Although Brian said publicly that it was a football decision, in my view he was strongly influenced by the fact that he would be closer to his family. His twin boys lived with their mother up there, and his partner, Val, had a senior job at Granada Television in Manchester. I think that influenced him greatly.

So I had to announce that he was leaving. The Albion fans were really upset by Brian's decision. He was a hero. I did a video called *Horton's Heroes* at

Christmas 1998, to celebrate the five away victories. That went down very well, it was one of the best-selling videos we ever did. Brian was very popular and he definitely got the team beginning to play. We'd become used to season-long relegation nightmares, and here we were on the edge of the play-offs. And there he goes, up and leaving.

For someone who had previously been manager of Manchester City in the top flight, the second level of English football ostensibly had a lot more appeal than the fourth. But basically we had revived his career as a manager and I felt a little bit let down because I'd given him a chance and he had a great affection for the Albion, and the fans had a lot of affection for him.

We had a home game on the Saturday, two days later, against Scarborough, who were bottom of the league while we were eighth. I went on the pitch to explain to the fans why Brian had left and that we wished him all the best. I said to the fans that there were family reasons as well as football reasons. They accepted that, both sentiments were well-received – and we wished him well. He was and still is a hero of the Albion, but we were all a bit disappointed that he left at that time.

As caretaker I appointed Jeff Wood, an impressive and likeable guy who had been a very good assistant to Brian and Steve Gritt through some difficult times. I'd even forgiven him for us almost missing out on one of the most important players of the Withdean era.

I had received a letter towards the end of the 1997/98 season from an Albion fan in Essex, about a young player playing for Stansted Airport Sunday team – a lad called Gary Hart. The letter said he was a forklift truck driver at the airport, but a striker worth looking at. So I gave this letter to Brian and said that Jeff, who had been a goalkeeper with Charlton, and was still playing in the Essex Sunday League, should take a look at him, if only as a courtesy.

After a couple of weeks I got another letter from the fan saying that we hadn't replied to his previous letter, and when I checked, Brian confirmed that we hadn't done anything yet as Jeff had been busy decorating his house. I said, "Tell him to take Sunday off, you never know." So the next weekend Jeff did go and on the Monday Brian rang me and said, "You know that kid who plays for Stansted? We've got him in today because Jeff says he's quite useful."

On the Wednesday we were playing Arsenal reserves at Worthing, and Brian put him in as striker up against Steve Bould, who was coming back from injury. Gary Hart from Stansted, up against a rock of the Arsenal, scored both goals in a 2-2 draw. Well, that was enough for us. I said to Brian, "Let's go and get him. Offer them £1,000, and we'll give them a sell-on if we ever sell him."

That was about the only player deal that I didn't do, because Brian came back the next day and said, "I got Hart for a thousand but I've given them a set of shirts instead of a sell-on." That delighted me – at one point I had an enquiry about him for a half a million quid, but we weren't interested in selling him. This is how we acquired one of the great Albion players of this period, a man the fans loved because of his unquenchable spirit.

He came in 1998 and played all the way through to the Amex. He didn't play at the Goldstone but he was there virtually from the beginning at Gillingham. So I'd forgiven Jeff the fact that it had taken him long enough to go and see Gary. And of course we never did sell Gary Hart.

Jeff started with a scrambled 1-0 win that kept us up around the play-off zone. And he won his second match as well so I decided to appoint him for the rest of the season. There were plenty of candidates but I felt that Jeff deserved a chance, the fans wanted him and the players were very keen, they wanted to play for him. He knew his football and he was a popular choice. That was at the end of January.

No one argued with Jeff being appointed. There was a good team ethic there, and we were playing some pretty attractive football without being the finished article. But unfortunately the two games when he was caretaker were the only two games that he won. By early April, we had dropped from eighth in the table to 18th.

We didn't win any games, and only drew a couple. Jeff was a hard worker, but I felt I had to make the decision to remove him from the job, because the club had too much to lose at that time, and we'd gone from being very much promotion contenders to being in real danger of getting drawn into the relegation battle again. Only one club went down out of the League still, but after having two years on the precipice I wasn't going to let that happen again.

Sadly it didn't work out for a very good man, and I fired Jeff on April 8. He had come under pressure from our fans at Gillingham, and I didn't really get criticised for the sacking. Well, maybe a little, delivered with the benefit of hindsight, for appointing him in the first place.

We still had half a dozen league matches to go, and I put head of youth, Martin Hinshelwood, in temporary charge, as a safe pair of hands. We were playing away at Plymouth, who were up in the play-off zone. And of course, as so often happens in a new manager's first game in charge, we won.

It was in March 1999, during that really bad run of results under Jeff, that I was approached by an intermediary who said that former Albion captain Steve Foster wanted to introduce me to a wealthy tycoon he'd met while playing for Luton Town. This tycoon wanted to invest in the Albion, so I arranged a meeting at my ad agency office in London. His name was Stephen Purdew, owner with his mother of Champneys, a chain of health spas.

In this meeting, Purdew told me that he had millions of pounds to invest in the football club in return for a controlling interest. The idea was that Steve, who seemed very nervous in my office, would be the managing director, Purdew would be the owner, and they would allow me to stay on as chairman.

I said to Purdew, "You say you will put millions in the club – what do you mean by that, and where's the evidence that you've got that sort of money?" I'd checked on the performance of his company and they had made £200,000 profit in the previous year. That didn't suggest the ability to put millions into the football club. I wanted to know whether this would be borrowings and what his terms for putting the money in would be. Would it be loans? He told me he wanted to build a leisure complex with a health spa in Brighton and he saw the Albion as being part of that project.

We had already identified Falmer as the only site for the permanent stadium, and I knew he wouldn't be able to put a health spa there because a perfectly good health club was already there, a joint venture between the University of Brighton and Esporta – which is still running to this day. His putting 'millions' into the Albion was conditional on getting his leisure complex, and that would have meant tearing up the plans for Falmer.

Purdew proved elusive in showing me any tangible evidence that he could support his financial claims. And anyway the timing was all wrong.

We had spent a lot of time demonstrating to the council that the club was being stabilised as we negotiated to get back to Brighton. Martin Perry and I had by now established a good working relationship with senior officers and politicians in the initially unwelcoming corridors of local power. The council had called a referendum with two questions: do you support the council's policy of wanting the club to find a permanent home within our area? And should the council support the club's bid to find a permanent site at Falmer?

This referendum was clearly designed to give the council a mandate to get behind the Albion's new ownership and new momentum. It was the idea of Steve Bassam, still the leader of the council, and quite clever from a political point of view because he called it on the day of the local council elections, on May 6 1999. He knew that if you held an Albion referendum at the same time as people went to vote for their local councillor, the chances were that it would significantly boost the turnout for the local elections. That was duly the case.

So we were a matter of weeks away from a delicately-balanced referendum held by a council who were finally beginning to see stability in the football club. Another change of ownership at that stage would have been ill-timed, to say the least.

Purdew also intended to be the majority shareholder and, after the traumas under Archer, I had already pledged to the supporters that no single person could ever control the destiny of the football club again. This was only a few months later.

Purdew was a sweet talker – but I'd met that type before. He kept telling me what he thought I wanted to hear: that he would allow me to be the chairman while he was the owner. He never showed any sensitivity about the football club. He didn't even know there was a referendum coming up. He failed to realise that the progress we'd made was at risk by his unsettling intervention. And one of the crucial things that made me dislike him, apart from the mystery about where his finance was coming from, was his claim to being a big Albion fan.

He told me he'd supported the club since he was a boy and had been to the 1983 FA Cup final. I said, "There are a lot of people who tell me they are Albion fans and the only match they've seen was that Wembley cup final, the 2-2 draw. So if you really are an Albion fan – how did we get on last Saturday?" At this point there was some uneasy shuffling and looks from the other side of the table. Steve mumbled something under this breath, at which point Purdew said that we'd lost 3-0. So I said, "Who was it against?' Silence. And then, "What was our team, if you claim to be an avid Albion fan?" He couldn't name one player. He'd failed on every criterion for being an investor in the Albion.

However, Purdew's hype did persuade *The Argus* into giving him a massive amount of coverage about what he wanted to do. Immediately following that meeting with me, Purdew went straight to the local paper – and they, for some reason, fell for it. Andy Naylor, the chief sports writer, repeatedly asked why I wasn't opening the doors to this guy, failing to appreciate the referendum, ownership and financial credibility issues.

It reached the stage where I demanded a right of reply to these stories, pointing out that it was exactly the wrong time for seismic change and also that Purdew had a business motive concerning this health spa. What was more, we were actively talking to other potential investors at the time – but they didn't want to take over. There was no way I was closing the door to new investors in the club; that was the last thing I was doing.

What was *The Argus'* motivation? There were references in match reports to "the sycophantic followers of Dick Knight", "Dick Knight's disciples" – that sort of thing. The fact that the fans related to me seemed to upset *The Argus*, the same paper that had feasted on back-page stories of the team struggling for survival and, at the same time, the front-page drama of the mismanagement and possible illegal behaviour of the club. It had given them scope for some really good investigative journalism. Paul Bracchi deservedly won an award and went to work in Fleet Street.

My policy was to tell the fans first, and to get news to them immediately, using the emerging technology. We created a club website and updated it daily, sometimes twice a day. We expanded the match programme content and had public meetings regularly. This was obviously a totally new style of Albion ownership. I was doing it my way, and I was very hands-on in terms of setting some standards and disciplines in the club that hadn't been there before, as well as guidelines about how we dealt with the outside world.

We had to make sure that we did things properly, that we conducted ourselves as a businesslike organisation. In the cataclysmic years the club had done anything but that. Any journalist in need of a story could pick up the phone, talk to anyone at the Albion, and more bad news would be in the paper the next day. I put a stop to that. I was open with the fans – and with the staff, to give them confidence – but there was now a more controlled relationship between the club and *The Argus*. We channelled all media contact through the press officer Paul Camillin, myself and Martin.

One of the main things that *The Argus* couldn't quite understand was why the fans and the chairman were getting on, something that was made clear on the night of the launch of our 'Yes, Yes' campaign for the referendum. It was another packed public meeting at Hove Town Hall. Paul Samrah made a speech, saying, "Despite the media campaign behind Purdew, we've now got an understanding between the council and the new ownership of the club, and the last thing we need right now is a media debate stirring things up."

The fans were totally supportive of the club's position. The days of the board and supporters being on completely opposing sides, the chasm between them, had ended. There was complete unanimity on this cause. Maybe that was so alien to *The Argus* that they just decided they didn't like it – not great for circulation, perhaps.

It was no doubt in the interests of *The Argus* to keep Albion at the top of their news agenda. Certainly Naylor almost got to a point over Purdew where he overdid it. *The Argus* were pushing the guy's case so hard that people were beginning to ask why; it was like a personal PR campaign for this fellow.

I wonder whether part of it was that I had started to use other avenues to disseminate club information. The internet was becoming significant. We were one of the first clubs to set up a website and I wanted to drive the fans there, and I was sure that there was an opportunity for a fanzine-type aspect to it as well. We were going through a media revolution, all of which was going against local newspapers. *The Argus* could see that if we had a dynamic website then people would be going there first for up-to-the-minute news about the Albion.

For the first time ever, there would be a 'fly on the wall' source of information about the club. We started beating *The Argus* at their own game and that had never happened before. We were at the forefront of the football communications explosion, which was only to be expected given my advertising background.

Purdew backed off when he realised he wasn't going to get control and ownership. Albion were still struggling on the pitch, as an organisation, and were definitely short of money, but the Champneys man came up short on proving that he could help.

After Jeff Wood's spell in charge, my search for a new manager was brief, because Micky Adams was already on my radar. I knew that he'd had a very successful period managing Fulham, where he'd got them promoted from Division Three. They'd finished runners-up the year we escaped on the last day at Hereford. And he'd had two interesting but short-term managerial appointments at Swansea City and Brentford.

I did some checking and found out why he'd left those jobs. At Swansea he'd been promised a lot of money by the chairman of the holding company that owned the club. When he arrived, he discovered from the chairman of the actual football club that the money wouldn't be forthcoming, and he left after three games. City chairman Steve Hamer, a good football man, was straight with him but Micky, a man of principle, wouldn't forget that he'd been misled by the owners. And then at Brentford he was working for Ron Noades, and I think they just didn't get on. A lot of people found it difficult to get on with Noades, and Micky walked out of that job as well.

That didn't put me off. I was more interested in what he'd achieved at Fulham. He had been very unfortunate to lose his job there. Mohammed al-Fayed had bought the club in the summer of 1997 and immediately installed Kevin Keegan and Ray Wilkins to run the playing side. So Micky was just shown the door.

I'd first met him at a reserve game at Northampton when he was assistant to Dave Bassett at Nottingham Forest, while I was with Brian Horton looking at a player. Micky happened to be sitting near us in the stand and I had a chat with him at half-time. I liked him and the way he talked about football and his passion for it. That short meeting had no significance for me at the time, but I remembered it, so when it was necessary to sack Jeff, Micky was really the only candidate in my mind.

By this time, he was in charge of the Forest reserve team because since we had first talked Bassett had been promoted upstairs, and they had brought in Ron Atkinson as manager. So when I met him at my favourite London inter-viewing hotel – The Grafton in Tottenham Court Road, which was central but quiet – Micky didn't take much persuading to come to Brighton, because he saw an opportunity to do the same thing he'd done for Fulham.

Over coffee, I made him fully aware of our recent history and the stadium battle ahead, but he didn't seem bothered by that. He wanted to talk football.

Micky is a very formidable, no-nonsense character, as he showed when I talked to him about the best way to get the team out of the fourth tier. He knew what he wanted to do, and he knew the way he thought the team should play. He also had a presence, a certain aura about him that I sensed would put players in awe of him and make them slightly scared of him.

He said, "I like my teams to play good football, but in the Third Division there are a lot of hard, big teams. You have to win the physical battle before you win the football battle." He was absolutely clear about that. He needed battlers, he needed strong characters, and physically strong people who could stand up when the going got tough.

I liked Micky's confidence and I was prepared to back him with a four-year contract. It didn't take us long to agree personal terms, but Micky was a stickler for having everything checked by the League Managers' Association. I liked that attention to detail.

When he joined, on April 12, we had five league games left and had just won at Plymouth. We had a press conference on the Tuesday afternoon at the Grand Hotel on Brighton seafront when he met the media, and then the same evening we had, coincidentally, that launch at Hove Town Hall for the first Falmer stadium campaign – the 'Yes, Yes' campaign. And I took Micky to present him to the hundreds of fans there.

The timing was perfect, and he received a standing ovation. I introduced him and he came from the back of the hall up to the stage wearing a 'Yes, Yes' T-shirt. Brilliant. He endeared himself to the fans immediately, because he stood up next to me at the lectern and spoke of how proud and privileged he felt to be manager of the Albion.

He knew Brighton had been a big club in the past. Born in Sheffield, he had been a gritty left-back for, among others, Coventry, Leeds and Southampton during the time when Brighton were playing in the higher leagues. Micky knew the potential of the club, but he was pitched straight into the battle we were fighting off the field, and quickly understood how vital it was to the club's future. His last comment brought the house down, "My job now is to build a squad of players as dedicated as the club's fans."

We went through the rest of the season and made ourselves safe, finishing in 17th place, but that didn't matter too much. I initially gave the new manager a watching brief to weigh up the squad, so that we could make the changes that he felt needed to be made at the end of the season. We had to get ourselves up to the right end of the division and I didn't think the squad was capable of it. I told him, "We have to make some significant changes. You've got training and a few games to make a judgement about the players, get to know the ones you think have some potential for us, and we'll get together immediately when the season ends and reconstruct the squad."

I drew up a list of the players who I thought weren't good enough and should be released. I had 16 names on this list from a squad of about 24 players. In other words, a drastic overhaul was needed – and Micky agreed with me because he came back with exactly the same number on the list he wanted to release, and virtually the same names. So there was an awful lot of work to do on the squad as soon as the close season began, and now I could promise Micky that there would be more money for the playing side.

We played our last game at Gillingham in May 1999 in a carnival atmosphere, mainly due to the tremendous 'Yes, Yes' vote for Falmer two days earlier. No one mourned its passing, but to be fair to Gillingham and Paul Scally, his club gave us a home when we had no other. I mentioned this to genuine applause when I went on the pitch at half-time to thank our fans for their beyond-the-call-of-duty support, while racking up new world record mileage for 'home' games those past two years.

The exile in Kent had ended. The battle for the right to play in Brighton had been won, and we were looking forward to our homecoming at Withdean. That meant that, relatively speaking, we were moving into a more promising period financially.

Although there was an improvement to 3,253 in the second season, we averaged crowds of only 2,791 at Gillingham, with all the heavy rental and travel costs. At the same time we had to carry the huge additional expenditure of getting Withdean ready to be a Football League ground – £2.8 million with all the planning and building work.

The excitement surrounding our return told us we were looking at getting sell-out crowds at Withdean. We very soon sold more season tickets – over 3,000 – than our average turnout at Gillingham, and there would hardly be a seat available on match-days. Capacity was still only 6,000, and we had enormous overhead costs associated with operating there, but I still had a few more funds to give Micky.

So that summer saw a lot of team strengthening and the arrival of players who were to become very significant in the next few years. Micky had in mind certain players who he had previously managed, including three who were no longer first-team regulars at Brentford – Danny Cullip, Charlie Oatway and Paul Watson. It made no difference to Micky. He wanted them all.

The transfer dealings I had over those three players were unusual. I agreed a fee with chairman Ron Noades of £50,000 for Danny, a really promising central defender, who, after an initial one-month loan period, finally joined us in October. I agreed this payment by instalments deal with Noades on the phone, and I briefed Derek Allan, the club secretary, on the terms of the deal, the way I always worked with Derek.

But Danny had a dispute with Brentford about a £15,000 signing-on fee that he'd been promised since he joined them, and when the details of the contract came through from Brentford, it said either Danny should waive his rights or we should pay him the £15,000 – if not, the deal was off. Obviously Derek picked up on this and said, "You didn't agree this surely? You didn't mention it." I replied, "I didn't agree it; definitely not."

I'd agreed to pay £50,000 for Cullip's signature, not to pay Brentford's debts for them, so I was quite prepared to back out of the deal. Danny and his agent got involved, and so did the Football League, and we got Danny, I'm glad to say, for £50,000 not £65,000.

The negotiations for Oatway and Watson were simpler. Micky told them he wanted them to come to Brighton, they didn't argue and we agreed a fee with Noades of £30,000 for the two of them. Both contracts were lined up on a table for the players to read and sign and I sat between them for the usual press pictures. Charlie was first and whizzed through the pages with hardly a glance, only pausing when he came to the final page – he seemed to be hesitating over signing.

To break the ice, I said, "So Charlie, how much of the £30,000 do you think you're worth?"

"About £29,950, Mr Chairman."

He later claimed that £20,000 was a fairer split, and Paul said it was £3,000 for Charlie and the rest for him. In fact we put it down on the paperwork as £15,000 each, but we had brought in three tremendous players, and three tremendous characters as well.

One player Micky didn't have direct experience of was Wigan Athletic midfielder Paul Rogers, but he identified him as someone to lead our squad. Paul was a wonderful acquisition, because he was such an intelligent man, and someone who was a quiet assassin on the pitch and made his presence felt in a very understated way. He'd come into the professional game late after working in the City while playing for Sutton United – including in their famous FA Cup giant-killing of top-flight Coventry City – so had a slightly different perspective on football life.

All the players absolutely looked up to him in the dressing room. He was a very good mentor to all of them. Paul knew we had some pretty strong characters in that squad, and they needed a firm hand. He was a natural leader and a very nice guy, but someone who immediately made his mark on the team and went on to score a lot of goals from midfield.

What Micky was brilliant at was identifying and acquiring strong characters, all through the spine of the team. That included another outstanding midfielder, Richard 'Chippy' Carpenter, even though we couldn't get him for a year. He was playing for Cardiff City, who had just been promoted to the Second Division, and he wanted to play at that level. He had a year with Cardiff but made a pledge to us that he would join Brighton at the end of the season.

Forward Darren Freeman, one of Micky's former Fulham players, came in, and we signed Andy Crosby, another very strong player, who would form an excellent central defensive partnership with Cullip.

Players who had been good servants left the club, Jeff Minton to Port Vale and folk hero Stuart Storer to non-League; the other players on our list were released and it was no great surprise to the fans that Micky and I both felt that a complete purging of the playing side was necessary. We kept some of the younger players, but we wanted a completely new attitude of mind. We were coming back to Brighton, we needed to start with a fresh squad.

Players who stayed, like Kerry Mayo, had to prove themselves. Obviously Gary Hart endeared himself to Micky because he was a real battler, and someone who gave 150 per cent every game, even though Micky had immediate doubts about whether he was a striker.

Most of the Withdean preparation costs, and for the coming Falmer application, were funded by all-too-frequent capital top-ups into the club from myself, some of the directors, and key backers Norman Cook and Billy Brown. The amounts were not small, but it was necessary if we were to keep the club on course.

We started the new season with a 6-0 win, but by Christmas Micky wanted to resign.

# CHAPTER SEVENTEEN

# THE SEAGULLS
# HAVE LANDED

T he first league match back in Brighton since the Doncaster game at the
Goldstone was a sensational 6-0 win against Mansfield Town, a result
that made all the hard work up to that point seem worthwhile.

It had been a long road. After all the resistance to the club playing at Withdean
from the local residents, the council had required more evidence of the public
support for bringing the club back to Brighton, hence the referendum that
Steve Bassam had called on local election day, asking the two questions: whether
the Albion should find a permanent home in Brighton & Hove, and then
whether they should play in a new stadium at Falmer.

I'd put together a poster campaign and created a video based on the posters,
saying 'Put Your Crosses In The Box', and showing a visual of a ballot form
with 'Vote Yes, Yes'.

Only Brighton & Hove residents were allowed to vote, and the election
turnout was well above the national average. The vote on the first question was
84 per cent (57,000 people) in favour of the permanent home in our area, with
68 per cent (45,000) voting 'yes' to us playing at Falmer.

These were encouraging numbers – showing a level of indigenous support
way above our normal crowds – but perhaps the most surprising finding was
that 16 per cent didn't appear to want us ever to come back – they wanted us
to die or keep playing at Gillingham, or anywhere other than Brighton.

The 68 per cent who voted in favour of us going to Falmer were obviously
the people who had voted for the permanent home in the area, minus those
who must have had an idea for some other local location. But there wasn't one.

We already had scale drawings of the Falmer stadium because we'd worked
out the complete spec and requirements for the planning application. Since we
were talking about a specific area, we had to have specific plans, in huge detail.

We'd started the project in 1998 when we appointed the primary architects,
KSS, a London firm who had worked on the Sydney Olympic Stadium and

later worked on a number of London Olympic venues. Martin Perry was aware of them and made contact with their principal director David Keirle. We had two meetings, commissioned them, and they allocated their senior people to the project.

Andy Simons, a founder director, basically stayed with the project through to completion of building and then again during the application to increase the capacity. He was the project leader. The architect, Adrian Holdstock, produced the original designs and later told me he had been thrilled to work on such a creative but demanding brief. We had made it clear that we weren't interested in ending up with four sheds around a football pitch.

The brief we gave them was to create a design with the wow factor, taking the location as an incentive to do something sensational. The only straight lines needed to be the pitch markings, so they could roll the lines of the building into the contours of the surrounding downland. I said, "Imagine a Henry Moore-style stadium, that's what we want. An iconic arena that reflects the style and flair of Brighton." Adrian nailed it, and although later the position of the roof arches changed a little, the fundamental design never altered.

We never took our eye off the Falmer ball because that was always the ultimate priority. But we had to walk before we could run and that meant bringing Withdean up to Football League standard, which cost the best part of £3 million.

We were helped by the Football Trust, who Martin and I persuaded in November 1998 to give us £500,000 towards the development costs of Withdean, and also promised us £2.8 million for Falmer when it was finally built – although we ultimately only got £2 million. The money for Withdean was a loan, to be repaid in tranches as we could afford it, but it was the only time the Trust had given significant money to a League club for anything but a permanent ground. But chief executive (now Sir) Peter Lee understood that we needed to get back to Brighton as soon as possible and these were exceptional circumstances. We have a lot to thank him for.

Peter and Dave Richards, the Trust chairman, created a precedent in our case. Although Richards has come in for criticism in his roles as chairman of Sheffield Wednesday and the Premier League, I won't hear a word said against him. He went out of his way to help us get money for Withdean and an amount ring-fenced for Falmer, however long it took to get there. He told me, "Football needs more chairmen like you, who support your local club and fight your corner. You have picked up the most poisoned of chalices. You have given everything for your club and now we are going to give something back to you."

We were grateful to get it, because Withdean needed a lot of work. Essentially it was a small athletics stadium with a Sunday League-standard pitch surrounded by a running track. The place was ramshackle. But it was a home, and most importantly it was back in Brighton. Little did I realise just how long we would be there . . .

Before we moved in, the stadium had only 1,000 seats, all on the north side. We put a narrow roof over them, because it couldn't cover the outside running lanes, and extended the north stand to seat 1,800, including a very basic directors' box and cramped press box.

The largest area of seating we put in was on the south side, where we installed 4,500 temporary seats on what had been a grass bank. At the end of every season, the seats went off to the Open golf tournament and various other sporting events. Because the Open is held in July and often in Scotland, we always had to ask the Football League for an away match for the first game of the season, in case the seats weren't back in time. The exception was that first season, when we kicked off at home.

This was all open seating, with virtually no cover. So we arranged to issue everyone with ponchos if it rained. We had them made in both blue and white, and gave the fans in each block alternate colours. So the first game it rained, the stands became blue-and-white stripes – which would later be repeated at the Amex. It became the uniform of Withdean, and some people still have their ponchos, as if carrying their battle scars.

At first, there was no seating behind either goal. That came later. Safety regulations restricted our actual capacity to just below 6,000. We also had to put in a police control HQ, toilet facilities, turnstiles and a hospitality area where we could welcome visiting directors and a few guests. Initially this comprised two Portakabins behind the east goal.

Regulars in the tiny boardroom in one of the cabins were the guys from Skint Records, our new shirt sponsors. When I took over, we still had a sponsorship deal with Sandtex, a hangover from the Archer days. I arranged for Donatello, the Italian restaurant in The Lanes in Brighton, to take over for the second season at Gillingham, and they have backed the club ever since.

Katie Price, aka Jordan, did a photo shoot wearing the Donatello-sponsored shirt. She's a local girl, and many of the men in her family are semi-Albion fans. Then her agent, whom she hadn't mentioned it to, tried to demand a huge sum of money to use the pictures. We couldn't afford it, but Katie, bless her, told her agent to let us have the pictures. So we sold these posters of Katie in her Albion Donatello shirt.

But ideally, I wanted a local sponsor who had national visibility, and I found it in Skint, the dance music label. It came from a discussion with my son David, who works in the music industry and had a connection with them. I knew they were based in Brighton, and I knew that Norman Cook – Fatboy Slim, a massive Albion fan – was on their label. Plus their name and our plight was a match that was too good to ignore.

David arranged for me to meet Skint co-owners JC Reid and Damian Harris, who was also one of their artists – Midfield General – so you knew where his heart lay, although he was an Arsenal fan. Andy McKirdy, their marketing manager, was there too. I sat with the three of them and persuaded them that it would be a great idea, but the important thing was their Skint Records logo. I said it would be much better if we could have just 'Skint' on the front of our shirts, because it would be funnier and get much more visibility for us both that way.

Being open-minded, and realising the marketing potential, they agreed to it. And they paid a sum of money that was very generous for what was initially a two-year agreement, which ended up being a partnership that lasted nine years, one of the longest-ever shirt sponsorships in English football.

It was great because Norman, their leading artist, got on board and started wearing the Skint-sponsored Albion shirts at his shows all around the world. At the 2002 World Cup in Japan and South Korea he played a number of gigs, often wearing an Albion top, which was great publicity for us.

For me, it was the perfect sponsorship. We could leverage it really well in terms of the name and the PR you could get out of it, and it was a local company that was also a young and trendy national and international brand. It reflected the whole Brighton city vibe and had a high-profile Albion fan helping to spread the word.

It also did something else. Here was a club, so recently mired in despair, and the Skint sponsorship put a smile on people's faces. Later when we played Barnet, the two shirt sponsors meant that it was Skint against Loaded – although in their case it was a claim that would never have got past the Advertising Standards Authority. We, on the other hand, were the Ronseal of football clubs!

I got on really well with Norman, and still do, and as I got to know him better, I explained to him the financial situation of the club and what had to be done, and my vision of the community stadium. He is very socially aware and never lost that although becoming a pop star. He is just a really good guy.

I asked him if he could invest in the club to help me keep it going while we had what was obviously going to be a big battle for the ground. And he was only too willing to help – on several occasions. He was never the major shareholder, but he still is one – he called it the most expensive parking space in Brighton. Norman's involvement made us part of the wider culture of the city rather than just a football club. And that was true nationally as well.

A couple of years ago, Norman invited me to do a guest DJ spot at the Audio Club on Brighton seafront to celebrate the 25th anniversary of his first appearance there. He knew I was into music, so I thought I'd have a go. I had to choose a few tracks, so I mixed up old favourites Aretha Franklin and Stevie Wonder with new bands such as The Killers, Magic Numbers and Vampire Weekend, who I'd seen recently at Glastonbury (yes, I've been to Glasto a few times, much to the delight of Albion fans I've bumped into there).

Anyway, the Audio was rammed with people who seemed to like DJ Knightman's music, and called for more. But knowing that I was being followed on the bill by a lady who'd introduced herself to me backstage as a porn star – goodness knows what she would be getting up to in her set – I decided to quit while I was ahead.

The next morning I was walking along Church Road in Hove, where people often come up to me and thank me for getting our wonderful stadium or for saving the club. This time a huge articulated lorry lumbering past slowed down, and the burly driver wound down the window and shouted, "Great set last night, Dick." Feeling cool, I waved a casual thanks.

Skint got 12 tickets for the Withdean boardroom which, with their unconventionally casual dress for such places, gave it a lively atmosphere. And they were genuine football fans. To make sure we filled the other 5,888 seats, I devised a campaign aimed at letting people know that the club was coming home to Brighton, and looking ahead to our fight for Falmer. It included stickers in the backs of cars that read: 'The Boys Are Back In Town', 'The Seagulls Have Landed At Withdean – No Sweat', and 'Permanent Home Wanted For Local Heroes'.

In July 1999, Martin Perry accepted my invitation to become chief executive and join the club full-time, cementing the working relationship we'd had with him at McAlpine since the takeover. Now that he was at the club, it formally severed any relationship with them. It was a good move for Martin, and the right move for the club, because I now had his specific experience to help me deal with the challenges we faced.

Nick Rowe, the general manager I'd appointed early on, continued to do a good job developing the commercial side of the club until leaving for pastures new later in 1999.

Our very first game at Withdean, on July 24 1999, was a friendly at home to Nottingham Forest, who were then in the First Division, what is now the Championship. David Platt was player-manager, and they had a very good team, including Mark Crossley, Chris Bart-Williams and Dougie Freedman. It would be a stiff test, not only for Micky's team but also for all our match-day planning.

Much of that centred around the travel arrangements that had been put in place, such as the mile wide no-parking zone within the Withdean area, which we had to steward, and the park-and-ride facilities at Mill Road, near the A23/

A27 Brighton bypass junction, and Mithras House in Lewes Road. All of that had to be tested, and everything came through very well.

Because we had informed the fans beforehand via meetings, leaflets, our website and the local media, they fully respected the situation. Of course the club were paying for all those ancillary costs. We were also subsidising free public transport within a 12-mile radius around Brighton. Match tickets included travel vouchers that spectators could use either on a bus, normal route and park-and-ride, or train, one inbound and one outbound. That cost us £2 per ticket – one reason why our tickets weren't the cheapest in the league, although they weren't the most expensive either.

I used the occasion of the first game back in Brighton for more than two years to address the crowd of 5,891. I adapted Neil Armstrong's classic line, saying, "This is one small step towards Falmer – but a giant leap for Brighton & Hove Albion."

Before the game we had the Brighton Silver Band playing 'Sussex By The Sea', and everyone began to feel so happy to be home. We had a few older players who came out on the pitch, including Peter Ward and Norman Gall.

When the game kicked off, the first goal at Withdean was scored by Gary Hart. We played several of our new signings, including local boy Darren Freeman who came on and put Albion 2-1 ahead. Near the end David Platt made it a very entertaining 2-2 draw.

The first league game on August 7 was a tremendous occasion. The ground was packed with a capacity crowd of just under six thousand, and we got off to a great start with Freeman scoring in the 15th minute and then again in the 20th minute to put us 2-0 up at half-time. It was one of those days when we could do no wrong. Freeman completed his hat-trick, Rod Thomas scored and Adrian Newhouse got two more near the end.

It was a beautiful sunny afternoon and gave our fans a lot of hope for the future. I had my oldest grandchild, Max, who was about 18 months old at the time, on my lap. He was fine until the first goal, when the loud cheering made him start crying. And when the second went in and the crowd was roaring, including me, he was in tears again. But by the time of the fifth goal, he was quite used to it, and when the sixth goal hit the back of the Mansfield net, he gurgled with delight. So in that one match he learned how to love the Albion.

My great niece, Natasha, 9, was one of the mascots that day and it started a passion for the Albion that was to see her queue up outside the dressing rooms after every single home game, to get the same players' autographs in every programme for the next five years! Our players got to know her well and knew exactly where they had to sign.

The 6-0 triumph was a great way to come back to Brighton and there was a tremendous air of celebration. It gave everyone, including the players, perhaps an artificial feeling that it was going to be a good season for us. The following Wednesday we lost at home to Gillingham of all teams, in the Worthington Cup, but we shrugged that off because after all they were in the division above us. The next Saturday we won 2-1 at Leyton Orient, so in the league we'd started with back-to-back victories, home and away, and a very good goal difference already.

But after that, performances just fell away, and from being top of the league after two games, the team just lost its shape. There were a lot of bookings, the team played in a very defensive system, with five at the back, and the midfield didn't really get into games. We were lacking up front. Hart was leading the line but it was clear we had a shortage of decent strikers.

By the time we came to early December we were in 15th position and had lost several home games. Everyone seems to remember in particular a game we played on a Friday night in December, against Rochdale in pouring rain in front of 5,049, the smallest crowd we'd had at Withdean up until then. Rochdale weren't much better than us, but went 2-0 up early on. We fought back and got level and then Hart scored a goal that put us 3-2 ahead.

However after that, defensive frailties allowed Clive Platt to score two goals for them in the last 10 minutes and we finished up losing 4-3. The crowd in the south stand were soaked to the skin so not in the best of moods and were subjecting Micky to some abuse. The team had created such high expectations with the 6-0 win, and that was the fifth home league defeat pre-Christmas. Long after the game Micky came to me as I sat in the boardroom alone, reflecting on events, and said he was thinking about resigning. He felt that perhaps he couldn't do what he'd done for Fulham, and he wasn't getting it right.

I wasn't having it. I said, "Micky, we've got some good new players." We had Danny Cullip putting in towering performances in the centre of defence, Paul Watson, Charlie Oatway and Paul Rogers were beginning to gel. There were good signs but we were missing something.

"We're playing the long ball too much," I said. "But I'm not accepting your resignation." I told him to go away and forget about football for the rest of the weekend and said that I'd meet up with him on Monday evening and we'd have dinner. And I wanted his partner Claire to come.

But before I could try to help put matters right on the pitch, there was something extremely important to deal with concerning the new stadium. It was on the morning after that depressing Rochdale defeat that we held the first meeting of what would become the 'Falmer For All' team, in Liz Costa's office near Queens Road. They were a patchwork group of Albion enthusiasts who together made up an almost seamless whole. They were a team of all talents.

I'd got to know most of them during the campaign for the return to Withdean – members of the supporters' club, the Independent Supporters' Club, fanzine writers, and a few other key fans. To get the new stadium would take much more effort, but I knew that we could count on some high-quality people.

What summed up the group was its extremes. There was Paul Samrah, the pinstriped chartered accountant, and John Baine, the punk poet, both passionate Albion fans who had been leaders of BISA. Paul was the general, who led the campaign with almost military precision. John would be first over the top, holding the flag, blowing a bugle, waving a cutlass and charging into the teeth of the enemy. Their intelligence and love of the Albion brought them together.

Tim Carder had an encyclopaedic knowledge of the history of the club but he also had an ability to analyse and plan meticulously. He was the master strategist who understood the logistics of distributing leaflets, with areas of the city divided up like theatres of war, but he would also put his own resources in, producing material to support the cause – forms, petitions, you name it.

Then there were the team of designer Bill Swallow and his wife Jan, Liz Costa and Sarah Watts, who knew other clubs' supporters, Ed Bassford, Roz South, Paul Whelch, John Hewitt, John Cowen, Peter and Wendy Near, Adrian Newnham, Ian Morley, Stuart Adams, Norman Rae – fans whose brilliantly resourceful efforts on the club's behalf have become an important part of its history. Their love of the Albion meant that they would never give up.

The original title was the Falmer Stadium Campaign, but although that told you technically what it was, it sounded formal, didn't convey any emotion. I suggested Falmer For All, because it had a nice alliteration, but mainly because it got to the heart of the issue. You're making a promise to people when you say Falmer For All. Everyone could instantly understand what it meant. It would be a community stadium for everyone to use and benefit from.

The Goldstone had never been that. It never played a part in the fans' lives apart from hosting the games. It wasn't used by the community in the rest of the week. I remember I would drive along Old Shoreham Road and see the North Stand roof, gaunt against the sky, the ground all locked up. Or if I walked from Hove Station along Newtown Road, you could see in through the South Stand. And you'd think, "Those empty terraces will be heaving with life on Saturday."

The Falmer For All logo featured two green hills. I worked with Bill Swallow on it. We wanted to reinforce the fact that we knew where we were, on the edge of the Downs, and that we would respect that.

And the important thing was that we made Falmer For All independent of the club. I said to Martin, "I won't be the chairman, and nor will you. Paul Samrah is the obvious chairman, a leader, a great spokesman, he knows how to deal with the media. He's perfect. We will be active members, but if we are in charge it will be seen as being a branch of the club. There are some talented people and we should let them run it, although we will be part of the team."

We already knew that we could trust everyone in the group, and they knew that they could trust us. They knew I was one of them. It meant that we could give them confidential information. Martin would say, "Okay now, put your pens down." That was the signal that the next part was confidential until Martin said, "Okay, you can pick your pens up again."

I came away from that first official Falmer For All meeting knowing that we had the best possible team of fans and planning experts working with us to deliver our major goal – the building of the new stadium. Now it was time to see what could be done about the team in stripes.

I met Micky on the Monday evening at an Italian restaurant in Preston Street. It was a very quiet night, with very few people around. I wanted Claire to be there, so that she could hear that I had faith in Micky, that I believed in him.

But I was quite unequivocal in saying that the team weren't playing the way we should be. We weren't playing out from the back, we weren't playing football in the Brighton way. I wanted to see it more on the ground, not being lumped forward.

Micky had felt that you needed to muscle the opposition and win the physical battle before the team played football, and that had largely been true a few years earlier when he was with Fulham. But now there were a few better players coming into the division and teams were playing better quality football. Part of the reason was that a lot of foreign players had come into the Premier League, which was forcing British-born players down the leagues. So even at our level we were seeing a better quality of play and more players who had gained experience in higher divisions.

We had good footballers too like Rogers, Watson, Oatway, Cullip, Andy Crosby – good players that Micky had brought in. But we weren't getting the best out of them, and we lacked creativity in midfield and going forward. We were relying far too much at that time on Gary Hart, who was still playing as a central striker. I said to Micky that we had to play the ball through midfield more, perhaps change the system.

I think Micky was looking for me to show confidence in him. We had a good heart-to-heart, discussed systems, and the meal ended with Micky in no doubt that I was backing him.

He decided to switch to 4-3-3, and towards the New Year results began to pick up as we adapted to the new formation. We brought in a centre-forward called Lorenzo Pinamonte from Bristol City. He was a strong, quite skilful player, very left-footed and not bad in the air. He gave us some physical presence up front that we had been completely lacking, a target man for Hart to play off.

On Boxing Day we played Barnet, who were top of the league, at home on a very heavy pitch. That was a bit of a turning point because we played well against a good footballing team. We started to pass the ball in that game and it ended 1-1. Then we went away to Rotherham, who were second in the league, and beat them 3-1 – the best performance of the season up to that time, or so I'm told. It was the one game I missed that season, with flu. And Oatway scored two goals so it was momentous for more than one reason.

The fact that we could win away but had lost five times at home drew attention to our growing problems with the Withdean playing surface. Micky, understandably, was complaining about it, but the management of the pitch was not under our control, but that of Ecovert South, who ran the stadium for the Council. We were only tenants after all. We had a groundsman, but he wasn't really allowed to maintain the pitch – they had their own people.

We were having to pay Ecovert a large hire fee but the pitch steadily got worse in winter and wasn't to resolve itself for some time further, certainly not during that first season. We were having regular run-ins with them as we attempted to get them to improve the quality of the supervision of the playing surface.

Essentially the problems ran deeper than who was maintaining the pitch, in more ways than one. They were in the drainage of a pitch that had never been intended for professional football. When there was heavy rain, the surface water stayed on the pitch. Although we felt that Ecovert could have done better, it wasn't until the 18 months later that we were able to afford the considerable outlay of digging the pitch up and installing proper drainage.

We began 2000 on a high note. When Darren Freeman netted two minutes after a midday kick-off at Withdean on January 3, he had the distinction of scoring the first goal of the new millennium in English football. We finished 4-2 winners over Exeter City and had won back-to-back league games for the first time since August.

At that first home game of 2000, the fans got a message from me in the programme welcoming everyone to the new millennium and a new era for the Albion, and they also got a questionnaire to fill in. It was a survey – the first work of our Falmer For All committee aimed at gathering a lot of information about Albion fans – asking how they travelled to Withdean, how they would travel to Falmer, and the money they would spend.

That all needed to be put into our planning application to emphasise the economic benefit that the stadium would bring to the city. We had evidence from the Goldstone days about away fans coming down for matches and staying for the weekend. All that information had to be brought together.

We suspected all along that the application would be controversial, even though the council were contemplating giving support to Falmer as the only option for a new stadium, and our fears were now confirmed.

Lindsay Frost, the director of planning at Lewes District Council, wrote to Brighton & Hove Council strongly opposing the stadium at Falmer on the basis that it was inappropriate for a sensitive countryside location. That was an early warning of Lewes' subsequent moves against the stadium several years later.

On the playing side, things were to get worse before they got much, much better. It started when we tried to buy Pinamonte after his loan expired at the end of January. Brentford's Ron Noades, possibly still smarting from not getting extra money out of me for Cullip, made a bid of £75,000 for Pinamonte. We decided we weren't going to compete with that.

So we were short of strikers again, but we did have David Cameron – a Scottish striker who Micky had signed from St Mirren, who collected more yellow cards (two) than goals (nil) in his 22 Albion appearances. Apart from later having a famous namesake, Cameron's claim to fame was being substituted after only 20 minutes of our 2-0 defeat at Hull on February 5.

Micky told assistant manager Alan Cork to attend the post-game press conference, and Corky publicly called Cameron "useless". I was very unhappy with that because it was a really poor team performance. Sure, Cameron wasn't playing particularly well, but I felt that we shouldn't be taking it out on one player in public.

The fans didn't like it either. Even though they probably thought Cameron wasn't much good, the whole team wasn't playing well, and it was really out of order – albeit Micky said he had told Corky to say it. It shouldn't have been said by Cork or him. Not said publicly at all, and I met with Micky after that incident and told him we shouldn't have to be justifying statements like that, because they should be kept in the dressing room.

I think to some extent it was frustration. Micky had brought Cameron to the club but he was not performing well. He was scoring for the reserves but did nothing when he played in the first team. The fans called him 'Silky' – because as a player that was the last thing he was. He was a bustling Scottish centre-forward with a first touch that wasn't great, but he gave it 100 per cent. He did his best. He just wasn't good enough. And unfortunately the management team decided to take it out on him personally.

That was a low point but, as they say, the darkest hour is just before dawn. With Pinamonte gone and Cameron out of favour, we were looking for a centre-forward again. And we got good vibes from a lanky 19-year-old at Bristol Rovers who we'd seen once when we were watching Pinamonte. His name was Bobby Zamora.

Zamora had made four substitute appearances for Bristol Rovers, but he'd never started a game, and had gone on loan to Bath City and scored some goals. He was six foot one and we knew that he had a very good first touch and held the ball up well, the type of player we wanted. And the irony is that if Noades hadn't outbid us for Pinamonte, we wouldn't have gone for Zamora. Thank you, Ron.

We brought him in on a one-month loan, and he played his first game on Saturday February 12, at home against Plymouth. He scored in that game, a 1-1 draw, and two weeks later he hit a hat-trick when we won 7-1 away to Chester City.

Chester were bottom of the league but it was still an amazing result, Albion's biggest away win for over 60 years. I wanted to rave about this rare diamond we'd unearthed, but I was the only Albion director there that day and decided to keep it to myself.

By the time Zamora had finished his loan period at the beginning of March, he'd made six appearances for us and scored six goals. He'd played brilliantly and quickly struck up an understanding with Paul Brooker, a talented winger we'd brought in on loan from Fulham, who could go either way, left and right, and also scored at Chester.

I knew Zamora was something special by that time, and so did Micky. We obviously wanted him to stay, and did everything we could to persuade him, but he felt he should go back to Bristol Rovers – hoping, and probably expecting, to get into their first team after his time with us.

However, he didn't actually make a start for their first team for the rest of the season and only came on as sub twice, late in games. Bristol Rovers had good strikers – Nathan Ellington, Jason Roberts and Jamie Cureton – so Bobby hardly got a chance, and I kept a very close eye on that, obviously.

But being Brighton chairman meant keeping several plates in the air at once, and it was time to go public with our plans for Falmer. We did so at a meeting at Lewes FC's ground, the Dripping Pan, on February 28. Our main aim was to outline the way forward, and we had some fantastic visuals of how the ground would look.

But we also knew we had to answer some criticisms that were being levelled at us by various opponents, to show that we had considered all the possible problems and could answer them. We were fully addressing the issues, not hiding from them.

For example, there were fears that the road system wouldn't be able to cope. But we had already proved at Withdean that our parking, transport and crowd-control worked and that our fans would co-operate. At Falmer we would have more car parking pro-rata than at Withdean, where there was none at all. We would be using the University of Sussex car parks that were unused on Saturday afternoons and midweek evenings, so not adding any more concrete to the area.

And we said that we would cordon Falmer village off on match-days so that no cars parked there. In fact, after the meeting, the Falmer residents began putting stewards at the entrances to the village so that university students couldn't park around the duck pond any more, as they had been doing, nose-to-tail. Then they took photographs of their unspoilt, car-free village to show what we were planning to 'desecrate'.

One of the fears was that the stadium would dominate visually, stand out on the Downs like a carbuncle. They had taken photographs of the Reebok Stadium at Bolton to show the visual impact of a new stadium. But the photographer must have lain on his or her back a few feet from the wall of the main stand, because the stadium looked as tall as a curved version of one of the World Trade Center towers. The reality is that there's hardly anywhere in Falmer village where you can actually see the stadium.

They also claimed that we hadn't properly considered other sites, but we had and they had all failed the various requirements immeasurably. We weren't saying that Falmer was a perfect site, but it was definitely the least imperfect. It was Falmer or bust. We made a lot of the fact that it was an area earmarked for development already. So we took a lot of heat out of many of the objections.

It was also around that time that the council made the decision to include the stadium in the local plan. There had to be a new local plan because Brighton & Hove had become a single unitary authority. And because of the results of the 'Yes, Yes' referendum, Steve Bassam felt he had an absolute mandate to include the Falmer stadium in the plan and support it. He'd had his eye on Brighton becoming a city, and I said to him on more than one occasion that a 21st-century city needs a 21st-century arena. Steve couldn't agree more, but all local plans are subject to a public inquiry, which would become incredibly important to us eventually.

Meanwhile, after the Chester game we went on an unbeaten run, even without Zamora. Having been down at 17th, we ended the season 11th, winning eight and drawing six of the last 14 games. Micky had sorted the team out after my meeting with him, the 4-3-3 system making us more compact but more fluid going forward. Danny Cullip deservedly won the player-of-the-season award, partly because in that late run we conceded very few goals.

It was an okay result, an improvement on the second season at Gillingham, when we finished 17th – but after the start we'd had it was underwhelming. It was also better than being involved in another relegation battle – and at one point it looked like we might be. What became clear was the squad still needed strengthening.

We let 15 players go at the end of that season and started signing players straight away. One who left was Mark Ormerod, the hero goalkeeper from the game against Hereford, who played really well in that escape season. Micky's first-choice goalkeeper was Mark Walton. He wasn't particularly popular with the fans and made a few errors and Micky was looking to improve on the goalkeeping front, so we signed Michel Kuipers in early June on a two-year contract. He had played a couple of trial games for us in March and we liked the look of him – like Bobby, from Bristol Rovers.

I made Brooker's deal permanent, for £25,000 in May, and we finally signed Richard Carpenter, who had wanted to see out his year's contract at Cardiff City. Despite interest from other Division One clubs, he'd made up his mind to come to Brighton. Chippy was a hard-tackling box-to-box midfielder who could score goals and took a great free kick. He was out of contract so it was a very good acquisition for us as he had been a regular in the Cardiff team. We also signed defender Adam Virgo, a late developer through the youth system, on a two-year contract. And he would have an important part to play.

And then there was Zamora.

# CHAPTER EIGHTEEN

# THE BEST SIGNING
# I EVER MADE

It was obvious that Ian Holloway, then the Bristol Rovers manager, didn't rate Bobby Zamora, at least in comparison to his many other strikers, because Bobby hadn't got into the Rovers side despite his exploits for the Albion. But he'd made a big impression on us and I told the board immediately after the season ended that I was going to make a serious bid for him.

The most we'd paid up to then in my chairmanship was £50,000, for Danny Cullip, the highest fee for many years. I said I was prepared to go above that. The board's reaction was that we all knew that we had to make a serious promotion challenge in 2000/01.

The fans were happy that we were back in Brighton, but they also needed to see good things happening on the pitch. There had been a false dawn at the beginning of the previous season when we had won the first game 6-0. It was important we made a genuine challenge in the second season at Withdean. The players we had already signed were very much evidence of that.

Geoff Dunford, the chairman of Bristol Rovers, was probably expecting a phone call from me, even though we'd had no contact since Bobby had gone back there in March. I'd said to Micky, "We should keep our powder dry, not show that we are particularly interested in him."

We certainly expected that he'd get into Bristol Rovers' first team, so when he didn't, I thought that £60,000 would be more than enough to get him. I was actually privately prepared to go to £100,000 – telling the board Zamora would be worth it.

But when I called Geoff shortly after the season ended and offered him £60,000 for Bobby, he turned it down flat. He said, "We're looking for a quarter of a million." I recoiled from that. I said, "How can you expect to get £250,000 for a player who has not started a first-team game for you?"

I thought he was trying it on because he was used to getting sizeable fees for their strikers. They'd sold Barry Hayles to Fulham, Jason Roberts had just gone to West Bromwich Albion for £2 million, and Nathan Ellington was beginning to attract a lot of interest.

Rovers must have thought that Bobby had attracted some attention when he was scoring goals for us, hence the figure of £250,000. For the right money, they were prepared to sell. Hoping to seal the deal quickly, I said I would go to £100,000 but not a penny more. But Dunford wasn't budging from his £250,000.

Although Micky and I were both very keen on getting Zamora, I decided to end the conversation. I said to Dunford, "The offer's there, it's on the table. You know you can get £100K from me." And I said to Micky, "They'll be back during pre-season." And we both agreed that we would wait. I wasn't prepared to let Bristol Rovers feel that they'd got me on a string. I'd made it clear I was not prepared to go above £100,000 for him.

Early in July I did talkSPORT's *From the Boardroom* show, a two-hour interview with host Chris Mann, during which I told listeners that our stadium planning application was now past £400,000 in cost, but was well-advanced and would be submitted shortly – an overly-optimistic forecast, as it turned out – and played down the Zamora story by saying I'd offered a six-figure sum, but he was not for sale. I wanted Bristol Rovers to think the deal was off as far as I was concerned, because they had no chance of getting £250,000 from me.

Anyway, the pre-season started, and we still hadn't heard anything. We got into August, and still no call from Bristol Rovers, by which time I was getting fidgety. I thought it would still happen, but that I might have to renew the dialogue myself.

We played a friendly at Withdean against Sheffield Wednesday, the Saturday before the season started. We won 2-0 and Gary Hart and Darren Freeman scored. So there we were with Gary, the previous season's top scorer, and Darren, who was suffering injury problems, as our main strikeforce.

We'd signed Lee Steele, who'd scored goals for Shrewsbury, as back-up in case the Zamora deal didn't happen. He had been swayed to join us rather than other clubs by the passion of Albion fans at Gay Meadow the previous season. But we still felt deprived.

After the game Micky said to me, "I thought we were going to get this tall striker and now, less than a week before the start of the season, I still haven't got him." I was ruminating that perhaps I'd been overconfident.

Then out of the blue, Dunford called on the Monday. "Are you still interested in Zamora?" Of course we were, but I played all hard to get. "I'll speak to my manager about it." But when I went back to Geoff, he said, "Well, we still want

From young man…

…to ad man…

It's all Business Class on this Fokker.

Gatwick-Paris, 3 times daily. Sleek new jets. 100% Business Class.

HELLO BOYS.

THE ONE AND ONLY
wonderbra

…always daring to be different.

Outside.

Inside.

The roomy new Micra. NISSAN

ACTION IMAGES

The last game at the Goldstone… with my daughter Amanda, son David, and Bob Pinnock (behind me) and his family.

THE ARGUS

Face to face with Bill Archer before the Football League EGM in 1997, when the Albion faced expulsion from the league.

STEWART WEIR

Saving ourselves at Hereford...                           ...Robbie Reinelt gets there first.

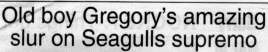

# Old boy Gregory's amazing slur on Seagulls supremo

KNIGHT POSER: This player's fee has given the Villa boss the bird, but who is he?

# Recognise him, Mr Chairman?

THIS is the picture Aston Villa manager John Gregory claimed Albion chairman Dick Knight would not recognise.

Gregory, the former Seagulls midfielder, is refusing to cough up cash Villa owe for Gareth Barry.

Gregory stormed: "Dick Knight wouldn't recognise Gareth Barry if he stood on Brighton beach in an Albion shirt with a ball tucked under his arm and a seagull on his head.

"We are being asked to pick up the bill for a football club so badly run that it nearly went to the wall."

But Knight today spiced up the war of words. He blasted: "John Gregory's cheeky chappie quips speak volumes for themselves.

"He by his own admission previously told the national press that Aston Villa had stolen Gareth Barry from Brighton.

"The timing of the tribunal was down to the tri-

TURN TO PAGE 31

THE ARGUS

The cutting from *The Argus* after John Gregory's jibe at me during the Gareth Barry tribunal.

My advertising career did not stop when I took over the Albion.

Micky Adams, Bobby Zamora and I when Bobby signed for the Albion in 2000.

Success at last after 36 years!

Delivering the Albion message in all the right places...

**Evening Argus**

NIGHT FINAL

www.thisisbrighton.co.uk

FRIDAY, MAY 7, 1999

**84% SAY BRING HOME THE ALBION
68% SAY LET THEM PLAY AT FALMER**

# VICTORY!

by MATTHEW JAMES

ALBION have won overwhelming public backing for their plans to build their new stadium at Falmer.

Jubilant Seagulls supporters were today celebrating a huge public endorsement of the proposals for the community-based development.

JUBILANT: Supporters celebrate this morning's referendum result at the Brighton Centre

FALMER FOR ALL

With Martin Perry at the launch of the Sven Goran Eriksson poster backing Falmer.

With Caroline Lucas MP, Steve Ford (left) and Alan Sanders (right) of Albion in the Community, at the House of Commons.

Addressing a public meeting at Hove Town Hall.

The Man Who Saved The Albion

I often took to the mic to address the crowd at Withdean.

It was a piece of cake for my grandsons, Max and Sam, (and Joyce Watts, daughter of Charlie Webb, Albion manager 1919-1947) at our centenary match v Bournemouth in 2001.

We came a long, long
way together…

….with Des Lynam,
Steve Coppell and
Norman Cook…

…through the hard
times and the good.

602

Still ho... after all these years    Our future in your hands,

Nationwide

402

Nationwi    PLAY-OFF TODAY
PLAY ON AT FALMER?

ACTION IMAGES

Plenty of uplifting occasions... winning the 2004 Division Two play-off final at the Millennium Stadium (left, above and, right, celebrating back in Brighton with my grandsons Max and Sam)...

.... and at King's House, Hove with Bobby Zamora and Peter Taylor after the Division Two triumph in 2002.

With John Prescott and Falmer for All stalwarts Liz Costa (left) and Paul Samrah (right) at the Hull City game at Withdean in December 2005, after the second Public Inquiry had gone our way.

ACTION IMAGES

Chris Kamara hands over the 'Coca Cola Kid' money at the Millennium Stadium in May 2005 (Mark McGhee can't wait to get his hands on it) with Aaron Berry, the Albion fan who won the competition.

With my son David and our fellow fans on the road...

Home…

...at last!

A great face for radio!

With Liam Brady at the Amex before our FA Cup fourth round match against Arsenal in January 2013.

Having a laugh with my good friend Steve Darby and Prince Edward at the Amex in July 2012.

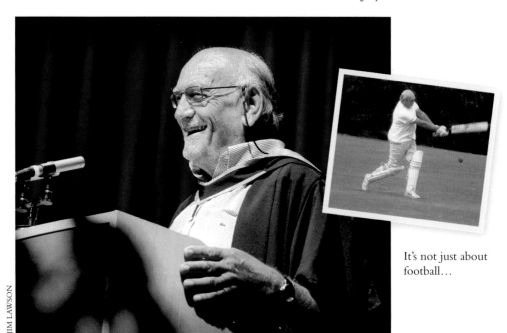

JIM LAWSON

It's not just about football…

Accepting an honorary Master of Arts degree from the University of Brighton at the Dome in July 2013.

*Special thanks to Bennett Dean, John Elms, Paul Hazlewood and Stewart Weir for use of their photos*

a quarter of million pounds for him." So I replied, "Well why were you on the phone to me? I made you an offer and there's no way I can increase it." He began to sound a bit more receptive.

By that time, Bobby knew that we had talked to Rovers, had offered £100,000 and they'd turned it down. He was now more than happy to come to Brighton because obviously he was disappointed that he hadn't got in Rovers' first team.

Then, infuriatingly, Geoff said, "The only thing is, I'm not sure we want to sell him. My manager maybe wants to keep the player." I said, "Why don't you let me talk to Ian Holloway?" He put me on to Holloway, who told me that basically he quite liked the player, but saw him more a left-sided midfielder than a striker. I couldn't believe it, but bit my tongue and replied, "I think Micky prefers him up front, we'll probably play him there to start with."

Holloway hummed and harred and said, "Well, you'll give him more chances" and in the end I said, "Look, are you prepared to do this deal, you and your chairman? I'm willing to pay £100,000 to get this deal done now – today. That's it, there's no more. Forget £250,000. I'm not going to get involved in any other payments or anything like that."

"We'll think about it," came back that familiar West Country burr.

I didn't want to go back to Micky until I had an answer. A nervous hour or so went by and then I got a call from Geoff, saying he was prepared to go ahead on the one hundred thousand, but wanted 30 per cent of any sell-on fee. That was quite high, but as far as I was concerned I was still getting a snip at £100,000. I was so confident of Zamora's ability – as a striker.

For us this was a huge sum of money, a major investment and an act of faith in the player and in Micky to get the best out of him. And of course it was a great story, just a few days before the season began. Bobby chose to keep the No.25 shirt that he'd worn on loan – the No.9 was Gary Hart's – and the pictures of him holding it up for the cameras really excited the fans.

It was an absolute coup that we had finally secured this player. I could only see good things in him, could only see that he would be a huge asset to us. Micky and I told him we felt he would play an important role in the club.

Holloway's view of the player confirmed a realisation that had been growing since I had come into the game: that, even at the top level, football is all a matter of opinions. There is little science to it. For me, Zamora was the best signing I ever made.

The transfer was concluded two days before the start of the season, and it was almost the perfect signing. It was no problem negotiating personal terms with Bobby. He was paid a decent wage, about £2,000 a week when he started, which put him at the top end of the club's wage scale. He didn't have an agent. His father was involved straight away and the terms were agreed with him and

Bobby. He got a goal bonus, which only one other player had. Gary Hart was the other, because when he first came to the club he was on low money but I gave him that incentive and he scored 12 goals in his first season.

Although Bobby didn't have an agent then, he very quickly interested a lot of them. Most of the players did have agents but they weren't troublesome, because they knew Brighton didn't have much money, so they didn't really consider us as a club they could get their teeth into. Another factor was that they would be dealing with the chairman, not the manager as was normal at most clubs.

I established certain negotiating rules for new signings. First of all I set the annual budget, with the board's agreement, determined never to exceed it. Contrary to practice at some clubs, our playing budget included all transfer fees as well as wages and bonuses. And I wouldn't pay signing-on fees to players. A lot of clubs did, as well as transfer fees to the clubs the players came from. In the Football League, signing-on fees would be five-figure sums – between £10,000 and £50,000. Normally in Division Three it would be £10,000.

We couldn't afford it. A fair fee to the selling club if a player was under contract, and a fair wage to be negotiated with the player – that was it. And I can't think of any players that we lost out on as a result of these rules.

Agents of established players coming in would try to get appearance money on top, but playing was what I was paying their basic wage for. Young players were different; they were on a very low basic, so I was prepared to pay them appearance money as an incentive for getting in the first team.

I knew the Albion had previously paid signing-on fees, despite not even making players live in the Brighton area, which was something else I insisted on – that players had to live within 20-25 miles of Brighton. When I first took over, the team bus used to leave Brighton for away matches with only about three players on it. It went through Hampshire and Wiltshire picking up players who played for Brighton. It was ludicrous.

The most infamous one was Nicky Rust, the reserve goalkeeper when I first took over. He lived in Cambridge and had been given a moving allowance in his contract. So he moved closer to Brighton – from north Cambridge to south Cambridge – and still claimed the allowance! There had been no stipulation about where he had to move to. I made sure that type of clause was taken out of future contracts, and made sure the players knew it. And I knew what my budget was.

I'd had something of a crash course in football wage levels during the months of negotiations with Archer. One of the things I learned was that you always talked about what people got per week. In business, people's salaries were an annual sum – £70,000 a year. But everything in football is based on the weekly wage – he's on £600 a week, etc. It goes back to the early days of the game and, like so much in English football, it had never changed. So today, when someone like Yaya Toure is reported to be on £220,000, it's per week!

Another thing for a club chairman to grasp is that the Football League standard contract stipulates that players be paid for 13 months in the last year of their contract, the extra month to cover the period when they're leaving a club. Respect to Gordon Taylor for negotiating that one!

With regard to playing bonuses, the Albion paid quite generously, particularly for big cup games. The bonus schedule was virtually unchanged since the halcyon days of the late '70s and early '80s, when players were given a share of the cup gate receipts. Any change to the bonus scheme in any club has to be agreed by a majority of the players. Of course, our players had never voted for a reduction.

For league matches, the bonus was based on performance, as it should be. When I took over, the amount depended on the league position, supposedly reflecting the fact that the club would be getting bigger gates depending on our position. Of course that was true at the Goldstone, but at Withdean we were getting the same crowd wherever we were in the league. So I simplified all that, making it a single payment for a win and single payment for a draw – in Division Three it was £240 for a win, and £120 for a draw.

Zamora, Paul Brooker and Richard Carpenter were given three-year contracts, and Kuipers two. It added up to a significant investment, because we'd already had one of the highest playing budgets in the league in our first season back in Brighton. It was in the top five after being the lowest budget when we were at Gillingham. All that had to be paid for, and we were able to do it because we had substantially improved the commercial side of the club.

In the second season at Gillingham we had lost more than £900,000 – not only because the gate receipts were minimal and we had to pay £150,000 in rent, but also because of the costs of the Falmer planning application, which were to prove an onerous financial burden for many years. The process went on and on, draining money from the club. But although we operated at a loss, it was a manageable loss because I, along with some directors and shareholders, put more money into the club.

Withdean was different. That summer of 2000, season ticket sales increased to more than 4,000, partly because we had finished the previous campaign so promisingly, but also because prices were lower if people bought them early. In addition I came up with the idea of a 10-year season ticket from 2000/01, and the take-up for that was really quite good – about 200 were sold. The point was to generate funds for the club now, and it was very good value, including cup matches for the next 10 years. It was a gesture really to say thank you to the fans, thinking that at least half of that ticket would be used to watch games at Falmer. Little did we know that the whole 10-year period would expire and we would still be at Withdean for another season after that.

Added to the season ticket income was the £500,000 that we had agreed with Aston Villa to settle the outstanding payments for Gareth Barry and Michael Standing. It was money in the hand, rather than sitting in Aston Villa's bank account on a promise of some date in the future. It was a no-brainer as far as I was concerned. No one on the board disagreed that it was the best option; the club needed it.

A couple of other things happened off the field. Early in 2000, I'd invited John Baine, otherwise known as 'Attila The Stockbroker' – who played a major part in the campaign to unseat Archer and was to play a big role in the Falmer For All team – to be the club's Poet in Residence. This appointment, backed by the South East Arts Council, was the first of its kind ever at a football club.

It was my idea because I liked his poems and his nuggety use of words, straight to the point. John had written the wonderful *Goldstone Ghosts* epitaph. He was obviously someone who had the Albion at heart, and he perfectly understood the magical relationship between fan and club. So I thought it was right to give him this position; it confirmed the club's individualistic style. To some extent it reflected the city, which Brighton & Hove now was.

We also announced the continuation of the kit sponsorship deal with Skint for a further two years through to 2002. The red-and-black striped away shirt was very popular, especially with the No.25 and Zamora on the back. He kept that number throughout his career with the Albion and on into the Premier League with each club he's played for.

So everything was in place when we opened the season at Southend. With Albion installed as pre-season promotion favourites, our 3,500 fans at Roots Hall started singing 'Championes' before kick-off, which was somewhat premature to say the least. It was a bit arrogant to assume that we would carry on from where we'd left off last season, on a long unbeaten run. And Southend proved the point by beating us 2-0.

One remarkable aspect of that game was that Kuipers was given his chance as first-team goalkeeper, and was then substituted at half-time. Not because of his goalkeeping, but because his kicking was so bad. It was the beginning of a long-running saga about his only fault as a goalkeeper.

Immediately after the game, I looked for Michel. I wanted to commiserate with him but also encourage him not to be put off by this setback. But I couldn't find him until I looked in the team bus, where he was already changed and sitting glumly alone on the back row of seats. I put my arm round his shoulder and told him he was a good keeper, and that Micky thought so too. So it was up to Michel to pick himself up and show Micky just how good he was. "Thanks, Mr Chairman," said a still doleful Michel, but he took my words to heart.

We might have lost that game but we soon started getting results, Zamora started scoring goals, and the team really began to gel. Micky moved Hart wide on the right and Brooker made a huge difference to the attack wide on the left. Paul Watson developed an almost telepathic understanding with Zamora from dead-ball situations, particularly inswinging free kicks on the right-hand side, usually curled into the near post.

Watson was that extremely rare beast, a left-footed right-back. And time and time again Zamora would spring the offside trap as Watson struck the ball into clear space, latch onto it completely unmarked and score. And Zamora worked exactly the same ploy when he was at Fulham, with the likes of Damien Duff on the right-hand side. But it was with Watson that he perfected that technique.

The team was performing like the champions the fans had already assumed we would be. There was a real feeling of bonding among these players, and they were a strong bunch of characters, with lots of leaders. And that included Zamora, although his leadership was mainly by example. He was quiet, and he was brand new to first-team football – he'd only previously started six league games. But he never showed any signs of being anything other that what we believed him to be. He knew we had faith in him and it gave him confidence.

Clearly the way they had dealt with him at Bristol Rovers hadn't. He once told me how disappointed he had been not to get into the team when he had gone back to the Memorial Stadium. Bobby is very professional. He had wanted to fulfil his contract there.

From the beginning of his Albion career, he showed exactly the qualities I was certain he would go on to show in the Premier League. His first touch was excellent, he held the ball up brilliantly, brought other players into it, and worked so hard for the team. And he scored goals.

As we got into that season, Zamora was playing with Hart to his right and Brooker on the left – nominally 4-3-3. But once the game was under way, Hart and Brooker were generally sitting in midfield. We basically played 4-5-1, with Hart and Brooker also used defensively and Bobby on his own up front.

There was a strong spine, starting in goal with Kuipers, who had quickly forced his way back into the first team. Then there was Cullip, with Charlie Oatway holding in front of him and two central midfielders in Carpenter and Paul Rogers. And Zamora at the sharp end.

The team spirit was good, almost too good at times, when it was 'all for one and one for all' – in other words, if there was a dust-up anywhere on the pitch, half the Brighton team would be over there. I said to Micky, "I don't want our team to behave like that." It started hurting us in the pocket because we were being fined by the FA for unruly behaviour. I warned him that next time, he and the players would pay. That sorted it.

It was Micky's team. The players related to him, but he never got too close to them. They respected him and even feared him a little. He had come out of the previous season's troubles with a lot of confidence, and had a real presence about him. With me, he knew that I had faith that we would get it right, and the players began to share that belief.

Micky relied on Alan Cork, his assistant, to be the bridge between him and his players but Corky left in September to join Cardiff City as assistant to Bobby Gould, renewing acquaintances with him and owner Sam Hammam from their Wimbledon days.

Micky knew immediately where to find Cork's replacement. Bob Booker, a former Sheffield United hero – which endeared him to Blades fan Micky – who has a lounge named after him at Bramall Lane and had worked at Brentford as a youth-team coach when Adams was there and impressed him. Bob was to prove one of Micky's best acquisitions and made the job of assistant manager his own, becoming the perfect link with the players. He had a lovely personality for arms-around-the-shoulder time, but was also a man they respected because he was an excellent coach. Bob fitted in straight away.

I went to all our away games, usually driving there and back in a day – the one exception being an overnight stay in the Lake District when we played at Carlisle United. One away trip was the most nerve-racking of all. On September 12 we were away at Blackpool, right in the middle of a nationwide petrol strike, with filling stations closed everywhere. Along with a few hundred hardy Albion souls, I decided to give it a go and set off with no guarantee I could reach Lancashire, let alone get back to Sussex afterwards.

Never before has a Porsche 911 been driven in such gingerly fashion, as I inched my way northwards with my pal Geoff Watts – and made it to Bloomfield Road with less than half a tank remaining. A goal from Rogers and a 20-yard rocket from Hart gave us a 2-0 win, putting myself and the other plucky Albion fans in good spirits as we crawled back south. Amazingly I made it with about a thimbleful left in the tank after a journey that ended just before dawn. I'm not aware that we lost any Albion fans on that mission.

One of the key games in the first part of the season was at Chesterfield, who were leading the table while we were second. On the way up the M1 we found ourselves stuck in a huge tailback 30 miles south of the town. I could see Albion supporters' coaches and lots of cars with blue-and-white scarves all crawling along, and I realised that we weren't going to make the kick-off.

So I phoned Ray Bloom, who always arrived at every ground early, and asked him to have a word with the Chesterfield chairman, explain that loads of potential paying customers were going to be delayed, and ask if he could speak to the referee and delay the kick-off.

Five minutes later, the chairman, Darren Brown, rang me back. He subsequently ran into problems with the law, pleading guilty to two charges of fraudulent trading, and Chesterfield were docked nine points for irregularities in player contracts. But he obviously knew about making money because that day he said, "Dick? It's Darren. I've spoken to the ref and that's all right. He's going to delay it half an hour. Your fans will be able to get here."

When we heard that, my son David wound down the window and started shouting to all the Albion fans inching along, "Kick-off's delayed!" This was greeted with jeers of disbelief until they saw it was me driving the car. Then all the cars and coaches started blowing their horns in celebration.

The game itself ended in controversy after the referee sent Oatway off very unfairly. Chesterfield were hanging on at the end, but then broke away to score the only goal in the last minute. It fired us up for the rest of the season and made our team determined to catch them. It wasn't so much the rumours that their players were getting illegal bonuses and so the club was cheating, as the unfairness of that result and the fact that Charlie had been unjustly sent off.

Other away games had their lighter moments. I had a bit of a reputation as a casual dresser, smart casual I preferred to think. I never wore a tie, which was ok in my own boardroom, but not necessarily in others. Once, I remember turning up at a northern ground with my friend Geoff, to be greeted by a stern-faced attendant standing sentinel outside the boardroom entrance. "You won't get in here without the right neckwear," he barked. "Geoff replied, "This is the Brighton chairman, he doesn't wear ties." "Oh, ok," he said and let us in.

We played at Mansfield that season, and when I drove up to the Field Mill car park entrance to report as usual, the steward on the gate said, "Mr Knight, I've got a present for you," and handed me a gift-wrapped package. It contained a Mansfield Town Supporters Club tie, bright yellow with the club logo embossed all over it. "We heard about your dress habits, you'll need that to get into our boardroom." I duly gained entrance, although the attendant was somewhat perplexed when, confronted with this bloke wearing a loud Mansfield tie, I told him I was the Brighton chairman. I offered it back to the car park steward on the way out, but he said "keep it." I replied, "It will go with all those other ties you get at Christmas but never wear." "No problem," he said, "It will improve your wardrobe no end."

Another top-of-the-table game was against Cardiff at home, when we won 1-0. Zamora scored early on and from that point we just defended. Usually the threat of a breakaway goal from Zamora meant that defences could never relax against us. He obviously made an impression on Hammam because early the next season he rang me up and said, "Dick, I'm going to give you a lot of money."

I said, "Thanks Sam, but why are you going to do that?"

He replied, "I'm going to buy Bobby Zamora."

"For how much?"

"A lot."

"It doesn't matter how much, actually. Bobby Zamora's not going anywhere. He's staying here."

"No, no, no, you need the money. I know your club is struggling for money. I have it and I'm going to give you lots of it."

I said, "Sam, there's more chance of me buying Robbie Earnshaw from you than there is of you buying Bobby Zamora from me. When Bobby leaves here he'll be going to the Premier League."

Sam didn't like that because Earnshaw was becoming a big name. Sam was obviously very confident. Somehow news of his bid had got into the local press in Wales, with a figure of £2.5 million mentioned, although Sam later told me he would have offered £3 million. Zamora now had an agent, Phil Smith, and Sam had made contact with him and had mocked-up pictures published of Bobby in a Cardiff shirt.

But I had an agreement with Zamora that I'd let him and his father know about any approach. I told them about this phone call, and Bobby said, "I'm not going to Cardiff, it's as simple as that." And when he found out about the mocked-up photos he was furious.

I knew he'd say that. Why would he go to Cardiff when they were in the same division as us? In fact we weren't that desperate for money. Zamora was far more important to me as a player, scoring goals and helping us up through the divisions, than cash would be. He inspired the club. He was the personification on the pitch of the fact that we were trying to do something a bit special, do things in style. He was the class act that I was trying to turn us back into.

He made the fans believe that the club was actually going somewhere again. I don't know if he realises how important he was and remains to this club. I met him in Portugal at an airport in 2010, long after he'd left, and he came over and said, "Mr Chairman, don't forget – one day I want to come back as player-manager."

But I'm not actually sure he will stay in football. He's a sensible guy. If he hadn't been a footballer I think he would have worked in social welfare, education or something similar. He comes from an interesting family, and would have made something of himself. When he was at his zenith at Brighton, the requests we got for him to visit schools, hospitals and go to prize-givings far outweighed all the other players together, but he was always amenable. He was never starry, never refused. I couldn't speak more highly of Bobby Zamora as a person.

I agreed with him that I would tell him when we got an approach. When we went up into the First Division in 2002, Phil Smith was very active in trying to get him into the Premier League. I said to him and his dad, "Stay another year. A season at the second level will give you more great experience. Then you'll have your pick of top clubs and will go with my best wishes."

With Bobby in Micky's team of strong characters, we took the occasional dip in our stride, and going into 2001, our centenary year, it became a question of when we would clinch promotion rather than if. And we were playing in a special centenary shirt that I'd designed with Errea, our kit suppliers, with the two town crests of Brighton and Hove embroidered on the front, and 'Brighton & Hove Albion 1901 – 2001' underneath.

It cost a bit more, but it was worth it. I think it's my favourite Albion shirt. It was a very complicated design and Errea's sales director, Fabrizio Taddei, moved heaven and earth to produce it. He had seamstresses in a little village in the mountains near Parma in Italy, where they're based, embroidering the crests on each shirt in time for the first game. That was on New Year's Day at home to Southend, who unfortunately did the double over us. It was the only game I missed that season, with flu, and everyone said it should never have been played because the pitch was totally waterlogged with rain.

But on normal surfaces we were almost unbeatable. We got to April and a match away to Plymouth on Easter Saturday, the first game in which we could technically be promoted. First we had to do the job – secure three points – which we did fairly easily, scoring twice early on, through Brooker and Zamora.

Our fans were now more interested in what was happening at other games. When Rochdale only drew and Hartlepool lost at home to Hull, we were up, for the first time in 13 years, and there were celebrations, if not perhaps as dramatic as I'd expected them to be. It was almost an anti-climax, because we didn't have to score a late winner – we just sat back and waited for the others to fail.

What we really wanted now was a trophy, because we hadn't lifted one since Albion had won the old Division Four back in 1965. And in our way were Chesterfield again. By now the League had imposed a nine-point deduction on them for financial irregularities, but because there was talk that they might appeal, there was an outside chance that they might be given the points back.

As luck would have it, they were the visitors in our final home game, and if we won we'd make sure that we finished at least 10 points ahead of them, enough to secure the title fair and square, even if they got the whole nine points back.

Well, we did win – a glorious header by Danny Cullip with 12 minutes to go when he threw himself full length at a Brooker corner: a typical Danny goal. At the end, everyone came on the pitch and I joined them. For me it was very emotional as fans hugged me and showered me with thanks.

We eventually got the pitch clear, the podium with the league winners' banner was rolled on, and the players were introduced one by one as they trotted up to collect their medals. I hadn't realised the time gap until a reporter came up to me and said, "How does it feel to win a trophy for the first time in 36 years?"

My other memory of that night was that before the kick-off, our fans on the south side passed over their heads an enormous brown envelope to repre-sent the illegal payments that Chesterfield had been accused of making to their players. To Albion fans, the 'Crooked Spireites' had more than lived up to their nickname.

We decided to hold an open-top bus parade because it had been so long since the Albion had had anything to celebrate. We went along the seafront, finishing at Hove Town Hall, on the balcony which was being used for the first time since the day after the FA Cup final replay in 1983. Thousands of people lined the whole route and there were at least 5,000 at the Town Hall alone.

It was a moving moment. As we went out onto the balcony, I hugged Bob Pinnock and Martin Perry. "We did it." I thanked the team and the fans and there was a tear in my eye as I looked down on the cheering crowd, a sea of blue and white as far as I could see.

We almost didn't know what to do with the trophy, because for years there had obviously been no need for a club trophy cabinet. So when we hosted the 'Centenary Evening of Legends', a sumptuous dinner at the Brighton Centre on May 18, attended by more than 1,000 Albion fans, to celebrate the club's centenary and the title, we came up with something special. Near the end, Steve, now Lord, Bassam and Ivor Caplin MP came on dressed as workmen in over-alls, carrying a brand-new trophy cabinet, and Micky and I proudly put the gleaming silver prize in its new showcase.

After a brilliant 'jumpers for goalposts' sketch that I had asked Albion fan Mark Williams (from *The Fast Show*) to perform, the trophy came out once more. We'd invited along players from every era of the club's history, including Harry Baldwin from the '40s, Johnny McNichol, Eric Gill and Dave Sexton from the '50s, Bobby Smith from the '60s, Alan Mullery's promotion team, and the 1983 FA Cup final side.

They went up on stage and were interviewed by Des Lynam and Peter Brackley, and for the finale we got the current team to come up and take a bow with our newly-won Division Three trophy which, it struck me, looked very much like the FA Cup. The stage was packed with players and at that moment I had a thought. I picked up the mic and called out to Gordon Smith to come up as well.

I'd seen Gordon a couple of months earlier at a league game up north – he was an agent representing some senior Scottish players at the time – and said, "Please come." He'd been a little bit unsure, thinking that, because of his famous cup final miss, some people might blame him for everything that had gone wrong at the club since then. But I promised him, "They absolutely won't, they love you." He was one of the most popular of all the former players. Anyway, when he came up on the stage, I said, "Gordon, I want you to pick up the trophy and hold it up to the fans – just as you would have done at Wembley all those years ago." He did it and the whole place erupted. It was brilliant.

I saw him when he was chief executive of the Scottish FA and he said, "I'll never forget that moment when you made me pick up the trophy." He had exorcised something and he was so pleased.

The whole centenary evening showed how much everyone had come together again, and how much potential we had to go forward after we'd so nearly lost the club entirely only four years before.

# CHAMPIONES (AGAIN)

While the team on the pitch was winning matches, the team behind the scenes was pressing ahead with the less glamorous task of pushing the Falmer planning application forward. We kept the fans well informed of progress because we had to get them on board to help, and nothing could be taken for granted about the new stadium.

Tim Carder from Falmer For All began to organise a massive petition to show that this was no ordinary application the council were being asked to approve. We had various meetings: there was a fans' forum that we held at the racecourse in July, a supporters' AGM, and a BBC Southern Counties Radio forum just before the start of the 2001/02 season.

I said at one of those meetings that I could see the club playing at Falmer in five years and there was no reason why we shouldn't be playing in the First Division in front of crowds of 20,000. I got the attendance numbers right, except that it was five more years on top of that.

After many delays we finally put in the extremely complex planning application, which was twofold – one for the stadium on Village Way North, the other for it on Village Way South (in case the University of Brighton didn't play ball) – both with the coach drop-off point on Village Way South. Are you still with me?

How complex was it? When we delivered the Falmer application to Brighton & Hove City Council on October 8 2001, the paperwork filled 32 boxes, meeting all the requirements of the planning system. It took the council nine months to evaluate that lot before it was put before its planning committee in June 2002.

The month before, we presented a petition containing 61,452 signatures in support of the Falmer stadium to the council leader, Ken Bodfish. These were huge numbers, much more than those who would actually watch the Albion. But that was the degree of support for the stadium.

And while all this was underway, we still had to fight for additional time and space at Withdean, which was costing more money. The original estimate of just under £3 million finished up at £5 million, because we were there much longer than we originally envisaged, incurring more legal fees when having to apply for tenancy extensions, and adding extra seating, including an away end behind the west goal and making what other improvements we could to our temporary home. I used to call the away seats 'the Worthing End' – because the seats were so far away that it felt as if they were literally in Worthing.

It was all part of Withdean's unique character. Okay, it wasn't perfect. It was the most unlikely of Football League grounds. Micky Adams came up with the psychological tactic of leaving a bucket in the middle of the away dressing room to suggest that the roof might leak if it rained, just to wind the visiting team up.

For many big clubs it was like playing a pre-season friendly in Norway, with all the trees. Derby came there for a league game a couple of years later with Fabrizio Ravanelli in their squad, and this former Italy forward obviously wondered where they would be playing the real game. He was warming up on a horrible drizzly day and suddenly pulled up 'injured'. I think he looked around, thought, "I've played at the San Siro and the Stadio delle Alpi, what the hell am I doing here?" and cried off.

We moved the boardroom into a little building just alongside the north stand which was used as a children's crèche during the week, with lots of books and toys in it, and when we played midweek matches the evidence of the crèche was often still apparent. We hastily put up some Albion pictures, but it wasn't difficult to see that there were ABC blocks and various children's drawings everywhere. Visiting directors would grin and bear it, knowing that was what the club was going through, and it certainly made for a friendly atmosphere.

It was a definite improvement on the first year or so, when the boardroom had been down behind the east goal, in nothing more than a large broom cupboard off the main hospitality area. That was where we hosted the visiting directors and occasional celebrities such as Helen Chamberlain, a Torquay fan, and the actor Alan Davies, who told me that he was a massive Arsenal fan, but he was intrigued to sample Brighton's "unique Withdean experience". It felt like the front room in a prefab, but we served decent grub.

'Hospitality area' makes it sound rather grander than it was – really quite a basic Portakabin – but one of the positives that came from that was a wonderful spirit amongst the people in hospitality, because we were forced to make it an open area. Most grounds had individual boxes for their corporate facilities, but we didn't have the space for that, so we just had open tables with everybody together. And what that generated was a great atmosphere. Friendships were made as people naturally networked, and it became a model for us for the future at Falmer.

I'd got to know David Dein, then vice-chairman at Arsenal, through my association with Liam Brady and from my negotiations getting players on loan from Arsenal, and I invited him to a game. He later told me that when they were planning the Emirates Stadium he remembered the Withdean open-plan hospitality and that is what they now have at Arsenal, as we do at the Amex.

I'm not saying we were the only ones doing it, but David Dein saw the spirit of the club was being strengthened because of this open hospitality area, where people were as much genuine fans of the Albion as the people who just turn up to watch the game.

The hospitality area was Withdean in microcosm – busy and cramped because it was so small, a shared experience in making-do, but also very informal, which suited me. I don't like regimented, uniform-type dress anyway. I tend to be more casual in my clothes. And bear in mind that Skint were our main sponsors and their staff, artists and guests were in the boardroom, quite a few of them at every match. Well, I couldn't get them wearing suits; it just wouldn't happen. I asked them to be as smart as they could be, but that meant being in nice jeans rather than bleached out ones with rips.

An air of informality was a style that I encouraged. The rules for getting in were strict and I wouldn't go as far as to allow replica shirts, but most visiting chairmen and directors took it in good spirits because they knew we were tenants in a ramshackle ground. About the only chairman who didn't join in the spirit of it at all was Roland Wycherley of Shrewsbury Town.

At the end of the 2000/01 season, Martin Perry and I went in the away end for our final game, at Gay Meadow, Shrewsbury. I had two reasons. First, because I'd decided that I would go in with our away supporters at least once a season, and that tended to be the last match of the campaign. But the other reason was in protest against Wycherley's boardroom policies at Shrewsbury. Certainly I never saw a woman in there, and he had a whole set of rules that included no cheering in the directors' box. I was told that in no uncertain terms by Wycherley when we were beating them 2-0 at half-time a couple of years earlier. I asked all our directors to pray that we got another goal in the second half, and sure enough Richard Barker duly obliged, off his backside, to wrap up a 3-1 win – a goal of drab ordinariness, but one which was greeted with the rapturous shouts of Brighton directors as if Gordon Smith had actually scored at Wembley.

When we played them at Withdean once, he came into the boardroom and looked in disdain at the surroundings. We won the game 4-0. We were 2-0 up at half-time. And when we scored the directors had cheered like everyone else. And he complained to Martin about this at half-time, saying, "You shouldn't be making that sort of noise." Our chief executive responded in the appropriate manner, with a phrase I couldn't possibly repeat.

Apart from that, the spirit in our boardroom was relaxed and friendly and, bearing in mind there were paintings by four-year-olds adorning the walls together with Albion heroes, it couldn't really be any other way.

I lost count of the number of visiting chairmen who said, "I never realised what you had to put up with". But that was Withdean, and we did have to put up with it. We had no choice.

Of course, as chairman of a club, I was now a regular attendee of the Football League meetings that were held four times a year at various grounds around the country – it was usually a trip to Leicester, Derby, Walsall or even points further north. And I was an active participant in these discussions.

At the AGM of the Football League at the Carden Park country hotel, near Chester, in June 2000, it was announced that the League had signed a contract with ITV Digital for live coverage of games on a new channel. As football boomed in the new satellite TV era, the League had secured a £315 million, three-year contract from the start of the following season, 2001/02.

They were talking big numbers about the sums each club would be paid per season: Division One clubs would get £3.3 million, Division Two £600,000, even every Division Three club would get almost £400,000 per year. Naturally this was received with tremendous enthusiasm by the assembled chairmen and chief executives of the 72 Football League clubs.

Or rather, 70 of them. The night before it was announced, Brian Phillpotts, the marketing director of the League, discussed it with me and Barry Hearn of Leyton Orient over a drink at the bar. Phillpotts had just tied up the deal with senior ITV people, and the figures he was quoting made us raise our eyebrows.

Barry is pragmatic, not an idealist in any way and, like me, he had some experience of television audiences. We were both sceptical and didn't think it all added up. It was all based on digital television growth and in theory it was a good idea because of the imminent switchover from analogue to digital television, which they thought this would accelerate. But for me the numbers didn't make any sense at all. The matches covered would have to attract big audiences for them to justify paying this sort of money out.

The money was going to be paid in two tranches per season, but I said to our board that we weren't going to rely on it turning up because I was very dubious about their ability to generate these levels of money. And so it proved – the whole thing went belly-up.

Coverage of live games started in the 2001/02 season as planned, but even as it got underway it was delivering seriously small nationwide audiences – less than 20,000 per game – because a lot of the matches they had on offer were not that attractive. No disrespect, but Macclesfield versus Torquay was not going to draw big ratings. And the deal ran into trouble during the first season; by March 2002 the channel was in administration.

The effect on a lot of League clubs was absolutely catastrophic because they had assumed they were getting this money for three years and had budgeted – and spent – accordingly. Eighteen Football League clubs called in the administrators following the ITV Digital disaster.

Brian Phillpotts left the Football League and went to the Premier League. He wasn't directly at fault that ITV didn't deliver on what they promised. He did the deal and got a lot of kudos as a result. But the outcome of the debacle with ITV Digital was that the League realised that it had to take a firmer grip on finances and governance. It formed a commercial committee as part of that strategy and invited me to join it.

The idea was that club bosses who had media and marketing experience would advise the new marketing director of the League – the others were Barry, Theo Paphitis of Millwall, Adam Pearson, the Hull City chairman, Barry Kilby, the Burnley chairman, and Mark Arthur, the chief executive of Nottingham Forest.

Of course, I knew Theo from our ill-fated Millwall groundshare project. I was aware that Barry was actively involved in snooker and boxing, but I found that he also talked so much common sense about football. He understands it. And he has a great sense of humour. He treats nearly everything as if there's a joke coming somewhere in the conversation. I met him at my first League meeting, when he came over to say hello and introduce himself. He'd been Orient chairman for a couple of years.

He said, "Allo Dick, nice to meet you, glad you finally won the battle against that bastard." Then he added, "You were in advertising, weren't you? Still work in the business?"

"Yes, I've got a consultancy, working with some of my old clients," I replied.

"How much of your time do you think you'll spend being Brighton chairman, percentage-wise?"

"About 60 per cent, I suppose – something like that."

"No chance. With the job you've got at Brighton, multiply that by 10."

Don't ever underestimate Barry, because he is a very shrewd businessman and goes straight to the point. He understands the business of sport probably better than anyone I've ever met. He's proved that in boxing, in snooker, and I've talked with him about his plans for developing other sports.

He's got some interesting ideas and he'll tell me, knowing I'll give him a point of view that might be different. He fights his own club's corner, as he has over West Ham's move to the Olympic Stadium in Stratford, but he also sees the bigger football picture.

The same was true of everyone on the committee. Theo, Adam, Barry K., Mark – they thought beyond the scope of their own clubs. They think on a global basis, and are strategic in their outlook. We were asked to guide the League on the best way to do deals, how to negotiate rights and so on. We were in the forefront of dragging the Football League into the 21st century in marketing terms, pushing it to present itself in a much more polished and professional way.

The League was slow to cotton on to the potential of football from a marketing point of view. 'Real Football, Real Fans', the main strapline on the League's website, came from the positioning that its clubs were the heart and soul of English football. That was my mantra and the mantra of the others on our committee.

The last marketing director that I worked with was Stewart Thomson, who sadly died in 2011 of cancer at the age of 48. He came from Glasgow Rangers and we worked well with him as a team, culminating in getting the Coca-Cola sponsorship of the League, starting in 2004.

As well as being on the commercial committee, I was asked a few times if I was interested in being nominated as a director on the League board, but I had my hands full with the club and the stadium. I just couldn't devote enough time to League matters. The commercial committee meetings were virtually all conducted via conference calls, but it worked pretty well and I think it helped take the Football League forward in a very relevant way from a strategic point of view.

At the end of the day the Football League is a big business, and has been transformed in the last 15 years. David Sheepshanks was a major player in that. He became the chairman of the Football League in 1997, and had put forward a proposal for the 1998 summer AGM conference which was to be of major significance. He wanted to appoint to a new post a chief executive – who first and foremost had marketing experience. There was a thorough headhunting process which produced a shortlist of candidates, who then met a few chairmen at our clubs who had the know-how to discuss the candidates' views on the way forward for the Football League – from marketing and the distribution of TV revenue to financial governance.

David gathered our conclusions and the collective view was that Richard

Scudamore was clearly the outstanding candidate. I knew Richard from way back in my advertising career, when he used to work for the Thomson Organisation (then the owners of the *Sunday Times*) as group ad director. He'd gone to work for them in the States and been over there for some time, and then had come back to England. I knew he had the credentials to do the job.

David decided to invite Scudamore to present his ideas to all the League clubs at the forthcoming AGM of the Football League, which was being held at Carden Park as usual.

However, at the beginning of the first day of the meeting on June 4, Douglas Craig, the chairman of York City, objected to Scudamore being allowed to make a presentation, and a lot of other old-school chairmen agreed with him. Douglas didn't think that we needed an outsider coming in and telling Football League clubs what to do. He came across as a typical dour Scot and, because he was a magistrate, he was used to getting his own way.

Sheepshanks looked despairingly to the floor for help; he couldn't fight this on his own. Now was the time for Barry Hearn and the rest of us to put forward our alternative view. Barry was then on the League board, representing Division Three, and he started it. He said that he didn't agree with the viewpoint put forward by Craig. He thought it was right that we had outside input. And that if Scudamore's presentation was good, then, subject to a majority vote and the right salary deal, he should be invited to become chief executive.

After Barry had sat down, I switched my red light on (indicating to the chair that I wanted to speak) and then explained to the audience that we needed fresh thinking and people with vision running the Football League. And as Richard Scudamore had devoted a lot of time to his presentation and interviews – and was a genuine Bristol City fan – the very least we owed him was the courtesy of listening. That was supported by a few of the other chairmen, like Theo, Barnsley chairman John Dennis, and Paul Scally and the mood of the floor changed. So Craig grudgingly withdrew his objection, even if he wasn't happy.

Scudamore's presentation was superb. He captivated the room with his thoughts and the way he delivered them. His approach was full of initiatives and he was forthright on the issues facing the League. As far as I was concerned it was a blue sky moment – we had to make sure that this guy was signed up.

We took a lunch break so that people had time to think about it and, during that break, Douglas Craig came up to me and had the decency to admit that he had been wrong to resist the presentation, saying that he had been very impressed.

"You were absolutely right, Dick," he said. "We should listen more to new people like you. You seem to have a good idea of what we need. I got it wrong. Mr Scudamore had some very interesting things to say."

When Sheepshanks called the afternoon session to order, Craig stood up straight away and said he had been completely convinced. It was clear that Scudamore had unanimous approval – any potential opposition had crumbled. I grew to like Douglas. Inside he had a heart of gold.

But Scudamore very nearly didn't get to start in football, and if change had not been forced on the Football League at that meeting, our cause would have been delayed, perhaps by years. It was a very momentous meeting as far as the future of the Football League was concerned.

Scudamore's League work soon became noticed and in November 1999 he moved to the Premier League as chief executive. But he would never have become English football's most powerful administrator if he hadn't been allowed to make that presentation at the Football League AGM.

In later years, the Football League annual conference was held near Albufeira, Portugal, rather than in that hotel near Chester – otherwise I might have died of hypothermia one day when I ended up in the swimming pool.

Lord Brian Mawhinney, former chairman of the Conservative Party, had become chairman and he was a stickler for procedure. So every time you wanted to speak you had to press your buzzer, the light went on and he insisted that you gave your full name and club. So I had to say, "Dick Knight, Brighton & Hove Albion" every time. And I was often the first to make a point after a presentation, and usually wanted to come back with a question again later.

I used to ramble on a bit, but usually there was some substance in what I had to say. And it would provoke debate, and of course I would want to add something. But Simon Corney of Oldham and Keith Haslam of Mansfield, both extremely humorous guys, decided they were fed up hearing "Dick Knight, Brighton & Hove Albion" every few minutes, and when I turned up by the pool sporting my latest pair of swimming trunks and showing off my six-pack, or 26-pack by that time, they grabbed me and threw me in head-first. I executed one and a half somersaults with tuck and got nine from the Russian judge, but splashed everyone on the loungers closest to the water.

Mawhinney frowned at that. He thought we should all be behaving ourselves. It probably wasn't the sort of horseplay most fans would expect of Football League chairmen, who are usually thought of as a pretty stuffy bunch. But at these meetings I found that quite a few people's preconceptions about chairmen were wrong. I take people as I find them and I got on well, for example, with Simon Jordan of Crystal Palace, although he made only sporadic appearances at the conferences. Some consider him arrogant and self-obsessed. I found him very friendly and knowledgeable about football and we never spoke about our clubs' so-called rivalry.

Michael Knighton of Carlisle was a charismatic and engaging fellow, and if he had been able to borrow another £1 million he would have ended up as owner of Manchester United. After my attempt to groundshare at Millwall had fallen through, he said, "Dick, I'll do you a good deal to share Brunton Park with us." I replied, "Thanks Michael. You're only slightly further away than Gillingham."

But most of the meetings were very serious. It was important that the Football League was healthy and strong, especially as the Premier League was getting more and more money from television. A few of us made them think about the true values of the world's oldest league, and how to capitalise on them.

Helping to reshape the Football League was important, but there were also plenty of things I could do to help the Albion. With the club saved, I was busy rebuilding its structures and activities, the need for money being one priority.

We brought in a number of new marketing initiatives. We relaunched the weekly Seagull Lottery in a joint promotion with Albion Bingo, called Double Booster, and that would prove to be pretty successful over the coming years. And the Withdean Wager became a popular revenue-earner as part of the match-day experience, due to the smiling sales patter of Julie Stavely and her team.

I'd taken on Kevin Keehan as commercial manager, as part of the rebuilding of the club on the business side, who was responsible for a number of projects, including launching our own insurance services in conjunction with Axa. It was a very good deal which gave Albion supporters all sorts of discounts, and gave us a percentage of the premium turnover.

Kevin and I came up with 'Friends of the Albion', which brought together local businesses who followed the club, for the supporters' and their own benefit. They paid a small subscription to us every year, and they were given specially-designed Friends of the Albion logos to display, so that fans knew they could get discounts. They were listed in the club programme and were invited to business breakfasts and so on, where they networked and did business with each other.

It became a very successful project which still runs to this day. It was an involving scheme and a great name. And it contributed to the momentum for generating revenue from every source that we could.

For example, even though we got favourable rates, we still had to find funds for a poster campaign that we launched in January 2002. Falmer For All posters went up at 15 prominent sites in the city as the council considered our planning application. They emphasised the stunning design of the stadium and the boost it would give to the local economy, and implored councillors to "move the boundaries of their imagination" following the powerful mandate they were given by the referendum.

On March 8, after discussions with the FA, in which I emphasised that our stadium would be built to the high standards needed to stage Under-21 and Youth international matches, we unveiled a new poster that carried an endorsement for our vision from Sven-Goran Eriksson, the England head coach, that he'd sent to me.

Using the proximity of the stadium site to the planned South Downs national park, the poster portrayed the stadium merging into the rolling downland land-scape under the banner headline 'International Park'. Underneath was a quote from Sven that read: "The beautiful new Brighton stadium is of national impor-tance. It is vital we have world-class facilities countrywide to support the national game."

By then he was not the only England manager on our side.

We started the 2001/02 season in Division Two with a fair amount of optimism and virtually the same squad – a strong bunch of characters whose team spirit was very apparent. We'd rewarded them for promotion with a trip to Marbella. Micky put in a very brief appearance and left early, ostensibly because he had a League managers' event – but I knew he never thought it was a good idea to mix socially with the team.

Paul Rogers was in charge of the players, along with Bob Booker. Paul laid down the rules. I remember after one splendid dinner at an Italian restaurant, Bob revealed his collection of masks for the first time – Michael Jackson, Freddie Mercury and the rest. Ray Bloom's nephews, Tony and his older brother Darren, were around too.

At pre-season training, the major new face was central defender Simon Morgan, who came in during the summer to replace Andy Crosby, who went to Oxford United. Micky knew Simon from Fulham. He was, in effect, a very experienced cripple – chronic knee problems meant that he couldn't train, could hardly run.

On the pitch he never moved beyond an area of about the size of my kitchen, but he read the game brilliantly, positioned himself perfectly to pick up every-thing that came into the box. I've never seen a player who used his brain more, apart from Bobby Moore. He was another strong, intelligent character, so we maintained the powerful spine of the team.

Simon was superb. What a player, and a great personality. He wrote a hilar-ious weekly column in *The Argus* about the escapades of the players, and he wrote it himself – it wasn't ghosted. I encouraged it because it was another way of showing the human side of the club. It revealed the players as characters, real people rather than distant idols.

Typical was Nathan Jones, the Welsh left-back with the unique stepover, who was to return to the club as assistant head coach in 2013. I always thought he had something about him and would make a good manager one day. A very bright and garrulous guy, he was like Liam Brady in that when he went abroad, to play in Spain with Numancia, he learnt the language and embraced the culture. He told me it was a formative experience. The value of my contribution to his maturity is debatable. I once did an ad for the club shop alluding to Nathan's forward sallies, headlined, 'One step, two step, trickery over there'.

All the players got on well together and they knew that they were in the presence of a great player in Bobby Zamora. So did other clubs, and we had scouts from Premier League clubs at every home match and most away games too. Naturally I expected approaches but when one finally came, it was not for Bobby but for another key member of our team.

We'd started off well, and by October were in third place, behind Oldham and Brentford, when I got a call from John Elsom, the chairman of Leicester City, who were then in the Premier League. They wanted Micky Adams to become their assistant manager. Dave Bassett, who had just taken charge of the team, wanted someone he knew and trusted to work alongside him, and there was the suggestion that eventually Micky would take over as manager.

I was in Spain and I spoke to Micky by phone and he admitted he knew they were interested. I said, "Do you want to go and talk to them?" and he said yes. I knew then he would go, and I didn't want to stand in the way of his chance to work in the Premier League. He had come, as a few more managers would, on the promise that we would be playing in our new ground within two or three seasons, and he didn't see much progress on that front.

While I was in Malaga airport on the way back, I got another call from John, saying he'd agreed terms with Micky, and I replied, "Okay, now we need to talk about compensation." I then negotiated on the basis of getting the full value of his remaining contract, around £300,000, which John eventually agreed to. That wasn't bad for a Second Division manager going as an assistant. As Micky pointed out, it kept the club running for a couple of months.

I went for a drink with him and wished him well. I said, "We're still friends, Micky – you deserve this chance. Even if they get relegated, you'll bring them back." We'd revived his career and he'd learned from some early mistakes and put together a tough but good footballing team, and a good backroom staff. Obviously Micky didn't take Bob Booker with him, because there was no vacancy at Leicester – Micky was going to be the number two there.

Initially Bob and the players were very upset that the manager was leaving. But they all understood and wished him luck, and thought the chairman had better choose a bloody good replacement because Micky would be a hard act to follow. I put Bob and Martin Hinshelwood – again – in temporary charge for a league game at Huddersfield, which we won, while I set about finding a new manager.

As soon as the news of Micky's departure broke, I knew there would be a lot of good applicants for the vacant job. We were already making waves as a club. There was the Gareth Barry coup, the fact that we had been on the brink of oblivion and were fighting our way back, and a new stadium on the horizon.

We had over a hundred applications from various people. Out-of-work managers with a track record usually send hand-written letters of application – you seldom see typed ones, perhaps because they no longer have secretaries. Managers who are in jobs usually make contact via an agent, who let you know that their client might be interested in talking. The bigger names wait for you to get in touch. There is also the strange circumstance where some managers may not be aware that their names have been put forward, but their agents have sounded out the ground just in case the situation is interesting.

There were three big names whose agents contacted me, with or without their knowledge – experienced former Premier League managers between jobs, including one who had won the FA Cup, one who was going to win the FA Cup and one who would take a club to an FA Cup final but lose. They or their agents knew that I understood football and was building something good at Brighton, and they probably all thought the new stadium was in the offing. In the end I felt all of them were a little too high-powered for us at our level and in our circumstances. We needed to be in the First Division.

Then you got the crazies – people who have played Championship Manager on their computers and believe that they can do the job in the real world. One guy was hilarious. He would apply every time the job came up and his letter would begin, "Since I last applied . . ." and then detail his most recent European Super League title and points total. "I will take your Seagulls to European games with Inter Milan within three seasons – and I'm also available to wash the team kit."

I knew that Peter Taylor, the former England, Crystal Palace and Tottenham winger and namesake of Brian Clough's old partner, was out of a job, coincidentally after being replaced by Dave Bassett at Leicester. But it was his work with the England under-21 team in the late 1990s that I was impressed by. That told me that he did good work coaching players, although his time at Leicester called into question his judgement in the transfer market. But I didn't need to buy any players.

He had also managed the full England team once, giving David Beckham the England captaincy for the first time. And he had taken Gillingham up from Division Two via the play-offs, so he knew the level we were playing at. He was already high on my list when his pal David Webb, the former Chelsea defender, made contact on his behalf.

I met Peter at the Grafton Hotel on Tottenham Court Road, and we got on well. He knew all about Zamora, and I went through the rest of the squad, detailing their strengths. Then I said, "One thing I should make clear is that this team virtually manages itself. There are so many leaders on the pitch that they hardly need any coaching in what to do during a game. They're a smart bunch of guys who know their roles and the team's way of playing."

"So I'm offering the job, but this isn't something that is broken – we don't need to fix it. And you have a ready-made assistant in Bob Booker. He stays, trust me on this. If you can't get on with him, let me know after a couple of months. And the youth set-up, with Martin Hinshelwood and Dean Wilkins in charge, stays the same." Peter didn't raise any objection. I knew in my heart that he saw it as a short-term job, and we did the deal very quickly.

By and large he kept to the brief, although initially he tried to tinker. I'd told him that Paul Watson was a left-footed right-back, which was unusual, but he couldn't play left-back – his view of the pitch just didn't work that way. So what did Peter do? Tried to move him to left-back and dropped Nathan Jones. It didn't work. And he wanted a more solid, conventional 4-4-2 than our naturally expansive 4-5-1 style, which had Zamora ranging all over the front, sometimes drifting wide, sometimes down the middle. It was to be expected that Peter had his own ideas, but eventually he and the players sorted it out on the training ground, ending up close to our normal style.

And Peter was very pleased with Bob Booker. "What a wonderful asset," he said. "He's been the bridge for me, told me everything I need to know about the players and their foibles. He's everything you could want in an assistant."

But he also wanted to make personnel changes, with mixed results. One player that he was desperate to bring in was his mate Dave's son, Danny Webb. He told me he was the next Teddy Sheringham, and that's what he obviously thought.

He said that he had known Danny since he was six and with the benefit of his coaching he'd be worth at least £100,000, very quickly. Peter always had a strong belief that he could improve lower-league raw material to Premier League level. We brought Webb in and he tried very hard, but after a few weeks I said to Taylor, "He's more like Terry Shedingham, who plays on Hackney Marshes, rather than the bloke who plays for England." He wanted to give him a chance, which we did, but really we had enough firepower with Zamora and Lee Steele. I loved Steele, what a character. But Zamora didn't really need anyone else.

If Webb wasn't a success, you couldn't say the same for Junior Lewis, whom Peter had previously taken from Gillingham to Leicester. Lewis was on big money at Filbert Street, which he hardly justified in the Premier League. But because I'd not stood in the way of Leicester taking Micky, we were able to get him on loan. Junior kept things simple but showed real ability to pass the ball and scored some key goals from midfield.

I can picture those long, gangling legs ploughing through the mud in the centre of the Withdean pitch, knocking the ball out to Paul Brooker. He was almost able to float above the mud. He played a big role in taking us over the line to promotion.

His best game was a 3-1 win over Reading at Withdean on a Monday evening in February. Reading were top of the league, unbeaten since December, but Lewis dominated the midfield. He started the move from which Steve Melton scored one of the best goals ever at Withdean, a dipping volley.

Peter also wanted to sign Michael Standing until the end of the season, but didn't want to put him under pressure by giving him a longer deal because he was my great-nephew. He wanted Michael to prove himself first. That worked against us because Michael was offered a long-term contract by Bradford so he took that.

Eventually it came down to us and Reading for the title. They didn't lose again after we beat them at Withdean, but they drew too many, especially at home, while we usually found a way to get three points.

On Easter Monday, for example, while Reading could only draw 0-0 at home to Northampton, Bristol City battered us at Withdean but Michel Kuipers was almost unbeatable, and then in something like the sixth minute of added time, Steele got the winner with a diving header. To this day I still believe he was miles offside.

The next Saturday we won 1-0 away to Peterborough, Zamora scoring the winner after having a first-half penalty saved, and when Reading failed to beat Tranmere Rovers on the Sunday, we were up. I was listening on the car radio.

After our game at Peterborough, in which Gary Hart had sadly broken his leg, I was standing outside the London Road dressing rooms talking to Bobby when Barry Fry, their manager, came up. He said, "Dick, well done mate. You deserve to go up." And then he turned to Zamora. "Now let me tell you something, young man. You're a fucking great player and you'll play for England one day, I'm fucking sure of it." Barry was not a bad fucking judge.

We became Division Two champions with a 0-0 draw at home to Swindon, one year after topping Division Three, a momentous achievement. Winning successive leagues was a feat only managed six times before in Football League history.

When we went up to Port Vale for the last game of the season, I went behind the goal with the fans, as was now my custom, and got a great view of Paul Watson's winner, direct from a free kick. Afterwards I went round to the main entrance at Vale Park to go to the boardroom and I saw what I took to be an old man struggling up the stairs. I went to offer him some help and I realised it was Simon Morgan, bent double with the pain from his knees, trying to get up to the players' lounge. I said, "Simon, I never realised how bad your knees were until now. And you've just put in another dominating performance."

He said, "I'm like this after every game, Mr Chairman. The joints just stiffen up the more the game goes on. But I don't usually have to go up a load of stairs afterwards."

The next day, a Sunday, we again had an open-top bus ride along the sea front, this time finishing not at Hove Town Hall but at the council offices in Grand Avenue where there was more space, rather than everyone cramming into Church Road. Bob Booker dressed up as Freddie Mercury to serenade the vast crowd. I made a speech but Peter Taylor had declined the opportunity to do likewise.

Peter had been different in the week prior to the last game. He normally spoke to me every day but now he had gone quiet, which I felt was strange. On the Sunday morning he called me and said, "Dick, I'm going to leave. I think it's the right time. I've got you promotion."

He added, "I've done my job here. You've still got a problem with the stadium and you're not going to have the resources I'm going to need next season to make the team competitive in the Championship. I feel I've got to tell you now to give you time to find a replacement."

He was quite open and honest about it, but what he didn't say, and what I believed, was that really he thought that he had shown, immediately after being sacked by Leicester, that he was still a good manager – and so he would quickly get another Premier League job offer. For that reason he wanted to make himself available early in the close season.

So he'd thrown a bombshell at me, but I wasn't totally surprised. I knew Peter was very ambitious and thought his place was at the top level. And at least he'd given us time to find a new man.

He was a good coach and he'd taken us from third place to first by the end of the season. He later became England under-21 coach again, from 2004 to 2007, and brought Adam Hinshelwood and Dan Harding into the squad. In a way that was a favour to us because it boosted Harding's value. But at the time Peter Taylor had left me in a difficult situation.

But if I was beginning to get used to managers quitting on me just when we were making progress, it was nothing compared to the massive quitting coup I was able to orchestrate myself that summer – when I finally removed Archer from the club, thus closing the book on the darkest chapter in the Albion's history.

True to form, following his resignation from the club's board in June 1998, Archer had given notice in November 1999 for the club to repay his full loan, with interest kicking in six months later as he knew we couldn't repay it then. For two years, it had been building up.

In May 2002 we decided to convert all the loans that people – myself, the other directors, who by now included Derek Chapman and Kevin Griffiths, plus Norman Cook and Bill Brown – had made to the club into share capital, to strengthen the club's balance sheet and develop the financial base. That meant everyone basically gave up their right to have their money back, while the share capital of the club would go from £100 in Archer's day to around £4.5 million on June 25 2002, when the conversion was due to go through.

When Archer learned about this he refused to convert, claiming that he was against further dilution of his percentage shareholding, and gave notice that he wanted his money out. He, of course, expected to get well over £1.4 million, the figure he was now owed, even after he'd got his £250,000 performance bond money back. And I, of course, had promised myself that he would never get back more than the £800,000 that Stanley had originally put in.

I knew that he was planning to take Focus DIY public, so I went up to Crewe to see him. To his surprise, I offered him much less than he was due, even less than Stanley had put in. I said, "You're not going to get nearly £1.5 million, you never were. I'm prepared to give you £700,000 – take it or leave it."

I basically spelt it out. I said, "You're taking your company public and I could make things very nasty for you with a few words in the right ears. You caused an almighty furore at Brighton, but this will be very different."

My words were not empty ones. I had always had friends in Fleet Street, and the last few years had won me a few more. All I had to do was suggest they checked the recent history of this guy who was planning to take Focus DIY public, a move of great responsibility.

That same month, *The Mail on Sunday* did a whole-page hatchet job on Archer, asking the question, "Is this man fit to run a public company?" The article reminded readers of everything he had done at the Albion – changing the club's articles of association, selling the ground and being reviled by fans.

The article quoted "an Archer spokesman" as saying, incredibly, "He got involved through a friend to save a near-bankrupt football club. When he left, its future was secure." It was – but despite him, not because of him.

But the final straw was in the last paragraph. "Ahead of the float, Archer has tied up a deal extricating him from the Brighton saga, writing off half of the £1.4 million he is owed." How magnanimous of him.

Archer had got wind of what was coming, and I warned him, "This can only

get worse for you." So he settled for a loss on his and Stanley's Albion investment. And he never did take Focus DIY public. I can only assume that the City
was wary of a man with his track record, looking after an institution that the
public would be asked to invest in.

For me, it was a pyrrhic victory. I had finally got rid of Archer, but he'd
taken £700,000 out of the club, which we could ill afford. Could I have haggled?
Possibly. But it was less than half of what he was legally owed. I was just glad
to see the back of him – and thousands of other people would be with me on
that.

The supreme irony was that when I stood down as chairman seven years
later, I received £400,000 of the almost £2 million of my own money I had
put into the club over the years. Some people might see an injustice there. But
more of that later . . .

# CHAPTER TWENTY

# DOWNS AND UPS

**M**y first thought when Peter Taylor left was that we needed an experie-nced replacement, and the name I had in my mind was Steve Coppell. At other times I might have considered someone who was emerging as a coach. I was aware of Roberto Mancini because Liam Brady, who had played with him at Sampdoria, told me he was interested in becoming a manager, possibly in England. I'd seen him play in Italy and knew he was a leader but, because he was totally inexperienced, decided not to pursue the idea.

As before, a lot of candidates offered their services, but I was very clear that we needed someone who could deal with the fact that we were going into the second tier with a smaller playing budget than anyone else. I worked out that we would have one-sixth of the average income of the clubs in that division. The average attendance in the First Division was around 18,000, while I couldn't rely on ours being more than 6,000. Plus, almost exactly half of our match-day receipts went on the park-and-rides, the transport vouchers, and additional stewarding in the streets around Withdean. Our budget was effectively based on crowds of 3,000.

I had always admired Steve as a coach. He had done great work at Crystal Palace and Brentford, and had been brave enough to quit Manchester City after only 33 days when he realised it was not for him. He had left Brentford at the end of the 2001/02 season, so I contacted his agent, Athole Still, who also represented Sven Goran Eriksson and some interesting Italian players and, alongside his football business, ran an opera agency.

We quickly developed a good relationship, because he was on the phone every day, apologising for not being able to get in touch with Steve, who had taken himself off to some remote spot in the Far East as he did every year at the end of the season to get away from football. Athole said that he might be away for three weeks.

But suddenly that was only one of my problems. We discovered that my little granddaughter Emma was desperately ill. She had been diagnosed with a brain tumour and was admitted to Great Ormond Street children's hospital. Her parents, David and Jane, needed my help so that we could maintain a 24-hour vigil. And within weeks I was due to get married to Kerry, my girlfriend, in Gibraltar, with the honeymoon to follow in Spain.

I couldn't just wait for Coppell to reappear. I was also interested in Winfried Schäfer. the German who was the manager of the Cameroon national team. The more I found out about him and the way his teams played, the more I liked the sound of him. He'd managed Stuttgart and won the African Nations Cup with Cameroon earlier that year. They were the only African team who knew how to defend, and they also had some good forward players.

I'd traced Schäfer's agent, Andreas Hohmann, who sent me his CV and said he was keen to manage in England – but Cameroon were involved in that summer's World Cup finals, which were taking place in Japan and South Korea, and he couldn't commit himself until they were eliminated.

So I was interested in two experienced managers but couldn't get to speak to either of them. Because of the wedding and Emma's illness, I couldn't fly to Japan, and no one knew where Steve was.

But of course, finding a new manager was only one of my concerns as Brighton chairman. On June 12 2002, Brighton & Hove Council's planning committee, consisting of 12 councillors, met to rule on the Falmer dual planning application.

In addition to legal guidance from our law firm, DMH, and project co-ordination by our architects, KSS, Martin Perry recruited a team of specialists in environmental and transport assessments, plus landscape architects, structural engineers, mechanical and electrical consultants, safety and security experts and cost consultants. The whole thing was extremely expensive and that was long before the public inquiries. There were so many issues that had to be taken into account, but with a combination of shrewd housekeeping and top-up capital injections from myself and some of the other shareholders, we managed to fund the Falmer project costs.

We had moved from a situation where the club had no rapport with the council to one where they understood what we were actually about – that we weren't just a bunch of new spivs who had taken over from the old spivs. We gradually won their confidence and Martin and I presented a very solid front. We were dealing with a very complex planning application and left them in no doubt that we were very serious about the project. We convinced them that we were not just saving a football club, but putting the city on a strategic road to the future with a 21st-century community stadium.

We had submitted the plans the previous October and over the following months they had been subjected to forensic examination by the planning and leisure development officers of the council, who would give their recommendations to the councillors. We had two officers allocated to us, David Fleming and Sue Drummond, who were always seeking a positive outcome. Sheila Holden was the head of planning, and was very precise and exact, as she had to be. It meant that every procedure was followed to the letter. If we needed a badger expert, then they had to be a properly-qualified badger expert. We had to tick about 5,000 boxes for the council even to accept and consider our application – but then they did not get one as big as this every day. In fact, the council probably hadn't had to consider an application of this magnitude for 30 years. So they were naturally cautious.

While the officers interrogated us on every aspect of the application, they were also guiding us. They had their own advisors, and we were dealing with their traffic and environmental experts, but it was so complex that they twice had to postpone the date by which they were due to make their recommendation to the committee. They needed more input and discussion with us. Finally, by early June 2002, they were ready for their report to go before the planning committee and they were recommending strongly in our favour. The officers were obviously convinced of the merits after all that hard work to fine-tune the application.

By that time we were quietly confident that they would recommend in our favour, although that didn't mean it would automatically be passed by the committee. Objectors had been writing to their councillors, but we had the 60,000-plus petition signatures on our side. Even so, I was amazed when the committee voted 11-1 to approve Falmer as the site for the new stadium.

We were pretty sure that David Smith, who represented Rottingdean, not far from Falmer – and had apparently once been on the Albion's books – would have concerns over match-day traffic and vote against, which he did. We thought there were other waverers, but they had clearly been persuaded by the planning officers' report. And by that time, *The Argus* was campaigning in our favour, having realised that we were now good news rather than bad and that getting behind the club was the right thing for the paper to be doing.

The next day there were few celebrations. Despite the overwhelming local council approval, Martin was certain that the application would be called in by the government for a Public Inquiry because the designation of the South Downs as a National Park was in the offing, and the Falmer site was still officially part of an Area of Outstanding Natural Beauty – although it had been earmarked for development in the Local Plan.

My instinct was more political and populist – that if we could demonstrate to the government there was a huge need and desire for the stadium, then that was what we should do. Environmental groups are good at getting their case over, and I was sure they would be lobbying strongly against us, so I said, "We've got such a convincing vote in our favour, we should do everything we can to make sure we don't have to face a Public Inquiry."

But I was advised against it. "Making a lot of noise now is exactly what we shouldn't be doing," I was told.

This reasoning was being influenced by the presence at Westminster of Lord Bassam and Ivor Caplin, who were now in the corridors of power. It was felt that John Prescott could be reached by them. It was also suggested that we shouldn't alienate Greenpeace, Friends of the Earth or the other environmental groups. I said, "But they're the ones who will be campaigning against us." However, I allowed myself to be overruled.

My instinct was telling me something different, but of course it sounds plausible when someone says, "I know how to do this, I've done it before" or, "How can Friends of the Earth have as much sway with the government as Ivor? He won Hove from the Tories for the first time ever, the result that convinced Tony Blair that he had won the election."

The government have a six-week period in which to decide whether or not to call in an application and, as the time went by, I kept being told that Steve and Ivor were taking care of business and it was all going to be fine. And then the mood changed. The messages from Westminster were mixed – "Prescott's not easy to get to, he's protected by civil servants" – rather than anything definite. I began to feel that this strategy was not going to deliver what we had hoped, and that proved to be correct.

On Friday August 9, the day before we began the 2002/03 season away to Burnley, our lawyers got a letter from the government office telling us that our Falmer planning application had been called in and that there would be a Public Planning Inquiry.

Martin and I sat down and we discussed what would happen next. We met with our lawyers and had to hire a barrister, Jonathan Clay, and prepare a case. It was basically the planning application plus additional information, expert witnesses who could speak in favour of our case, and it now had to be in person rather than written evidence.

I was hugely disappointed, but not surprised. And I was furious years later when Prescott told me that, if he had known about the huge local support for the stadium rather than hearing only lobbying from Greenpeace, Friends of the Earth, the Campaign for the Protection of Rural England, the Society of Sussex Downsmen and the rest, he would have had a totally different perspective on the Falmer stadium application.

We could have answered the opponents' objections as we did later with our

'Fans of the Earth' initiatives. The Falmer For All logo had two green hills on it. With our Withdean experience, we approached everything about the new stadium fully aware of the environment and the need to protect it.

Martin Perry would have made it clear that we would protect the village at Falmer as we had protected the local area at Withdean – no car parking in the village and most spectators coming by bus and train. The good practice we had learned at Withdean was our obvious blueprint for Falmer, and something we would strongly have lobbied Prescott with.

We would have challenged the protesters' cases. They were able to get away with continuing to refer to the site as an Area of Outstanding Natural Beauty, which had been true when there was nothing there 40 years earlier except the University of Sussex beyond the main road. But since the University of Brighton campus had been built there, the site become an area planned for development – educational development. None of that case was made to Prescott when his advisors were telling him that our plans should be called in.

Prescott didn't categorically tell me he wouldn't have called it in, but he said, "I had no idea there was this vast public support for your stadium. I was never made aware of it."

As a politician, he naturally wanted popularity and to confirm that New Labour was the party of the people – Brighton and Hove now had three parliamentary seats that were all Labour-held marginals. And from what he was being told, the people didn't want the stadium. As the process went forward, I definitely had the feeling that there was an anti-stadium lobbyist among the civil servants in his department; the whole way they dealt with us, and Tony Allen and Peter Rainier, our lawyers. John Prescott himself confirmed to me that he had been strongly advised to call it in.

"What I was being told was that everyone was against it," he told me. "I was being shown various letters coming in from all these bodies that were lobbying – the Ramblers' Association, Friends of the Earth and so on, all complaining about it.

"The message I was being given was that there was no strong public support for the stadium. Your club was a dreadful club that had been mismanaged, sent to Kent and now wanted a new ground but didn't deserve one – all these points were made to me and I never heard your story.

"Of course, for all I know, you did lobby and I was never allowed to hear about it."

Sadly, I could only reply, "We didn't, John."

It was a mistake we would not repeat.

Within days of being admitted to Great Ormond Street, my granddaughter Emma had two successful operations, one to save her eyesight late one Saturday night, and the other to remove the brain tumour. Thank God, thanks to the brilliance of the surgeons, she was on the long road to recovery. Nothing mattered more that summer.

I had been frustrated in my efforts to replace Peter Taylor, although it had seemed there might be a breakthrough on the eve of the council vote on June 11, when Cameroon were knocked out of the World Cup by Germany in their final group game in Shizuoka.

That meant that Winfried Schäfer was now available for interview, but he was still on the other side of the world. What was more, the Cameroon FA had taken a very roundabout series of flights to the finals to save money and hadn't booked the return trip.

Undeterred, Schäfer somehow managed to persuade the US military to get him back to Europe. He got on a flight down to Clark Airbase in the Philippines, and then via a C-130 Hercules to Wiesbaden in Germany. By now I had moved on to Spain in preparation for my wedding, but he took two more flights to get to Malaga and met me at the Marbella Club.

He proved to be a most interesting guy, but I soon realised an obvious problem – his English was very poor. His agent did most of the talking, although I could tell that Winfried was intelligent, and that I could have got on with him.

We had a second meeting and I liked his ideas about football, but I thought, "If only this guy spoke English better. Because I need someone who can get a grip of the team straight away or we'll have our work cut out in Division One." He'd obviously swotted really hard, and it was so heartbreaking because he desperately wanted the job and I really wanted to give it to him, but it was just so exasperating for both of us. Of course I knew that Kerry, who is good with languages, has studied German – although having my wife alongside me every time I wanted to speak to my manager might have been a problem. It could cause confusion as to who was really the boss!

Pre-season was approaching and we still hadn't heard from Coppell, so by this time, in my mind, I began forming a back-up plan. Martin Hinshelwood had done a good job in youth development, had coached the first team more than once and had stood in as caretaker manager a couple of times. He was third choice but, if things didn't work out, I was prepared to give him a chance.

Meanwhile, there was the little matter of the wedding. The day we got married was June 21, the day England were beaten by Brazil in the World Cup quarter-final. I was watching the game in a bar in Gibraltar over the full Monty English breakfast. Michael Owen put us ahead, Brazil levelled after David

Beckham jumped out of a tackle, and we all know what happened in the second half – Ronaldinho's freak free-kick winner for Brazil.

After the game my best man, John Gold, tried to cheer me up by reminding me that I was getting married, so I decided I'd better find out if Kerry was in Gibraltar yet but when I tried to call her, I found my mobile had been stolen. I didn't know where the registry office was, but Gibraltar was so small that we managed to find it. After that, the day got better.

Athole called a few days later and told me that Steve had finally picked up the messages that he hadn't been able to get while up-country in Thailand. He'd be returning the next day via Hong Kong, landing at 10am on Saturday, and would be very happy to meet me at the Grafton Hotel on Tottenham Court Road the same morning. That was very convenient for the Great Ormond Street hospital, but I said to Athole, "He'll be jet-lagged."

"No, he'll be fine. He knows you've been trying to get hold of him and have been very generous in keeping the job open for him and he's very keen to meet you."

So I flew back to London, he met me at the hotel and I said, "Black coffee, Steve?"

"No, no, I'm fine," he replied.

But within minutes of us starting to talk, Coppell was nodding off and I realised it was pointless going any further. We spoke for about 45 minutes, but it wasn't really getting anywhere. So I terminated the meeting and said I'd get back to him. Although I later saw the funny side of a candidate falling asleep in an interview, was the prospect of managing Brighton really that unexciting, or was it more a comment on my interviewing style? I was so irritated after waiting all that time that I decided not to delay any longer.

I'd been under pressure from the fans to make an appointment. They must have thought, "Oh, he's in Spain getting married instead of finding a manager", unaware of the serious family problem, my misgivings about the stadium lobbying, and the difficulties I'd had with Coppell and Schäfer.

I'd asked Hinsh and Dean Wilkins to take pre-season training while our search continued, and I made a decision in the Grafton Hotel as soon as Steve Coppell had left. I rang Hinsh and asked him to meet me at my house in Haywards Heath and told him I was going to give him the job. He came to the house and took it in his stride.

Martin Hinshelwood is unflappable and he had been an important member of the staff since 1998. The first thing I'd done when Brian Horton took over from Steve Gritt was develop the way our youth system was being run. I had Hinsh top of my list because I knew he had been a good first-team coach under Barry Lloyd when we reached the 1991 play-off final, and we also interviewed Dean, who had captained that team. Both had passed with flying colours and were welcomed back into the club. They worked with the heads of the two centres of excellence, Vic Bragg at Worthing and John Lambert at Seaford, and began to produce players.

By 2002 players they had developed were on the verge of the first team and Hinsh was keen that they should be given their debuts, three in particular: Shaun Wilkinson, Dean Marney, and his nephew Adam Hinshelwood. But I thought we needed more fresh blood than that, and the first thing I said to Hinsh after giving him the job was, "Martin, we need to get this organised very quickly but we're short of quality players. There are one or two opportunities at the Arsenal."

I had an arrangement with Liam Brady that we could have our fair pick of loan players from Arsenal now that we were in the second tier, and so Hinsh and I went up to see a Saturday pre-season match between the Gunners reserves and Charlton at Barnet's Underhill ground.

Liam had already talked to Arsène Wenger on our behalf about Steve Sidwell, who had played well against us the previous season while on loan to Brentford – managed at the time by Steve Coppell – so we drove up to Barnet in Hinsh's car. Liam and Arsène were there and we said hi. Hinsh decided to go around to the other side of the ground to watch.

The game began and Sidwell was in central midfield, very recognisable with his ginger hair, doing exactly what I knew he could do. But even more notice-able was a big black guy playing on his right – very powerful, getting forward, tackling back, making strong runs. The shirts had no names on them, only numbers, so I had no idea who this No.7 was.

At half-time I was raving about him to Liam and we went over to Arsène.

"Ah, Dick, are you happy with Steve?" he said.

"My manager's over the other side of the ground, but yes, we'll definitely have him," I replied. "But who's the No.7? Could I have him too?"

Ignoring my first question, Wenger adopted his slightly quizzical look. "Why? What do you like about him?"

"He's such a powerful player, gets on the ball and looks to pass it – athletic, although he's quite bulky. Where did you get him?"

"His name's Kolo Toure. We got him from Beveren in Belgium, he comes from the Ivory Coast. We're not sure yet about his best position. You're a good judge. But if you think he's good you should see his brother."

By the end of the game I was absolutely certain that I wanted these two players and I said so to Arsène. "We'd love to have them – shall I get my manager to call you, Arsène, or Liam?"

He said, "Ask him to call me on Monday."

Arsenal were not only prepared to let us have both of them on loan, but for the whole season, so that gave us two terrific midfield players to strengthen our squad. I met up with Hinsh after the game and as we drove away from Underhill towards the motorway, I said, "We saw some real talent there, Martin. And guess what – we can get not only Sidwell but that No.7 as well. His name's Kolo Toure. Isn't that great?"

To my amazement, Hinsh paused and then replied, "I didn't really see anything here today that's better than we've got at Brighton."

I could hardly believe what I was hearing. I said, "Martin, these are quality players, they are way above anything we've got."

He said, "I honestly don't think we need them. We've got Shaun Wilkinson and Dean Marney."

I didn't put my foot down. He was my newly-appointed manager and I wasn't going to overrule him or impose those Arsenal players on him. I knew he would be reluctant to play them or would find reasons not to, and we had to make sure that anyone we took on loan would get to play, not sit on the bench – that was the whole point of loaning them out. Maybe once he'd seen them in training he'd have changed his mind, but I couldn't guarantee that to Arsène and Liam.

I was just astonished but I knew that Hinsh wanted to give our youngsters a chance, so I phoned Liam and explained. He said, "Dick, I think in the circumstances it would be better if you tell Arsène rather than me."

Arsène was fine about it. "That's okay, you have deferred to your manager and I understand," he said. Privately I was furious, but we began the season away to Burnley and Martin started Adam Hinshelwood, blooded Marney and Wilkinson off the bench, and we won easily, 3-1.

It was a perfect tonic, coming the day after the planning application had been called in, and the margin of victory could have been greater – a classic Bobby Zamora flicked header from a quickly-taken free kick by Paul Watson, which would have given us the lead, was wrongly disallowed for offside, but Steve Melton put us ahead before half-time, Paul Brooker scored a brilliant solo goal and Zamora got the third. We absolutely outplayed them and Martin had made a perfect start.

Adam Hinshelwood played like a veteran of 100 games, so it seemed that Martin's decision was being vindicated straight away, and good luck to him. But in fact his luck from then on was all bad. We drew 0-0 at home to Coventry, who played for 50 minutes with 10 men, then lost at home to Norwich on the Saturday – and kept on losing.

And in that game against Norwich, Zamora picked up a knee injury that sidelined him for weeks, which was very significant, and a huge blow to Hinsh.

The players didn't have the one man they knew they could always play the ball to, who would hold it up and make something happen. They had got used to playing with this talisman up front and he wasn't there. Naturally results suffered, and morale plummeted.

So it was a combination of negative factors. The team were playing at a higher level, missing their best player, and missing the experience of Simon Morgan, who had retired. Guy Butters came in at centre-half, but was clearly unfit, although he was to prove his worth later.

I began to think of the two guys sitting up at Highbury, where Arsenal still played then, who could have made such a difference. Our decline was a very sad thing to see. After 10 league defeats in a row, we were five points adrift of safety and I had to act because otherwise we might have been relegated by January.

I felt really sorry for Hinsh, but I didn't have any other choice. I told him I wouldn't be firing him, which most clubs would do, but I would be relieving him of his duties as first-team manager, and was offering him his old job back as head of youth development, which he gratefully accepted.

Steve Coppell was now helping out with coaching at Swindon under Andy King and I contacted Athole and arranged to meet Steve again. We met at the same hotel but I gave him a different sofa to stretch out on this time – not needed because this time Steve was sharp as a new pin. We talked about his football philosophy and I offered him the job there and then.

I said: "You know as well as I do how difficult your task is. The first thing you've got to do is install some morale back in the team, make them believe in themselves again. Zamora's back but we still need strengthening. It's unfortunate what happened in the summer, but let's not worry about that now, let's get on with it."

He accepted the job, and I immediately knew I had a real professional who analysed everything. He studied the opponents, he studied his own team, looking at weaknesses. One of the first things he said was, "I need some decent video equipment, because I disappear in the afternoons. From 2pm I'm at home looking at us and looking at the opposition."

I also said, to my third manager in a row, "I want you to work with the existing assistant manager." He had heard about Bob Booker and was fine with that. I explained that Bob was the perfect link-man between players and manager. He was a very good coach as well as being a good guy – funny, and a real personality. You need personalities in every walk of life, and Bob fitted into the ethos of what I was trying to create – a professional club but a friendly one.

We went about our work with huge determination but also with a sense of fun about it, because I find that gets you through all sorts of problems. I tried to run the club with very little of the politics that you find around most other organisations. I tried to let everyone be themselves. An open environment encourages people, knowing that they have been given the responsibility to get on with things. I wanted a team that was happy in their work both on and off the field. If people are happy they will do a good job. I wanted people to come up with ideas, think outside the box.

But I also kept standards high. I was very careful about the grammar in our publications, how the players represented the club – as regards their responsibilities. A standard player's contract talks about being required to make appearances in the community, but it's very vague. I went out of my way to stress to every new player that we were a genuine community club and that they would actually enjoy getting involved in helping people to improve their lives. In my book, the public, the fans, had risen up to save the club in the first place, so I was determined to give something back, to use the power of football to make a difference in our community.

Unfortunately, our community didn't witness an immediate upturn in our playing fortunes. Steve soon started giving the players back their confidence, but he also saw the scale of his task. We lost his first game in charge, snatching defeat from the jaws of victory at home to Sheffield United thanks to two very dubious penalty decisions from Phil Prosser, the referee.

Prosser was listed as being from West Yorkshire, which incensed some fans, including Ivor Caplin, who threatened to bring the matter up in the House of Commons. Then Prosser accused our fans of racism, which was a cheap trick and completely unfounded. The black player he alleged had been abused said he hadn't heard a thing. Next up was Crystal Palace away, Steve's old club. Police helicopters hovering over Selhurst Park made it feel like *Apocalypse Now*, and there certainly would have been the smell of napalm in the morning, or the late afternoon, if some of our fans had got hold of me.

We lost 5-0 and deserved to. Kerry Mayo was given a real roasting by their wide players, and Andy Johnson scored a hat-trick. They absolutely annihilated us, and it was the only game ever when an Albion fan really turned on me. The directors' box at Selhurst has no division from the rest of the seats and a guy came up to me, stood right in front of me and said, "You're a fucking arsehole – you appoint that ex-Palace wanker Steve Coppell and we've got a crap team, so put your hand in your fucking pocket and sort it."

He was vicious and very unpleasant, spitting venom at me because we'd lost a game against Crystal Palace. He was in a suit and looked as if he'd just come from the office and I thought it was sad that football could make people feel like that. I certainly didn't respond in kind. I just ignored him.

But I did think, "You ungrateful bastard. We've saved the club and we're now in the First Division, not the Conference. We're already more than 'Halfway between the Gutter and the Stars'" – the title I'd borrowed from a recent Norman Cook album for our first promotion season's Christmas video.

But those two defeats meant we were even more embedded at the bottom of the table, five points behind 23rd place and nine from safety. After that, Steve started changing things. He brought in Dean Blackwell in central defence, a solid, reliable centre-half who had played for Wimbledon in the Premier League, to play alongside Danny Cullip, and Simon Rodger, a former Palace player but an Albion fan, to give us know-how in midfield.

With all of us dreading a thirteenth successive defeat, my niece Michele came up with a winner. She decided to loan me her lucky '13' gold pendant her mother had given her and said that that would do the trick. It worked. Bobby scored twice in the next game, a 3-2 win at home to Bradford – thanks Michele – and the confidence began to spread to the other players.

After the Palace game, Steve had said, "That left-back . . ." meaning Kerry Mayo, and just shook his head. But Kerry fought back because he's a good footballer and a brave one. He had to prove himself over and over again, to a series of managers. "Time to do it again, Kerry," I'd say to him when a new man took over. But he did it. All the managers he worked with got to know that they could rely on him to play the way he'd been asked to. And, unlike some players, he cared about being a professional footballer and worked hard at it.

Three weeks later, Kerry scored the only goal of the match against Derby at Withdean, a late winner for our second victory in three matches, either side of a magnificent 1-1 draw at Wolves live on Sky. Zamora scored with a clever chip at Molineux and Michel Kuipers made an unbelievable double save. Both incidents are still shown on the big screen before games at the Amex.

We gradually started clawing our way back towards the pack, and I said to Steve, "Hopefully we can get Sidwell and Toure now, but bearing in mind what happened before, let me speak to Liam and Arsène Wenger."

Steve was happy with that so I spoke to Liam first and he agreed that I should call Arsène. I said, "Arsène, it's Dick Knight from Brighton. I've made a change of manager, so could we now have Steve Sidwell and Kolo Toure for the rest of the season?"

Wenger chuckled. "No. I said you were a good judge of a player and I was right. I'm turning Toure into a centre-half and I will be playing him in the first team very soon. Sorry, but you had your chance. But Sidwell, okay."

In retrospect, Kolo Toure's career at Arsenal and later Manchester City and Liverpool was probably helped by not coming to Brighton, although I'm absolutely certain that if he and Sidwell had both been with us from the start, we would never have got relegated that season. And who knows how we would have progressed from that point?

If we were battling against the odds on the field, then the same proved to be true off it. The Public Inquiry into our application for Falmer opened in February 2003 at Hove Town Hall, and we began in a spirit of optimism. After all, the city council had overwhelmingly approved our complex and extremely well-prepared planning application. It was as comprehensive as it could be, even though we would still have to augment it with expert testimony at the inquiry.

And we were over one of our biggest hurdles – or so we thought. Even before Brighton & Hove Council had officially earmarked Village Way, Falmer as the site for a community stadium in the draft Local Plan back in August 2000, we had begun discussions with the University of Brighton over the prospect of being their near neighbours, and the issues and opportunities arising.

The vision which Martin and I had presented to the university's vice-chancellor, Sir David Watson, and his colleagues was a Sport Falmer complex, featuring the stadium and a separate indoor sports arena, providing basketball, squash and other indoor sports facilities for student and public use, with the prospect of integrating the university's sports science and sports medicine faculties, then housed in Eastbourne, into the scheme. After we showed them plans as to how Sport Falmer would be part of a new campus layout, the university informed us they couldn't take it further as they had other plans for the site. Disappointing – but we weren't going away.

We had more meetings, and the main stumbling block became the price we should pay for the small piece of land we needed from them. I formed the view from the beginning that Sir David didn't want football fans anywhere near his halls of academe, so he demanded a huge sum that was either designed to put us off, or was an attempt to get many more millions from us than the land was actually worth. Either way, that wasn't going to happen. And by October 2001, we had made enough progress in negotiations with the university to allow us to submit our planning application to the council.

Further negotiations followed, with me reminding them that I was one of the residents whose council had given the University of Brighton the land free 40 years earlier, and by the time of the council vote and then the Public Inquiry, we had an agreement in place to pay the university what I considered was a reasonable sum for the land, way below what they had originally wanted, but still a financial win for Sir David and his institution.

The inquiry got under way on February 18 2003. I was there about 80 per cent of the time, while Martin was there every day. Every expert we had spoke very professionally about the traffic impact plan, the environmental assessment plan, whatever, under rigorous questioning from not only the inspector but also barristers from Lewes, Falmer and all the environmental groups represented in the inquiry. Martin and I were also interrogated by the same people.

We went through our evidence in advance with Jonathan Clay. We were schooled as to how the questions would come at us and how best to respond, but we both knew the case back to front. Jonathan also told us to be ourselves, that we were both convincing people and he didn't want us to come across as slick business suits.

In one of the sessions Charlie Hopkins, the very experienced barrister for the Falmer residents, who looked like a long-haired hippy straight out of Woodstock, was questioning me about the Goldstone. I knew he was a Newport County supporter, so I replied, "If you like I'll tell you about my all-time favourite game there, when we beat Newport 9-1 and Johnny McNichol scored four." That brought a smile from Charlie.

The fans who gave evidence were all very convincing, as were Des Lynam and Peter Lee, from the Football Trust, when they spoke. And David Davies came from the FA and gave evidence, which was very telling. He said, "The blame for this football club's position does not lie with those who are trying to resurrect it now but with those who mismanaged it in the past. The whole of football wants them to get the stadium." Davies's and Lee's statements were very supportive, coming as they did from the top levels of football.

Unfortunately, the proceedings ground to a halt in June. The University of Brighton had thrown another spanner in the works. I think they saw the Public Inquiry as a further chance to stop the stadium development happening.

When we had started negotiating with them over the Section 106 agreement, which is the operational way of making a planning application work, Brighton & Hove Council was the majority landowner and the third partner in the agreement. We went to the inquiry with an entirely reasonable 106 document on the table for all parties to sign up to. But now the university wanted to revisit the deal and wanted more control themselves, stating they didn't trust the council to enforce traffic regulations on the stadium properly. I think they hoped that if they could spin things out we might give up or go out of business completely, as we were still losing money even though we were in the second tier.

But Martin and I were made of sterner stuff. With our team we came up with a plan to circumvent the university's objections by submitting an additional application to the council for a new access to the coach park/drop off area at the stadium, which would keep traffic further away from the university. The council would play ball, but we still needed extra time to prepare it. So John Collyer, the inspector, adjourned the inquiry with the resumption set for October.

While the meticulous procedures of the inquiry frustrated the life out of me, there were more promising signs on the field. We signed Ivar Ingimarsson, a fine central defender and another of Steve's former Brentford players, on loan from Wolves in February, and in the same month 43-year-old Dave Beasant, still a fine goalkeeper, and effervescent striker Tony Rougier joined. Rougier immediately endeared himself to Albion fans by scoring the only goal against Millwall two minutes after coming on, for our third win in a row.

But no one did more than Sidwell to help us close the gap. Two games stand out. One when we were 2-0 down at home to Burnley at half-time on December 28 and Alastair Campbell, the Prime Minister's press secretary and a big Burnley fan, was crowing about his team's display at the break. Sidwell pulled one back a minute from time and then equalised in the last few seconds. We were very pleased with that point, even though Burnley were only mid-table at the time, because of the fighting spirit it showed in the team and our fiery redhead.

"You lucky bastards," Alastair said afterwards. But he added, "That Sidwell is one hell of a player."

The other game was at Preston, another match in which we came from behind. Sidwell played a one-two with Zamora on the halfway line as he broke out of defence on a quick counter-attack. Zamora, wide on the left, instantly controlled the pass and stroked the ball 30 yards between two defenders, right into Sidwell's stride, and he hammered it in from 20 yards. Bobby remembers that goal as "the best pass I ever played".

Eventually, on the last day of the season, we had got ourselves off the bottom of the table. To stay up, we needed to win at Grimsby, who were below us and already down, and hope that Reading could do us a favour by winning at Stoke. But they lost, we drew and we were relegated.

It was a sad day for another reason too. It was Zamora's last game for us. It was the right time for him to go, and he went to the top flight with my best wishes. He had done a season with us in the Championship, which I had asked him to do. He had scored 14 goals even though he missed a large chunk of the season. For all the outstanding ability he'd displayed for us, the only offer we had at that time came from Tottenham. Their manager, Glenn Hoddle, had been to see Bobby so many times that I thought of issuing him with a season ticket. He never spoke to me or Steve Coppell.

I'd turned down an offer from Bill Kenwright, the Everton owner, the previous season. Bill is a great guy and was the only Premier League chairman who wrote to me in 2011 congratulating us on the opening of our new stadium. Walter Smith was the manager and had watched Bobby a few times – once with Bill – at Withdean and a couple of away games, but I got the feeling he wasn't that keen. There was one occasion when Zamora was a bit off his game and Smith left 20 minutes into the second half. I thought, "Good – that's another club that won't be trying to buy him."

Bill, though, had said to me at a couple of functions that he liked Zamora, and one day I got a call from him. He was anxious to buy Bobby and he would have gone up to £3 million. Both his two main strikers, Duncan Ferguson and Kevin Campbell, were injured.

I said, "Your manager isn't certain about him at all, is he?"

He replied, "It's me pursuing this, Dick."

I had an arrangement to inform Bobby and his father of any bid, so I told his dad, but I added, "He'll get in the team initially, but once Ferguson and Campbell come back, Bobby will be out of the team, playing in the reserves, isolated in an unfamiliar area. It's not like going to a London club." He didn't disagree.

I got back to Bill Kenwright and said, "We're not interested, Bill. The player is going to stay here and help us into the second tier."

And of course he did, scoring around another 25 goals, but when we were relegated it was time to give Bobby his chance in the Premier League, which meant dealing with Tottenham and their chairman, Daniel Levy. His negotiating style is to play hardball, take it or leave it. If he's buying he likes to give you the impression that he's doing you a favour and couldn't care less whether the deal comes off or not. I think in this case there was an element of truth in that. It was Hoddle who wanted Bobby, but he wasn't in a 100 per cent solid position as Tottenham manager.

So when Levy called me he was even more offhand than usual, despite Hoddle's regular appearances being widely reported.

Levy said, "There's been all this press talk about Zamora. Where do you stand on it?"

I started by saying, "We're looking for £2.5 million pounds."

Levy replied, "You've got to be joking. We're talking about £750,000."

Bearing in mind that I could have got £3 million from Everton, I thought I was being reasonable. And also in the back of my mind was the fact that I had to pay 30 per cent of any profit to Bristol Rovers. At that level of sell-on, it has an effect on your negotiations. It makes it very hard to get a fee that is worthwhile. So anyone who thinks they are being clever in negotiating a 50 per cent sell-on clause, think again. Even at £2.5 million I would only be getting £1,680,000 – 70 per cent of the profit on the original £100,000. Rovers would be getting £720,000 extra for a player they hadn't really reckoned at all. But that was the deal.

And in any case, Levy wasn't offering anything like that. I said, "Sorry, I'm not selling at that price."

It would have helped if Tottenham had had any competition, then I could have played one club off against another. But there was none. I wonder whether other clubs had been scared off by me turning down Everton, or whether it was that they knew Tottenham were determined to get him. Either way it was good news for Bobby's agent, Phil Smith, because it left more money available for personal terms negotiations.

There was a further complication in that Paul Kemsley, a Tottenham director, knew a relative of one of the Albion directors. When Levy called me again, he started telling me things about the Albion that he must have got from somebody close to the club, and Kemsley's name cropped up. "You need this money, and I know you'd accept £1 million."

I said, "Your man Kemsley may be friends with [I named the person I suspected] but that doesn't mean you have any idea what I'll take for our biggest asset."

In fact, Levy was right in that we did need the money to fight our continuing planning battles. But although he was a tough negotiator, so was I – and I wasn't giving away our crown jewel for £1 million and ended the conversation. I intended to hold out for £2.5 million and I went away on holiday to Sardinia.

The Italian season had just ended, and the resort that Kerry and I were in, Forte Village, seemed to be full of Serie A stars and their families. Alessandro Nesta and Fabio Cannavaro were there and I joined in a five-a-side kickabout in the sports area with them and their kids one evening.

Levy phoned a couple more times and I gradually inched him up to £1.5 million, at which point I realised that I had squeezed all I could out of him. And of course Zamora was desperate to join Spurs; his agent had been in discussions with them for weeks. I finally agreed the deal over the phone on a terrace in Sardinia, 20 yards from where Nesta was playing keepy-uppy with his kids.

It was frustrating to settle for half the amount Everton had offered, but the consolation was that we had benefited from Bobby's talents for another season and a half, or slightly less because of the injury he suffered. Even so, the £1.5 million transfer broke our club record. Sadly we had to give £420,000 of it to my friend Geoff Dunford at Bristol Rovers, much more than the £250,000 he'd originally asked for, and all because we'd done the hard work of nurturing a great player and helping him fulfil his potential. He'd scored 83 goals for us in 136 appearances.

I told Steve Coppell, who had assumed a deal would be done. I knew there wouldn't be any problem over personal terms for Bobby who was joining a big London club where he knew people like Ledley King, having played with him for the Senrab boys' club in east London.

Unfortunately Bobby's career at Tottenham never got under way because Hoddle was sacked, after he had only made six appearances, and replaced by David Pleat, who obviously didn't rate him. He never scored a league goal for Spurs and went to West Ham in February 2004 in part-exchange for Jermain Defoe.

Bobby is a tremendous player, a dedicated professional and a very likeable person. He knows his worth as a top striker, and he's made the most of his talent. He was unlucky not to play for England more than he did. He would have gone to the World Cup in South Africa if he had been fit, but he played for Fulham in the Europa League final in Hamburg because he felt he owed it to the club, and it killed any chance he had of going to South Africa. He told me that Fabio Capello had phoned him more than once with advice, anxious to help him get fit. Zamora would have done well in internationals for the same reason he played well in Europe for Fulham – his touch is so good and he flourished in a quick-passing environment.

Steve was very low after our relegation, but he had come close to pulling off an amazing escape and had only grown in my esteem over the season, even though I couldn't say I got as close to him as I did to some other managers. Steve was a very private person, who very rarely revealed anything of his personal life. The only insights I was able to get happened because his family, who were still based on Merseyside, would come to some northern away matches. It was obvious they were very proud of him.

At Withdean he would come and sit next to me in the first half, but would barely say a word. He said it was so that he could watch the game from an elevated position – all of six or seven rows back! All you'd get out of him was the occasional grunt, and if I made even the smallest of small talk – and always about the game – he'd just say, "Yep." He wouldn't even say, "See you after the game" at half-time. He'd just disappear a few minutes before the whistle so that he would be in the dressing room when the players got in there. He never sat with me in the second half, but always went straight to the dugout. He had his routine and never deviated from it.

Coppell was a great analyst. He would tell you things about the opposition before a game and be proved absolutely right. He would spend hours watching videos. He'd say, "I missed out on dinner last night because I was still watching Watford at 10pm." He is still the most intelligent and the most cerebral manager I've met. He could talk about anything – not that he usually wanted to.

But Steve had a humanity about him. While we were compiling the retained list before he went off to the Far East again, Dean Blackwell's name came up. Dean was unlikely to be fit, but Steve said, "Look, this guy did a good job for us and wasn't on much money. If we give him a four-month contract, it gives him a chance to find another club." So I did and Steve said, "That's really good of you, Dick." When I next saw Dean he thanked me. The other directors thought it a waste of our precious playing budget.

When Coppell got back from Asia, we had the job of filling the hole left by Zamora. Replacing him like-for-like was impossible, but we did our best with Leon Knight from Chelsea – no relation. He was only 5' 4", but a handful on and off the pitch, as Steve knew. But he also told me that he was a really good player.

So we knew what we were getting, and after a short and successful loan spell, Knight joined us on a permanent deal that I negotiated with David Barnard and Gwyn Williams at Chelsea. They sold him to us for £100,000 plus a 20 per cent sell-on clause, which they considered was doing us a favour. It was still a lot of money, but we had just received more than £1 million net from Tottenham for Bobby.

Our other attempts at signings weren't so successful. I'd already said to David Dein at Arsenal that I wanted to buy Sidwell, but they'd had an offer from Reading, of £300,000. I said I'd match it, and David said he'd leave it up to the player. Steve and I spoke to Sidwell but Reading had offered him Championship football in a stadium the like of which I could only promise in the future.

Steve also wanted to buy winger Stephen Hunt from his old club, Brentford. He had shown some moments of magic against us in their 4-0 win at Griffin Park a couple of years earlier. "He's got this devil in him to hurt defenders, to humiliate them," Steve said. But I wasn't convinced about him and said that £25,000 was too much to pay for such an unpredictable player. Steve was later proved right, and we missed out thanks to an error of judgement by the chairman.

When the 2003/04 season started, the team didn't look very different except up front where we had the pint-sized Knight instead of Zamora. But he did just as well. He scored 27 goals in his first season. In the opening game at Oldham, he scored twice – once with a header – and could have had a hat-trick when he was brought down for a penalty early on. But as he was about to pick the ball up to put it on the spot, big Darius Henderson, who was on loan from Reading, grabbed it, put it down and drilled it into the corner of the net for the opening goal. Knight was still remonstrating with him as the team came off, having won 3-1.

Early in the season, Gordon Strachan came to see one of our games and said to me, "That Leon Knight, what a good player, but damned difficult to manage."

He'd taken a Coventry City youth team to a tournament in Singapore, which Chelsea were also playing in. And Gordon had seen Leon in the plush Shangri-La Hotel, in the bars and living it up. His attitude seemed to be, "I'm a footballer, I can do whatever I like." Strachan said, "He'll never make the most of his talent" and he was right. That was his best season. By 2006 I'd sold him to Swansea because we'd had enough of him.

We started pretty well and looked reasonably well-placed to challenge for a return to the Championship when, in late September, Alan Pardew left Reading for West Ham and I soon got a call from John Madejski, Reading's chairman. I wasn't at all surprised. Madejski had said to me at the Football League conference that summer how impressed he had been with the way Steve had nearly kept us up. "You made a great move getting Steve Coppell, he almost saved you."

There had been nothing in Steve's demeanour that said he wanted to leave. But I knew that he wanted one more crack at the Premier League. One lunchtime weeks earlier, I had sat with him and said, "Steve, you and I get on pretty well, we have the same footballing ethos, and we know this club is heading in the right direction. I want to offer you a job for the next 10 years. I want you to be manager for as long as you like, then develop your successor. By the time we go to the new stadium I want you to be director of football. To control our entire football strategy."

He said, "Thank you, Dick. No one's ever made me an offer of that scale. But I still hanker to manage in the Premier League again. And I know that the only way I'm going to do it is to take a team there from the Championship, rather than be appointed. I'm past it as far as Premier League clubs are concerned. If you were going into your stadium now, it would be different."

The Falmer thing was rumbling on with no sign of a conclusion. Steve understood the issues and the frustrations we felt. But it meant that I knew what would happen when the call from Reading came through. I like Madejski and he told me, "I'm ringing about Steve. I'd like to take him off you. I know I'm going to have to pay compensation, so tell me how much."

I said, "Have you spoken to him?"

He answered, "Officially? No. But unofficially, Alan [Pardew, who had played for Steve at Palace] has." Madejski told you straight, which I appreciated.

"Fine, John, but I'm going to want a decent amount of compensation because, as you know, he's done a good job for us, and I recently offered him a long contract. I'll speak to him and if he's interested, I'll give him permission to talk to you. I know – and you probably know this already – he wants another crack at the top flight and he's got a better chance with you than with us at the moment. Not only because we've just gone down, but because you've got a stadium."

Anyway, the value of the remaining period of his contract was around £200,000. I said, "I want the full value of his contract, which is nothing in player terms, and you'll be acquiring a snip for that sort of money, assuming Steve wants to join you."

John didn't haggle, although he sounded tempted, "I thought you might ask for £100,000."

I replied, "John, do I look naive?"

He knew that I would stand my ground, but I hadn't tried to bump up the price either. "You can check his earnings on his P60 when it comes to you," I said. "That's what I want – and I want it all in one lump." He agreed.

The cash would help to pay the wage bill, which was always an issue given our costs at Withdean.

So I told Steve who of course knew that I would be getting that phone call from Madejski. He said, "I'm sorry, Dick, but I have to go. This is that last chance I wanted."

Yet again the absence of a resolution to the Falmer question had cost us a manager.

# CHAPTER TWENTY ONE

# "CAN WE HAVE ONE OF THESE PLEASE"

As usual, we got a great number of applications for our once-again vacant job but I very quickly narrowed the field down to two – Leroy Rosenior, who was managing Torquay United, and Mark McGhee, who was out of work at the time, having recently left Millwall. He had also done a good job as a pundit on Sky's *Soccer Saturday* and spoke a lot of sense, as my wife Kerry told me.

The key for me with regard to Mark was that he had taken Millwall up from the division we were in, as recently as 2001. We were in second place, on the verge of bouncing straight back after relegation, and we needed to maintain that momentum. I spoke to Theo Paphitis about Mark, with some trepidation as he had just sacked him, but he confirmed that Mark knew his job.

I interviewed both Leroy and Mark, twice, and in the end decided to give the job to McGhee. He was experienced and a very mature guy. But it was a close thing. I talked to the Torquay chairman, Mike Bateson, a real character, about paying compensation for his manager. I was very impressed with Leroy. He spoke very intelligently about the game and I liked the way his team played, bringing the ball out from the back, passing it, almost in the style of West Ham, where he'd played.

But because we were in such a good position, and I'd seen how Steve Coppell's savvy had got the team organised and motivated quickly, once again I opted for experience over promise and potential.

As with Steve, Mark was very articulate and could talk intelligently about a wide range of subjects. He completely understood our financial situation and that there would be no point knocking on my door asking for a bigger transfer budget. And he instantly accepted, as had Peter Taylor and Steve, that he would be inheriting Bob Booker and the rest of the coaching staff.

He was also very much his own man, evidence of which was the fact that he had fallen out with Alex Ferguson when he was manager of Wolves, over Alex's son Darren. Up to then, Mark had been one of Alex's blue-eyed boys, one of his favourite sons, and perhaps even an intended successor.

Mark had been a key member of Alex's Aberdeen team, and what a school for future managers that club turned out to be. But he dropped Darren Ferguson from the Wolves team and Alex was on the phone almost immediately, but Mark stuck to his guns. "Darren wasn't playing very well so I dropped him," Mark told me. "I caught it – I got the hairdryer treatment down the phone."

It was a fairly seamless transition. It had been a difficult choice to make, but now Mark needed to get on with it. When Coppell left, we were in second place, but with Bob Booker in temporary charge, after initially going top following two straight wins, we had slumped to seventh on the back of a poor run by the time McGhee arrived in early November. As Christmas approached, he had us back up to fourth.

Bob Pinnock retired from the role of finance director in September 2003 after six years' sterling – if you will forgive the pun – service to the club. He was replaced by Robert Comer, partner in a local firm of accountants, who was known to Derek Chapman, Ray Bloom, my brother-in-law Michael, and was also Tony Bloom's personal accountant.

Bob's accounts team stayed on: another of my former agency colleagues Ian Andrews, financial controller, our very own Johnny Cash man, who always dressed in black, played in a rock band, and walked the bottom line very skilfully. And Edward David, diligent and always willing, who was everyone's idea of the old-style friendly local bank manager.

When the public inquiry resumed on October 14, the coach park/drop off application was approved and in place, and the University of Brighton finally withdrew its objections to the stadium and signed agreements with the club and council to proceed.

On October 23 John Collyer, the planning inspector, brought the Public Inquiry – 39 days spread over nine months – to an end. The mood in our team was super-confident; our barrister Jonathan Clay's closing submission had been superb, the case for the stadium had been presented as robustly as could be imagined, and all the points raised by the opposition appeared to have been answered – surely nothing could go wrong now.

But I'm certain the rift with the university had an effect on the planning inspector. In Collyer's subsequent report, it said that the partners were clearly not together. That was to prove more damaging than the delay.

On December 1, Des Lynam, Norman Cook and I, along with Lord Bassam, Tim Carder and Paul Samrah, delivered more than 6,200 letters and a summary of the 61,452-signature petition to 10 Downing Street. It got good press, but we didn't get to enter the inner sanctum, we just handed them in at the door to be passed on to the Office of the Deputy Prime Minister, John Prescott. But it was a good way to make sure we kept our case before the politicians and public.

After the Public Inquiry, our advisors were absolutely satisfied that we had done everything possible and we were going to get the right outcome – approval from Collyer. But even now I was adamant that we should make sure that Prescott got the message, even while the inspector was mulling over his findings.

Collyer wasn't the only one doing that. During the inquiry Charles Hoile, the Local Plan inspector, had been sitting alongside Collyer, we all thought just as an observer. The inquiry into the Local Plan, which included the Falmer stadium, was just coming to its conclusion. Hoile never said a word during the whole stadium inquiry, apart from the occasional whisper to Collyer, and was very po-faced. You could never tell what he was thinking.

The strong opinion of our law firm and barrister was that we would win, but sadly they were wrong. That was suddenly made plain to us when, through pure good fortune, Hoile announced his findings first. When he issued his Local Plan report on February 4 2004, he included in it a damning attack on the stadium at Falmer.

He said the site was too small, and that "a provincial city's professional football club was not a national consideration and should not override planning policy which restricts development on the South Downs. Only limited university expansion could be contemplated on the Falmer site". He listed four possible alternative sites: Brighton Station, Withdean, Toads Hole Valley and Sheepcote Valley, which he seemed to favour.

From that conclusion it was obvious that his colleague, Collyer, would come out in his report with similar findings in the near future. But this time I had learned the lesson of the weeks of inactivity before the application was called in for public inquiry; we had to start some real campaigning – and we had to do it fast.

The mood of the first Falmer For All meeting after Hoile's report was unbowed. We'd already had so many knock-backs, and experienced the University of Brighton's delaying tactics. This was a huge blow. But I wasn't down. I was used to the feeling that this was never going to be an easy ride, inured to it. It was my job to make everyone quickly realise that we would fight on, up our game even more.

It was a massive stroke of luck that Hoile reported six weeks before Collyer. It gave us a six-week window of opportunity and, although it was unlikely we could change Collyer's mind, his recommendation would be going to Prescott, the man we had to influence. We might have missed the chance to lobby him after the Brighton & Hove Council 11-1 vote, but now it was critical to make him and his political advisors fully aware that the inspector's recommendation would be going against the democratic will of the people – nationwide, not just Brighton fans.

In the succession of Falmer For All meetings that quickly followed, the atmosphere was inspiring. Everyone just gritted their teeth and said, "We're not going to be beaten by this" and then came up with lots of good ideas for giving the campaign real bite.

We started by sending emails out to all Premier League and Football League clubs, getting them to put messages on their websites and in their match programmes – giving them the contact details of Falmer For All for more information so that their fans could send appropriate emails and letters to the Office of the Deputy Prime Minister. We wanted people around the country to bombard his office.

A few days after Hoile's plan came out, we played away at Wycombe Wanderers on Saturday February 7. There was a sit-in on the pitch after the final whistle, joined by myself, Martin and our players – very peaceful, because our fans had approached Wycombe and told them what we planned to do. It was in most of the Sunday papers.

On February 10, Prescott's department email crashed, swamped by the weight of thousands of messages from all over the country. Boy, did that make an impact, as he later told me. Suddenly he realised this was a huge issue. The same day, 89 bouquets of blue flowers, one from every other league club – except Crystal Palace who didn't answer FFA's calls and Southend United who also had a stadium application in at the time – arrived in his office in Whitehall.

On Valentine's Day, we were away to Grimsby Town, just across the Humber Bridge from Prescott's constituency, Hull East. The Falmer For All team made a huge Valentine's card and a group of fans going to the game took a detour to be there when it arrived at his constituency office, Bill and Jan Swallow having borrowed the team's kit van to deliver it. Prescott wasn't there but his constituency workers took it round to his house and he put it up in his kitchen.

The front of the card had two big hearts on it – one red, one blue-and-white stripes – with the words: "Be our Valentine, Mr Prescott. Roses are red, violets are blue, our club's future is all down to you. Please say YES to our new stadium."

I know he loved that. It really got to him. He told me when I met him that he'd said to Pauline, his wife, "That card, what a nice touch. Those fans at that football club in Brighton, aren't they clever? They're all together, they're not fighting the club. All they want is a football stadium and they deserve a slap on the back from me." As opposed to a slap in the face from Collyer.

If the initiatives had come from the club rather than the fans, it would have looked like nothing more than a vested interest, and the voice could not have been so loud. It was the voice of hundreds of thousands of fans from all around the country. No club had ever mobilised that sort of response before. It was an example of what fan power can do when supporters believe a cause is just.

That was the first time that John Prescott became aware of the huge support for the stadium. If we hadn't taken action, it would have been all over. When John Collyer recommended against Falmer, Prescott would have simply killed the whole thing.

Sure enough, Collyer's report came out in March, strongly condemning our plans for Falmer, as we expected. If we hadn't mounted that huge campaign, Prescott would have followed his inspector's advice and rubber-stamped his recommendation. And that would have been the end of it.

For some reason Collyer ignored the compelling evidence for Falmer. Instead, like Hoile, he wanted us to go to Sheepcote Valley, which was ridiculous because of the transport problems. There was no railway access, and all traffic coming from the east and west along the A27 would have turned off onto the B2107 – and gone through Falmer! On top of that, central Brighton would have been gridlocked by local match-day traffic.

But I needed to rally the troops again – to convey to the Falmer For All team and all the fans after the publication of Collyer's negative report that the club was going to fight this to the absolute end. We were not going to bow down.

We never let up on Falmer, the tempo of the campaign was maintained. Everywhere John Prescott went, he later told me, in this country and even in places like Hong Kong, people would come up to him and ask him what he was going to do about Brighton & Hove Albion.

On the field, the team was in touch with the promotion places, and we got five very valuable goals in 10 games from Trevor Benjamin, who came on loan from Leicester City in January – coincidentally a player Peter Taylor had signed for them. But they wouldn't let us keep him so we had to look elsewhere.

In March we got Chris Iwelumo, who was to play a vital role, on a free transfer from Stoke for the rest of the season. I went with Dean White to see him play a reserve game at Newcastle-under-Lyme against Bradford City and my great-nephew Michael Standing was playing as he was recovering from injury. I was impressed by his partner in central midfield that day, Paul Reid, so I phoned Michael up on the way home and asked him about Reid. "He was better than you," I said. "I agree – on the day," came the reply. And we ended up signing him.

And we'd seen enough of Iwelumo to know that he could do a good job alongside Leon Knight. Two days later, on his debut away to Chesterfield, he scored an absolute screamer, cutting inside from the left and walloping the ball into the far corner. He told me it was the best goal he had ever scored.

In the end, we fell short of automatic promotion by six points, but we made the play-offs. We went to Swindon for the first leg of the semi-final on a scorching-hot Sunday, and I have to say that they were unlucky. We were dangerous on the break, but they struck the woodwork more than once. It was Chippy Carpenter who broke the deadlock fairly late on with a volley that was deflected in, at the end where all our fans were, to make it 1-0 to the Albion. So we came back to Brighton, our high spirits somewhat deflated by huge traffic jams caused by a terrible accident on the A23 at Pyecombe.

We faced the home leg, on May 20, with huge expectation and an assumption that if we had beaten Swindon in Wiltshire, we'd have no trouble finishing the job and going on to the Millennium Stadium in Cardiff to play Bristol City, who had beaten Hartlepool in the other semi-final.

But in fact the pattern of the match was very similar to the first game. Only this time they scored, through Sam Parkin nine minutes from time, and the game went into extra time, when they scored again, through Rory Fallon. We were staring defeat in the face, and I always remember Danny Cullip recounting the story of Parkin winding him up near the end of the game by telling him that he'd text him from the Millennium Stadium in Cardiff on the day of the play-off final.

Parkin's jibe, of course, only made Danny even more determined and he pushed forward. He had this inspirational cry of "Winner, winner, winner" and it rang out at the now otherwise quiet, rainy Withdean. Extra time was just going into added time when we got a throw-in on the left. Charlie Oatway took it, Danny headed it on and Adam Virgo made up yards of ground, threw himself at the ball and nodded it in.

Pandemonium. I was good friends with Willie Carson, the Swindon chairman and famous jockey, but he had been really lording it, yelling at me, "We've done it, Dick, we've done it" until the 121st minute, and suddenly he was absolutely crestfallen.

So it went to penalties. I remember saying to Mark when we were having lunch before the play-offs that I had a feeling penalties would be involved at some point, either in the final or semi-final. He said, "I agree. I've got the players rehearsing them."

I asked if he'd chosen his five penalty takers and he said, "I have in my mind, but I'm doing it with all of them. You could get to nine or 10 penalties."

I said, "One of the things that must be most nerve-racking is the walk from the halfway line. The tension building up with every step."

He replied, "We're covering that too. We're giving them positive ideas, things to distract them from everything except the kick."

It was very well thought through, and of course when the moment came we scored every one. I remember Virgo's penalty: if it hadn't gone in, just under the bar, it would have been a menace to Gatwick air traffic control. It almost ripped the net out of the ground.

Our goalkeeper, Ben Roberts, who I really liked, was a very interesting char-acter − a natural backpacker at heart who regularly took himself off to remote parts of the world such as the High Andes. Now it was Ben's chance to be a hero and he took it, saving Tommy Mooney's penalty. It wasn't Mooney's night − he'd been voted Swindon's player of the season, but he'd missed his penalty, and he was supposed to be marking Virgo when he scored. And when Andy Gurney hit their fifth against the post, we were on our way to Cardiff. Cue a further eruption and, despite the teeming rain, everyone went on the pitch, including me. Danny sought out Parkin and told him, "*I'll* text *you!*" Brilliant.

The media wanted to talk to me and I was doing a Sky TV interview under a couple of umbrellas when, out of the corner of my eye, I saw a sad-faced Willie Carson emerging from the Swindon dressing room. As the interview continued, a bedraggled Willie came over, prodded me in the chest and shouted, live on national TV, "You lucky bastard." I put my arm round his shoulder and hugged him.

By reaching the final, we had not only given ourselves the chance to be promoted, but also to present our case for Falmer on a big stage. We made part of that case simply by taking 31,000 fans to Cardiff. Even we had only expected 27,000, and the only time Withdean ever got gridlocked because of the Albion was when we sold those tickets at the ground on the previous Saturday.

Falmer For All made the most of the exposure live on national TV, making sure that banners with our message were draped from every tier at our end of the stadium, 'Please, Mr Prescott, can we have one of these?' And postcards had been given out to the queues of fans buying tickets for the final. The cards, with a picture of our Falmer mock-up with the words 'Wish we were here', were to be sent to John Prescott, of course, posted from Cardiff.

It had been Martin Perry's wedding in Surrey the day before the play-off final, which was on Sunday May 30, after which I took my children David and

Amanda and grandsons Max, Sam and Louis down to Cardiff. We stayed at the St David's Hotel in Cardiff Bay – very trendy and very expensive.

Eddie Izzard was also staying there, because he's a Crystal Palace fan and they'd won the First Division play-off final against West Ham on the Saturday – when even some Palace fans had displayed a banner calling for our stadium to go ahead, which just proved how universal the support was. Eddie came up to us in the bar and said, "Good luck tomorrow, although I'm not sure you deserve it."

I replied, "You're from Bexhill, Eddie. You should support the Albion."

On the day of the game, Cardiff seemed to be full of Albion fans. The sun shone, and there was the promise of a great occasion. As one-off games go, it was completely different from the dire mood of Hereford. Albion fans were just thrilled to be there whatever the outcome.

I was asked to do a BBC Radio 5 Live interview in the tunnel 10 minutes before kick-off, with the teams literally lining up ready to go out. I remember shaking hands with Mark and Danny Wilson, the Bristol City manager and a great former Albion midfielder and captain. The players of both sides were yelling and shouting as usual, ostensibly to give their team-mates confidence, but really to give it to themselves.

The interview was with Mark Pougatch over headphones and, completely out of the blue, he immediately struck a jarring note, "Why do you keep pursuing this Falmer stadium thing?" he asked. "Surely your club doesn't need a ground as big as that?" He basically started challenging me on our choice of Falmer, almost as if speaking on behalf of someone who was against us going there, because his questions were so specific. Maybe he was just trying to put a different angle on the usual pre-match interview – and if so, I apologise Mark – but I lost it.

Live on radio, I said, "Why are you asking me these ridiculous questions now, just as my team is about to go out and play one of our biggest-ever games? We've got 30,000 fans here." He said, "Every club that goes to the play-off final takes a big crowd." The teams had started to go out, the roar of the crowd increased and I was missing all that. I ended the interview, angry that Pougatch had riled me at such a magical moment in my Albion journey.

It was a terrible game, but we shaded it. Iwelumo won a penalty near the end when he cut in from the right and was tripped by Danny Coles, the City defender. We might have had doubts about Leon Knight's attitude and application, and he wasn't the most popular player in his own squad, but he had fantastic ability. He took nine penalties that season and converted them all. There was never any doubt that he would score. Ice-cool, he despatched it in clinical fashion.

There is a famous image of him with his shirt off celebrating after he had scored. He threw it up in the air but there's no footage of it coming down. Years later when I was having a hip operation in the Nuffield Hospital in Woodingdean, a nurse said to me, "I've got some really important memorabilia from the Millennium Stadium."

I said, "Really? What is it?"

She said, "My husband caught Leon Knight's shirt after he scored. And then at the end when the players came round with the trophy, he took off his boots and gave the right one to me of all people, the one he scored with. I've kept it. It's like a little kid's."

When the players were on the podium receiving the trophy, I was on the pitch nearby. Captain Danny Cullip jumped down with the cup and said, "Go on, Mr Chairman, you deserve to have this" and handed it to me, but between the two of us we managed to drop it against the edge of the podium and it bent. It can't have been made of very strong silver. Michel Kuipers hadn't played, but he had been on the bench and obviously had plenty of energy so he grabbed the trophy and bent it back into shape – almost.

In front of us, rising up almost to the sky, was a panorama of blue and white and noise, while behind us were empty seats and complete silence in half the stadium where the Bristol City fans in the 65,000 crowd had already melted away.

As I lifted the slightly damaged trophy high in celebration, hogging the glory as we walked slowly round, I couldn't help noticing that so many of our fans' replica shirts bore sponsors' names – Sandtex, Nobo, TSB, British Caledonian – from many years earlier. Even at that moment I realised just how many fans we had lost over the years because of the damage of the Archer regime, our exile in Kent and our restricted lodging at Withdean – it wasn't just youngsters, it was their dads as well. At least we were now giving them reasons to come back.

It was perfect, a national stage. It was a wonderful day out for Albion fans, and no one who was there will ever forget it. Going up via the play-offs has a lot to be said for it. And we'd picked up another trophy, albeit one that was slightly the worse for wear.

We made Iwelumo an offer to stay that was good, but he also had an offer to play for Alemannia Aachen, a club in Germany, and he took it. Chris has had an excellent career, including playing in the Premier League for Wolves, and almost everywhere he has gone, the club and the fans have liked him, because he's a good guy – Scottish, with many of those strong Scottish character traits, a real footballer, very professional. But he wanted to play abroad.

Perhaps we could have fought harder to keep him, but I'd singled out Danny's old friend Sam Parkin as the ideal target man to play with Knight. I offered Willie Carson £500,000, hoping to get back in his good books, but he was holding out for £750,000. No one was that friendly, however. Swindon sold Parkin to Ipswich for £550,000 a year later.

But all the preparation for the upcoming 2004/05 season and our return to the second tier were secondary in importance to Prescott's decision following the Collyer report. If that went against us, the long-term future was bleak.

In the programme for the Swindon play-off match I'd written an open letter to Prescott, a copy of which I sent to him. In it I pointed out the contrast between the "quaint, ramshackle" Withdean where the match was being televised live to the world and the "magnificent" Millennium Stadium that we were battling to reach, and reminded him of the "rejuvenating social, emotional and economic effects of new stadia on towns and cities across the UK".

I summarised our arguments for being granted planning permission and explained why there were no other viable sites than Falmer. I restated our reasons for wanting Falmer, "a facility that will be of real benefit to the local community, which is why we have always called it the Community Stadium".

I finished the letter by saying, "It is no understatement to say that you hold the future of this club – indeed the future of top-class sport in this city – in your hands. Please say 'Yes' to Falmer, and give us a sporting chance."

We had done all we could. Had the letters, emails, flowers, Valentine's card, postcards, clever slogans and all the rest made the difference?

# CHAPTER TWENTY TWO

# "YES"(ISH)

T he only feedback we were getting on the stadium situation was that John Prescott was very conscious of the swell of opinion because of all the campaigning that had gone on, and that he was beginning to listen. Prescott was due to deliver his verdict six weeks after Collyer's report came out, but it ended up going well beyond that. He was weighing up a strong recommendation against Falmer from his inspector on the one hand, with the weight of public opinion on the other. Very rarely do ministers go against the recommendations. After all, the inspectors are supposed to be the experts.

What did we expect from Prescott? We knew that it was on a knife-edge. But I never had any doubts that we would get there in the end, and so there were never any doubting Thomases among the Falmer For All committee. We all believed that what we were doing was right, and we were sure that we had done everything possible to make our case.

Prescott later told me that the early evidence of the support behind our application had been kept from him. He was almost accusing his civil servants at the Department for Culture, Media & Sport (DCMS) of not making him fully aware of the situation until the torrent of emails, flowers, cards suddenly alerted him, four months after the Public Inquiry had ended.

As it was, Prescott had been sufficiently affected by the campaigning, and by a letter we had instructed our lawyers, DHM Stallard, to send to his office immediately following the publication of John Collyer's report, detailing the errors and omissions in his judgement. These representations produced a further series of letters and comments through till June 2004 as Prescott gave all parties the opportunity to comment on developments since the close of the inquiry. All the time he was gaining a clearer picture of the true situation.

Finally, on Sunday July 25, we learned that the letter from the Office of the Deputy Prime Minister containing the decision would arrive the next day, Monday July 26. It arrived in the office of our lawyers in Queens Road, and

# "YES"(ISH)

Tony Allen called Martin in our offices 100 yards away at around 9am. "The letter has arrived," he said. "Come up."

He had opened it, because it was addressed to him. He didn't tell Martin the contents, because it wouldn't have been right to do so, but he managed to convey that it wasn't bad news. We almost ran up the road.

In fact it was good news. Prescott had rejected the conclusions of Collyer's report. The letter explained that he had decided to re-open the Public Inquiry, because he wanted to explore whether there was any better site than Falmer within Brighton and Hove. He had clearly recognised there was a need for a stadium in the city. If he'd wanted to accept the recommendation of the two inspectors, he would have said no to Falmer.

Instead, he wanted the other sites to be evaluated under the strict set of criteria that had been applied to Falmer: Brighton Station, Hove Greyhound Stadium, Sheepcote Valley, Shoreham Harbour, Toads Hole Valley, Waterhall and Withdean Stadium. He also challenged the inspectors' conclusions that it was not in the public interest to build at Falmer – 'public interest' being a justification for building in an Area of Outstanding Natural Beauty (AONB). In the absence of any alternative location, the landslide of support from across the country had clearly demonstrated to him that it was.

We interpreted the decision as an 'amber light' for Falmer; that unless a better alternative site could be shown to exist, the stadium would be built there. That way, if he decided in favour of Falmer, it couldn't be challenged. And that is why the Albion are playing at the Amex today. If John Prescott hadn't been brave enough to go against the first Public Inquiry inspector, and if we hadn't campaigned so strongly after the Hoile Local Plan report came out, it would never have happened.

*The Argus* front page the day after Prescott gave his verdict had the headline 'YES(ish)' but the various opponents seemed to believe it was a No, because they were on TV and photographed drinking champagne as if they had won. The chairman of Falmer Parish Council said, "As far as we are concerned, it is a red light for the Falmer site." They assumed the re-opened inquiry would find a better site as proposed by the inspectors and they celebrated – as they had when Hoile's and Collyer's reports came out.

On a busy day with the media I told Sky Sports News: "It doesn't take a great brain to realise that, if there was another site, we would have saved ourselves years and hundreds of thousands of pounds going through a Public Inquiry and made the decision long ago to go to that site. I'm confident the re-opened inquiry will demonstrate that there is only one site in Brighton & Hove, which is Falmer."

The Falmer objectors may have been encouraged in their view by having someone on the inside. Prescott, remember, felt that someone was massaging the reports he was getting and keeping pro-Falmer information away from him. It may have been the same person who also helped the later Lewes fight.

We soon had another Falmer For All meeting, and the mood was good. We had to prove that none of the other sites were viable, and that was where all the previous work we had done in ruling out sites such as Shoreham Harbour would pay off. We already had chapter and verse on all the difficulties of each location – the traffic and access problems, the insurmountable costs.

But we were taking nothing for granted and the campaigning continued until the reopening of the inquiry in February 2005, with a new inspector. The Labour Party Conference was in Brighton in September 2004 and we took maximum advantage. We held a march along the seafront from the Palace Pier to the conference centre and hotels. Some people estimated the number of people on the march at 8,000, a great snaking line that was headed by me, the directors, and former manager Micky Adams, still showing his feelings for the club.

We couldn't get close to the conference itself because there was heavy police security but I gave a speech on the seafront outside the Grand Hotel and John Prescott came out on the balcony for a quick wave to the massed Albion fans below. If he wanted proof that we weren't making it all up about the huge support, he got it then.

We attended a fringe meeting where we lobbied MPs, and we had a banner on the derelict West Pier – 'What do this pier and the Albion have in common? Past, historic; present, tense; future, conditional – and in your hands'. The marchers carried placards that read, 'Enjoy your Conference – Don't condemn us to ours' (not bad for an old ad man, I thought). Even though it had been more than seven years since we had narrowly escaped dropping into the Football Conference, there was a distinct possibility that, without a new ground, we could sink back downwards.

Also at the Conference we had blue-and-white sticks of rock with 'Falmer For All' running through them put in the delegates' hotel rooms. We distributed pledge cards, echoing the pledge cards the Labour Party had produced to remind everyone what they had promised at the 2001 General Election. Under the injunction 'Please make a stand for our stadium', we promised 600 new jobs, education and skills training and other community benefits – plus 'dreams, pride and motivation for generations'.

We were aiming at the heart of government on this key issue, and by luck we got right to the centre. There was a fringe meeting at – where else? – the Royal Albion hotel, and Paul Samrah and Tim Carder were in the lobby at the right time to hand Tony and Cherie Blair postcards and pledge cards, which they took, with Cherie saying, "I know about this. What's happening with the stadium?"

We were lucky that Labour had chosen to come to Brighton, and it helped that all three city MPs were now Labour, but we made the most of it. One political historian said that it was the first time that a local issue had been protested about at a Party Conference. We couldn't miss that opportunity, and we didn't.

The club was losing money at Withdean and although the losses were sustainable, that was mainly because I was putting money in along with some other shareholders – directors plus other backers such as Norman Cook and an interesting guy named Billy Brown who I've already mentioned briefly. I was aware of Billy, a city entrepreneur who had made a lot of money in satellite re-insurance, a very specialist area. When a Japanese company launches a satellite, you can be almost certain that Billy's company is spreading the risk.

There's a great story about him. Apparently Bill went to lunch with one of his best mates in the City at Le Caprice in Mayfair. After a big lunch they were walking through Berkeley Square and stopped outside the Rolls-Royce showroom. There were a couple of new Phantom models and they went in to have a look. The story goes that Bill then said, "Don't worry I'll get these; you got the lunch."

He is a Londoner, a real larger-than-life character, and his company has boxes at Chelsea, Arsenal and Tottenham. But he has a big house in West Sussex and used to bring his son, Harry, to Withdean and I was introduced to him by Robbie Raggio of Hove Car Wash – a mover and shaker in the town. He said, "Billy wants to meet you" and so I met him and we got on straight away.

He basically said he wanted to help me and support what I was doing at the club, but not get actively involved. He loved coming to the Albion and liked the friendliness of Withdean after the prawn sandwich treatment at Chelsea. Billy supported me to the tune of about £1 million in total and helped keep the club going although, like Norman, he was happy to be a shareholder but never wanted to become a director. Billy is ill now, but his wife Tracey comes to the club AGM every year.

Despite our shortage of money, we still had our principles. So when the Football League negotiated a three-year sponsorship deal for Championship clubs with Wickes Home Improvement Centres, I stood up at a League meeting and said Brighton wouldn't take the £20,000 per season on offer, because Wickes were part of the Focus Wickes Group, whose chairman and chief executive was Bill Archer.

"It was not a difficult decision for us to turn down this money, even when the club is strapped for cash," I said. "We do not feel it is appropriate to become associated with a company run by someone who our supporters hold responsible for the position we are now in."

The other clubs applauded my stand. The League, however, said we were putting the deal in jeopardy because it was conditional on all 24 clubs being involved, but I stuck to my guns and eventually Wickes backed down, possibly because I'd suggested to the League that Wickes' marketing director had a word in the ear of his boss. Six months later, when Archer's Focus group sold off the Wickes chain, I was only too happy to enter the sponsorship deal, much to the amusement of the other Championship chairmen.

Also that September we launched the 'Alive and Kicking' fund, to help the Albion to continue doing just that as we entered the seventh year of our battle for a permanent home.

By now the board and shareholders had put in over £7 million in share capital and loans, but as I explained at the launch press conference, the costs of converting Withdean, the Falmer planning application and the Public Inquiry had eaten most of that up. Then there was the small matter of struggling to keep the team competitive in the second tier of English football while playing at an inadequate ground.

Supporters were invited to donate what they could afford at this crucial period in the club's history: if they pledged £100, they got a commemorative certificate, signed by me. From £250, they got the certificate and their name on a seat at the new stadium when we got it. 'Alive and Kicking' generated over £330,000 in a few months. I'd come up with the madcap idea of giving a free season ticket for life to the five lucky winners of a prize draw for everyone who donated over £100, so that may have had something to do with it.

I was told that one of the winners was in hospital in Haywards Heath so I went to see him to give him the good news personally. He was so overjoyed that he almost jumped out of bed to hug me.

Most of the £250 donors wanted the seat plaques for their late fathers, uncles or grandparents who had loved the Albion and could be remembered at the new stadium. I think it was very sad when the club later decided to put their names on bricks in front of the West Stand reception instead. Unfortunately, the names on the bricks soon wore off, so a new site had to be installed. The club honoured the pledge to provide a memorial, but people can buy the same thing today for £99.

We were just a few weeks into the Championship season – as it was now known – but at least I had had the luxury of knowing who my manager would be when we planned for that campaign. I had increased the playing budget by almost £1 million and had met Mark at his flat on Brighton seafront well before pre-season. We both had a wish list of players and on top of my list of wide players was Darren Currie, who had just been released by Wycombe Wanderers. Mark showed me his list and Currie was at the top too.

Currie didn't have a lot of pace but he could get a cross in from anywhere, jinking down the wing and curling his foot round the ball. And he was completely two-footed. He had always caused us problems whenever he had played against us, and incredibly he was available as a free agent. Wycombe were in the bottom division and they had let this quality player go, perhaps because they thought that at 29 he was a bit old for a winger. We took him on at middling wages, and both club and player were delighted at the prospect.

For the new season I had changed the colour of the stripes on our shirts to a lighter, more of an Argentina, blue. It ruffled a few feathers, but it sold a lot of shirts, which we needed to do. The yellow away shirt just had a black seagull on it, with an aggressive-looking bold black 'SKINT' (our sponsors didn't mind), and that proved very popular too.

We played away in the first game, at Reading, managed by Steve Coppell. We scored after 12 seconds when Maheta Molango, whom we'd got from Atletico Madrid, took a pass from Paul Reid, came in from the left and drove the ball into the roof of the net. Reading equalised almost immediately and we nearly went straight back ahead with an almost identical move to our first, but Adrian Williams hacked Molango down for a blatant penalty and the referee just waved play on. Perhaps he didn't fancy a 1-2 scoreline after two-and-a-half minutes.

We lost that game 3-2 and only scored once in the next three games, a late free kick from Adam Virgo to rescue a point in a 1-1 draw at home to Coventry. Molango never lived up to his first few minutes in an Albion shirt and Leon Knight, after scoring 27 goals the previous season, never got going in the higher division. He only scored four goals and started playing up, both on and off the pitch. A couple of times at Withdean he had run-ins with fans or opponents, and the fans began to get on his back.

The bright spot was Darren Currie. The problem was that we had no one to finish off all his good work. There was a midweek game in late August, at home to Bristol Rovers in the League Cup. They beat us 2-1 but Currie must have put in almost 30 crosses from both sides. We had Knight and Molango up front and neither of them got on the end of a ball all evening.

I used to talk to Mark a lot. On the Friday after the Bristol Rovers game I was having lunch with him when he asked, "Do you think Adam Virgo can score goals?" Well, of course he could. He could hit a mean low free kick, as he had against Coventry, and it was his header that had taken us into the play-off final. But I didn't quite appreciate what Mark was driving at. I assumed he meant from dead-ball situations.

"Yes, he's got a helluva shot on him and he's very decisive and fearless."

I knew he liked Virgo, thought he was intelligent and often talked to him about football and about leadership. The next day, we were at home to Preston, who were play-off contenders. As we tucked into our pasta, Mark continued, "I've got a hunch about Virgo. I'm going to play him at centre-forward tomorrow."

I chewed on my tagliatelle as I thought about Mark's bombshell before replying, "Well," I said, "He's strong and can certainly get his head on Currie's crosses, and will probably make his presence felt among their back four."

Preston had one of the meanest defences in the league with the likes of Claude Davis, Chris Lucketti and Marlon Broomes. We prepared to kick off and there was this buzz of incredulity around Withdean when Virgo lined up at centre-forward, and at first he misplaced a couple of passes and there were rumblings – "He can't play there" and "McGhee, you don't know what you're doing."

But then Adam started closing their defenders down and harrying their back four, running himself into the ground. Mark hadn't told me that would be part of the game plan, but Adam was naturally quick and aggressive and wouldn't let them play the ball out from the back. After half an hour he put Broomes under so much pressure from a cross that the Preston defender put the ball in his own net for the only goal of the game.

Adam went off at both half-time and full-time to a standing ovation. It was a huge boost to morale because it was our first win of the season, at the sixth attempt. Two days later, Bank Holiday Monday, we went to Leicester and won our first away game, also 1-0, and this time Adam scored, as he did in the following game to grab a late point in a 1-1 draw away to Watford. So it was a bit of a masterstroke by the manager.

Mark did think outside the box and was unusual in other ways too. For one thing, he had a stylish flat in the exclusive French Apartments on Marine Parade out near the Marina rather than the more conventional football manager's four-up, four-down. His two sons were both at university, one up north and the other in America, and both very popular with everyone, especially the girls, and intelligent. They got all of that from Mark. He was a mature man of the world, knowledgeable about a lot of things. He was even writing a novel, which is unusual for a manager, to say the least. He'd played for many teams including Morton, Newcastle, Aberdeen and Hamburg. In Germany his best friend was Felix Magath, one of the great midfielders of his time.

Of course, competing in the Championship with our resources was always going to be a struggle, but there were lighter moments along the way. For our home game on October 2, I got special permission from the Football League to turn Withdean into 'Palookaville' to mark the release of Fatboy Slim's CD of the same name.

Palookaville means the pits, the definition of a dead-end area, which comes from a line in the Marlon Brando film *On The Waterfront*, where Brando's character talks about "a one-way ticket to Palookaville". So we put up various signs and images to make Withdean look like some downtrodden downtown area of an American city. It didn't take much dressing-down to achieve that, to be honest.

I got Errea to produce an all-navy strip with just the Palookaville lettering in white instead of Skint, and it became one of our most successful kits. We drew the game, against Sheffield United, but the cool kit quickly established itself with the fans. We wore it when we won 1-0 at West Ham in November, Guy Butters scoring the only goal in a game where they attacked us incessantly. Steve Claridge played for us that afternoon. He worked so hard up front, socks round his ankles as usual.

One notable incident in that game was Bobby Zamora's first appearance against us. He had moved to West Ham from Tottenham as a makeweight in the deal that took Hammers favourite Jermain Defoe to Spurs, so that didn't make him popular at Upton Park even though he was a boyhood fan. He was warming up to come on as a sub for Matthew Etherington and was being booed by some West Ham supporters, but when our fans spotted him they started cheering. And when Zamora came on, he got a standing ovation and thunderous applause from the away fans and stony silence from his own supporters.

Our 2-0 defeat at Millwall on Saturday December 11 gave rise to one of the funniest incidents of that or any other season, despite the result. On the Monday after the game, *The Sun* newspaper ran a sensationalised double-page spread in the news pages, alleging rampant racism at the game and headlined, 'Nazis alive and well in English football'. They'd sent Raymond Enisuoh, the sports editor of *New Nation*, a paper aimed at the black community, to the game to report on any suggestions of racism. He wrote that he'd heard chants of 'Sieg Heil!' ringing round the ground. So there it was, all over the country's biggest-selling newspaper.

I had got to hear about this pretty early in the morning. Then Theo Paphitis phoned me and said, "Have you seen *The Sun*?"

"Yes, Theo – it's absolutely ludicrous. And hilarious."

"No it isn't – it's bloody terrible for our reputation, it's bad enough already!"

"Theo, I know you're only ever thinking about your team when you watch a game, but who were you playing on Saturday? What's our nickname?"

Then it clicked, and he burst out laughing. Obviously the reporter hadn't known Brighton's nickname and somehow misheard our 'Seagulls' chant as 'Sieg Heil!'

I said, "You do a statement and I'll do one too, but we need to make sure we both get an apology from *The Sun*, because they're painting our fans as Nazis. Yours get accused of a lot of things, but calling Millwall or Brighton fans fascists is too much."

Later in the day, *The Sun* realised they'd scored a huge own-goal. The reporter had got it completely wrong. The following February they published a very humble apology, albeit very small and on an inside page.

We lost that game and soon after we lost two key players. Danny Cullip had been wanting to move for some time and departed for Sheffield United. He didn't get on particularly well with Mark, who thought Butters did most of the central defensive work. Adam Hinshelwood had come through and Mark would play him and Butters together sometimes and drop Danny. I got £250,000 for Cullip, but I was sorry to see him go. He'd been a great motivator and a great leader. Every Brighton fan loved him because he gave everything in every game, like a defensive version of Gary Hart.

But if that move had been coming, the other was out of the blue. One day David Sheepshanks, the Ipswich Town chairman, came on the phone, urbane and charming as ever. We had always got on well, particularly since I was one of the few people who stood alongside him at the Football League AGM over Richard Scudamore.

He said, "Dick, our manager Joe Royle is very interested in your player Darren Currie."

I replied, "I'm not surprised, David; he's playing well. And he's vital to our chances of staying in this league."

"Come on, old chap, you need the money."

"No we don't."

"Well, I'm duty-bound to make an offer."

"What's the offer then? I'll tell Darren if it's of any significance at all."

"£75,000."

"Forget it, David. You tell me your manager is very interested in this player but you've offered a paltry amount. You're in the same league as us, pushing for promotion, and you want me to virtually give you my best attacking player?"

"Well, what sort of figure would you be looking for?"

"Four times that, £300,000. But I'll give you a discount. I'll take £250,000, cash on the nail, no conditions on appearances – and a sell-on. But I know you won't pay that, and I'm glad the discussion is over. Because as far as I'm concerned he's worth far more to me. He's going to help us stay in this league."

Old Etonian murmurings of discontent came back. "Dick, dear boy, you're such a tough negotiator. I'll talk to Joe again and come back to you."

When he said that, I thought, "Bloody hell, he is going to come back to me."

I phoned Mark and said, "You won't believe this . . ."

He wasn't surprised that Ipswich were interested, because they played good football and had Darren Bent and Shefki Kuqi to get on the end of Darren's crosses. But when I told him that Ipswich were offering £75,000, he said, "You're not letting him go for that are you?"

I said, "Absolutely not" and told Mark what I'd quoted them.

Mark said, "Good deal, Mr Chairman, if you can get it." He knew the financial situation at the club and that a quarter of a million pounds for a player we'd picked up for nothing only four months previously would be too good to turn down. We didn't want to sell Darren but for that money it would seriously help the cash-flow.

Later that day, David came back and said, "Okay, you've got a deal."

I replied, "For £300,000?"

"Really, dear boy – you said £250,000."

"Well, I'm not sure I want to sell him now . . ." I said, feigning second thoughts.

"Come now, Dick – you're a man of your word."

"Of course I am, David. And I'm sure Darren will be thrilled to come and play for Ipswich in front of 20,000 people. We haven't said anything to him at all. Unless, of course, your manager has spoken to him, which does happen, as you know."

Darren is a very straightforward guy, and when we told him he said, "It's a fantastic opportunity, but I'm really loving it here. I like this club and the way the team plays. But I could be in the Premier League next season."

Darren's departure was still a loss, even though it was fantastic money for a signing who hadn't cost a penny and had just turned 30. But we got 23 appearances out of him, most of them excellent.

Danny and Darren both left before one of the highlights of the season, our FA Cup third-round tie away to Tottenham. We hadn't had a tie away to a London Premier League club for ages, so I was thrilled that our fans could enjoy a day out at a big ground – and we would also get 45 per cent of the gate.

The team did us proud. Ledley King put Tottenham ahead but Chippy Carpenter equalised with a precisely-placed free kick early in the second half, right in front of our fans. We looked good value for a draw until Robbie Keane won the match late on, but the goal shouldn't have stood. Keane barged Adam Hinshelwood out of the way but made it look like he'd simply spun him before scoring with a tremendous shot on the turn. We should have had a free kick, and a replay at Withdean.

The team showed in that game what they were really capable of, but it was that sort of season – plenty of interesting and even uplifting moments, but those high points made you wonder why we were struggling in the league. Leon Knight had his best game of the season, but that was probably because he wanted to show his mates in the Tottenham squad, like King, that he was just as good as them.

But if the players hadn't quite hit the headlines, the Falmer For All team did in the same month when the CD *We Want Falmer* by Seagulls Ska got to No.17 in the singles charts. John Baine had been annoyed by other clubs playing the Piranhas' *Tom Hark*, which is really a Brighton record, so he re-recorded it with different words and got the Falmer For All team singing on the choruses. One of the lines was, "Playing at Withdean is like Albania division eight".

January is well-known to be a poor time for music sales, so it was the perfect time to make an assault on the charts. I imagine it was the first, if not the only, football protest song to make the UK Top 20, and as a bonus it made £7,000 for the Alive and Kicking fund. But again it was an attempt to get to people's hearts through humour rather than aggression, which was the hallmark of the campaign.

There was another funny incident in our 1-1 draw at Leeds late in January. Michel Kuipers had been badly injured in the previous game in a collision with Andy Reid of Nottingham Forest and after our reserve keeper also dropped out injured, we took David Yelldell, a German, on short-term loan from Blackburn. He knew nothing about Brighton, the club or the city, and met up with the team for the first time in the hotel in Leeds on the Friday.

We were 1-0 down at half-time, and I'd noticed that at least twice our players had passed to the linesmen. We were wearing the dark blue Palookaville kit and the officials were in black. I went into Ken Bates's inner sanctum within the boardroom and spotted Andy Williamson, the operations director of the Football League. I said to him, "Andy, did you notice our players passing to the referee's assistants?"

"Yes, I did actually."

"Do you mind going and asking the ref and linesmen to change their shirts?"

"No problem,' he said, and Bates totally agreed. Five minutes later Andy came back and said, "It's sorted, they're changing into yellow."

"Hang on," I said. "Our goalkeeper's jersey is yellow."

"No, it's all right, they've got another colour jersey for him."

So we went back to our seats for the second half and there was Yelldell walking towards the goal in front of the Don Revie Stand at Elland Road, packed with Leeds diehards – wearing a pink jersey. You can imagine the reaction – you know, that up-and-down 'wheeeooowoooh' sound people make (and this was 12,000 of them) when they're poking fun at someone – especially bearing in mind that Brighton has the largest gay population in Europe.

Yelldell, knowing nothing about this, waved to the Leeds fans, obviously pleased to be getting what he thought was a warm welcome. And within a couple of minutes he'd made a fantastic save from a 25-yard piledriver by Garry Kelly, getting up into the corner and flicking it over the bar. Even the players were applauding him, and Kelly patted him on the back. The crowd took to him, and he responded with a series of saves as Leeds pressed hard for a second goal, although it spoiled their mood when Guy Butters headed a late equaliser.

Yelldell's performance had done at least as much to earn us the point, but our players were hooting with laughter in the dressing room as they hadn't told him anything about Brighton's reputation as the gay capital of Europe. When he twigged, he said, "Thanks guys. You bastards." Unfortunately, in the next game, at home to Derby, he gave away two of the goals in a 3-2 defeat and we replaced him with first Rami Shaaban from Arsenal, then Alan Blayney from Southampton on loan for the rest of the season.

But, as ever, we were fighting on two fronts and the second Public Inquiry, as I always think of it, started in early February 2005, at Brighton Town Hall this time and with a different inspector, David Brier. Brier had a more specific brief – to prove that there wasn't a better site than Falmer. He also didn't stand for any delaying tactics and was very concise.

We made our submissions based on a lot of the evidence that we'd already produced, which Hoile and especially Collyer had overlooked, it seemed. And we were able to add more information to the exhaustive site analysis that we'd already done. The inquiry had also added two other sites to the original list: Shoreham Airport and Beeding Cement Works, which was really clutching at straws – both in the Adur district and both about 10 miles from Brighton & Hove. They never had a cat in hell's chance because they were either too expensive or not available. If an airport has aspirations of growth, you don't want large planes landing near football stadiums.

Both Hoile and Collyer had wanted Sheepcote Valley, but we had already shown that the build and decontamination costs would be prohibitive and that the transport problems would be massive. The opponents of Falmer claimed that supporters could walk from the centre of Brighton, around two and a half miles, in 25 minutes. A group of our fans tried it by the quickest route to Sheepcote, along the seafront, and it took 58 minutes. The same was true of another route, from Moulsecoomb Station, which was closer. Brier himself walked the route, which included long, steep climbs, most challengingly a flight of stairs called 'Jacob's Ladder'. Brier actually told the inquiry, "I climbed it and it was a killer."

The owners of Toads Hole Valley, the Cook family, pushed the case for a stadium on their property. Robert Stiles, their lawyer, had apparently been in support of Archer's original proposal there, but we went into far more detail about the A27 congestion problems, which Archer had hardly touched on when he effectively bet the club on going to Toads Hole Valley.

Now Stiles stood up and told the inquiry, "We want the club to come back to Brighton and we believe that our site would be ideal for the stadium," which must have been music to the ears of the objectors until Jonathan Clay, our barrister, questioned him and brought out the fact that the owners would only release the land if they could build a retail park on the rest of it. The council had long since rejected that idea.

We picked the sites off one by one as Brier kept the pace of the inquiry going – submissions from consultants, experts, all at great expense, just to prove again what we thought we had proved in the first inquiry.

It had been six years since we had identified Falmer as the only viable site. Nothing had changed since then. It wasn't 100 per cent perfect but, in a city squeezed between the sea and the Downs, it was far and away the most sensible and achievable of all the potential locations. We were going over old ground, so to speak, again and again. It cost us a lot of money, but that was the process we had to endure.

I mentioned all of this in a match-day programme article when the second inquiry opened and added, "We trust that the new inspector – unlike his predecessors – is not oblivious to the needs of this community, and recognises Falmer as the one and only realistic site for our much-needed stadium."

The second Public Inquiry finally ended in May 2005, after 63 days in total with the first, spread over 28 months. No football club in England, probably the world, had ever been through such a relentless and cripplingly expensive ordeal.

To some extent the inquiry was a diversion from the poor form of the team in the spring. Mark had almost tempted fate at the end of February when, with 11 games to go and 44 points in the bag, he pronounced that we were virtually safe from relegation. After that statement, we lost the next six league matches which meant that, with five games left, we were down in the bottom three.

In our penultimate home game we played West Ham in Bobby Zamora's return to Withdean. He came on as a sub and you could tell that he did not want to play – I remember he missed a really easy chance. But Teddy Sheringham was excellent for West Ham, as was the emerging Dean Hammond for us, scoring both goals in a 2-2 draw.

It was a fantastic match that deserved to have been played in front of a big crowd. Instead I remember seeing a photo in the paper taken through the back of the net and down the Withdean pitch that showed Sheringham and Zamora, and you couldn't see one spectator. It looked like a park game.

Then we went up to Rotherham and won 1-0. In the last game of the season, with our fate still uncertain, we played Ipswich at home, who would be promoted to the Premier League if they won and Wigan didn't. There were two early goals, one for each side, with Adam Virgo – who else? – scoring for us.

There was no further score before results began to come in from the other grounds as our game continued. When all the other games had finished, we knew that a point would keep us up, and we had to hang on. Ipswich were throwing everything at us, playing four centre-forwards – Bent, Kuqi, James Scowcroft and Pablo Counago – going all out for the win they thought would take them to the Premier League, not knowing that Wigan had already won, claiming automatic promotion themselves.

The nightmare would have been Darren Currie setting up or, worse still, scoring the winner for Ipswich to send us down, but as it was he'd gone off after 64 minutes. Even so we had to sit biting our nails for four long minutes of added time until the final whistle blew and we were safe.

Staying up was a remarkable achievement as we were punching way above our weight on, once again, about a sixth of the average budget for the division. But I'd expected Knight to get at least 10 goals, maybe more. Virgo finished as our top scorer, with nine extremely valuable goals, justifying McGhee's gamble.

I wished David Sheepshanks the best of luck in the play-offs, but Ipswich lost to West Ham in the semi-finals with Zamora scoring three goals over the two legs. Having West Ham sympathies, I went to the final in Cardiff to see them play Preston. And there we got a very pleasant surprise.

There had been a 'Win a Player for Your Club' competition organised at the beginning of the season by Coca-Cola, the Football League sponsor. The winning fan won £250,000 for their club to spend on the player of their choice. A Brighton fan named Aaron Berry had entered a few times and when the draw was made, he was the winner out of 1,092,110 entries. He also won £10,000 for himself. And he was even luckier than that. The winner was notified by text and had 10 days to respond to Coca-Cola. Aaron had been in the USA, landed in Gatwick on the morning of the 10th day and turned on his phone – just in time. Thank God the plane wasn't delayed!

There was a special presentation to the competition winner on the Millennium Stadium pitch before the Championship play-off final. Mark McGhee and I were invited onto the pitch along with Aaron to receive the cheque from Steve Summers, the Coca-Cola marketing director. The players were warming up and I saw Bobby Zamora about 25 yards away so I shouted over to him. He heard me, did a double-take and came over, still dribbling the ball, carrying on his warm-up routine, and said, "Hello Mr Chairman, what are you doing here?"

I said, "Bob, I'm just picking up a big cheque that I'm going to use to buy you back. You know it's your destiny to come back to Brighton."

He laughed and said, "Do it!"

I hadn't realised that we'd gone live on Sky while I was chatting to Bobby and so Chris Kamara, who was waiting to start the ceremony, tapped me on the shoulder and said, "If I'm not interrupting you, Mr Knight . . ."

When the game got under way I was sitting up in the royal box behind Terry Brown, the West Ham chairman, and Paul Aldridge, their chief executive. They also asked me why I was there so I told them. And I added, "I'm going to cross out 'Brighton & Hove Albion FC' on the cheque and make it payable to West Ham United instead and you can give me Bobby Zamora back. He's hardly got into your team."

Terry replied, "He's been doing quite well, but if we don't win today I could do with the money."

They seemed to be in a good mood, but as the game wore on they were sweating and not because it was a hot day. I later found out that they were deep in debt and would have been in danger of going into administration if they didn't get back into the Premier League.

It was 0-0 at half-time and as we left the royal box, Terry said, "Your offer's looking good." But after 57 minutes Bobby went and spoiled everything by volleying in Etherington's cross to score what proved to be the only goal of the match to take West Ham up.

Terry turned round, gave me a hug – he knew I'd always had a soft spot for West Ham – and said, "By the way, that price for Bobby Zamora – add a nought to it!"

So Bobby had played himself out of a move back to Brighton and would be going back to the Premier League, where he belonged. Who would we spend the Coca-Cola windfall on? I was already pretty sure I knew.

I had a pal up in Middlesbrough who kept me informed about players up in the north – kind of like an unofficial scout. Les had tipped me off about a player playing for Bury called Colin Kazim-Richards and I'd got some DVDs of a couple of games that he'd played and liked the look of him. He wasn't an out-and-out goalscorer; he just looked a good player, confident and held the ball up well.

There was no agent involved. His father took care of him. His mother is Turkish Cypriot, his father is Jamaican, and devoted to his son, a caring dad. The chairman at Bury, Fred Mason, was quite open and said they wanted £100,000 for him. He saw a lot of potential. But I was also told that he had a bit of a wild side off the field. Having said that, Colin was very polite and absolutely committed to making a mark as a footballer. He wanted to be taught to be a good player and Mark McGhee, as a former international striker, was a perfect manager for him.

I went to see Colin in a game and although he was only a sub, he did enough in 20 minutes to show me he was a cut above the others. He'd come from the East End of London via some player trials and had only played half-a-dozen games for Bury. But he struck the ball cleanly, everything he did was decisive, and he was quite quick. Not that tall, but strong.

I decided to take a punt on him with some of the Coca-Cola money, although I was going to go for him anyway. The initial deal was for £55,000, with add-ons up to £100,000, because he was pretty unproven. That was a deal I was happy to do based on appearances. We introduced him at a press conference at Withdean and the papers immediately dubbed him the Coca-Cola Kid, a name that has stuck with him ever since.

With Colin signed up, I went on holiday to Cyprus with Kerry. But little did I suspect that I was about to pull off the best deal I ever did as Brighton chairman.

# CHAPTER TWENTY THREE

# THE BEST DEAL
# I EVER DID

dam Virgo had scored the goal that had kept us up, and had attracted quite a lot of interest because he'd got nine goals after being converted from a defender. He'd even been picked for Scotland Futures (also known as Scotland B) because his grandmother was Scottish. He gained two caps and did well.

I knew one person who particularly admired him was Gordon Strachan, who had become Celtic manager in June – one of the biggest jobs in British football. Before that, Strachan had taken a 15-month sabbatical after leaving Southampton, going to look more closely at football overseas, in Spain and the French coaching centre at Clairfontaine. I'd spoken to him quite often because he came to Withdean games a lot during that period to see Mark McGhee, his friend and former teammate with Aberdeen and Scotland.

Kerry and I were going on holiday to a very nice hotel in Paphos and two days before I left I got a call out of the blue from Peter Lawwell, the Celtic chief executive, saying that they were interested in Adam and asking if we would be prepared to sell him.

I said, "No. He's just been voted our player of the season and we have no intention of selling him."

He replied, "Well, our new manager is very interested in him."

"That doesn't surprise me because I know Gordon has watched Virgo a lot, but he's not for sale."

But Lawwell wouldn't give up and said, "Well, I can assure you we are very interested. What sort of figure would you be looking for?"

In my mind, Adam was worth probably around £200,000 in the open market – but to me, to Mark and the team, he was worth more than that. Probably more than any other player he had been responsible for keeping us up; he was a hero because his last-second goal against Swindon had kept us in the play-offs when we were promoted; and he was a local lad, part of that new group of players coming through.

So in reply to Lawwell's question, I said, "Well, it would have to be a lot. But I haven't got a figure in mind because I'm not interested in selling."

We finished the conversation, and I assumed that would be the end of it because I'd made it pretty clear that Virgo wasn't for sale, although I hadn't added "at any price". Nor had I mentioned that I was going on holiday because I didn't expect to hear back.

But only two days into my holiday I got a call from Sally Townsend, our office manager. She said a fax had come through from Peter Lawwell at Celtic offering £600,000 for Adam Virgo.

He was probably expecting me to react to that straight away. I was absolutely certain that Celtic had not contacted Adam through a third party because they are not that sort of club; Peter is a real gentleman and does everything the right way, and Gordon was a friend of Mark's. So I called him back and told him that I was on holiday, adding, "Peter, I've told you I'm not interested, and my wife is expecting me back next to her on the beach."

Peter replied, "Dick, we are very interested because our new manager is very keen to make Virgo his first signing for Celtic."

Well that, of course, gave me a bit of leverage. So although I said I was going back to the sun-lounger and I still wasn't intending to sell, I knew that I could play hardball a bit. Over the next couple of days I got two more calls and it wasn't too difficult to push the money to £850,000, although my standpoint was that I didn't want to let Adam go.

Finally Peter said, "Look, Dick, it's going to be out of my hands now. Dermot [Desmond, the owner] is going to get involved. He wants to tie up this deal. He wants it done."

I said, "That's fine by me, Peter, but make sure it's only one call."

A few hours later, my mobile rang and it was Dermot Desmond. An Irishman and business associate of John Magnier and JP McManus, the racehorse owners who sold their share in Manchester United to the Glazer family, he was very friendly and chatty. "Hello Dick, I hear you're having a nice holiday."

"Yes, Dermot," I said. "Get to the point."

"Okay, this lad Virgo you've got down there – our manager really likes him. We see him being part of our assault on Europe."

"I'm sorry, you're going to have to go north of £850k – into seven figures."

He said, "Okay, but if we agreed, it would have to be broken up into instalments and with achievement conditions."

"Listen, Dermot – my wife has been getting steadily more fed up with me over the last few days. I've been spending rather a lot of time on the phone to your chief executive when she thinks I could be spending time with her. We're going to have to end this. I'm not going to sell Virgo to you with all sorts of strings attached.

"I'm going to tell you a figure. It's a ridiculous figure and you won't want to pay it, and you won't pay it – it's £1.5 million. That's what I want, end of subject. Give me that and you can have Adam tomorrow although, knowing him, that isn't necessarily the case. He's a very independent-minded person. But you will certainly be able to talk to him.

"And there are no conditions. That figure doesn't depend on appearances, or Celtic's achievements, or him scoring the winner in the Champions League final, or anything. It's all cash up front. The only thing I'm prepared to give you is that I'll take one million now and the rest at Christmas.'

There was a "hmm" at the other end of the line. And then he said, "I'll think about it" and the phone went dead.

But something told me that I'd got the money – they were going to pay it. Adam was a good player and very important to us, but this sort of money was impossible to turn down. I called Kerry's mobile and told her I'd be back on the beach in a while, but I thought I'd be able to tie this up quickly.

Half an hour later Peter Lawwell phoned me and said, "You've got a deal." It was exactly as I'd asked for it – well, almost.

He added, "Would you mind splitting it 50/50 between now and Christmas?"

I answered, "Peter, are you telling me Celtic Football Club haven't got a million pounds in the bank?"

He laughed and said, "All right."

I told him I'd call Mark McGhee, tell him what we'd agreed and ask him to inform Adam. "I assure you the player will think about it, but he'll be flab-bergasted. Mark will get back to you and I'll also brief our club secretary, Derek Allan. And please can I spend some time with my wife now?"

I got on the phone to Mark. He knew that Gordon and Celtic were inter-ested, but he hadn't heard anything more from them or me for several days, so when I told him I'd sold Virgo to them, there was an "oh" of disappointment at the other end, because he was an important player for us.

But then I said, "For £1.5 million" and there was a noise that I think was Mark dropping his phone.

"What?"

"£1.5 million. I know – unbelievable, isn't it? Not only that, there are no conditions."

"Bloody hell. How the fuck did you do that? Can I have it for new players?"

"No." Then, "Well, maybe a little."

Mark already knew the score, because we had Falmer to fund. But I told him to tell Adam and deal with Lawwell and arrange for Adam to go up there, see them and agree terms, which I didn't think would be a problem.

In fact, when Mark told Adam, he discovered that he was actually a big Celtic fan and had supported them as a boy, and had grown up with pictures of Jimmy Johnstone and Bobby Lennox on his bedroom wall. And now he was being given the chance to go and play for them.

Even so, it took Adam a few days to agree. Being a thoughtful guy, he didn't just jump on the next plane. He talked to his brother, who was in America, and other members of his family, and his girlfriend, who was at university. And in the end he went up to Glasgow and signed.

It has to be the best deal I ever did. All cash, with no conditions.

Nevertheless, it was a blow to the team. However, even while I was still on holiday, we thought we had a natural replacement in an exciting player from Argentina. But if the Adam Virgo sale was a triumph, Federico Turienzo turned out to be one of my biggest mistakes.

A striker, he'd been recommended to Liam Brady by Zbigniew Boniek, the Polish forward who he'd played with at Juventus. Liam phoned while I was still in Cyprus and said, "There's a player you've got to look at who wants to come and play in England."

Liam got Boniek to send me a video of Turienzo to my hotel and I borrowed a video player so that I could watch it. It showed Turienzo scoring against Boca Juniors and other big teams in those tight, steep Argentinian stadiums, packed with screaming fans setting off flares – volleys, powerful shots, spectacular headers. It was very impressive. Boniek and I were taken in by it, at any rate, and I remember saying to Kerry, "This guy looks very good."

I phoned Mark and told him, and asked him to call Turienzo's agent to get the player over to England for a trial. Mark was sent a copy of the video and he played Turienzo in a pre-season friendly at Lewes and thought he was a bit rusty, but was only too happy to sign him.

So as soon as we got back from holiday I met up with his agent and we went into negotiations. His agent was a charming Italian, Luis Ruzzi, and he owned Turienzo's rights, which was the first time I'd encountered that sort of arrangement. He'd bought them from his previous club, Gimnasia La Plata. So I did a deal with Luis for £150,000 based on appearances and gave Federico a two-year contract.

He was the most likeable young man, very willing to learn. If he hadn't been a professional footballer, he'd have been a doctor like his father and two of his siblings. He was very well-educated – he spoke Italian and French as well as Spanish, and was speaking some English very quickly. Then he got injured and wasn't available for the beginning of the season, so he never quite got started. He was used mainly as a substitute.

I felt really sorry for him. He wanted to play in English football and was grateful for the chance. His agent did everything possible, his girlfriend came over from Argentina. He worked so hard and did everything he could but he never adjusted to English football, although he was a tall, strong centre-forward and good in the air.

Often we see foreign players coming into our football and they just can't fathom the pace and power and Federico was one of those. He seemed unnerved by the hurly-burly of it. He wasn't used to being hassled on the ball. He wasn't slow but the game often passed him by. He was tall but got knocked off the ball too easily.

His attitude was good, his behaviour was impeccable, everything should have worked. If Mark had been able to start him in more games early on he might have gained more confidence. Strikers in particular lose confidence quickly. It just goes to show that, in football, nothing is certain.

So we ended up with Leon Knight and Colin Kazim-Richards up front most of the time. Knight began to look as if he was recapturing his old form, although his off-the-field problems began to plague him and us.

A natural replacement seemed to be Jake Robinson, a small, quick local boy who'd scored goals for fun through his development years in our youth set-up. He'd been the subject of a huge amount of hype even before he broke into our first team with one journalist hailing him as "the next Michael Owen". He made 29 appearances for us that season, as Mark gave him his chance, but he scored only two goals. Although Jake has made a career in the lower leagues, I think weight of expectation on him early on was too much and he never quite came to terms with the physicality of League football. A good lad and a great shame.

We'd lost Dan Harding, who had gone to Leeds after his contract expired. He'd been picked for the England under-21s by Peter Taylor, and was egged on by his agent about his value after talking to players with bigger clubs, on bigger wages, while on international duty. Early on, I offered him a sizeable contract renewal but he sat on it. He kept saying he wanted to stay, but I don't think he had any intention of doing so.

Because he was under 24, we were entitled to compensation. Shaun Harvey, the Leeds chief executive – who became CEO of the Football League in July 2013 – tested me with a couple of paltry sums before finally offering £250,000, which I rejected. It was time to put my Football League tribunal cape on again.

In the end I got a total of £850,000 for Harding, some of it based on achievements, with a 20 per cent sell-on. Leeds claimed that we'd had little input into his development, even though he'd come through our youth system and in fact had started more league games than any other player the previous season. That and his four international caps formed pretty conclusive evidence that we'd brought him on and made him worth more than £250,000.

But if that weakened the left side of our defence, we strengthened the centre when we took Paul McShane, the Irish centre-half, on loan from Manchester United. He ended up being voted player of the season and provided arguably the highlight of the campaign when he scored – well, claimed, at least – the only goal when we beat Crystal Palace 1-0 at Selhurst Park on October 18.

That night we were wearing an all-white kit for the first and only time because both our home and away strips clashed with Palace's red-and-blue stripes. That season was the first time we'd let the fans vote for the away kit and, of the options, my favourite was a green-and-black striped shirt with black shorts and socks – which would have been a precursor to the away kit we wore in the first two seasons at the Amex and proved to be highly popular with the fans. But the vote went to an all-maroon version of the Palookaville kit that I must confess I didn't like as much. The only time I think I enjoyed watching us play in it was when we drew 3-3 at Leeds on September 10, but even that was a mixed blessing because we'd gone 3-2 up with seven minutes to go. Seb Carole, a French winger we'd signed from Monaco a few days after the start of the season, played extremely well and scored our second goal and was so impressive that Leeds eventually took him from us.

But whatever shirt McShane wore, he put in maximum effort. He was a very determined player and a winner who went for every ball. I remember going into the dressing room after one game and looking for him to congratulate him on his performance only to spot him on the table in the treatment room with the doctor, Tim Stevenson, and Malcolm Stuart, the physio, bending over inspecting his knee, which was swollen. They suspected cruciate ligament damage, but the red-haired defender looked up at me and said, "Don't worry, Mr Chairman, I'm all right. I'll be playing next Saturday." I could see Malcolm and Tim shaking their heads, but he was right – he played.

Most of the time he was alongside Guy Butters, Mr Consistency, who played 46 games, using all his experience to compensate for a lack of pace. Jason Dodd, from Southampton, was an influential signing, lending experience at the end of his career, but he got injured and only played a few times.

The rest of the team, apart from Gary Hart, was pretty young. Dean Hammond played over 40 games, Adam El-Abd broke through and Joel Lynch made his debut away to Southampton, a left-footed central defender who we all liked and was very confident in his own ability – sometimes too confident. At Carlisle the following season he lost the ball on the edge of our area to an opponent, who quickly passed out to the wing. Joel chased the winger down, won the ball back, took it towards the striker who had won it from him, nutmegged him and calmly strode forward to start an Albion attack.

In the meantime, the stadium campaigning kept going, the tempo never relaxed. We couldn't afford to let it.

I got Des Lynam to come to Withdean one day in August. I said, "We want to photograph you with some fans of other clubs." I didn't tell him what was going to happen. The idea was that the fans were going to drench him with buckets of water, to show what spectators at Withdean had to put up with every time it rained – away fans too, of course. We gave him one of those Withdean ponchos, so he was marginally protected. Des was worried about his hairstyle, let alone catching pneumonia, but he saw the funny side and it got us a lot of coverage, keeping our fight in the public eye.

Also in August the Falmer For All team delivered another giant postcard to John Prescott's constituency office in Hull, where the staff were by now beginning to be on first-name terms with our fans.

The Labour Party Conference returned to Brighton in September 2005. There was another march and this time it was 10,000-strong. Steve Coppell joined myself, directors and staff at the head – it spoke volumes that he was prepared to come from Reading to support us.

Because of the paranoia over security – did they think I would incite our fans into a riot? – I had to address the crowd from a strange place. "Good evening everyone, this is the chairman, speaking from a police van near you." I used Tony Blair's words from the speech he made in Singapore to help London win the 2012 Olympic Games, in which he spoke about the Brits' love of sport – "That's our passion" – to remind him that there were issues much closer to home.

The crowd cheered when I implored him, "We have the love, we have the passion – please give us the stadium to consummate it." They behaved in the good-humoured manner I had come to expect, and were in great spirits and large numbers thanks to leaflets the Falmer For All team had come up with that read, 'The last chance to make Mr Prescott say Yes' and 'The fat lady is about to sing'.

And in wonderful voice too. On October 28 2005, John Prescott wrote to our lawyers saying that he was approving Falmer, subject to the statutory 42-day appeal period. He was in no doubt that there was no alternative. And that Falmer was a viable site.

The letter arrived at DMH Stallard, addressed to Tony Allen, and it also went to all interested parties. It was actually sent by messenger to the councils and the opponents, but by normal post to us. It didn't matter – we had final approval. Or what we thought was final approval.

*The Argus* photographed me, Martin, Norman Cook and Paul Samrah opening champagne on that beautiful sunny autumn day outside Donatello's in The Lanes in Brighton. *The Argus* headline under the photo the next day was 'Falmer Fizz'. I held a press conference in the restaurant's upstairs suite although even then I was cautious. I warned that there was a 42-day period in which objectors could appeal and, after everything that had gone on, we should remember that.

The letter from Prescott was 16 pages long, and I reread it in its entirety that evening. But as I did, I realised that there was a mistake in it, a pretty basic one at that. It said that the entire site was within the Brighton & Hove built-up area boundary. It wasn't. A recent decision by the City Council had marginally altered the boundary – and a tiny part was now in Lewes District. No one in the government office had picked that up. And the error was repeated twice. Martin and Tony had spotted it too.

It wasn't Prescott's fault, and it wasn't a determining factor in his decision. How could he have known that one point in a 16-page letter had been incorrectly drafted before he signed it? It was a technical error made in the DCMS but of course I just knew Lewes would latch onto it. And so did Martin. They would get their lawyers on to it as soon as they received the letter and we knew that they would spot it as we had.

But in the meantime, we had to put on the most joyous face because, as far as our fans were concerned, it was the best possible news. And it was. We'd got over the big hurdle. I knew there wouldn't be any more public inquiries. So, the following day, Saturday October 29, we celebrated at the home game against Ipswich.

I said to Martin and the board that we should do something no one else had ever done. It was our fans who had won it for us so why don't we serve them champagne? Not just in the boardroom or the hospitality area, but to the whole crowd – almost 7,000 of them, except children of course. No one worried about the cost. They just said, "Great idea."

I think it worked out about £6,000, and organising it was tricky. We didn't want to use glass, so it was clear plastic cups, and we set them out on trestle tables at the entrance to the north and south stands. Everyone was given a pouring of genuine bubbly. Not Krug or Brut, but a decent quality champagne. Plus there were non-alcoholic drinks for kids.

David Sheepshanks was there, of course, and Peter Cobbold, a member of the legendary brewing family who had owned Ipswich for generations. When David saw what we were doing, he said, "Dick Knight, what a club."

Cobbold said, "What a splendid gesture."

I replied, "Peter, we do this at every match."

"Do you really?" He looked very impressed until he turned round and saw David grinning all over his face. But I think he was jolly impressed anyway. I don't believe he'd ever been to a top-class football match at which everyone was served champagne before the game.

Although we were half-expecting a legal objection to Prescott's letter, I was confident that we would win out. The objectors surely couldn't win what was at best a frivolous challenge on a technicality. The fundamental reasons why Prescott had made his decision still stood.

But our opponents waited, and waited. Finally, on November 24, almost at the end of the appeal period, Lewes District Council mounted a legal challenge in the High Court. Everything they did was aimed at dragging out the process. I think they hoped that we might eventually run out of cash.

The ruling Liberal Democrat group on Lewes District Council had been opponents of the stadium from the start, and now they took the decision to spend council tax-payers' money on this appeal without any public consultation. It was going to cost them a lot of money that we estimated at a quarter of a million pounds.

So the Falmer For All campaign group swung back into action and within seven days we had a petition from 5,000 Lewes residents protesting against their own council's decision. We don't have 5,000 fans in that area, but we lobbied and appealed to people's sense of outrage at this money being spent in their name.

From December onwards, numerous questions were asked by Falmer For All members Ed Bassford and Roz South, who lived in the Lewes area, at council meetings, and council leader, Ann de Vecchio, didn't like it one bit. And there was the drearily predictable Nimby cry of "Of course we want the Albion to have a home, just not at Falmer." It didn't matter if it went to Sheepcote Valley, somewhere hopelessly less suitable.

In June 2006, FFA formed the Seagulls Party to fight local elections for Lewes Council seats in the coming months. We had three candidates and none of them won their seats, but they made a serious impression, causing De Vecchio's controlling Lib Dem party to lose seats.

Fellow Liberal Democrat Norman Baker, the Lewes MP, had also been an extremely vocal long-term opponent of the stadium. In 2001, when Lewes FC had been drawn against Stoke City in the FA Cup, they couldn't stage the game at their small ground, the Dripping Pan, so it was switched to Stoke's Britannia Stadium. I made the point to Baker that if a similar situation arose in the future, Lewes giving up home advantage wouldn't be necessary – we would gladly stage the game down the road at the Falmer stadium. But I don't think he wanted to hear that.

Under Parliamentary privilege, Baker strongly insinuated that there were dubious motives behind John Prescott dining with us at the Brighton v Hull game in December 2005 – as if giving him some club steak and kidney pie at a trestle table in our temporary boardroom-cum-children's creche with a glass of ale constituted some form of bribery. And it was after the decision anyway.

Baker must have thought that the old pals were getting together and I was rewarding Prescott with lavish entertainment for the decision he had made. But I hadn't even invited him. The Falmer For All team had mentioned to his constituency office that we were playing Hull and had asked if he would like to come. I wasn't going to be seen inviting him for the very reason that it might be misconstrued.

But Prescott had enjoyed himself. He'd turned up wearing his gold-and-black scarf, with his son and some of his advisors. Then he must have told them all to make themselves scarce because when we sat down for our pie, they had disappeared and it was just him and me. That was when he told me about the information he had never been given and of his suspicions that someone in his department was working against Falmer. "Someone was keeping the information from me," he said.

We were still talking until just before kick-off, and when we strolled round to the very public Withdean directors' box he was instantly surrounded by fans who started thanking him. Then there was a chant of "Johnny Prescott's blue-and-white army" but he held up his scarf and shouted, "I'm Hull, not Brighton."

Anyone who has a bad word to say about John Prescott should understand that it was only him going against two Public Inquiry inspectors that got us to Falmer. Hard as they tried, our political advisors, Steve Bassam and Ivor Caplin, had little influence on the outcome. Perhaps lobbying at Westminster isn't all it's cracked up to be. Okay, we did the job thoroughly, we found every needle in every haystack to cover every argument, we showed beyond doubt that Falmer was the best site; we admitted that it wasn't perfect but promised to do everything we could to protect the area and treat the neighbourhood and the residents with total respect. But having seen the way the planning system worked, or in some cases didn't work, I know that it was John Prescott who made the difference.

The other thing that came across to me was how smart he was. The image the media like to portray, that he is a buffoon, is total nonsense. To rise from working on a ship, up through the union ranks to become Deputy Prime Minister, he had to be sharp. He is very sharp. He couldn't just be a bully. He's a politician and a man of the people. We were lucky he came down on our side.

Ironically, Prescott wasn't going to be around to see us through the final green light for Falmer. In a government reshuffle on May 5 2006, he handed ministerial responsibility to Ruth Kelly, the new Secretary of State for Communities and Local Government. But I'd come too far to be shaken by this. Once Prescott had made his decision, it was always going to be an incredible u-turn for any other Secretary of State to argue the other way.

Sadly for Prescott and happily for us, we beat Hull 2-1 in that December game, the winner coming from Charlie Oatway. But Charlie broke his ankle in the next game, cruelly at home to QPR, the club he supported and after whose 1973 team he was named (he has 11 middle names which are the first names of all the stars of that famous side). We won that one as well, 1-0, thanks to an early goal by Guy Butters. But they were the only back-to-back wins the whole season.

We were 20th or lower from October onwards and in the relegation positions for most of the new year. There was the isolated success of a 2-1 victory over Leeds at Withdean on January 14, but the next win didn't come until April 1.

We sold Leon Knight to Swansea in January. Despite his great season in 2003/04, he couldn't repeat it in the Championship. He only scored four goals the next season and, after a brief flurry in autumn 2005, the goals dried up again.

I liked Huw Jenkins, the Swansea City chairman. He has quietly built Swansea up from a position of turmoil to the formidable and exciting reputation the club has today, and he always sympathised with our problems regarding Falmer, even though the Liberty Stadium was built with no planning problems from the Welsh Office.

So when he asked about Knight, I told him, "He is an extremely talented player and scored a lot of goals for us in his first season. He has tremendous natural ability. He can show someone the ball and then go past them. And he's got a good eye for goal. The figure is £125,000, when it should be at least double that." I was making a small profit on the £100,000 we'd paid, and he'd basically taken us to the Championship, and for me it was a good deal.

I explained to Huw, "He'll start off like a house on fire but I'm warning you, he is a problem. I don't want you coming up to me at a League meeting in six months' time saying, 'You bastard, you sold me that absolute so-and-so who is a thorn in the dressing room.' So I am telling you in advance that that's the type of player he is: bloody good, but a problem."

We did the deal, Leon was delighted to go to Swansea and, true to form, he scored a hat-trick in his first game for them, at home to MK Dons. Huw called me afterwards and said, "Well, the first part of what you said is right."

I replied, "Let's hope the second part doesn't turn out to be true this time."

But of course it did. I saw Huw a few months later, and he said, "Yes, you were spot on."

Our team didn't gel all season. We lost all five games in February, scoring only two goals, and we finished 24th and bottom at the end of the campaign.

It was perhaps only to have been expected with our small budget, but it was made worse because Mark McGhee had issues in his private life that appeared to be affecting his work. He might disagree but I felt he lacked the same will and was distracted in that second season in the Championship and began to take things for granted. Bob Booker was also going through some difficult private issues.

I was very annoyed when Arsenal arranged a friendly for us so that we could watch Quincy Owusu-Abeyie. I'd gone with Mark to Highbury to see him play in the League Cup the previous season against a full Everton team that had lost 1-0 at Chelsea on the Saturday. Owusu-Abeyie had played wide and was lightning-quick. He'd come on as a substitute and run Tony Hibbert and Joseph Yobo ragged, scoring five minutes after his introduction. Arsenal went on to win 3-1. I was excited and said, "Mark, we could get this guy."

Mark replied, "I don't know. I'm not sure." Liam told me more about the player and that Arsenal were now happy to let him go out on loan in the Championship. The player himself, who was born in Amsterdam and went on to play for Ghana, was almost over-confident in his ability.

So Arsenal fixed up the game, against Charlton at London Colney, so that we could have another look at Owusu-Abeyie. Thanks to Liam our relationship with Arsenal had always been good. We were once invited to send our reserves to play in another of these behind-closed-doors friendlies when Arsene Wenger wanted to give Gael Clichy and Philippe Senderos a run-out after injury. I was there talking to some of our players when Dennis Bergkamp came out of his personal dressing room in full playing kit and Tommy Elphick's eyes widened when he realised who he'd be playing against. Theo Walcott was also in their line-up. Tommy marked Bergkamp and Sam Rents, who was coached throughout by Jason Dodd from sweeper, played Walcott out of the game. Wenger said to me, "We've still got an awful lot of education to do with Walcott. He has to learn the team ethic."

The game against Charlton kicked off at midday, so I went along and arrived at 11.30am. Owusu-Abeyie played, and McGhee and Booker turned up at 1.15pm. Wenger was furious, because he'd laid the game on especially for us.

Mark said, "Well, we've been training."

I said, "What do you mean you've been training? You could have left Bob there to take it. You should have been here. Mark, this is totally out of order. You should apologise to Arsene Wenger."

I don't know if he ever did. I certainly did. One of the top clubs in the world was helping us out. The player was told by his agent that the Brighton manager hadn't turned up until late, so he said, "I don't want to go there." He eventually went to Spartak Moscow, but came back to the UK on loan to various clubs. We were not one of them.

So that was a negative against Mark, but he achieved a lot for us against the odds. He organised teams well and he was good at reacting to situations in games. He was prepared to take chances – a bit of a visionary, a bit of a gambler. But that second full season was more of a slog. The fans were getting at him and I came under pressure from the board to sack him. I thought Mark had done a tremendous job to keep us up the previous season.

I called a board meeting that was held at the Gatwick Hilton, rather than Withdean. It was an unusual meeting in that some of the directors were actively in favour of sacking Mark and some weren't.

I'd canvassed the opinions of four senior shareholders beforehand. They didn't have votes, but I thought I should have their input. They were Tony Bloom, who had been helping to keep the club afloat financially, Norman Cook, Billy Brown, and a long-term supporter, a key member of the Falmer For All team, who has always wanted to remain anonymous, but who had received a large legacy from a relative and put it all into the club.

This supporter had come into the club offices one day in January 2004 with an envelope addressed to me and handed it to Sally, asking her to give it to me. She said I was in and asked if he would he like to see me. But he declined and was on his way out when I spotted him and invited him into the board-room, where I always worked, not having my own office. He gave me the envelope and I opened it and inside was a cheque made out to the Albion for £170,000, signed by a solicitor. He told me that his aunt had died and left all her money to him, and he wanted me to have it for the Alive and Kicking fund. He hadn't taken a penny for himself.

I said, "This is unbelievable – above and beyond the call of duty for any fan."

He replied, "Well, I haven't got any children, so I want you to have it for the club."

I insisted that he should become a shareholder in return for the money, although even then he took some persuading. And he still holds the shares through a lawyer – he didn't want to have them in his name.

The four shareholders' opinions were split – two were for sacking Mark and two against. So I took that to the board meeting, which was held on a Saturday evening at the end of April, before the last match of the season the next day, at home to Stoke City.

The meeting began at 7pm and went on until 1.30am. The four other directors – Martin, Ray Bloom, Derek Chapman and Robert Comer – were as split as the four non-voting shareholders had been. It was the only time in my 12 years as chairman that I had to call a vote, and the only time I had to use my chairman's casting vote. We would normally discuss an issue democratically, often with a heated debate, and come to a consensus opinion.

I used my casting vote to keep Mark in the job. My argument was that, although he had been a bit distracted in his private life, he knew how to get teams promoted from the division we were going back into. I thought that, with a very stern warning from me, he could turn the team back around.

Mark knew that the board meeting was happening, and of course he guessed what the main item on the agenda was. I got in my car to drive back to Brighton at about 1.40am and switched my mobile on. There were three texts from Mark. The first two, sent earlier in the evening, asked, "How's it going?" and "Any news yet?"

The third, sent at 1.15am, read simply, "Coward."

He obviously thought that the meeting was long over, the news was bad, and I hadn't had the balls to tell him the outcome.

I got on the phone and called his mobile. It rang and rang and there was no answer. So I rang off and called again, and eventually he answered, in a sleepy sort of voice.

I said, "You're tucked up in bed after accusing me of being a coward. You don't deserve to have a chairman like me, because I fought for you and, for your information, you're still in your job because of me. There was a lot of opposition to you staying on. Don't you ever call me a coward again. Go back to bed and you and I will talk again tomorrow. Or later today."

Of course, the next day Mark was very apologetic, and you could imagine that he thought the meeting would have finished by 10pm. When he didn't hear anything by midnight he obviously suspected the worst.

But sadly it was to be only a stay of execution.

# CHAPTER TWENTY FOUR

# FALMER, YES!

I f anything proved that the Liberal Democrat majority on Lewes District Council were not interested in a sensible resolution to the stadium issue, it was the fact that they had refused an entirely reasonable offer from government lawyers to resolve the matter soon after Lewes had lodged their appeal. The government would withdraw the original planning permission and re-determine it, correcting the technical error and also taking into account the other 15 issues that Lewes had subsequently raised.

Instead Lewes insisted that they wanted a full hearing in the High Court on all their objections, most of which were spurious, in addition to their original complaint about the mistake in the approval letter. It was clearly a delaying tactic, designed to stretch the whole process out as long as possible.

By happy coincidence, the Liberal Democrats had selected Brighton as the venue for their annual conference in September 2006, so we were marching on the seafront again. We held a rally on the Sunday as all their delegates were gathering. It was a very sunny day and again several thousand fans turned up.

The Falmer For All team, Martin Perry and I met with a group of senior Liberal Democrats including Lord Kirkwood and Don Foster, their spokesman on sport. Like the Labour party before them, they were surprised to be confronted with a local issue at their national conference.

What came over in an open and sensible meeting was that they couldn't understand what their own party's group on Lewes District Council was up to or even why their own MP, Norman Baker, was on the same side. The national party could see the merits of our argument, not least because it was a vote-winner. Or a vote-loser, if Lewes continued their tactics. It made social, sporting and economic sense. There was no reason not to support it.

To ram the point home at the conference, we lobbied the delegates with leaflets and posters against the local party's stance. We also explained why the Seagulls Party would be standing against their candidates in Lewes.

The piece de resistance was the spoof menus that John Cowen of the Falmer For All team came up with. Paul Samrah and Adrian Newnham, dressed in dinner jackets and dicky bows, handed them out to guests going into the Lib Dem Gala Dinner. They included dishes such as 'Unappetisers – Lewes Hand-raised Porkies', 'Canard de Lewes avec Nimby Sauce', 'Just Desserts – Baker's Fruitcake Fool' and 'Bellotti Career Brulee'.

Sir Menzies Campbell, the party leader, arrived in a limo with Lady Campbell and Paul shook his hand and gave them the menus. Sir Menzies asked, "Are you security? I understand there are protesters due." Paul replied, "We are the protesters." Priceless.

Of course, we knew that our battle for a stadium didn't affect the party on a national level, but we'd wanted the hierarchy to look into what the local party in Lewes were doing and to try to make them see sense. We had been able to get over to the highest level of the party that the Lib Dems were risking a lot in Sussex.

Baker, the Lewes MP, agreed to go on the local BBC radio post-match phone-in on Saturday October 14, after our away game at Scunthorpe. I suppose he expected that he'd easily be able to see off some inane questioning from blinkered football fans. But we ambushed it. We had six or seven fans including members of the Falmer For All team sitting around a table in the Withdean boardroom, passing the phone around. Several of them got through and put challenging questions to Baker, most of which he struggled to answer. He was taken to task on everything he said and resorted to the normal political escape route of bluster.

A typical Baker tactic in his campaign against Falmer was not only to question John Prescott tucking into our Withdean hospitality, but also to make a serious insinuation – behind the shield of parliamentary privilege – against club director Derek Chapman whose company Prescott had visited to hand out an Investors In People business award they had won, three months before the Falmer plans were even called in by the government. Whatever Derek was supposed to have done clearly hadn't worked. By now Baker was stooping to new lows in his efforts to denigrate us and the Deputy Prime Minister.

He latched onto and exploited a report leaked by a hotel consultant – 'hotel-gate' – which criticised the choice of Falmer and said we should have looked at other sites. Where had the author been during the two public inquiries? The writer also claimed that we were going to build a hotel on the site. Baker again used parliamentary privilege to make a big thing of this, but all the plans were in and there was no sign of a hotel. In October 2013, to my surprise, the club announced its intention to build a hotel behind the Amex East Stand, but it was never part of our original plans.

In the end Martin and I held what was described as a 'clear-the-air' meeting with Baker at Withdean after we suggested a get-together. He agreed, wanting to be seen to be open-minded and approachable, but came over to me as condescending.

This was supposedly a 'round-table' discussion, but Baker sat at the table as far away from us as he could – as if he were granting an audience to us in our own boardroom. He conceded nothing at this meeting beyond a vague promise that he'd be prepared to work with us towards a solution.

That was pretty rich, as we already had a solution, but it was purely a political, opportunist move by him. He wasn't interested in a reasoned discussion or an explanation of why thousands of his constituents were in favour of our plans, or that there was no other deliverable site in Brighton & Hove. Baker had continued to quote the Nimby excuse, "Of course the Albion should have a new stadium, but not . . ." and talked up Sheepcote Valley as the best site in the city, and even proposed Gatwick at one point!

All he was doing was moving his position politically slightly towards the club so that he could say, "Well, I've met Dick Knight and Martin Perry and I'm trying to reach a solution with them."

The strange thing is that Baker espouses some valuable public causes, but he completely misjudged the Falmer issue. He thought he was endorsing what the majority of the people who voted for him wanted. In reality, hardly any Lewes residents wanted their council pursuing expensive legal action, costing £250,000, to take it to the High Court.

I believe Lewes were hoping that our money would run out before theirs did. They may well have been aware that Oxford United's finances for a new ground had run out in mid-build. We had spent way north of £10 million on planning surveys, planning applications, submissions, consultancies experts and two planning inquiries. In truth, this was hurting our football club. We were scrimping along, but I never resorted to begging publicly for another £300,000 to help us get by. It would have encouraged the opposition to believe that we were in a weak financial position.

Conversely, I often wondered whether Lewes had a financial benefactor. I don't have any evidence for that, but their will to take the fight to the High Court seemed very strong. I think they were delighted that we had been relegated to League One, because it enabled them to depict us as a club in decline, who couldn't possibly need a 23,000-capacity stadium.

It was because of his record of getting teams promoted from that level that I had resisted the pressure on me to get rid of Mark McGhee. But I wanted to freshen up the coaching, and because we had a number of young players coming through such as Adam El-Abd, Lynch, Elphick, Robinson, Joe Gatting and Dean Cox, it seemed logical to promote Dean Wilkins, who had been in charge of them in the youth team. Dean deserved his chance to coach higher than youth level, and some people wondered whether he was being groomed to be the next Albion manager. Although a good coach doesn't necessarily make a good manager.

Mark may have sensed the same thing and was initially resistant because it seemed like a slight, but I said, "Mark, sit down with Dean and talk it out between you. I'm not forcing this on you but I think it makes sense." And after he'd spoken to Wilkins he saw that it could work. Dean White, who had looked after the reserves and also did some coaching and scouting, became chief scout, in charge of rebuilding the scouting network in the UK and abroad. The only problem was that Dean hated flying, so if I asked him to go to Poland or Bulgaria it was a hardship for him – but he did it, because he's a good guy.

We brought in striker Alex Revell from Braintree Town, and he scored the only goal in the first game of the 2006/07 season, away to Rotherham. It was quite an eventful match – Dean Cox was sent off after receiving a second yellow for taking his shirt off to celebrate, and Colin Kazim-Richards played his last game for us. He came on as a substitute but was so ineffective that Mark took him off again.

Colin gave me a letter after that game asking for a transfer, dated the following Monday. He had it typed and ready, which told us he had already made up his mind, so we let other clubs know that we might be interested in selling him.

Showing how well I now got on with Paul Scally, Kerry and I had been invited to his wedding the following day, and what a splendid affair it was. Paul and his lovely wife Sara arrived in a horse-drawn carriage and Guy Butters and Andy Hessenthaler, also guests who of course had both played for him, told us that the only time they'd seen Paul look so happy was when Gillingham took three points off Brighton.

A lovely lady on our table was Helen Chamberlain, the Sky *Soccer AM* presenter, with whom we had a lot of laughs. Helen is so down to earth and seemed to have a lot of time for Brighton – perhaps surprising for someone who supported the other Gulls, Torquay United, but she had gone out with our player Nathan Jones for a while and he must have told her what a nice chairman I was.

Later that month I was watching our reserves play at Worthing's ground at Woodside Road with Mark and Dean White, while Bob Booker was looking after the team. Colin Kazim-Richards was playing, or rather going through the motions, really. I went to get something from my car at half-time and my mobile rang. It was Terry Robinson, the chairman of Sheffield United, who had just been promoted to the Premier League. He said, "Dick, I'm very interested in taking Colin Kazim-Richards off your hands."

"Hi Terry, I'm all ears."

I agreed the deal there and then, sitting in the car park at Woodside Road. I asked for £150,000 and got it with a 25 per cent sell-on. That turned out well when he joined Fenerbahce for around £1.275 million 10 months later, giving us £431,500 in all. Not bad considering that Colin had originally cost us £55,000.

But I was as honest with Terry as I had been with Huw Jenkins over Leon Knight. I said, "Let me explain to you. Colin is a difficult player. He might do well under a down-to-earth manager like Neil Warnock, who tells it straight, but his father has a big influence, so tell Neil that when he talks to Colin about terms, his dad will be in the conversation as well.

"I'll tell my manager and secretary that the deal will be happening, but I'll ring off now, Terry, because Colin is actually playing in the reserve game I'm at – so I'd better get him off the pitch in case he gets injured!"

So I got back just after the second half had started and said to Mark and Dean, "Sorry I took so long guys, but I've just sold Kazim-Richards."

"Brilliant!" Mark said.

I added, "To Sheffield United for £150,000 and add-ons. We'd better get him off."

So Dean White set off round the pitch to the dugouts, which were opposite the main stand, and told Bob what had happened. Bob signalled Colin to come off and told him to go and get changed, although he didn't say why. Colin ambled back round the pitch and scowled at me and Mark as he went into the dressing rooms.

After a while, I said, "I suppose I'd better go and tell him." So I went down to the dressing room and Colin was there in a towel, having just come out of the shower. I said, "You want to leave this club, don't you?"

"Yes, Mr Chairman."

"Well, I've just done a deal for you to go to Sheffield United. If you can agree terms you'll be a Premier League player."

At this, Colin yelled, "Wow, brilliant – thanks Mr Chairman" and rushed across the dressing room and gave me a big hug. His towel had fallen off, so there was I being embraced by a stark naked footballer. All I could think of was, "I just hope no one comes in now."

I pulled him off me and said, "If you fancy it, which it sounds as if you do, tell your dad and you can both go up to Sheffield and see Neil Warnock tomorrow. We wish you all the best."

The next day, Mark got a call from Neil Warnock, "I know your chairman mentioned it to Terry, but that kid's dad – I had to send him out of the room!" The sad thing was that, during his time with Brighton, Colin's agent was Mike Drew, a real professional who works hard and looks after his clients very well, but then he dispensed with his services when Mike didn't get him to Manchester United, Liverpool or Arsenal.

In the first month of the season we had three wins, but then lost badly, 4-1 at home to Crewe, and were very poor. The game was played on a Sunday because Sussex were playing Lancashire in the final of the C&G Trophy at Lord's Cricket Ground on the Saturday. We moved it with the co-operation of my friend John Bowler, the Crewe chairman, and his very likeable and lovely daughter Alison, the club secretary.

Sussex won thanks to a great bowling performance from James Kirtley to complete the first leg of the Trophy and County Championship double, and there were Albion shirts everywhere and chants of "Dicky Knight's blue-and-white army" at the revered headquarters of cricket.

The next day the mood was very different. Thanks to Crewe's help in moving the game, there were nearly 6,000 there to witness our capitulation rather than 3,000. We went ahead through Dean Cox but were 2-1 down by half-time. There were vociferous calls for Mark's head and some people were having a go at me for keeping him. At Withdean you were in such close proximity to the fans – they could walk straight up to the dugout and I had to walk through the crowd to get to and from the boardroom. You weren't cocooned. You have to take the rough with the smooth as a chairman, but it wasn't pleasant.

There was something about the way we had given up against Crewe which concerned me. Then we lost at Bristol City the following weekend and were poor again. I felt Mark had lost his way and that the younger players were following Dean Wilkins. It was hard to sack Mark, but we had to have a change.

I thought about it a lot and finally made my decision. On Thursday September 7, I met Mark at Topolino's at 3pm when there was no one there and gave him the bad news. And I decided that this time I had to sack Bob Booker too because, like Mark, he had too many distractions from elsewhere in his life. It had affected his performance.

It was a difficult decision. There was strong vocal opposition to McGhee, but also a large, less noisy element who were behind him. So we had a divided crowd, a divided dressing room and, going back to the end of last season, a divided board.

Martin Perry was with me at Topolino's, not because I needed moral support but because he wanted to be. He had already established a friendship with Dean Wilkins, the obvious successor, and I think he wanted to make sure I went through with it. Mark was surprised, because he knew there was an element of fan support that he still had, and I think he assumed he still had me on his side as well.

Mark generated a lot of emotion. Everyone recognised what he had done in taking up and keeping up a team that was not that great, to be honest. Hats off to him, he had done a terrific job. And he is a very intelligent, personable guy. We had long talks about all sorts of subjects, and he was very good with the fans. He always had time for them, always came to fans' meetings, always made them laugh. Some people thought that I had been swayed by the fans who had shouted loudest rather than the silent majority, but I had done what I thought was best for the club.

The only candidate to replace Mark was Dean Wilkins. I was always going to give him the chance to do the whole job with the big boys' team. He was always very animated at the side of the pitch and a perfectionist, pointing out where someone could improve. I remembered how he had been disappointed when we had beaten Blackburn 1-0 at Ewood Park in the fifth round of the FA Youth Cup. He was haranguing the players for not scoring more – away from home against the youth team of a Premier League club!

Perhaps I should have been more wary of the fact that he was more likely to be telling players where they were going wrong. I'm not sure how good he was at putting his arm round them. Certain players who had come up with him respected him hugely but some of the older players found his methods strange.

When Brian Horton and I originally gave him the job as youth coach he said he had a vision of us playing in the Premier League with a team of young Sussex-born players, and he said the same thing again now, which was admirable – up to a point. In the back of my mind, I thought, "Let's get real here", but for now there was a good group coming through, and they wanted to play for Dean.

Wilkins brought in Ian Chapman as his assistant, a popular former player and local boy who had played in Barry Lloyd's team with Dean and who proved himself a competent operator. We started with a few good results, including a 4-1 win over Leyton Orient, and a 2-1 win away to Scunthorpe, the division leaders. Jake Robinson scored a perfect hat-trick – right foot, left foot, header – in a 3-0 win at Huddersfield. But we also went on some bad runs, which emphasised that we were short of strikers.

I had tried again that summer to get Sam Parkin, who had been at Ipswich, but he went to Luton instead, and Danny Dichio from Preston, who was interested but then had an offer from FC Toronto in Major League Soccer. He was what Turienzo should have been – a striker who held the ball up well but also scored goals.

In the January transfer window, after a bad run up to and over Christmas, I tried even harder to land a goalscorer. Leon Constantine was banging goals in for Port Vale. His agent was Eric 'Monster' Hall, who turned out to be a lovely guy. I agreed a fee of £135,000 with Vale and the player's personal terms with Eric, but then he told me, "I like the sound of what you're doing at Brighton and it would be a good club for Leon to go to, but there are Championship clubs interested as well."

I had a chat on the phone with Leon and he told me that Eric had advised him to come to us, but he then said, "I'm 28 and I may not get another chance to play in the Championship." So he decided not to come, but in the event he didn't go anywhere in that window. In August he moved on a free transfer to Leeds, who were in the same division as us and he never made it to the Championship.

Then I turned to Millwall's Darren Byfield, a Leon Knight style player but a very together guy, whose girlfriend was the singer Jamelia. That was when I first met Ken Brown, the Millwall chief executive, who later joined us as managing director. They wanted £300,000. I offered half that, then upped the offer to £165,000, which was a lot of money for us. Ken said, "Dick, we're going to get £300,000 for him from someone." But, like Constantine, he didn't move that January, and when he went to Bristol City in the summer it was for an 'undisclosed fee' and I'm sure Millwall didn't get the £300,000 that Ken had said they would.

I always got on well with Adam Pearson, the Hull chairman, and they were desperate for money so I did a £75,000 deal for Nicky Forster, one of the most consistent scorers in the Football League. I agreed it with Adam and Nicky but then Phil Brown, who had become Hull manager in December, didn't want to let him go. Forster, whom I saw as an out-and-out central striker, was being played by Brown, who was short of players, on the right of midfield. He did well there, incidentally, and was runner-up in Hull's player of the season award.

In the end I completed the Forster deal at the end of the season. But even though I had been pursuing three top strikers throughout January, all three fell through and we were left with a strikeforce of youngsters Joe Gatting and Robinson, and Alex Revell, who was injured.

I came in for a lot of criticism from Andy Naylor in *The Argus*. We'd scored one goal from open play in six weeks, true, but his criticisms that we never spent money on players took no account of my efforts to do precisely that – agreeing fees on two of my three targets, still to no avail. He knew about Byfield and Constantine, but not Forster.

On February 1 I told *The Argus* that the transfer window had been frustrating, but I said, "We set our targets pretty high as far as the quality of strikers is concerned. There is no doubt we need an experienced goalscorer and ideally two; that is what we targeted. We have offered big money but that is not a factor."

Naylor appeared to concede the following day that our failure to land a striker had not been for the want of trying. But he had begun to give a lot of space in his match reports to knocking me, so that they became more like opinion columns, but with teams and referee at the end. He barely mentioned the games. We lost at Brentford on Saturday February 10, our fourth game in a row without scoring, and what he wrote in the Monday paper was spiteful and the fans thought it was over the top.

"The chairman has . . . messed up by dragging his heels during the January transfer window," Naylor said. "He is in danger of being remembered for doing the dirty on Steve Gritt, not landing Steve Coppell when he first had the chance, not giving Martin Hinshelwood enough backing and losing his nerve when prematurely abandoning McGhee. Crowds, like the team, are falling. Most damning of all, Knight is in danger of being remembered for steering a club that reached for the stars, but came back down to earth with an almighty bump in the basement division of English football against a backdrop of accelerating apathy."

But as well as accusing me of being unwilling to spend money on strikers, Naylor suggested that I had tried to interfere in team matters. "Yet another change of manager is not the answer when the man doing the firing is part of the problem. In my view, the chairman of any club should leave the football to the football experts. He should back the manager's judgement in the transfer market to the best of his financial ability, without his own opinion of players clouding that process. From past conversations with previous managers . . . the recurring theme is that he tries to exert too much influence."

Pretty heavy stuff which showed a distinct lack of understanding of recent events, as well as the fact that managers were no longer exclusively responsible for player recruitment and transfer policy.

Naylor's comments certainly didn't reflect the feelings of the majority of the fans, and when we played away to Leyton Orient on the Tuesday evening, they made their feelings known with some pretty strong anti-Naylor chants.

The crowd was around 5,000, and a lot were Albion fans. The travelling supporters are obviously the most dedicated fans, who follow every aspect of a club more closely, and at Brisbane Road they were seated close to the press box, near their target. I don't think I'd ever heard of a fans' protest against a journalist before.

The special partnership between fans and club came sharply to mind a few weeks later when Liverpool manager Rafa Benitez suggested that reserve teams of Premier League clubs should be allowed to play in the Football League. I reacted strongly against it in an interview on the BBC website, saying it insulted the League's history and stature, which echoed views I'd expressed a few years earlier during a BBC Radio 5 Live *Any Sporting Questions* programme. Compere John Inverdale asked me if, bearing in mind Brighton's recent troubles, I'd ever thought of making the Albion a 'nursery club,' along the lines of the apparent relationship between Crewe Alexandra and Liverpool.

"Our fans would rightly string me up from the nearest lamppost," I replied. "We're proud of our traditions and we're fighting our way back. You can't take away the hopes of supporters – it's amazing what a club can do with belief, unity and using their talents."

Premier League clubs have touted the idea again recently of nursery 'feeder' clubs, but I am as much against the principle now as I was when I first became chairman of Brighton. The dreams of smaller clubs that they may one day make it to the big time should never be extinguished.

As if to answer Naylor's point about striker recruitment, we won that match against Orient 4-1 and one of the scorers was Bas Savage, whom I'd just signed – on the day Naylor's piece came out in fact. He was a free agent, and he scored six goals for us over the second half of the season and celebrated every one with his famous 'moonwalk'.

I remember I took my grandsons to Northampton, where Savage scored both goals in a 2-0 win – our ninth victory on the road, a record bettered only twice in Albion history at that point. We were down in the tunnel area when Bas came out and the boys shouted to him, "Bas, do us a moonwalk." He turned round and peered towards them with his eyes screwed up. He was only 10 yards away and he couldn't see where the voices were coming from. I asked him, "Bas, is your eyesight really that bad?"

He replied, "Yes, Mr Chairman. I can only see the ball when it's a few yards away from me."

He did the moonwalk, autographed their programmes and went off.

Over lunch on the Monday I said to Dean Wilkins, "Bas Savage's eyesight is terrible, isn't it?"

"Is it?"

Dean White was there and he said, "So that's why he always sits at the front in tactical meetings when everyone else sits at the back. He can't see the tactics board otherwise. And he leans forward . . . I thought he was extra keen."

But Bas was a great character who we would have liked to keep but couldn't, even after relaunching his career when Gillingham let him go. He was misled by an agent who told him what he thought he wanted to hear, then struggled to deliver it.

We got through to the third round of the FA Cup that season and were handed another excellent money-making draw, away to West Ham. We lost 3-0 and Carlos Tevez was the outstanding player, beating us virtually single-handed. Later, of course, West Ham were fined £5.5 million by the Premier League for irregularities over his registration and that of Javier Mascherano, and when this came out I raised the legitimacy of West Ham's cup win over us with the FA.

In May I wrote to Brian Barwick, the FA chief executive, whom I knew from his career in television and because he is a friend of Des Lynam. I pointed out that Tevez had been the most influential player in our defeat. And if Tevez, as the Premier League had ruled, had been improperly registered, that should equally apply to the FA Cup and we should be given the £40,000 third-round prize money that West Ham got for beating us. I also said that by rights we had claim to West Ham's share of the gate for their fourth-round defeat by Watford.

I got a letter back from Jonathan Hall, the FA director of governance, who said that they had to wait for the outcome of a request for arbitration from Sheffield United, at whose expense West Ham had stayed in the Premier League. Eventually Sheffield United got £20 million from West Ham in an out-of-court settlement, but the FA wriggled off the hook in our case, and we got nothing. In November I got a letter from Hall saying it had subsequently been ruled that the original fine was for a breach of Premier League rules rather than registration, and that it would be "entirely inappropriate and unfair" for the FA to give us West Ham's Cup money – a decision seemingly favouring a big club over a small club as usual.

It seemed the FA would rather not get involved in protecting the integrity of their own competition – whatever the legal word play, West Ham were clearly at fault in the Premier League, otherwise they wouldn't have paid the Blades £20 million – but apparently not so in the FA Cup. I came to the conclusion that if West Ham had played, and beaten, other Premier League sides in the cup that year, the outcome would have been very different.

That wasn't my only clash with the authorities. In many ways Lord Brian Mawhinney was one of the best ever Football League chairmen. In his reign the League finally dragged itself into the 21st century. He was responsible for improving governance, pushing for points deductions and made clubs more accountable for their own actions. But perhaps inspired by those changes, he went what proved to be one step too far.

On the day of that 2-1 win at Scunthorpe in October 2006 he collared me in the boardroom and put an idea to me. "What do you think of this, Dick? I've got an idea that will be as revolutionary, as significant to football as three points for a win. There are too many draws. And everyone loves penalty shoot-outs. So I propose that when there's a drawn game after 90 minutes, there will be a penalty shoot-out and the winner will get an extra point."

"But Brian," I said. "The two best games I've ever seen have been draws – Tottenham against Burnley, 4-4, and Chelsea versus West Ham, 5-5. Even a goalless draw can be a tremendous game. People don't need a falsely-contrived ending. One reason people like penalty shoot-outs is because they're so rare. And why should one team get half as many points as another when they've proved that they're just as good?"

But he was absolutely convinced that it was a winner. And over the next few months I heard that he was lobbying clubs throughout the League for this idea. And it appeared as a firm proposal on the agenda of a Football League club meeting in March 2007, with a view to implementing it for the 2007/08 season.

On the morning of the meeting, which was held in Leicester, I was heading north on the train when I got a call from Mark Arthur, the Nottingham Forest chief executive, who was on the League board. He said, "Dick, you are going to take the lead as usual on this penalty shoot-out idea, aren't you? Because everyone's against it."

The club chairmen and CEOs on the League board usually kept quiet at League meetings, perhaps because they were told to. I always felt happier outside the tent as I was one of the most vocal of the people on the floor of meetings. So I said, "Have any of you actually said that to Brian Mawhinney at a board meeting?"

"Well, you know what Brian's like, Dick – he loves to get his point over."

"So Brian is going to make his presentation even though everyone knows it's crazy? Well, if I have to I will. But it shouldn't just be coming from me and one or two others; it should be coming from you as well. He'll be looking for a reaction from the floor. Why don't some of the board speak up too?"

"Er, yes, okay Dick."

That afternoon Mawhinney made his presentation and then asked for comments. "Over to you guys," he said, obviously expecting a hugely positive response.

There was Mark Arthur looking at me from the platform behind the chairman as if urging me, "Come on Dick, knock it down." And I was looking back at him, waiting for him or one of the other directors to say something. Nothing. So I pressed my buzzer and said, "Dick Knight, Brighton & Hove Albion.

"Brian, I sense that the room is not with you on this. I told you some months ago that I thought it wasn't a good idea. Not only does it go against the very essence of football, but with all those extra points you'd be handing out a team could technically win its division with 92 points without actually winning a single game – by drawing every one and then winning all the shoot-outs.

"Equally, under your scheme, a team could possibly get relegated with 46 points without losing a single game, if they drew every match but lost every shoot-out."

By this time the laughter was starting around the hall. "Dick, you're always so negative," Mawhinney said, expecting the other clubs to pile in on his side. But when the buzzers started sounding, everyone more or less agreed with me. But Mawhinney kept protesting that it was a great idea and that the fans would like it until Barry Taylor, a Barnsley director, who was also a member of the FA Council, was especially direct, "Brian, you bloody well never know when to take no for a bloody answer; it's a bloody stupid idea."

After that, Mawhinney, being a politician, suggested setting up a working party to look into it further, rather than risk a 72-0 defeat. And, like most working parties set up by politicians, it was never heard of again. And the members of the Football League board, who had wanted me to speak up and promised to back me? They sat on their hands and kept their mouths shut throughout. But at least now if a team wins a hard-earned point they don't risk the disappointment of losing a penalty shoot-out immediately afterwards.

That was a minor victory, in a sense for the Albion, but all in all, 2006/07 was a disappointing season. Our excellent away form didn't compensate for an appalling home record of only five league wins and many lacklustre displays, resulting in an unsatisfactory 18th place at the end of the campaign.

But there was light at the end of the tunnel on the stadium issue because no hearing at the High Court ever took place. In October 2006, Lewes withdrew their appeal and accepted the long-standing government offer to rescind the original planning permission and re-determine the application, correcting the boundary mistake and addressing the other points they'd raised. It seemed reasonable to assume that our initiatives at the Liberal Democrats conference a month earlier had played their part.

But of course that didn't mean that we were home and dry. Nothing was ever that simple – it had been over four years since we had got local approval. And now we had to deal with the new Minister in the driving seat, Ruth Kelly, and convince her that our cause was just.

We produced a series of postcards for fans to send to her. We couldn't assume that she would have the same attitude or awareness of the issues going back over months that Prescott had. Kelly was not particularly sport-orientated although she purported to be a Bolton supporter, so we had to make sure that the pressure on that office was maintained.

There were 10 postcards, featuring different images, superbly designed by Bill Swallow. One showed fans in the rain at Withdean wearing the pointed-head ponchos, the white ones, looking a bit like Ku Klux Klan members now I think about it. Others showed the busy Falmer Road interchange and the Brighton University outbuildings with 'Falmer's Country Lanes' with the slogan 'Area of Outstanding Natural Beauty?', and so on.

Rather than deal with reality, in their literature Lewes had put out an image of the stadium photoshopped into the wrong position, to make it appear that it would be far closer to open downland and a hilltop path. Peter Near of the Falmer For All team spotted that they had already used the downland image in a previous leaflet, but now it was next to the stadium! It was blatant misrepresentation.

We distributed almost 40,000 of our postcards to other clubs and visiting fans so that a big pile of cards would be landing on Kelly's doormat from everywhere, not just Brighton. Hibs, Sheffield Wednesday, Bristol City – the cards came from all over Britain. It was an incredible logistical exercise promoting them in club programmes but we had the people to do it. By now we were all old hands.

We had no real indication of how well we were getting through to her, but we were confident that the legal case for her repeating Prescott's decision was strong. Amazingly, she gave all parties the opportunity for further submissions, even though there was no reason why she would come to a different conclusion.

It beggared belief how low our opponents were willing to stoop, when Falmer Parish Council made some very crass comments about the residents of the nearby Moulsecoomb and Bevendean estates, stating that they would not benefit from employment opportunities at the stadium because the people who lived there were only suitable for very low-level jobs. That would hardly play well with a minister whose role it was to improve communities. Brighton & Hove Council published their submission to Ruth Kelly and in it was a scathing dismissal of Lewes's claims for Sheepcote Valley's accessibility, and our fans had proved the point.

At last we received notice that there would be a decision on or by July 9, but then there was yet another delay – like a referee adding on another minute at the end of the second period of extra time. On June 27 2007 Gordon Brown succeeded Tony Blair as Prime Minister and reshuffled the cabinet, putting Hazel Blears in Ruth Kelly's job. So she needed to get on top of the brief, but we felt she was unlikely to change anything, and so it proved. On Monday July 23 we were told that the Minister's final decision would arrive the following day and that the letter would be sent direct to us as well as to everyone else involved.

We gathered in the club offices at 7am, ready to receive the letter. It was "Where's the postman?" "He's gone into the lift." "He's on his way up." Sally Townsend and Becky Mitchell, my secretary, who worked on the Alive and Kicking campaign, were ready and eager to welcome the red-letter man. He delivered the usual pile of mail and we frantically went through it, but there was nothing.

So there were Martin and I and several other directors and the media all wondering what was going on. *The Argus* had a picture of Martin and me sitting in his office, taken through the frosted glass of the club crest – a moody shot of us looking very pensive, which we were. Then the phone rang, and it was the University of Brighton calling to congratulate us. And then the Council rang with the same good news. They'd both received letters, but we hadn't.

The government had posted our letter to our lawyers, DHM Stallard. They faxed all 40 pages of it over to us at 9.04am. The news I'd been waiting ten years for appeared in paragraph 84, on page 22:

". . . accordingly, for the reasons given above, the Secretary of State agrees with the conclusions of the second inspector and disagrees with the recommendations of the first inspector. She hereby grants planning permission for: 'A Community Stadium at Falmer with accommodation for class B1 business, educational, conference, club shop merchandise, entertainment and food, and road works, pedestrian and cycle links, coach/bus park and set down area, shared use of existing car parking space at the University of Sussex and shared use of land for recreation and parking at Falmer High School'."

And three other permissions for the coach and bus interchange, the widening of Village Way, and the new roundabout at the University of Brighton campus entrance. It was signed by Andrew Lynch, 'authorised to sign for Hazel Blears'.

Oh, and we could also play football there.

Hazel Blears's conclusions rejected all of the 16 legal points Lewes had raised in the final stages of their Machiavellian manoeuvres, which had cost us over 18 months of delays and a lot of extra costs since Prescott's approval letter back in October 2005.

Champagne? Not yet.

Paragraphs 85 and 86 set out "the circumstances in which the validity of the Secretary of State's decision may be challenged by making an application to the High Court within six weeks of the date of this letter". So we could only sip a cup of warm tea rather than a glass of bubbly. Lewes, or anyone else, had until September 4 to appeal. We still had six weeks to wait.

*The Argus* front page the next day showed me and Norman Cook celebrating again, but in reality our rejoicing was fairly muted. We knew that we had achieved our ultimate goal but on this project we never took anything for granted. Who knew whether Lewes wouldn't come up with another reason, another scheme for pouring council tax-payers' money – and ours – down the drain?

Even though Norman Baker had now woken up, smelt the political coffee, and told Lewes that enough was enough and they must now work with us, it wouldn't have surprised me if they had claimed to have found the grave of Richard III under the coach park site.

We'd run almost the full mile but we still had a few yards to go before we breasted the tape. Martin and I were thinking, "They could still appeal but really we've won and it's all over, isn't it? Isn't it?"

We played the waiting game, but the deadline passed on September 4 2007, with no challenge. And we really had finally won. Ten years and a day after I had officially become chairman of Brighton & Hove Albion.

My reactions were mixed. By now we were a decade out of the Goldstone. All the money and time that we had wasted could have been put to far better use. The delays hurt us in many ways. We got a letter from the Football Stadia Improvement Fund, part of the Football Foundation, previously the Football Trust. It explained that the rules for grants towards building of new stadiums had changed and that £800,000 of the £2.8 million funding we had been promised in writing way back in 2000 was now no longer available. Nor were other loans and extra grants that we could have got if we'd been able to start a few years earlier. The Anfield Kop and the Stretford End at Old Trafford had benefited in the early days of those stadium improvement grants. Far wealthier clubs had been given far more, but we would miss out because our application had been bogged down in the planning process and dragged through two public inquiries.

Then there were the massive costs of that ludicrously protracted marathon. By the time we completed all the agreements and were ready to go on site at Falmer, the bills were almost £14 million – for the planning applications, for upgrading Withdean, the unbelievable range of experts and all the legal costs.

Of course, there was also time to reflect that there were lasting benefits that came out of it – the bond of the club and supporters working together with one voice: an army of willing crusaders and campaigners. No other club in English football has shown more togetherness. But it was born of desperation and absolute necessity. No sane chairman would ever want it to happen that way.

There was no euphoria, more a sense of relief, combined with the knowledge of how much work lay ahead. Only now could Derek Chapman step into the role I had brought him onto the board for years before. We had to tender for the building contract straight away. We had to revisit our business plans and make sure they were still robust, which they were. We had to reinforce to the council that this was still a viable project that they would not have to bail out.

And what we didn't know was that the delays had taken us to the building phase just as the worldwide credit crunch was about to hit.

So it was like the famous Churchill speech. Even after 10 years, it wasn't the beginning of the end. It was the end of the beginning.

# CHAPTER TWENTY FIVE

# BOXING DAY WITH THE GLOVES OFF

**W**e didn't have an auspicious beginning to the 2007/08 season, losing three of the first four games, but Nicky Forster then showed what he was capable of when he scored twice in a 3-2 victory over Southend. He had been raring to join us even though he had enjoyed a wonderful second half of the 2006/07 season at Hull City.

He didn't have an agent. He is an intelligent guy and acted for himself. He was 33 and I offered him a three-year contract as an incentive to stay fit. I was certain he could still score goals and, unlike Hull, we had no intention of playing him as anything but a striker.

Dean Wilkins was keen, because he realised that we had some way to go before we could achieve his goal of an all Sussex-born first team, and here was an experienced player who could bring something to the squad.

I hadn't anticipated that Paul Duffen, who had taken over as chairman of Hull, his first job in top football, in July 2007, would try to go back on the deal I had done with Adam Pearson to buy Nicky for £75,000. When I called him to activate the deal he said, "We don't really want to sell him, so the price is now £250,000."

I told him, "Well, I have a deal with your predecessor, both clubs and the player agreed to it, and as far as I'm concerned that is written in stone."

He said, "Forget about what my predecessor said, the price is £250,000."

I replied, "I'm not going to forget it. That is the agreement I had with your club, and you will soon learn that in football, if two chairmen agree something over the phone, then that is a deal and the contract is only rubber-stamping what's been agreed. I have been working on the understanding that Nicky Forster is coming to Brighton for £75,000. And, just as important, so has he."

Duffen said, "My manager, Phil Brown, doesn't want to sell him."

"That may be the case, but you are going to have a very disgruntled player on your hands. Your club's word is its bond, a new chairman honours what his predecessor agreed. I'm going to insist."

To an extent I was being the wise old head telling the new kid on the block how things are done in the big leagues. But I knew that Nicky would back me up. He had just got married, to the mum of future Albion player Jake Caskey. Jake, now Forster-Caskey, was a young lad at the time. They lived at Lingfield, just over the Sussex-Surrey border, and he wanted to come back south. So Duffen gave in.

In my heart, I knew that from the way Nicky had played in the second half of the previous season, he was good enough to keep playing in the second tier, certainly worth more than £75,000, and here I was taking him into League One. But we had a deal.

After a slow start, Nicky kept on scoring all season and easily justified our outlay. He was a single-minded guy who knew how to put the ball in the net. An absolute professional hitman who scored with the minimum of fuss. He found space in the box and could score with his head as well as his feet. He was strong-willed, straightforward, knew his own mind – all the qualities that made him a predator on the pitch. He kept referring to the third year I'd offered him – which would be at a lower wage – but I said, "Three years here at your age is a hell of an incentive, and it's up to you to prove you are worth it. And then I might reconsider the salary." And it was soon obvious that he intended to make me pay him a higher rate when he got to that third year.

I was concerned that fans had been deserting us in droves at Withdean. That was obviously to do with our dismal home record in 2006/07 and football that hadn't been entertaining. I wasn't prepared to accept another season like that, so I had a chat with Dean Wilkins and made it plain that we needed a more attacking style and to be competing at the right end of the table, playing the sort of football that the fans wanted to see.

Forster got into his stride in November, when we were in the top 10. In one month he scored two goals on four occasions, and we were up to seventh by the end of the sequence. And I had appointed Barry Lloyd as the new chief scout, bringing him back into the club because I remembered all those unusual and interesting players he had signed back in the early 1990s – people like Mike Small, John Byrne, Sergei Gotsmanov and Stefan Iovan. He could spot a player and, instead of sending him to Russia, I sent him up north to look for another striker.

Barry came up with two gems, but not before things reached a new low. Bas Savage was seeing out his calendar-year contract, which expired in December. I think his agent, Kevin Horton, had thought that if his contract ended at a different time from everyone else's he'd be able to negotiate a special deal. I made Savage an offer of a very decent pay increase and a two-year contract but Horton ignored it and started talking to Wilkins instead of me. Dean wanted to appear to be on the players' side over negotiations, but that sometimes meant that he went against the club's best interests.

*The Argus* gave Horton space to rant about us not respecting Savage, saying his client was, as he had previously told me, a "leader of men who should be captain of the club". He also made it clear that the money was not enough, even though it would make Bas one of our best-paid players. Well, every agent has his job to do, and Bas was a likeable character, but *The Argus* were very happy to print Horton's claims, encouraged as he was by Dean Wilkins.

We played at Millwall on Boxing Day, lost 3-0 and were a disgrace, playing as if we were the worse for wear after Christmas. This was Bas's last game for us because his contract was about to expire and we were sure he wasn't going to sign the new one. And to cap it all, he played with his hair dyed in red-and-blue stripes, the colours of Crystal Palace. That smacked to me of sticking two fingers up at the club and the fans, and so the dramatic gesture he made at the end, taking off his shirt and giving it to the fans, seemed pretty hypocritical.

In the post-match press conference, Savage and George O'Callaghan, an Irish ball-player on loan from Ipswich, were nominated to speak to the media and used it to have a rant about me. They said I'd treated them unfairly, and O'Callaghan said the club didn't respect its players. "There are a lot of lads who are important to this team that don't know if they are coming or going and it's about time the club got a grip and sorted it out. It's funny that other clubs are speaking to me and the one I'm playing for at the moment hasn't spoken to me much. The team could fall apart – it's just a disaster really."

In his case, it sounded like bluster intended to cover up his appalling performance that afternoon. Dean admitted that O'Callaghan had been "off his game".

As I was driving back from the New Den I got a call from Andy Naylor asking for a comment on this outburst – which I hadn't heard – and I said the match had been the only time I had ever been genuinely ashamed of the Albion. "It was a complete debacle. I think certain players should be looking at themselves before trying to deflect the criticism elsewhere. George O'Callaghan is totally out of order."

And I spelt out the Savage situation. "He has been made an extremely generous offer. I even slightly increased it recently. I gather even his agent has now told him he should sign it. We are not going to pay the sort of wage demands that he is making. Our offer puts him above several other senior players. What was he doing with a red–and–blue stripe down the top of his head? If it was what I think it was, that is sad and disrespectful.

"He seems to think he is worth a whole lot more. If he doesn't want to sign the contract, and he still has a few days to do it, then we will move on. I have been negotiating with him and his agent since October. He hasn't been treated badly by us; he has been treated well. Why is he deciding to leave? It is his decision. He obviously loves the fans, up to a point, but he is walking away from a very fair contract."

The first repercussion was that David Sheepshanks heard about O'Callaghan's outburst, immediately recalled him to Ipswich and terminated his contract. Incredibly, there was talk before the end of the season that Dean wanted to bring him back.

Mindful that we were likely to lose Savage, a new strike partner for Forster was vital. Barry Lloyd had been working hard and had come back from the north with two names: Glenn Murray of Rochdale and Will Hoskins of Rotherham. I saw Murray twice before Christmas and knew I was watching a goalscorer and a very talented player. He was laid-back but I'd heard good things about him as a pro.

It was also possible that we would lose Dean Hammond, the club captain, and a contributor of valuable goals from midfield. After Mark McGhee had fired a warning shot across his bows with an offer of a very short contract, he had got his head down and become an important player. But his contract was due to expire at the end of the 2007/08 season. In the autumn I'd had a couple of meetings with him and Dean Wilkins and separate meetings with Tim Webb, his agent. I made an offer that would have made him the highest-paid player at the club and, bar Bobby Zamora's, the biggest contract that I'd ever proposed – demonstrating that, contrary to rumours, I had a lot of faith in him.

But Webb was telling him that he was worth a lot more and that he could get him to a Championship club. Webb always used to remind me that he was a qualified lawyer, and was fond of saying, "I'm not like other football agents", which of course told you that he was exactly like other football agents, because so many agents say that. They all know that the reputation of their profession is so bad that they try to distance themselves from the others.

Hammond kept telling the local media that he wanted to stay and sign a contract, but I think he was being encouraged to hold out for more money. And I was getting feedback from other chairmen that Webb was touting him around. Terry Robinson at Sheffield United was one who marked my card and asked if I knew about it. It was naïve of Webb to assume that chairmen didn't talk to each other.

I was a little annoyed when Nicky publicly questioned us in *The Argus* over the Hammond situation. "I want to get back up to the Championship and at the moment the ambition from the club doesn't seem to mirror that, and I think that is the reason why Dean Hammond is reserving judgement," he said.

"I think it would be with a very heavy heart that he would leave this club but, for the sake of his future, he might feel he needs to." Thanks for your under-standing, Nicky.

I told Dean Wilkins that we needed to get Hammond to sign, because if he didn't he wouldn't be worth a penny to us once the transfer window shut at midnight on January 31. He could walk away for nothing at the end of the season. The player kept saying he would sign, but the agent kept procrastinating while he still shopped him around.

On January 30 I told Webb, "Right, we're selling Dean Hammond. I know what you've been doing. You'll be able to tell us who's interested, so which of the Uniteds do I sell him to: Sheffield, Colchester or Leeds?"

I didn't want to sell Dean, but I was forced to. I finalised the deal with the new Colchester chairman, Robbie Cowling, late on the evening of January 31 for £250,000 – £50,000 more than he had offered me for him the previous summer. In normal circumstances I might have got more, but time was running out. Sheffield United, I found out, were not that interested. So I had to be a bit nifty, and the maximum I could get was from Colchester, who were splashing the cash a bit.

Bearing in mind the Hammond situation, I had also lined up an experienced, creative midfield player who Barry had found – Steve Thomson, 29, from Falkirk. And results around that time bore out my view that we were short of quality midfielders. By the end of January we'd only won one game out of six, including an embarrassing home defeat by Mansfield Town, 92nd in the Football League, in the third round of the FA Cup. We made a dreadful showing and it meant we missed out on £40,000 prize money, and a home tie against Middlesbrough in the fourth round. Keith Haslam, the Mansfield chairman, was delighted, but he knew what sort of reaction I would face, and he was right.

Immediately after that game I was scheduled to go on the BBC Southern Counties radio phone-in, hosted by Ian Hart. I'd agreed to appear a few days earlier, but after that result it seemed a foolish idea, like being thrown to the lions. But the buck stops with the chairman, so I went in for the mauling. And I was basically abused for an hour by people who seemed to be mates of Hart. The carnage began with a caller demanding that I should stand down right now. Someone else told me the same thing, more bluntly. It was pure car-crash radio, so I was genuinely surprised by the messages of support I received after the programme.

Inevitably there were callers adamant that we would still be in the cup if we had kept O'Callaghan and Savage. I repeated the explanations I had given earlier: that Savage had turned down a very good offer, and that O'Callaghan had been recalled by Ipswich and wasn't coming back. I said I was negotiating to bring in five players, but some callers dismissed that. "We hear that every season. We always miss out in the transfer window."

I was asked by other callers about reducing ticket prices, which we simply couldn't afford to do, and I made the point that I and the other directors and shareholders had had to put more than £13 million into the club and we were unlikely ever to see that money again. One fan's response to that was to say, "I think you've done a really good job over the years but it's time for you to move on. We need some new investment." I thought, "You ungrateful, unthinking so and so. Do I really put myself through all this for people like you?"

He mentioned Stephen Purdew, and I explained why he had been a non-starter, but he also mentioned David Gold – a far more credible potential investor.

In September 2007 stories began to appear in the local paper that Gold, the chairman and co-owner of Birmingham City, had sold some of his shares in the Midlands club to Hong Kong businessman Carson Yeung, might be selling up completely, and was interested in investing in the Albion.

David is a wealthy man, and the link to Albion was that his fiancee lived in Hurstpierpoint, just north of Brighton, so he was regularly in our vicinity.

I knew David from Football League meetings, where he was extremely sociable, and I liked him. We got on well and had in common an affection for West Ham – a lifelong passion in his case. He was a down-to-earth football man, and the fact that he had made his money in some eyebrow-raising pursuits was irrelevant as far as I was concerned.

Occasionally we'd wave to each other as our cars passed on the M40 if I was on my way to a game in the Midlands or North and he was going to St Andrews, me in my Porsche, David purring along in his chauffeur-driven, 'DGOLD' number-plated Rolls-Royce.

Had David let it be known that he was interested in investing? An *Argus* exclusive claimed that "people close to the Seagulls" had "sounded him out". Whoever these people were, they certainly were not on the board, so they had no authority to sound anyone out.

I waited to see if David was going to get in touch, but nothing happened, although *The Argus* kept insisting that he was "keen" to get involved. Of course, the fans were curious so I put them in the picture – not that there was a picture, really. I had a statement read out at Withdean, categorically denying that there had been any contact between David and the club, which was definitely the case.

That seemed to annoy *The Argus*. In a back-page 'comment' column on September 26, they asked, "Why is Albion chairman Dick Knight so touchy about David Gold wanting to invest in the Albion? We know for certain that he [Gold] is keen to do so. Gold's interest has been welcomed by an over-whelming majority of fans. Knight has to be careful of leaving supporters with the impression of a man desperately clinging on to power."

I was getting annoyed. I replied on our website, saying I had always known that once we got the green light for the stadium, the club would instantly become attractive to potential investors and that we would need and were seeking further investment. But David Gold had not made contact with me or anyone directly connected with the club about investing.

And I added, "It's quite clear that *The Argus* haven't actually spoken to David Gold because if they had, it would have been fully reported, even if he'd made no comment. So this is all at the moment idle speculation."

I should have expected this sort of press gossip. Two years earlier *The Argus* had run a story that Diego Maradona and Ossie Ardiles were interested in investing if we got permission for the stadium, after Ossie's former Spurs team-mates Steve Perryman and Paul Miller had identified Brighton as "an English club with potential".

Of course, planning permission had been delayed, so that story was not pursued, but I decided that I had to speak to David Gold face to face about this one. I would be happy to sit down and discuss things with him, because if he was interested I needed to know what his level of interest was and what he envisaged in return for any investment.

So I called him and arranged to meet him at his house just off the M25. Well, his mansion to be exact, with its own golf course and lake. We sat in his vast lounge, full of elegant furniture, looking out over the lawn, on which was parked a helicopter, black with gold lettering, with tea served from antique silverware in bone china by his maid.

We had an excellent discussion. David is very straight and you know where you are with him. He explained that he had been at a charity fund-raising event in Hurstpierpoint and had given an interview to a local radio station in which he mentioned that the Albion had made itself an integral part of its community. Yes, he had said he was interested in the club but had only been putting out feelers.

*The Argus* had interpreted that as him definitely wanting to invest in the club and me deliberately holding it back. But David emphasised that he still hadn't in any way done the deal to extricate himself from Birmingham, and we both knew that League rules prevented ownership of more than one club. He asked me about our stadium business case, which I said was very strong, and he said, "This is your club. I don't think it's right for anyone to barge you out of the way right now. If I did go into another club, I would want to take over as owner and chairman."

He was perfectly open about it, which didn't surprise me at all. But I said, "I don't think it's the right time for me to stand down or for a new major investor to take over. The existing board and I have got this far and built relationships and a level of trust with the council and all the partners. We have a job to finish."

David was remarkably complimentary about what we'd done at Brighton and asked, "I just want to know – do you need any help?"

I said, "I don't think we do at the moment, David. We've still got to put together all these agreements with the council and the universities and I don't think it's the right time."

Then he said, "Tell me if you'd like to take it further", but he also told me that he had spoken to at least one other club, and that that was quite well advanced. I had my suspicions about which one it was but, as we know, he and his partner David Sullivan later succeeded in buying West Ham, which was the fulfilment of a dream.

On Friday October 5, David and I put out a joint press statement which read: "Birmingham City FC chairman David Gold has poured cold water on reports that he is keen to invest in Brighton. Gold has met Brighton chairman Dick Knight to clarify the matter. Gold said, 'An interview I gave on a Sussex radio station has been blown up out of all proportion, probably because my fiancee Lesley and I have a house near Brighton, but I have not expressed an interest in investing in the Brighton club'."

Incredibly, that did not prevent Michael Beard, *The Argus* editor, claiming on the paper's website, "The facts are: David Gold has expressed an interest in the club. He has been contacted by people close to the Seagulls. Other clubs have expressed an interest in him joining them but Albion are Gold's first choice."

Who were these 'people close to the Seagulls'? There are 30,000 people in Sussex close to the Seagulls.

David and I were, and remain, friends. But, outrageously, *The Argus* were, in effect, saying, "Knight, you've done all the hard work. Now move over, mate, we need a big name." It didn't matter whether it was Maradona or David Gold, they were both more famous than me. I was being invited to step aside in favour of someone who would sell more papers.

Now, in response to another question on the BBC phone-in after the Mansfield game, I reiterated the fact that I was happy to talk to anyone who was genuinely interested in investing. But we needed new blood now, on the field, and I let the audience know that I intended to do just that, by making some signings of better-quality players than the ones who had chosen to leave.

Dean Wilkins, though, saw it another way. He felt that what we had was pretty good and we didn't need to change much, even though results suggested otherwise and I was prepared to spend money. He didn't come to watch Murray with me or Thomson at Falkirk with Barry. Rochdale wanted £300,000 for Glenn Murray but I thought I could beat them down, and if it was by enough I might be able to squeeze in a bid for Hoskins too.

I liked Rochdale and respected the way they did business – Colin Garlick, the chief executive, took charge of most of the negotiations. They knew they had a quality player and wouldn't budge and we ended up paying them £300,000 plus add-ons, the highest fee we had paid for a player since Mickey Thomas came from Everton in 1981. But I felt Glenn was worth it.

We arranged to pay in instalments, which I always did when we were buying. When we were selling I always wanted everything up front! Glenn signed a three-year contract that made him the highest-paid player at the club, which tends to happen with top strikers, like Bobby Zamora before him.

So Thomson and Murray came in, and I also tried to get Darren Currie back, but it fell through, as many last-minute transfer window deals often do. Hammond and Alex Revell went out, the striker to Southend for £150,000. I told Ron Martin, their chairman, "He'll score goals when he's fit, but he's very injury-prone." As with Leon Knight and Colin Kazim-Richards, I was open about the player I was selling, but that didn't stop Ron telling me at a League meeting, "You con-man, you got £150,000 out of me for Revell and he's always getting injured."

I said, "Ron, did you record what I said to you? Because I did [which was a total bluff]. I distinctly remember telling you he was injury-prone!"

"Okay, maybe you did actually."

Two-footed and a good header of the ball, Murray started scoring as soon as he came into the team and got nine goals between mid-January and the end of the season. Thomson had captained Falkirk and been man of the match in a recent victory over Celtic. The fact that he had once played for Crystal Palace was irrelevant. He was consistent and reliable and we needed that after the shenanigans with O'Callaghan. He was a natural captain, anchored the midfield and the two of them had a great effect on the team, despite Dean's misgivings.

But by the end of March I had received written transfer requests from both Thomson and Murray. Thomson was more forthcoming in his reasons. He called Dean Wilkins's methods into question. He said, "I feel like a junior who has come straight from school. The squad are treated like schoolboys. We are never asked our opinions despite our experience."

Glenn said he was homesick and wanted to move back closer to the Lake District, where he comes from. But I knew that he had once been called out by Wilkins in front of the entire playing staff, including the juniors, and accused of being lazy. His style is languid and unhurried, but he is certainly not lazy. And that cannot have helped any homesickness and must have made him more keen to leave.

Also in March, Barry told me about a French midfield player called Therry Racon, whom Charlton had signed for a lot of money. He needed experience of English football and I went to see him play in a reserve game at Brisbane Road – the man from L'orient playing at the Orient. He was absolute quality, getting on the ball, spraying it around. We had already been trying to get Ian Westlake on loan from Leeds, and almost as soon as Racon agreed to come to us on loan, Westlake decided that he'd like to come as well.

So I was able to present Dean with the addition of two quality midfield players, if only for a month in Racon's case. But in that month we played nine games, winning four of them and drawing three. Nicky scored seven goals. Dean played Racon at the base of the midfield diamond, Westlake on the left, Thomson right. David Martot, whom we'd got from Le Havre in January, was furthest forward. Not a bad League One midfield.

We pushed on to the end of the season and got to the fringe of the play-off positions. There was a game at Leeds when we had a corner a minute into added time with the score 0-0, and the chance to convert one point into a priceless three. Young defenders Joel Lynch and Tommy Elphick, who was to be voted player of the season, went up but Dean waved them back when we should have been going for the win. We finished in seventh position, just outside the play-offs.

The last game of the season was a 1-0 home defeat by Swansea City, who finished as champions and were presented with the trophy after the game. To mark the end of the 10-year Skint sponsorship we wore a special version of our blue-and-white striped shirt with the inscription under their logo, 'Team mates 1999-2008'. I introduced all the Skint team to the crowd in the centre circle at half-time.

We'd improved our league position greatly over the previous season. But I thought that we'd underachieved. Dean's eventual acceptance of more experienced players came too late, and his regular use of youngsters like Joe Gatting in brief substitute roles with little chance to be effective seemed more designed to ensure they got their appearance money. I made a real effort to sign Racon permanently from Charlton because he had been highly influential, but he proved to be out of our financial league, which only added to a feeling of frustration.

And after all the turmoil around the turn of the year, it was clear that the manager and I weren't on the same page. He had taken some players' sides against the chairman in contract talks, while creating divisions in the dressing room. In my opinion, his man-management skills were lacking, which was why I made the decision I did after the end of the season, which was to remove him from the manager's job.

Meanwhile, the process of moving to the next stage of the stadium development was also, inevitably, a source of further vexation. We began to prepare the planning implementation contracts, which required tripartite agreements between the club, the council, and the University of Brighton. At the same time we began the tendering process for the design-and-build contract for the stadium.

That took us into 2008 because it was a very detailed spec, as you can imagine – a unique stadium design, not an identikit off-the-shelf version like one or two around the country, where the only difference is the colour of the seats. The main building contractor would then sub-contract to other suppliers and specialists. By the time we got into spring we had narrowed it down to three contenders.

Inevitably, the process was dragged out. But, experienced as we now were, why would we ever be surprised that the planning agreements were taking longer than expected? According to Martin Perry's monthly reports to the board, the University of Brighton were still causing problems, even under a new vice-chancellor.

There was one particular period where the process seemed to be lying completely fallow regarding moving the 106 agreements forward. Martin said the university were being awkward and demanding things that they had no right to.

After we'd heard this for the second or third board meeting running, I said, "We have to unblock this." Martin had told us the next meeting was in a few days' time so I said I'd come with him. He said, "You don't need to do that, I'll resolve it." But the board was unanimous that I should go. We needed to sort it.

When I turned up with Martin and our architect, Andy Simons, at the university property department offices in Hollingbury, I found that what the university were 'demanding' was something not very unreasonable at all to my mind. They wanted to see the materials that were going to be used in the construction of the stadium, especially the exterior, which was understandable as we were going to be very close neighbours.

Martin was sticking to the letter of the law procedure-wise which, as far as he was concerned, meant that the university weren't entitled to see the materials. But in the spirit of good neighbourliness, not to mention common sense, I said, "Right, let's all convene one week today and we will show you all the materials that you want to see.

"Because we have been resisting, you probably think we have something to hide. But we haven't. Where you will have a problem with me is if you object after we have shown you the materials. Our stadium spec is absolutely top-notch. Every material is better quality than it needs to be to meet minimum requirements. We are going to build a stunning-looking stadium – that's why the materials are the best. You should have no problem with any of them. If you do, you will be doing it simply to be obstructive."

Martin wasn't happy. He felt I was undermining him but I thought he'd just been bloody-minded. He may have been right in theory but we needed to move the whole thing on. Martin had done a great job, but because he had previous experience of stadium planning procedure I think that sometimes he was inflexible in his way of handling things.

I knew Martin had samples of some of the materials in his office, and Andy Simons said he could get the others without delay. So we turned up a week later and of course the university didn't have a problem with any of them. Property manager Rob Mallender and university second-in-command David House were delighted with the quality. The hold-up was over.

They still wanted us to put grass on the roof at the ends of the stadium, as per their earlier suggestions, but that would have been totally impractical. You'd have had to mow the grass by helicopter. The idea made us chuckle. There hadn't been many other laughs in a difficult season.

# CHAPTER TWENTY SIX

# KOMPANY & CO. LIMITED

Although I had lost confidence in Dean Wilkins's abilities as a manager, I still admired him as a coach so, as I had done with Martin Hinshelwood, I decided to offer him his old job back – in this case, first-team coach, the position he had held under Mark McGhee. I intended to bring in an experienced manager, and I had the person in mind.

On the face of it we had done well to improve on our finish in 2007 by 11 places, but it was only a qualified success. We had started winning matches at home again, but there had been a turbulent spell in mid-season when the team had almost unravelled. Wilkins had not helped calm the unrest among players.

In addition to the transfer requests from Glenn Murray and Steve Thomson, Paul Reid, who had been released, came out in *The Argus* with a strong attack on Dean's methods, saying, "You would think someone who has played would know how to man-manage players."

Dean's response in the paper was to say that, "I always knew a big part of the job would be to bring to a close a very successful part of the club's history", by which he meant letting go popular players such as Chippy Carpenter, Guy Butters, Kerry Mayo and Reid. But the way he went about it, with curt dismissals, upset a lot of people.

But I knew my decision to sack him might be an unpopular one. The fans remembered him as the player whose late free kick had taken us into the play-offs in 1991, and they knew the job he had done with the youth team, as I did. What they didn't know was the effect his poor relationship with some of the players was having on the squad.

I asked Dean to join me and Martin Perry in the boardroom at Withdean on the afternoon of May 8 2008 and told him that I wasn't happy with the way things had developed – and that I was relieving him of his duties as manager.

His reaction was unbelievable. Before I could tell Dean about the offer to stay on as coach, he started losing it. To say he didn't take it well is an under-statement. "You can't do that to me," he said, looking to Martin for support. "After everything I've done for this club!"

He began ranting at me and, in a sense, the way he reacted confirmed my judgement. He was known for using colourful language with the players – not just the senior players, but the youngsters as well – and a torrent now poured out. He stormed out and drove away across the park-and-ride car park.

I looked at Martin and he looked at me and said, "Well, he's a very emotional guy."

I replied, "Fine, we're all emotional. But the way he reacted was immature, to say the least."

About 45 minutes later he came back and I assumed he had calmed down so I started to explain my intention. But he was almost as truculent as before. It was as if he'd thought of some further retorts. He didn't take it well at all, although I suppose he felt he was fully justified. He was fuming after what was obviously a big blow to his pride. But finally I said to him, "You don't have to give me your answer straight away, Dean, but I'm giving you the chance to stay on as first-team coach under someone else."

The 'someone else' was Micky Adams.

Micky had been doing some scouting for Stoke – and informally for us as well – since leaving Colchester, where he had been assistant manager. I had been in fairly regular contact with him since he had left, so when my name came up on his mobile, he was probably not surprised. But when I asked him to come back as manager, he certainly was. He hadn't been expecting that particular call.

But I'm not sure he would have been surprised that I was planning to make a change. He kept his ear to the ground, so he must have realised that I wouldn't have been happy with Dean after all the unrest with players and agents. Micky always knew who was boss with me even though we talked all the time and worked things out.

He'd taken us up before, from Division Two as it was then known, and it had been his team that had gone up again the following season from the divi-sion we were now in, even though Peter Taylor had been in charge for some of the campaign. So I offered him the chance to do it again in the coming season. With Falmer now on the horizon we needed to be in the Championship, and I thought that having Micky as a leader, someone who knew how to deal with players, and Dean as coach, would be an excellent arrangement.

Bringing back one of the most successful managers in Albion history – he had been promoted with Fulham and Leicester as well – seemed like a no-brainer. He knew the club and its potential with a new ground, so I gave him a three-year contract, at exactly the same money as before ("We're still at Withdean for the moment, Mick," I reminded him), with a view to him taking us into Falmer.

At the press conference to re-introduce Micky, a seasoned hack asked him what I had said to tempt him back. He replied, "Exactly the same thing he said in 1999 – that we'd be playing in a new stadium in two years."

That brought the house down, but I confirmed it was true, adding, "And this time it might well happen." Of course, others wanted to know if it was wise of either of us to try to repeat Micky's earlier success. "There are examples such as Stoke, where Tony Pulis has gone back and done a great job," I said. "Also Paul Sturrock at Plymouth. We're not looking back, we're looking forward."

The reaction both among the local media and the fans was, "Brilliant, Micky's coming back." He was a hero, everyone knew what he had done and there was no good reason why he shouldn't do it again.

Micky tried to persuade Dean to stay, still on decent money. They talked football, and Micky was happy to work with him. But Dean hummed and hahhed and eventually I had to give him a deadline because if the answer was no Micky would need to make alternative arrangements. The writing, though, was on the wall when Ian Chapman resigned as assistant manager, stating his disagreement with the decision regarding Dean Wilkins. Eventually Dean decided he wasn't going to stay and that was unfortunate but understandable.

Andy Naylor summed it up in *The Argus*. "The sadness of Wilkins's departure was that Albion lost not a manager, but a gifted coach. Wilkins was not cut out for management."

Micky set about bringing in some new players, but I began to get a bit uneasy at that point. Before he'd been very sure about the type of players he wanted, and where to find them. His knowledge seemed encyclopaedic and his judgement was excellent – Cullip, Rogers, Watson, Oatway, and so on.

So it was very disappointing when he brought in defender Colin Hawkins whom he'd known at Coventry, and winger Kevin McLeod from Colchester, players who were no better than the youth-team products we already had such as Tommy Elphick, Joel Lynch, Jake Robinson and Dean Cox.

Micky always wanted experienced players, and he went to the opposite extreme from Dean. He brought back Adam Virgo, who had played at Coventry after Celtic and was by then a bit injury-prone. The worst signing was midfielder David Livermore, from Hull. He'd had a good start at Arsenal then went to Millwall, Leeds and Hull, and he was always injured. There was a player I liked much more at Chesterfield called Peter Leven, slightly overweight but a terrific passer of the ball with great vision and a fantastic long throw – another who was spotted by Barry Lloyd and his team.

I'd asked Micky to look at Leven when he was doing some scouting, but he wasn't impressed. He said Livermore was better. I replied that he was injured all the time. Micky said he was over all that, but it turned out he wasn't. And when he did play he was a shadow of his former self. There was no one who set your pulses racing. So that did worry me, although I wasn't going to over-rule him. I trusted Micky to make the right judgements.

The 2008/09 season started with high anticipation and at one point early on we were top after taking eight points from the first four league games, and also recorded wins in the League Cup and Football League Trophy. After beating Barnet we drew Manchester City at home in the second round of the League Cup. They had just been taken over by Sheik Mansour and become the richest club in the world. Needless to say, the game attracted a Withdean record attendance of more than 8,700.

Des Lynam's cartoonist friend Mike Payne did a cartoon of Robinho at Withdean wearing his light blue No.10 shirt, looking perplexed while I explained, "The dressing rooms are over there behind the bike sheds". I've got it framed, signed by the Brazilian star, in my office. It summed up the haves versus the have-nots nature of the tie. In the end, Robinho didn't play, but their team did include Vincent Kompany, Daniel Sturridge, Pablo Zabaleta, Stephen Ireland, Jo and Michael Johnson.

Often these ties don't live up to the hype but this was a terrific game, full of end-to-end attacking. Gelson Fernandes put them ahead in the second half, but Murray equalised on 89 minutes to send it into extra time. Substitute Joe Anyinsah, who had arrived on loan from Preston, put us ahead before Ireland made it 2-2. So it went to penalties and we won the shoot-out 5-3. Michel Kuipers saved their penultimate kick from Michael Ball and Matt Richards scored our fifth to win it. City manager Mark Hughes said to me afterwards that we had deserved to win.

It was one of the most memorable games we played at Withdean and of course the result attracted a lot of national attention. It gave writers like Paul Hayward another opportunity to make the point that we had been in the wilderness for so many years that we had lost out on home gate receipts worth an estimated £38 million to date.

Afterwards I had a cheeky word with Paul Aldridge, who was then City's chief operating officer, and asked if they might be able to waive their share of the gate, which was 45 per cent. It would be a superb gesture to a club that really needed the money from the wealthiest team in the game. He said, "I'll talk to them. They're very good people and I wouldn't rule it out. Drop me a line."

I didn't waste any time and wrote to him the next day. He got back to me and said that the owners were genuine football investors and owning City wasn't a vanity purchase, but they didn't want to set a precedent. However, they would be prepared to send their full first team to open our new stadium without charging us a penny, not even their travelling expenses or asking for their share of the gate. For all they knew they might be European champions by then, so it was a very generous offer on their part. Their share of a full house at the new stadium would represent a couple of hundred thousand pounds more than their cut of the Withdean gate, which I worked out was £56,000.

At the time, the other directors and I were delighted, but ultimately the offer was ignored and Spurs were the opponents for the official opening match at Falmer. I don't know what the financial arrangements were but I assume they charged their usual fee or we would probably have heard about it.

In the league, though, we began to slip down the table dramatically. Virgo scored three goals early on but fell away after that. And McLeod never really imposed himself. Forster and Murray proved what a good strikeforce they could be. Murray scored 11 goals before Christmas but then got injured. The team weren't playing well and we were hitting too many long balls.

We needed fresh blood and learned that Robbie Savage, whom Micky knew, might be available on loan from Derby County. He was, of course, a hard-tackling Welsh international midfield player with a reputation for annoying opponents and their fans, but was known to be a great guy to have on your side.

Robbie was interested and said he would come down to Brighton. When he told my old friend from Hull, Adam Pearson, now the chairman of Derby, Adam said to him, "That means I have got to deal with that Dick Knight, he'll screw me into the ground!" He was right – Robbie was on £24,000 a week and I got him on a month's loan for a weekly payment of less than one-tenth of that.

Robbie didn't want us to sort out accommodation for him; he said he'd do that himself. We arranged to meet him on October 1 and he asked us to meet him at his hotel rather than the club offices or the training ground. So I went with Micky and Derek Allan at 7pm that evening to the address he'd given us, which I immediately recognised as a trendy boutique hotel in the heart of Brighton's gay quarter, which Robbie's personal assistant had unknowingly booked him into.

We soon spotted Robbie's white Lamborghini parked in the square and walked into the small hotel to find Robbie in the bar, standing in front of a neon-illuminated stained-glass window of Marilyn Monroe in the famous *Seven Year Itch* pose with her white dress billowing. The barman looked very interested in Robbie, with his flowing blond locks backlit by Marilyn's provocative pose.

I introduced myself and Derek – Robbie knew Micky – and asked, "Are you settling in okay?"

He replied, "Yeah, it's great here. You've got to come and see my suite."

We followed Robbie, assuming we'd be going up to a penthouse. But instead he led us along a corridor and opened a door leading downstairs – most of the suite was below ground. It was like a scene straight out of *Saturday Night Fever*. The stairs down were like that illuminated coloured-panel dancefloor. And there was even a mirrorball. All it needed was Robbie, strutting in his white suit a la John Travolta.

Derek just said, "Bloody 'ell." But Robbie was chuffed to bits. So we went down into the suite and he had about four rooms, with high-bling décor and a jacuzzi.

I said, "Robbie, I need to tell you something. You've heard about Brighton's reputation as a gay capital?"

"Yes?"

"Well, you're right in the centre of it."

"Really?" It hadn't dawned on him. "I still think it's great."

We went back up to the bar to go through the contract paperwork, while several of the hotel's regulars congregated at the bar to ogle Robbie.

The next day Robbie arrived at the training ground at Falmer in his Lamborghini. While he was meeting the squad Bob Booker, whom Micky had brought back as coach and reserve-team manager, spied the car and from somewhere found some parking tickets, which he proceeded to slap on Robbie's windscreen, and a clamp that he put on one of the wheels.

At 12.30pm Robbie came out, saw the car and Bob, dressed as a traffic warden, and stormed back into the building, shouting, "I came here to help this club out and look what happens" – until he saw all the players laughing their heads off and Bob following him inside. Robbie took it brilliantly and immediately hit it off with the rest of the players, because there was nothing big-time about him (apart from the car). He never considered League One to be beneath him and told me he was quite embarrassed about the wages, because he didn't think he was worth that amount of money, but he'd been offered it by Derby so he'd taken it.

Unfortunately it didn't really happen for him on the pitch in his seven games for us. He hadn't played for a month and wasn't match fit, although he could still read the game, pass the ball and snap into a tackle. He admitted he was trying to use his head more because his legs weren't what they had been. But he had been a breath of fresh air and lifted the morale in the squad.

To give you an idea of what a decent bloke Robbie Savage is, a couple of years later Derby County were having some rest and recreation in Marbella during one of those early-season international weekends. Robbie, by now the captain, and some of his team-mates were hanging out at Buddha Beach, one of the resort's cool beach clubs. We happened to be out there on holiday too and my grandson Louis spotted him.

He walked up to Robbie and said, "My granddad knows you."

"Does he? Who's your granddad?"

"His name's Dick Knight."

"Dick Knight? From Brighton? Where is he?"

And Louis led him down to the beach where Kerry and I and my other grandchildren were sunning ourselves. He spent half an hour talking to us when he could just have said to Louis, "Tell him I said hello."

Robbie's last game for Brighton was against Leicester on October 28 when he was booked and then came off at half-time when we were 2-0 down. But we came back to win 3-2 – Bradley Johnson scoring two cracking goals on his debut after joining us on loan from Leeds. It was one of only four games Leicester lost all season, and then we beat Millwall 4-1. But we didn't win again in the league until December 28.

On the stadium front, there had been plenty going on. We had to get so many ducks in a row at once – there were the 106 agreements, the often small but irritating issues that all three parties had to agree to, and the tendering process for the design-and-build contract, which meant advertising in construction journals. We had a good response; Alfred McAlpine could have tendered but never did.

Martin narrowed the shortlist to three construction companies and then Derek Chapman and I conducted the final negotiations and tied up a deal with the Buckingham Group at the end of October as main contractors for a £66 million design-and-build contract. That didn't include the planning costs that we'd incurred or all the roadworks that would be needed.

And of course, there were more delays that put back our intended ground-breaking – a ceremony to mark the start of the construction process – from October to December. The first actual work that would take place on the site was the widening of Village Way and the excavation of the chalk hill to make room for the West Stand. We had to get more planning consents to cart 20,000 tons of chalk spoil across the road, to approve design changes to the roof support beams, and to redesign the roofs of the North Stand and South Stand. But by now the council was anxious to grant us approval.

However, looming on the horizon were the grey clouds of the global economic downturn. All the stadium business cases that we had done, all the range of scenarios, were based on historic attendance percentage increases that had been achieved by other new stadiums – 19 in total – in the previous 10 to 12 years, in a relatively buoyant economic period. No one had seen this hurricane coming. But the sky was darkening. And I had to tell the board that we could not start the building of the stadium until we knew that we had all of the money.

In the meantime I was getting feedback that Tony Bloom would be prepared to put more money into the club. By this time he had already put in as much as I had, getting on for £2 million, and now he let it be known that he would underwrite the building if we ran into problems with the banks. He had made a lot of money out of his online betting businesses, successful property investments and other ventures, and was now an extremely wealthy man.

Tony's growing influence had been flagged up, for those who notice these things, in an interview with Ray Bloom in *The Argus* back in June 2008, in which he had spoken about his family's involvement with the club, and justified his staying on the board during the Archer/Stanley era.

"I was being misled by Bill Archer, who was telling me the Goldstone wasn't being sold when, in fact, he had done a deal," he was quoted as saying. "It was only when I knew that, I resigned from the board [the Goldstone was sold in July 1995, Ray didn't actually resign until October 1996]. The other directors took their money out. It was a matter of principle for me not to take anything out from the proceeds of the ground [sale]. I would rather have lost it.

"It was an honour to be invited back. I think it is a very well-run board. Everybody has their say. It is very democratic. Dick's role over the last 10 years is impossible to exaggerate. He has ensured the survival of the club. His unshakeable belief that we were going to get permission for Falmer and to build Falmer, again with others, will go down as the greatest achievement of all."

That was very kind of him. But, significantly, he added, "I cannot predict the next 20 years but I have every intention of staying. I don't know whether Tony [my nephew and a major investor in the club] will eventually become chairman. What I am very confident of is that the support he has given the club will continue long into the future."

"Chairman?" I obviously noticed that, although I, and perhaps Ray, did not know was how soon "eventually" might mean. But when Tony made his offer to underwrite the stadium construction, it was sufficient for me, with the board's agreement, to give the green light to begin building.

So we were able to hold the groundbreaking ceremony on Wednesday December 17 2008 – an historic moment in the stadium saga.

We invited 200 or so people to meet at Withdean before we took them to the Falmer site: dignitaries, fans, people who had been involved in the planning at the club and council. I made a welcoming speech and later, at the site, Martin and Des Lynam also spoke.

I looked back as well as forward. "On April 26 1997 the Albion played their last ever game at the Goldstone Ground, the home of the club for almost a hundred years. We're gathered here today to see history in the making – to ensure the next hundred years and a wonderful asset for not only the football club but also the whole community. It is groundbreaking in more ways than one.

"Not a brick has been laid yet, but our stadium already has a history of its own. No stadium in the world has been so hard fought-for. It is unique because of the battle to get to this point and every one of you, and thousands of others, have played a part in that."

There were tears in plenty of eyes. No club had suffered what we had been through to get to that day. It was a momentous and joyful day for so many of us.

Then everyone was bussed up to Falmer for the official ceremony. The work that was to start the project was the widening of Village Way, but we had also marked out the actual position of the pitch on the site. Because of the topography of the land, it made the old sloping Yeovil pitch look flat by comparison. It was an uneven, mud-clogged landscape, but to me it looked very dramatic. By lining up mechanical diggers facing each other we had made an impromptu goal exactly where the real one would be at the North Stand end. Norman Cook looked at some of the university prefabs that were due to be demolished and said, "I used to study in there."

It was a beautiful winter's day, freezing but very sunny, and it was a very moving occasion. I was going to take the first ever penalty at Falmer, with the diggers forming the goal. In 'goal' we had John Sullivan who, the night before, had saved a vital penalty from Grant Holt in a shoot-out to win us a Johnstone's Paint Trophy tie away at Shrewsbury. That game was notable because I agreed to do the match summarising during the game on BBC Southern Counties Radio alongside commentator Johnny Cantor. I really enjoyed it but they never asked me again – I probably talked too much.

I put the ball on the spot and shouted to John, who was still buzzing from the night before, "Remember you've got a contract renewal coming up, so you'd better not save this."

The 'goal' was about four times the size of a normal goal, so I hit the ball with my right foot and scored – just. But there's no excuse for what happened next except that I was too cocky and decided to take another penalty with my left foot. I managed to plonk the ball against the caterpillar of the digger on the left – an amazing miss.

Martin, who had hardly ever kicked a ball in his life, was due to follow me. Everyone was laughing, thinking, "Where's this one going to go?" And Martin absolutely slotted it, top corner, well out of John's reach. So we had some fun, but we had also got the stadium building process actually started.

The day ended on an unnecessary sour note. In my speech I had mentioned that it was ironic and very sad that two councillors in Woodingdean were still against the stadium when Woodingdean Primary School had the largest number of members of the Young Seagulls in Sussex, over 150. They had written poems and stories about the stadium and also made a beautiful model of it.

In the afternoon Martin, very flustered, told me that Mary Mears, the Tory leader of the council, had been incredibly offended by my remarks and the way I had 'politicised' my speech by attacking two Tory councillors. I pointed out that I hadn't even mentioned what party the two came from – this event was way above politics – but Martin said I'd have to phone or write to her and apologise. I said to Martin that not only did I have no intention whatsoever of doing do that, but nor must he.

The next day, December 18, the Football League had called an EGM at Pride Park, Derby, to vote on a proposal to bring in what they called the home-grown players' rule. The new rule would insist that at least four members of the 16-man match-day squad must have been registered domestically for three seasons before their 21$^{st}$ birthdays – in other words, developed through an English club's youth system.

Because they were conscious of European law, the League had to allow foreign players to be included, but of course the rule was really aimed at increasing the number of English youngsters in the playing squads.

The national press reported that only one chairman voted against the proposal.

Charles Sale of the *Daily Mail* found out that it was me, and took the mickey out of me in his Sports Agenda column. He thought that I was so blinkered that I was resisting it because I wanted to bring more foreign players into my club – that I was against a rule whose whole point was to increase the number of young English players coming through into the upper levels of the game.

In fact, I'd said at the club meeting that the measure didn't go far enough. It should be about the quality of young English players at clubs. Four was paying lip service. Make it eight and then all clubs would be forced to provide better coaching resources.

"Sixty per cent of the players in the most recent senior England squad originally came from Football League clubs," I said. "But the FA's last England under-16 squad had less than 30 per cent. That shows the drift of young players towards Premier League clubs. Quality young English players would be far better served learning their trade playing in the Football League rather than being seduced into Premier League clubs to play in the reserves or the Carling Cup or to sit on the bench watching foreign players."

Some clubs agreed with me, but not one other chairman was prepared to vote against the rule when it came to it. The consensus was, "Just let's sign it off, Dick. We must make sure we get the money we're given for youth development from the Premier League."

What Charlie Sale had failed to appreciate was that I was demanding more dramatic regulation, not less. He has a large readership, among other sports writers as well as the public. But he misread my intentions completely on that one.

We couldn't repeat our success against Manchester City in the next round of the League Cup. Derby County put us in our place. And we went out of the FA Cup to Hartlepool after a replay. The spirit that had been the hallmark of Micky's previous reign didn't seem to be there at all. He was getting abuse during games from the South Stand, nearest the dugouts, which didn't help.

In January Bradley Johnson went back to Leeds, but we signed Jimmy McNulty from Stockport, a player I'd seen who bombed forward from left-back but could also play centre-half. Jim Gannon, their manager, accepted our second offer of £150,000 and McNulty quickly became a fans' favourite because of his buccaneering style.

We also signed Craig Davies from Oldham, but although he went on to score plenty of goals for Chesterfield and Barnsley after leaving us, he never hit it off at the Albion. We paid £135,000 and he scored in his first game, and McNulty scored too, but in each case they were the only goals they were to score for us. Davies seemed almost timid for a striker and although he worked hard and was experienced – he had played in Italy – it never happened for him with us.

But we should have had a heck of a strikeforce with him, Murray, Forster and Calvin Andrew, whom we got on loan from Crystal Palace. Yet things scarcely improved and the pressure was building on Micky. People on the board with the gift of hindsight were saying, "We should never have re-appointed him." And perhaps I should have known that whenever you go back to the scene of former glories, you are deliberately tempting fate.

Micky thought everything was going to be as it had been before, but it wasn't. The club was different, the players were different, perhaps even I was too. I didn't have quite the same overall influence that I'd had. Ever since I used my casting vote to keep Mark McGhee in his job, I'd invited Tony Bloom to attend board meetings, as he now had significant funds in the club.

One of the most surprising outbursts against Micky came from John Baine. Until then he had never expressed any negative views about the team, only the previous owners. But he knows his football. He shared the match announcing with Paul Samrah and Richard Lindfield and on January 20 2009 we drew the home leg of the Johnstone's Paint Trophy semi-final 0-0 against Luton Town. Afterwards he went on the radio phone-in and talked about the team's "pitiful" attempts to play football and said, "I want my old Micky back." It was a significant moment because he had been one of Micky's biggest fans. All the Falmer For All team had always got behind him.

By the time we played the second leg of the Johnstone's Paint semi-final in February, we were 20th in the league and in danger of relegation despite all that early hope and a squad including some decent players. Micky just couldn't pick them up; it seemed the spark had gone.

The Football League Trophy, played for by lower-division clubs, was often ignored by managers and fans until the late rounds, when the fact that the final was played at Wembley (and previously the Millennium Stadium) made it attractive and lucrative. When Johnstone's Paint took over as sponsors from LDV Vans in 2006, I made the suggestion at a Football League meeting that the competition should be called the Johnstone's Paint Pot. The trophy itself, instead of being the traditional cup shape, would be a mounted beautiful gold paint tin with a silver brush sticking out of it. That would have attracted a lot of publicity, given the competition a boost in the early rounds and put a smile on people's faces. Some chairmen liked the idea, but it was probably thinking that was too far out of the box and I doubt if the idea was ever put to Johnstone's Paint themselves.

I had assumed that we would win through to the Wembley final against a team which was struggling in League Two. We would have taken 30,000 for our first visit to the new Wembley, no doubt, and we would have got around £20,000 for winning the semi-final. It would all have been very useful, but instead it was a big disappointment.

We drew the second leg at Kenilworth Road 1-1 so it went to penalties and we lost, but in my opinion we had deserved to lose in normal time. We were terrible. Luton were a poor team but we hardly created a chance in either game. Could it get any worse?

That second leg was on Tuesday February 17 and we had a game at Millwall on the Saturday. I'd been telling Micky that we had to turn it round, and had been coming under increasing pressure from the board to admit that it had been a mistake bringing him back. I defended Micky to give him a bit more time, because he had previously done wonders for us, but equally I knew that the last thing we needed was to open at Falmer back in League Two.

I arranged to see him on the Friday for a clear-the-air meeting at the Little Chef on the A23 at Hickstead, well out of Brighton & Hove to minimise the risk of encountering any fans. Someone ranting at Micky wouldn't help at all.

I went there to give him one final round of encouragement, "We've got to start picking things up, Mick. I can't keep defending you much longer." But it soon became clear that the pressure was getting to him. He was hugely disappointed that he didn't have the directors' confidence any more. He always came to the boardroom soon after a game for a chat to the directors and he had picked up the vibe. He knew that I was coming under pressure. Directors who had wanted to be his friend years earlier and had welcomed him back with open arms were now uncomfortable with him.

Micky said, "You've been a great chairman to work for. But I'm putting your position in jeopardy now because you're defending me. I don't want to put you through it any more. And I don't want to put myself through it − to feel that I've got to win the next two matches or I'm out. It would be better if I leave now."

I was shocked but, knowing the man, not totally surprised. I said, "Micky, is that what you really want?" He replied, "Yes, that's what I want." I nodded, "Then we'll make it by mutual consent." I hadn't gone to that meeting on a Friday afternoon intending to sack him. If I had, we would have met the day after the Luton game.

Now I suddenly thought, "I haven't got a manager. If we'd been playing up north tomorrow, we'd already have left." So I called up Dean White, gave him the news, and told him to meet me with Bob at the training ground, which would be deserted. When we met, I told Dean I was putting him in temporary charge, and that Bob would assist him. I put out a press statement on the Saturday morning saying that I was very sad, as all Albion fans would be, that things hadn't worked out for Micky.

Once again, in the game immediately after a manager had left, we won, Adam Virgo scoring in a 1-0 victory over Millwall. Afterwards I went on Southern Counties Radio and Ian Hart asked me if I had expected Micky to be in the dugout. "Yes, I went to our meeting yesterday to give him a boost, not to sack him."

After the game I was standing outside the New Den reception area when Nicky Forster approached me and asked if he could have a quiet word. There and then Nicky said, "It's sad that Micky has gone, but would you consider me as the next manager? I know that I could do the job."

I respected Nicky as an intelligent guy, a step ahead of the average professional, and I half-expected what was coming when he asked to speak to me. I replied, "Nicky, you might well be a future Brighton manager, but I can't give you the job now. We're in a relegation fight and we need you out there on the field concentrating fully on scoring goals. You haven't got your coaching badges, although I know you're taking them. It's not the right time."

The need for experience also ruled out Dean as a permanent manager. The speculation started immediately, but I had one man firmly in my sights and that was Jim Gannon of Stockport. I'd seen his team play a few times while watching McNulty and I loved their fast, attacking style. He was calm and collected, spoke well, and struck me as a considered and studied character. In fact he was a qualified accountant as well.

I'd had a few dealings with Stockport's chairman, Martin Reid, and he told me they were in financial difficulties. The money I'd paid them in January for McNulty had helped. I was prepared to pay compensation for Gannon, which would probably pay the wages for a few more months, so Martin encouraged him to talk to me.

I met Gannon at the Gatwick Hilton at 11am on the following Wednesday and had a most engaging discussion with him. He had booked a flight back at 4pm and that seemed to give us easily enough time, but our talks went so well that we ended up rushing back into the airport so that he could catch his plane to Manchester.

I went with him and we kept talking until we were on the shuttle train that connects the south and north terminals. And then, in a surreal moment bearing in mind how well discussions had seemed to go, he suddenly said, "Dick, I don't think I can take the job. I really love Stockport. Not just the club, but the town. It's a wonderful place to live, and my wife and her family come from there."

I couldn't believe what I was hearing. Where had this come from? Why had he even bothered to come down? Maybe he had suddenly realised the implication of going home and telling his wife he was uprooting her and their kids and moving the family to the south coast. There was nothing to be ashamed about if that was the reason. Or maybe he felt he had to give me an answer there and then.

The shuttle arrived at the north terminal platform, the doors opened and I was saying, "Jim, I don't understand. We've just had this really good discussion."

He replied, "I don't want to let you down, I have to tell you now. I've really thought about it and I can see your club's potential and I wish you well but I can't take the job. I feel a duty to Stockport County."

He texted me when he got back, thanking me for seeing him, but repeating that his decision was final. Sadly his loyalty to Stockport wasn't rewarded as he later lost his job as part of cost-cutting measures.

There was another name on my list which was that of Paul Ince, who had been sacked in December by Blackburn Rovers, unfairly in my view. Michael Standing knew Paul, and his agent had sounded Michael out and asked if I would be interested in talking to Ince, which I was. But it was soon made clear that Ince wouldn't move down south and would expect to keep living in Cheshire. I never actually got to meet him. All the discussions were via Michael and Paul's agent. It was like communicating with Archer at CEDR. And I got the sense that he might be waiting for another club closer to his home to make an offer.

The delay in replacing Micky had been costly in terms of results. After that win at Millwall, we drew at home to Northampton then suffered a 4-0 home defeat by Crewe at the end of February that was not only depressing, but also nearly tragic when Jimmy McNulty suffered a horrendous injury. On a rock-hard pitch he challenged for a ball almost on the halfway line, just in front of the directors' box. The Crewe player was innocent of any malicious intent, but Jim was struck in his side and the whole North Stand heard him scream in agony before he even hit the ground. He had ruptured his right kidney.

It was upsetting and a lot of kids saw and heard it. The Crewe player was distraught. Jim was rushed into intensive care and later had the kidney removed. He was out for six months and was never really a regular again for us. But I'm glad to say that he's still in football and was voted player's player of the 2011/12 season at Barnsley, becoming their captain. A decent young man, I still follow his career, wishing him well after that setback.

My next managerial target was Russell Slade, who had recently left Yeovil Town, and was in dispute with them over his contract payment. Yeovil tried to claim that we had tapped him up before he left them, although obviously I didn't because I'd been going after Gannon and then Ince and only contacted him on March 5 and appointed him on the 6th.

I'd always admired Russell because his teams played football and he was a calm, articulate man. I invited him down for a chat. I said to him, "You are my third choice, but you are only third because of Gannon and Ince. I'm going to offer you a contract to the end of the season with the promise of a bonus of £10,000 if we stay up." Russell was up for the challenge.

However, he didn't start too well. We lost his first game, 2-1 at Leyton Orient, and the second, at home to Southend. But the third was an extremely satisfying 5-0 win over his previous club, Yeovil. Dean Cox, who thrived under Slade with us and later at Orient, scored two, as did Forster, while Murray converted a penalty.

But we took a bit of time to win again – four games, including a 2-0 defeat at MK Dons on April 4. That was remarkable for something unusual that happened in the lounge at the Milton Keynes stadium where visiting directors were entertained. Dennis Wise was there with his agent and I saw him shaking hands with a number of Albion directors, including Ken Brown, our new managing director, who had been at Millwall when Wise was manager there.

I thought nothing very much of it until the following weekend, when the *Sunday Mirror* and other red tops ran a story saying that Wise was "set for a shock return to management with lowly Brighton". And one line said, "He will be helped out by his old ally Gus Poyet." The writer had once been *The Sun's* man in Yorkshire, where he had no doubt got to know Wise while he was in charge at Leeds. So it could have come via Wise, but it quoted "a source high up in the club" and I had my suspicions who that might be.

I immediately challenged the story and denied it absolutely. I made it plain that I wouldn't consider Wise even if Russell left. I didn't like his style and a lot of fans agreed with me.

I was asked about the story when I invited questions from the floor after the club AGM the following Friday. One shareholder, Alan Gower, a long-term fan who had backed me with £10,000 he put in the club some years earlier, asked me whether there was any truth in these stories about Wise. If there was, he said, he and other fans who sat near him in the North Stand at Withdean would be returning their season tickets. "We don't believe that someone with Dennis Wise's record should be associated with the Albion," he said. "And I speak for a lot of season ticket holders in our block."

I promised that Wise would never manage Brighton while I was chairman. "There is absolutely no chance of that happening."

But Ken Brown, who had been going red in the face, butted in and said to Alan, "What possible qualifications do you have to judge whether or not Dennis Wise is a good manager?" He was very annoyed that a shareholder had the temerity to ask this question.

Alan said, "I know he has been a manager. But he's not the sort of manager we want at Brighton."

Then Ken came out with a classic. He said, "You don't know anything – Dennis Wise got me a cup final, that's how good a manager he is." Not "Millwall" but "me".

"I didn't realise you owned Millwall," Alan retorted.

But the feeling among some other directors seemed uneasy at the anti-Wise mood among the supporters and me. I don't think Ken would have said what he did unless he had some backing from other people on the board.

Ken had come in when I had decided that Martin needed to concentrate solely on the stadium project, and give the day-to-day administration duties of the club to a new position of managing director. I had been doing quite a lot of it myself, but now I had to devote more time to the bank negotiations that would be part of the funding package for the stadium construction. Martin was a little reluctant to accept the idea, but I insisted and so did the rest of the board.

Ken Brown had applied for the job and Martin, who had met him at a few league meetings, pushed for him to be given it. I knew he had worked at Millwall and had some dealings with him over Darren Byfield, so I gave Theo Paphitis a call. Theo had left Millwall and Ken had departed soon after. Theo gave him a great reference: "The best administrator who has ever worked for me. He's a football man, hard-working, a clear thinker." So I went on my mate Theo's word.

But it wasn't long before I realised I had a problem. Ken's way of dealing with fans didn't accord with mine. There was a game at Withdean against Gillingham when he decided that, because of the high number of visiting fans likely to attend, we'd charge more for the away end than for the home fans' cheapest areas. This despite the fact that I'd previously promised that the cost of tickets for the 'Worthing End' would always be at least £1 lower than any other ticket in the ground because the view was so bad.

The supporters' club got into a row with him about that and I was forced to get involved. I had to point out that the Gillingham fans who went to their away games were most probably the ones who had written letters in support of the Albion's stadium planning application, and we certainly weren't going to create a money-making opportunity at their expense.

The talk of Dennis Wise may have come up because of Russell Slade's slow start, but the day after the Sunday paper reports we won 1-0 away to Colchester – Dean Hammond and all – with Lloyd Owusu, a Slade signing on loan from Cheltenham Town, scoring the only goal. Owusu was a stylish striker who knew where the goal was and we were unbeaten after that for the rest of the season, winning three games and drawing the other, Owusu scoring four more times.

Gary Hart played probably his best game for the club in the 2-1 win at Bristol Rovers. He launched a brilliant run all the way down the right after picking the ball up just outside our penalty area, and crossed for Calvin Andrew to throw himself in at the far post and head home. Andrew went straight to Gary, giving him an almighty hug because he knew he had created a special goal.

In the end we needed one point from our last game, at home to Stockport of all teams, to stay up. We got three thanks to Nicky Forster's goal after 73 minutes. I didn't want to make my traditional last-home-game-of-the-season speech before kick-off because we might still have been relegated. And I couldn't do it after the match because the pitch was full of people celebrating.

And that was a shame. Because it turned out to be my last game as chairman of the Albion.

# CHAPTER TWENTY SEVEN

# IT'S NOT JUST ABOUT FOOTBALL . . .

On March 4 2007, at the Grosvenor House Hotel on London's Park Lane, Albion won a title that was as important in its way as any of the four trophies hoisted by Danny Cullip and Gordon Greer at Withdean or Cardiff. The occasion was the Football League awards, and the prize was our recognition as 'Community Club of the Year'.

I am as proud of Albion in the Community (AITC), the club's charitable arm, as I am of anything else that I have done at the club. That award was recognition that we had become one of football's best community schemes, but I believe it was one of the best schemes in the country, full stop. We went on to win four national awards between 2007 and 2010 as our scope for helping to improve people's lives widened.

The idea of AITC was born very early on. From the moment I took over as Brighton chairman in 1997 I understood that it was the community, the fans themselves, of whom I was one, that had risen up to save the club.

Years later I was asked about what the Albion had done for the community while at the Goldstone and the answer was nothing. The club didn't have any dialogue with the fans; they just expected them to turn up every other Saturday to read programmes that told them very little apart from what their favourite player's meal was – usually steak and chips. They were expected to shout their heads off for 90 minutes and then shut up for the rest of the week.

Most clubs did a bit of football coaching but that was all, and all anyone would expect. And that's what we were doing when I took over in 1997. In a small portakabin at the Goldstone, against all odds, Steve Ford, who was a local lad, an ex-Hove Grammar School boy who had somehow slipped the Albion net and ended up playing for Stoke, had been running an embryonic scheme since 1990. He had a bag of footballs and went into local schools and did some coaching. In those days it was just called 'Football in the Community' because that's all it was.

After the takeover was finally concluded, within a few weeks I sat down with him. "Steve, let me assure you we're going to continue," I said, because he might have thought his job was on the line. "Not only that, we're going to expand, because it's time this club gave something back to the community that has supported it and saved it. Despite the fact that we have very limited resources, I'm going to divert some of those resources to help you develop a proper community scheme.

"You'll be in charge of this and we need to open our minds about what it can be, how we can harness the power of sport to help people and hopefully make a difference to their lives." I wanted to develop that side of the club despite all the other battles that were going on. Steve took hold of that baton and ran with it.

While we were at Gillingham we expanded to include disability and health projects. It gave us a continued presence in Brighton & Hove even though the first team was playing in Kent. But as far as I was concerned it would also be a key part of the strategy to get the stadium planning permission – to demonstrate what the club did and could do for the people of Brighton & Hove and the county of Sussex.

My vision of the club was always about community. I sensed we had this vast untapped resource that could use the power of sport, especially football, to attract and involve people in a way that other forms of communication couldn't. It engaged disadvantaged people, it interested otherwise uninterested people; for example, kids who were opting out of the formal education system.

When we got to Withdean in 1999, we were able to develop things a lot more. It wasn't a charity in those days, although it acted in a charitable way, but Steve, Martin and I knew that we should be able to access public funds if we expanded our community services.

Steve brought in Teresa Sanders, an enthusiastic volunteer, full-time to help develop the special needs and disability section, so that more youngsters – and not just youngsters – could get more involved in society.

Obviously the football coaching continued and expanded, but we gradually developed the scheme into the core of a bigger social structure, including working with the NHS and adding social inclusion programmes.

The administration was squeezed into the cramped club offices at first Queens Road, then North Road. The equipment was either stored there or kept in the boots of the cars of the people who were going out and doing the work. We had started hiring qualified coaches and community specialists, some part-time, and volunteers. The work itself was all done out in the community, at schools, social clubs, church halls etc.

One area of provision we saw a great need for was education. Alan Sanders, who is an experienced educationalist with a PhD in Social and Applied Sport Studies, joined us in 2002 and he rapidly developed the education side – adult education primarily.

Alan approached the Learning & Skills Council and we were awarded a grant to open a study support centre at Withdean. We started with a range of very basic post-school education. The people who attended were mainly kids who had somehow missed out on school – disadvantaged or completely uneducated youngsters whom we taught basic English, mathematics, geography and some history. The acronym they use is NEETs – Not in Education, Employment or Training. People who have somehow slipped through the system.

Because it was linked to a football club and not a school, AITC learning was automatically more interesting to them and that was the whole point. We could teach them maths with league tables, the points system, transfer fees and percentage sell-ons. We built in geography and history by talking about European competitions and World Cups. You start relating it to things people are interested in and you start teaching them.

In the first year we enrolled almost 1,000 students in our various courses, adding IT to the literacy and numeracy work. We promoted the courses in the local papers, on our website and in the match programme and we started going out with social inclusion and special needs programmes into different areas of Sussex.

The Albion's catchment area is not generally thought of as containing poor areas, but some council wards in Sussex are among the most deprived in the country. And we went into them because the club had a power to help them that some other organisations didn't.

But we also had senior citizens. One of our first graduates was an 87-year-old chap who had wanted to do an IT course so that he could communicate with members of his family who had emigrated to Australia. And we enrolled lots of women who had had children and now wanted to get back into the workforce.

Along the way we also became proficient in applying for grants. First in sport, then education, and next in health. Working with the local NHS we received funding to develop and deliver their projects for them. We had smoking and cancer awareness programmes and promoted them during games. Men with bowel cancer have been saved because they picked up a leaflet at Withdean or at the Amex.

In 2003 Alan secured a £1.7 million grant from the Learning & Skills Council and Interreg, the EU link-up, to open another eight study support centres around Sussex, linking up with local clubs like Eastbourne Borough, Worthing, Bognor Regis, Hastings, etc. So by now the 'community' really meant the whole of Sussex. Between 2004 and 2006, over 3,000 students qualified from the various courses on that project.

In 2003 we went overseas. Some AITC people went to Kosovo, helping with mine-clearing. We started working with an international project run by the British Council called 'Coaching for Hope' and I was asked to find a patron for them to succeed Bianca Jagger. I suggested that Fatboy Slim might be interested and, when I spoke to Norman, he was. The Skint link worked because it dovetailed with what the club was doing. The project was using football to help educate youngsters in Africa about AIDS. We started coaching in Mali, Burkina Faso and Lesotho, our coaches training local people to coach football so that during the football sessions they could give the kids HIV/AIDS education. Norman went on a couple of these trips and made many new fans. It was slightly surreal, Brighton & Hove Albion taking its community programme into Africa, but why not – it was another example of our power to help.

In 2004 something happened that might well have been unique, when one of the club's top players became a client of the club's community scheme. I saw Charlie Oatway in the offices at Withdean one afternoon and he said, "I've signed up for one of your courses, Mr Chairman."

I asked him, "Is that an IT course then, Charlie, so that you can keep up with your kids?"

To my great surprise, he said, "No, it's a literacy course. I can't read or write." He was quite open about it. "But you're right that I'm doing it because of my kids. They come home from school with their homework and want me to help them and I can't. And I feel so bad about it. So I've got to learn."

He was enrolling for one of our basic courses, and I just thought how brave he was to tell me.

Then I remembered the day that we'd signed him from Brentford and he'd joked with me about how much he was worth relative to Paul Watson. We'd had the two contracts on the table ready for them to sign so we could do the usual photographs, and while Paul had gone through every clause of his with a fine-tooth comb, Charlie had whizzed through his very quickly.

He'd signed it with just a squiggle. Now it dawned on me that he hadn't really read his contract at all, but just cast his eye over the pages. We could have put anything in there and he wouldn't have known.

But now he said, "If I pass, then maybe we can do something about it, talk about it."

He'd obviously spoken to Alan Sanders, who had helped him and become his mentor, later helping Charlie write his book, *Tackling Life*. Alan had raised the possibility of going public with it in order to help raise awareness of what AITC was doing, which would have been a hugely courageous thing for a professional footballer to do.

I said, "Charlie, just go and do the course and we'll think about that afterwards."

So he took the course and passed. He was still willing to put his story out there, a very brave thing for a local hero and role model to do, but it was as the latter that we knew Charlie's story would have the greatest impact.

We could have taken the story to *The Argus* or held a press conference, but we decided to go straight to the national media, because we knew that *The Argus* would pick up the story anyway. Paul Camillin, our press officer, offered the story to Nick Szczepanik of *The Times* (who has collaborated with me on this book), knowing that it was the broadsheet that gave the most coverage to football and – this was significant – was widely read in Whitehall.

Nick is a lifelong Albion fan so we knew that he would not only treat Charlie sympathetically but also understand the reason why Charlie had agreed to go public and how it could help the club. It was a feel-good story that would attract publicity, but also make the point that we could do even more community work when we eventually got permission to build our new stadium.

We weren't disappointed. On March 1 2004 *The Times* made Charlie's admission the lead story in their Monday morning football supplement, *The Game*, and although the story led on Charlie's experiences, it also mentioned the other work our community scheme was doing and included a pointed prod in the direction of John Prescott.

One paragraph read, "The study centre operates in a Portakabin that doubles as a hospitality suite on match-days. Brighton are sweating on the decision of John Prescott on their bid to build a stadium at Falmer. A positive response will let them expand the educational programmes. A negative result may, in the worst case, mean the end of the club and its community initiatives." Alan was quoted, "It shows you what we could do if we did have a proper stadium."

We asked *The Times* for permission to reproduce the piece in the match programme for the next home game, which we were given, and as we expected *The Argus* followed the story up, as did *The Times Educational Supplement* and regional and national broadcast media. Not only did Charlie come across well, but we were able to show that we didn't only want a new stadium to play football – it was needed for other reasons too.

It was incredibly positive news for the club and its community activities. It was a perfect example of what a football club could do to help someone improve their life. Needless to say, it provided a huge boost to the number of people signing up for our courses.

At the Footballer of the Year dinner later that season, I was sitting with a writer from *Corriere dello Sport*, the Italian paper, and he'd heard about Charlie and his story. "Ah, Brighton, you are the club who had the player who couldn't read and write." They'd done a story on him too. Charlie was never going to star in the Juventus or Inter midfield, but his fame had spread to Turin and Milan all the same.

I can't speak highly enough of Charlie. Going public about something so personal and potentially embarrassing said everything about the man, and was why I told him, "Even if you finish your playing career with another club, there will always be a job for you here. You're exactly the type of strong character and role model that we need to go out and work for AITC in the community."

I saw the possibility for key players to have a role with the club off the pitch and even beyond their playing days. Paul Watson qualified as a physiotherapist and joined the club's medical staff. Danny Cullip, Guy Butters, Chippy Carpenter, Gary Hart and Michel Kuipers have all made an important contribution to AITC. In recent years our Basque defender Inigo Calderon has carried on the tradition and wholeheartedly embraced it. Muchas gracias, Calde.

In my time as Albion Chairman the club provided free office space but we never had to bail out the community scheme financially – Steve Ford saw to that. The number of permanent staff increased to 20, then 30, then 40, with up to 130 part-time coaches and volunteers – and it was self-funded by the public grants, education contracts and local sponsorships that we obtained. It never made a loss in 20 years.

I officially became the chairman of the community scheme in 2005 and we decided to formally become a charity. And I suggested that by that point we needed a name that reflected all that we were doing more accurately than Football in the Community, so we changed the name to Albion in the Community. And I added the supporting slogan: 'It's not just about football. It's more important than that.'

It was making its presence felt. In 2007, Alan McCarthy, the Brighton & Hove Council chief executive, said we were their largest partner in social programmes. "AITC is an essential part of the strategy to deliver education and skills training in a unique way."

In the autumn of 2011 we launched a groundbreaking initiative called 'Want to Work', aimed at educating youngsters and retraining older people and getting them work experience placements and into jobs, working with local businesses and colleges of further education. In the first year we got work placements and employment opportunities for over 200 people.

I always saw the new stadium as a standout addition to the city's community culture. It would not only host sporting events but also be the focus of many other community activities. It would create jobs. It was an inherent and vital part of our strategy to the council throughout the long quest for planning permission – what the stadium would do for the community. The stadium would be the ultimate expression of our community scheme.

And so it proved. In 2012, the first full year after the opening of the stadium, a total of 52,823 members of the public directly benefited from AITC programmes.

But for me, it was the small things that mattered. About how we gave our young disability apprentices like Keiran Green and Ben Doehren the confidence to stand in front of an audience of local business people and give a speech about their work. What made the work of AITC's dedicated staff so important was their unending ability to help people discover themselves and get more out of life.

Inigo Calderon delivered a lecture on sports psychology to participants in our pioneering Want to Work programme, and also gave a motivational speech to local unemployed groups. He was a deserved recipient of the Football League's Community Player of the Year award, following up the club's earlier awards. What a tremendous role model as a professional footballer. Calde understands what a club can do for its community.

AITC health manager Dan Lawson broke a world record by running an incredible 518 miles non-stop (20 marathons back-to-back!) and raised £13,000 for the charity.

The delegates to the first-ever conference at the Amex were 30 coaches drawn from Africa, India and the Middle East, some with learning difficulties or disability problems, as part of the HIV/AIDS project.

And of course the London 2012 Olympics and Paralympics captured the public's imagination and appetite for the magnificent possibilities of sport to motivate and inspire people.

What happened on the world stage in London was something we'd been doing in Brighton for 15 years.

In 2008 our community involvement was the key to me pulling off the coup of securing one of the world's most powerful brands as the sponsor for our new stadium. Don't forget that the full name of the Amex is the American Express Community Stadium.

Stadium naming rights are a very important source of funding – that was why the stadium was never going to be called the New Goldstone – and once we had secured planning permission to build at Falmer I knew that I needed to pull off a big naming-rights deal for our new home, and that I was capable of doing it.

To get a feel for the market, Martin Perry had invited sports marketing agencies to come up with proposals for selling the rights. One produced a flashy, quick-cutting Sky Sports-type video that had nothing to do with the soul of our club. It was as if it was trailing a Premier League game at the Emirates or Old Trafford. The one he chose produced estimates of the sort of money we could expect to get: between £30,000 and £70,000 per year over a five-year deal. They said, "The most you could possibly get would be £80,000–100,000 a year because of your stadium, but we're pretty sure that no League One club has ever got that."

Their judgements about long-term sponsorship deals were stabs in the dark bearing in mind the actual market, and they were based on media exposure figures that were way off the mark. I know something about media coverage and the way to analyse it. And this company that charged us £35,000 for a market appraisal and recommendations had made errors that were laughable. Their 'expert media analysts' thought that our new stadium sponsors would get more coverage from the Scunthorpe local paper than from *The Argus*! You could drive a bus through the holes in their numbers.

I wanted something much better so I called in my own media expert, David Cuff, a big Albion fan who had worked for Virgin Media and big advertising companies and did a lot of work for me for nothing. We came up with our own projections of the huge national coverage we would get, and they could all be fully justified.

We had registered the stadium company as The Community Stadium plc back in 2002, because from the day the search for a new home began I had always intended that the naming rights would be tied to community. Albion in the Community was the link. I had pledged to develop the scheme, knowing that would be the way forward for the future. Clubs would need to have meaningful relationships with their communities, and AITC had led the way. It was all part of the vision for our stadium.

I knew that consumer champions such as Ralph Nader were encouraging the public to challenge big organisations over the safety, contents, production methods, etc of their products, and I knew from my advertising experience that there was a big consumer backlash going on. Big corporations were having to react to that and come up with a more responsible approach to their customers and their markets.

I targeted American Express for the naming rights. It was pure coincidence that they had their European headquarters in Brighton – I was thinking globally. I knew where the company had positioned itself in world markets, and I understood their company ethos. In their mission statement, they had four different audiences that they wanted to reach: their customers, shareholders, staff – and the communities they operated in.

With Bill Swallow's excellent graphic input, I put together a presentation for our stadium that talked about a unique marketing opportunity for American Express, on the theme of 'corporate social responsibility'.

Through business contacts I was able to arrange a meeting with Peter Godfrey, the American Express president of global network services – probably more through my marketing background than my credentials as a football club chairman. My contact, Richard Lewis, told Peter that I had a great opportunity that I'd go and sell to someone else if he didn't meet me. He agreed to meet on Friday June 13 2008 at the American Express headquarters in London.

After 20 minutes of the meeting, Peter's secretary came in and said, "The President of the Bank of China is on the line." I sensed this could be a code allowing him to halt the meeting if it wasn't going anywhere interesting. But Peter said, "Tell him I'll call him back" and our meeting continued. The secretary clearly knew the procedure, because then she returned with coffee and biscuits, knowing the meeting would be a long one. Peter said, appropriately, "You've got 90 minutes."

I presented my community thinking and the media evaluation that David Cuff had put together, which was extremely robust.

Peter's response was very positive and I could see he was buying into the social concept.

If I had gone in asking for a conventional sponsorship deal, he would have taken that 'call'. Just after the coffee arrived, he said, "If you had come in and started telling me about your shirt, I would have thrown you out by now. We could have sponsored the Emirates Stadium or Stamford Bridge. We had approaches. But nobody came to us with the proposal that you have about community."

The mistake that Arsenal and Chelsea had made was to approach American Express for shirt and stadium sponsorships, promising brand awareness through television coverage. But American Express were already one of the most recognised names in the world and hardly needed extra brand awareness. They'd get virtually none from a League One club. What they were interested in was projecting their brand values. They could see that I understood that and that I was offering an involving new way to convey them.

So, because I understood their corporate aims, I was confident in what I was saying as our meeting continued and I told Peter that if they went ahead, the name would have to be the American Express *Community* Stadium. I said: "The whole vision of the stadium is community-based, and I'm afraid it will be a deal-breaker if you want to call it the American Express Stadium. Everyone will shorten it to the Amex, but the name on the side of the building must include the word 'community'."

The reply, as I knew it would be, was, "You'll have no argument from us on that."

I was giving them a global blueprint for the future. I knew that they were expanding in the Far East, and this could be a way forward as part of their marketing strategy. Peter could see the potential and said he would be talking to Amex's worldwide chief, Ken Chenault, who set great store by the company's community involvement and who Peter thought would be very interested in my ideas.

I proposed a 10-year contract minimum, and Peter asked why. I explained that there was no value in doing it for a shorter period. Five years spent firmly establishing the name in the public mind would be wasted if the contract ended there, rather than going on and capitalising on that awareness in the coming years.

That set me up to ask for the amount of money I had in mind. The figure is covered by business confidentiality, but I can tell you that it was many times greater than £30,000 a year, and was based on a reach of millions of people.

Peter had no problem with my asking price. The meeting ended very cordially, with him promising to go away and consider the whole proposition with other top people in the company. Meanwhile he would get Amex's media experts in New York to check our coverage projections and, after their thorough analysis and me clarifying a few queries over the phone, they validated them 100 per cent. So far, so good.

We had another meeting, at Withdean. I had said, "You've got to come and see where we are now and what we have to put up with, and look at the new stadium site and the detailed plans." Martin was in his element then, and they could see that an immense amount of professionalism had gone into our plans.

I saw that there could be another opportunity. I said to Peter, "I never asked you for shirt sponsorship, but you could also be the title sponsor for our community scheme."

I gave a brief outline of what we did in AITC and he said, "There could be more money for that. We could be very interested. What sort of amount are you talking about?"

I suggested a sum that, added to the figure for the stadium contract, would add 25 per cent to the 10-year total. Peter replied, "No problem, but let's get the stadium deal tied up." He had already got his legal people to start drawing up agreements.

But in autumn 2008, I got a letter from him saying, "We're going to have to put this all on ice." Despite several meetings we'd had with his people to thrash out the agreements, American Express would have to call a halt because of the gathering financial clouds over Wall Street and the City. But when I spoke to him Peter promised, "This is just going on ice. We will do this deal, unless catastrophe strikes."

And American Express were true to their word. The stadium naming-rights deal was revived in 2010, exactly as I had negotiated it, although I then had to make a separate pitch to the head of Amex's Albion team, Michael Edwards, for Albion in the Community.

Peter had retired from American Express, and he subsequently accepted Tony Bloom's invitation to become a director of the club.

In 2012, AITC's unique partnership with American Express launched a number of community projects, including taking over 500 disabled kids on special 'Gully's Days Out', and running school masterclasses in a true-life work environment. More than 700 Amex staff worked with AITC's experienced people to ensure 11 different initiatives made a difference to a lot of lives.

# CHAPTER TWENTY EIGHT

# STEPPING DOWN

T he feeling at club board meetings was now very different, and I didn't feel I could rely on every director's loyalty.

Soon after the official green light had been given to Falmer in September 2007, I had begun, with Martin Perry and our advisors, Price Waterhouse Coopers, exploratory talks with a few selected banks for medium-sized funding for the project. These carried on into 2008 and were encouraging due to the strong stadium business plan and our other sources of public and corporate funding planned or already lined up.

But as the worldwide credit crunch began to bite, in autumn 2008, it became clear that we would need to take Tony Bloom up on his offer to underwrite the building of the stadium. It had also been proposed that, because Tony was going to have a substantial investment in the club, a couple of his business associates should join the board. These were Marc Sugarman, a banker and a school friend of Tony's at Brighton College, and Adam Franks, an accountant who worked for Tony's Blue Lizard company.

There was quite a lot of discussion about that. They were coming onto the board to safeguard Tony's interests. I was never scared of a vote, but it was very clear that Tony, although up until then he had never wanted to be a director himself, was manoeuvring things so that he would have three financial people on his side in the boardroom – Robert Comer, the club's financial director, was Tony's personal accountant. It had been Robert who had tabled the idea, as a sensible move to give more stability to Tony's financial investment. And the rest of the board, which included Tony's uncle, Ray, were not disagreeing.

It was a significant time. On Wednesday February 4 2009, the council planning committee had passed our final planning applications concerning some stadium roof design changes and site management issues, by 10 votes to nil. Two councillors, whom I won't name, abstained. I told *The Argus*: "Committee members have certainly got the message about how important the stadium will be for everyone in the city – they understand it's not just about football fans on a Saturday afternoon, but about improving people's lives with state-of-the-art community facilities – in other words, a real community stadium!"

It showed faith in the club that the council, despite the economic climate, had given us an overwhelming mandate to go ahead. They didn't want a half-built stadium disfiguring the north-eastern entrance to the city, but they had seen our business case and trusted us to deliver. They knew how important this was to the city, so they gave us the conclusive go-ahead. They were saying, "Let's get on with it."

With the final barriers all overcome, this was potentially a great moment for the city and the club. All we needed now was the money in the bank.

We had a board meeting at Withdean scheduled for the morning of Monday April 27. Although this was before we had escaped relegation, Russell Slade was there to confidently outline his plans for the future, and there was also an impressive Albion in the Community presentation by Steve Ford and Alan Sanders.

Tony had asked if he and I could meet up afterwards. So we sat down in the early afternoon and Tony came straight out with it. "If I'm going to put the money in, I want to take over as chairman now."

He had laid his cards on the table.

I replied, "That's a pretty big step. I'll have to think about it, Tony."

I suppose I had known it was coming. It had been building up. But while I fully expected him to want to come on board as a director, and even put his foot in the door of the chairman's office, I hadn't expected him to want to kick it open and suddenly dispense with my services.

However, stepping down completely from the role I had held for 12 years – the 12th anniversary of the last Goldstone game had been the day before – was not on my agenda. Three days later, on April 30, my birthday, and two days before the final game against Stockport, I had scheduled a presentation from architects KSS on the interior design of the stadium – the décor, the imagery. I had given their head of design a very open brief and she responded in kind. We were shown some exciting ideas for how the lounges, the ceilings, the concourses would look. I had been, and still was, very involved with that.

A few days after we had beaten Stockport and easily escaped the drop, I gave Russell Slade a two-year contract which, as far as I was concerned, he thoroughly deserved and would see out under me. I told the media, "Russell has done a fantastic job pulling off a great escape, and I know all Albion fans will agree that he has earned this opportunity to lead us forward."

Tony, by this time, was also keen to get more involved with what was happening on the playing side. We had a scheduled meeting the following Monday about the scouting network with Russell and Barry Lloyd, so I invited Tony along. I wanted our reporting systems modernised and made more comprehensive. I wanted us to make more use of aids such as Prozone in the future. Tony was very interested and asked a lot of questions.

The next day I met Tony again, this time in the rear dining area at Topolino's. Now he was more insistent about becoming chairman. And this time I was prepared.

The meeting the previous week had given me plenty to think about. If I turned down Tony's offer of funding, I knew that I would have to go to the fans and explain that we would have to delay moving ahead with the stadium. I could have told them, "You all know that there is a worldwide credit crunch going on. Liverpool's proposed stadium has been postponed indefinitely, so has Everton's. There isn't another major stadium in Britain being built apart from the Olympic Stadium."

The fans could see all that for themselves. I would have been arguably justified in telling them that we would have to wait a few more years while the economy rode out the financial storm. We had waited 12 years. Would another two make such a difference?

The Falmer For All team had been shown the stadium business plans, so they knew they were strong, but they were bound by commercially confidential agreements, so were unable to disclose details to other supporters. If they had, the glass-half-full fans and members of the team would have said, "This is only a short-term problem." The glass-half-empty ones might have thought, "With everything that has gone on before, something else is bound to go wrong." I had enough trust and credibility to carry the positive ones with me – I was sure of that. For the gloomy ones it would have just been prolonging the agony.

Because I knew that the business case was strong, I was sure that when the credit crunch was over, the banks would lend us the amounts we had originally targeted. They weren't huge sums relative to other projects, such as the over 90 per cent mortgage on Arsenal's Emirates Stadium. We had the planning approval, so I was confident the banks would go for it when the economic horizon was brighter.

But the difference was that Tony was offering the money now, not at some time in the future. And I knew that, if he wanted, his PR machine could make that point and claim that I was clinging on at the expense of the club moving forward more quickly.

I went through that dilemma in my mind and came to the only possible conclusion. For the fans' sake, I could not stand in the way of Tony putting the money we needed in then, so that we could proceed with the stadium build without any hold-up, despite the economic chill. His offer was tremendous.

I felt for the fans after what they had been through. It was already a dozen years since we had left the Goldstone. Did I have the right to delay the new stadium even a couple of years? I decided that I did not.

The fact that, in my opinion, we should have been in the new stadium already was irrelevant at this point. We had been delayed by the Public Inquiries and the Lewes appeal. It was just my bad luck that the delays had taken us into the midst of a global economic meltdown, especially after I had negotiated the exciting naming-rights deal with American Express.

But I could not hold the club back.

The detail would be in the timescale for the transfer of power that had begun to seem inevitable. Martin and some of the other directors had changed in their attitudes to me. I can understand it − I guess they sniffed a change in the air and felt that it was time to call a taxi for Mr Knight.

When I had used all my experience in marketing and powers of persuasion to do the deal on the stadium naming rights with American Express, the nature of which was pioneering for English football, the other directors were delighted. But even then the reaction was relatively muted. I don't think they realised the breakthrough significance of what had been done, but I suspect there was also an element of frustration that it was me who was able to pull it off

The writing, in a sense, was on the wall. So I went into that meeting at Topolino's prepared to give Tony what he wanted. And I made what I considered a very reasonable proposal. I said, "While I respect what you're putting in, I think the best thing would be for you to become vice-chairman initially. Everyone will know why you are taking that role and be very pleased and grateful.

"The stadium build will take 18 months. Here we are in 2009, with the opening in August 2011. During that time you can stand alongside me as vice-chairman. I will show you the ropes of running a club, and introduce you to the top people in football. I didn't have the benefit of anyone teaching me how to become a football club chairman, but I can do that for you. And then you will be able to hit the ground running. It will be a natural progression.

"There's something else. I know you spend a few months every year in Australia, so you won't be as hands-on as I have been."

"No, I won't," came the reply.

"There's an issue there because − and I have to be honest with you − Martin is a very good planning expert and he has done a tremendous job and is still needed in that area, but he wasn't fully able to do the job of club chief executive on a day-to-day basis on top of all his stadium work. I did a lot on the major stuff myself. Because you're not going to be so hands-on, you're going to need someone very good to run the club – and I'm not sure Ken Brown will be able to cope with it." Tony said he would bear that in mind.

I had one more thing to add. But pretty important to me.

"The stadium project is my baby. I started it the day we left the Goldstone, so it is only fair and right that I lead the club into the new stadium. It would make great theatre for you and me to walk out onto the pitch alongside each other before the first game at Falmer, and I hand the keys of the club to you. That would be the perfect closure to my time as chairman."

Tony looked at me. It was an odd look as if to say, "Why?"

He said, "I don't need to do that. I'm going to run the club in a very different way from the way you have. I don't think I need your advice."

I was surprised to hear him say that. He obviously thought his money would do all the talking. With hindsight, various things fell into place. I said I'd think about it, but he said, "I need a decision, because I need to know where I stand."

He clearly didn't want to go into an interim partnership, and because I didn't want to let the fans down, I felt I was being pressured into agreeing. But I arranged to meet him again the following day, the Wednesday, at the same place, and then I picked up the bill; it felt like paying for the bullets for your own firing squad.

There was no one else in the restaurant the following afternoon. And now he said, "It's time for you to stand down and let me take over. I've got the money to build the stadium, I'm prepared to do it – and you know that I'm Brighton through and through."

I said, "I don't have any doubt about that, Tony. Your Albion credentials are impeccable, unlike those of so many people who could have tried to come in at this time." He was certainly far better qualified to become my successor than, even say, David Gold – than virtually anyone, in fact. But it was the way he was going about it. I said, "In the circumstances, I'm going to need some of my share money back."

At that point I had about £1.8 million (including loans) in the club. He offered me a sum for a small number of my shares which was unacceptable. I said, "I will stand down now, but only if you make me a reasonable offer." I knew that now we had planning permission the shares had some real value, but I added, "I'm not looking for a profit on my shares." Bearing in mind that I was handing over control of the club that I'd saved and now had a very bright future, I thought I was being entirely reasonable.

We parted with Tony promising to get back to me to sort out the financial arrangement for the transfer of power. Until he did, publicly I carried on as if nothing had happened. I met up with Russell a couple of times, for example, to discuss team strengthening. He would need to do that, with or without me.

Martin, though, was very aware of developments. He came to see me the day after my second Topolino's meeting with Tony. I had a flat in Third Avenue, Hove, and when he arrived I got the impression he was trying to let me down lightly. He started by saying, "This was always going to happen, Dick. It has been coming for some time. As you know, Tony has been putting money in and helping us . . ."

I thought, "*Et tu, Brute?*" As far as I was concerned, we had worked together brilliantly. I had brought Martin into the club, we had been a very good team. He had been my confidant and I felt really let down. He had read the lesson at our wedding, and before that Kerry and I had been a shoulder to cry on when Martin was going through his divorce. He tried to be sympathetic but it seemed almost patronising. Looked at one way, Martin was merely being prag-matic. But I found the meeting hurtful. Perhaps he felt he was being nice to me but it left a sad feeling in the pit of my stomach.

I arranged to meet Tony again, in London at lunchtime on Friday May 15 – in fact, at the Grafton, where I had interviewed managers – and we had the final discussion. Bearing in mind that I had said I would stand down, it was now a question of him upping his offer to a reasonable level.

He said he would give me £400,000, for that number of £1 shares that I held. He wanted to pay it in two instalments – £200,000 now, when I stood down, and the rest in a year's time. And he agreed to pay back a loan to the Co-op Bank that I had taken out and given to the club, who were paying it back bit by bit.

I said that £400k was still nowhere near enough considering that he was investing millions in the stadium construction, only made possible because of the efforts of myself and the people who had supported me. But as far as Tony was concerned, that was it. It crossed my mind that if I had sold out to David Gold when he put out feelers about taking over, I would probably have got about £5 million for my 1.6 million shares in the club. I'd given up a lot when I told him the Albion wasn't for sale.

Even Bill Archer had got £700,000 after all the grief he'd caused in almost destroying the club. I was going to get £400,000 back for 12 years of hard work, inspiration, refusal to give up, motivation and whatever else I contributed in saving and rebuilding it. I had taken on a club in the bottom of the gutter and was passing it on with its huge potential reawakened and with full planning permission for a new stadium.

I stood down so as not to delay the building of the stadium, but Tony got control at a very cheap price.

I said to him, "If you don't want to give me back what I put in, then at least give the less wealthy shareholders back what they invested. Their money helped ensure that this club survived for you to take over."

I was thinking particularly of people like the Falmer For All team member who had given us that £170,000 legacy, but also others who had put sums between five and fifty thousand pounds into the club: Alan Gower, John Vickers, Neddy McDonnell, John Gold, John Town, Edward David who had worked for the club over a long period, an Albion fan in the States, Peter Hirschel, and others. They had helped keep the club alive and deserved their money back. There was also a case for former director Kevin Griffiths, who had hit hard times, to get part, if not all, of his £500,000-plus investment repaid.

But Tony was putting all this money in for the stadium so probably thought he was being generous in offering to pay me £400,000 on top of that – of almost £2 million that I had put in – and I don't know if he even considered the other shareholders.

We had kept our talks private, but suddenly that changed. On Sunday May 17, the *News of the World* carried the story that Tony was taking over. "Gambler Tony Bloom will be the man holding all the aces at Brighton next season. And the 39-year-old millionaire poker star and football betting expert is set to take control of the club from long-serving chairman Dick Knight."

On the Monday at 10.30am, May 18 2009, the Albion put out a press release, parts of which I knew nothing about, whereas normally I would have overseen it. The heading was, 'Stadium Funding Secured'. It began: "The club is delighted to announce full funding has been finalised for the new community stadium at Falmer. The full cost of the stadium project is £93 million, the majority of which will be funded by Tony Bloom. Bloom will take over as Albion chairman, with Dick Knight taking on the role of life president, ending a very memorable 12 years at the club's helm."

The 'life president' title was not a surprise. Tony had said he would give me that – and five more years in the club's health scheme. But the impression given by the press release that he would be paying almost all the £93 million himself failed to take account of the millions we had already paid out on planning and the millions secured in public grants and corporate naming rights. And I was amazed to find myself quoted as saying, "This is the natural progression for the football club."

There were some quotes that I was okay with and I went on to say, sincerely: "Tony's investment will mean no need for external financing, which is absolutely superb news for the club and its fans.

"Being chairman of the Albion has been the most rewarding period of my life. To be able to give something back to the club I've supported since I was a boy has been a privilege. Helping to save it, building a forward-thinking reputation, developing our youth system and encouraging Albion in the Community to spread its wings – I've enjoyed it immensely. And all of this while we fought the long and relentless battle to secure our new home against all the odds."

A few words from Tony followed. "I would like to pay tribute to Dick Knight. Nobody should be in any doubt that he saved the club from almost certain extinction at a time when no one else was willing to come forward, and under his leadership we have had some very memorable times including our successful nine-year battle to secure the go-ahead for Falmer."

*The Argus* website reported that Tony had converted £18 million of loan stock into a 75 per cent shareholding and had been "unanimously elected chairman by the directors with immediate effect".

I must have missed that meeting.

Brian Owen, writing in the next day's *Argus*, summed up my time in charge. "It has been a battle most of the way – and usually a battle against the odds. From the first and biggest conflict of them all, to wrest control from Bill Archer and potentially save the club. To the ongoing struggles to move back to Brighton at Withdean Stadium, then on towards a brighter future at Falmer. To his tussles with bigger clubs for what he felt were fair transfer fees or, in the case of Gareth Barry and Michael Standing at Aston Villa, compensation for players emerging from Sussex. To the regular searches for new managers, and trying to tell them Withdean really was the place to be, as the incumbents left (usually) for better things or (occasionally) because of poor results. To the challenge of making ends meet at spartan Withdean.

"There was a power struggle or two. 'Knight will not give up control' screamed the headlines as Stephen Purdew flashed the cash in 1999. He has even been known to have an occasional disagreement with *The Argus* over issues close to his heart.

"Knight might find it tough sitting back and watching the blue-and-white stripes do their stuff from a luxury box at the new Falmer stadium a couple of years from now. No matter where his place is in the main stand at the community stadium, it will feel like a back seat." Shrewd observation, Brian.

Of course, Tony was right that the fans would be delighted when they heard that the stadium build would be going ahead and there would be no more hold-ups despite the credit crunch. Many who'd become my friends held a marvellous celebration dinner for me at Donatello's when I stood down and presented me with a superb crate of my favourite Italian red wine and the colourful pop art painting of me (featured on the front cover of this book) that hangs in Dick's Bar. None of the other directors were invited.

Tony was being presented as a man with a lifelong mission to pick up the mantle of his grandfather, Harry, and build the stadium. That was fine, but I thought the way I was treated left something to be desired. When I was offered the life president title, I naively assumed that my name would be at the top of the list of the club hierarchy in the match-day programme – as it is at all other clubs. I found myself nearer the kit man.

I'd talked to Kerry and my children, David and Amanda, after the first meeting when Tony made it clear that he wanted me to stand down. To no one else. Kerry felt that this had always been going to happen once Ray had come back and Tony had started putting money in the club. My kids hoped Tony would come round on the financial settlement, bearing in mind I'd given the club most of their inheritance. But I had no choice other than to accept his offer of £400,000, meaning I still had a lot of shares in the club for the future.

I'd lost potential allies on the board when Bob Pinnock retired, and when Chris Kidger left. He was a local guy who was the founder of the Friday-Ad empire and put in £500,000, the going rate for a seat on the board. I valued Chris greatly as a good businessman and a fair-minded guy who loved the Albion and never promised something he couldn't deliver. But he resigned after four years when he felt we should never trade at a loss because we could always trim the playing budget. I told him that football didn't work like that. We wouldn't have such a good team, gates and receipts would fall, we would lose out on quality players and would slip back down the leagues. And we needed to keep people coming to Withdean, so that we didn't lose the umbilical cord to the community for the future. But Chris found that my reasoning went against all his business instincts.

I was very sorry about that because, of all the people on the board at that time, I saw him as the best possible successor to me. He was sharp, intelligent, had a presence, a likeable way with people, and was Albion through and through. And he had the money if necessary, although it was unlikely he would need it to bail the club out in the way I had. I gave him an early indication of my thoughts, but it wasn't enough to persuade him to stay on. And from his objective position, I think he saw the writing on the wall with Ray's comments about the Bloom family building their links with the club.

As a result, not only was I not in a position to determine my successor, I was on the way out myself.

But it was plain to me that I could never have lived with myself if I had let the fans down by refusing to accede to Tony's demands. I knew that we could press forward, because Tony had shown that he had the wherewithal to do it.

And he had been hugely helpful to the club in the past few years. His family's history of involvement with the Albion was undeniable. I was not handing our fans' club to some imaginary sheik whose money would turn out to be as much of a mirage as he was, as Portsmouth had done. Or to a businessman who wanted to change the club's name, or colours, or move it to another city.

Tony's funding allowed us to move forward on the stadium straight away, although my certainty about the business plan meant I knew that his offer was never a case of 'Without my money the stadium will never get built', however anyone might have liked to present it as such. But I knew that to cause any further delay would not be fair on the club, its aspirations, the players and, above all, the supporters.

In the end, I let go for the sake of the fans.

Because, since that December day in 1946 when I first stood on the Goldstone's rainswept East Terrace to watch the Albion beat Mansfield Town 5-0, I have always been one of them.

# CHAPTER TWENTY NINE

# ONE KNIGHT STAND?

A fter I stepped down as chairman, I wasn't involved in the day-to-day running of the club or the building of the stadium any longer, but it wasn't as if I suddenly woke up every morning with nothing to do. I was still very much involved, as chairman of Albion in the Community.

There were two years between me stepping down and the opening of the stadium, but it didn't seem like any time at all. I was still working very closely with Steve Ford and Alan Sanders on something that was a vital part of the club, and we were full of ideas for ways to develop it for the benefit of the community and the image of the club – not the financial benefit.

I was invited to the press conference when Gus Poyet was announced as the successor to Russell Slade in November 2009 and met him beforehand in a suite at the Grand Hotel. He had obviously done his homework on the club, because he knew who I was and was very knowledgeable about the Albion story. He came across as proud, charismatic and intelligent, as he had when he played.

The only jarring note he struck at the time was in describing the Albion as "a fantastic stepping stone in my career". I don't like to hear anyone describing the Albion as a stepping stone. But on reflection, it was just Gus showing how ambitious he was, and it was that drive that took the club to new levels of quality performance and achievement. I could hardly blame someone for being ambitious.

He treated me with great respect, especially when he saw that I was around a lot and went to every game, home and away. And I was pleased when he chose Charlie Oatway to be his bridge to the first-team players as coach, and Charlie, of course, made sure that Gus appreciated what AITC was all about.

A word about Russell Slade, as hard working, honest and down-to-earth a football manger as ever you'll meet. He was never going to compete with Gus's charisma and was sacked by Brighton, but I was so pleased to see Russ having such great success at Leyton Orient at the start of the 2013/14 season when they had an amazing unbeaten run with two ex-Albion players, Dean Cox and Romain Vincelot, in the team. Barry Hearn has got a good one there.

I was up at Falmer pretty often even before the club's offices moved up there permanently. As the steelwork took shape, it was obvious that the stadium would look every bit as awe-inspiring as we had imagined when we produced the first visuals.

Every time I drove up there, it was like gradually filling in a painting-by-numbers image, as the frame was clad. From the roundabout on the University of Sussex side of the bridge over the A27, the view was an exact replica of the video I had made for the 1999 referendum campaign with Norman Cook's track *Right Here, Right Now* building up. Over the image through the trees to the empty field we gradually morphed on the stadium, looking like the spaceship in *Close Encounters of the Third Kind* landing, yet blending perfectly into the landscape. Unlike the proverbial Spanish hotel, this artist's impression was eventually finished and looked exactly like the architect's drawing.

Each stage of the stadium build was photographed every 15 seconds by the time-lapse webcam we had set up at the site, and there were regular hard-hat tours for supporters who were very happy just to walk around what was basically a building site. I went on several. We put on wellington boots, hi-visibility jackets and hard-hats and Martin Perry showed us how work was progressing.

A superb coffee-table book, *Stadium Yes!*, was produced showing every stage of the build, with photographs taken by Paul Hazlewood, the club photographer, Laura Collins, who was Martin's PA, and Graeme Rolf, a fan who worked near the stadium and regularly posted high-quality photographs on *North Stand Chat*, the fans' internet forum. Graeme also produced three calendars of stadium photographs, with some of the proceeds going to the Brighton & Hove Albion Collectors & Historians Society.

The stadium literally bears my signature. The supporters' bar is named 'Dick's Bar' and the sign on the wall outside is in my handwriting. I gave Laura a sample of my signature and they made the logo from that.

We had a few laughs about other possible places where my name could appear at Falmer. It was never going to be called 'The Stadium of Knight', because, as I knew more than anyone, we had to do a naming-rights deal. I mused with Derek Chapman that they might name a stand after me. Just one, I wasn't greedy – the 'One Knight Stand' perhaps.

I suppose it was a dilemma for the new regime: what, if anything, do they do to acknowledge my role? But the fans were delighted and the club were happy with the bar name, which was one I came up with. My first name is actually Harry, and there's the famous Harry's Bar in Venice. So why not Dick's Bar in Brighton? Even though the ambience and settings are pretty different.

We had always promised that the supporters would have their own special bar at the stadium because we owed it to them. There had been various discussions about the location; at one point a separate building that was going to house Brighton City College was suggested as a possible location. That building never materialised, so the bar would have to be within the stadium. It had to be the fans' own place, where they could decide what beers they had, for instance, and it needed a capacity of at least 250.

I remember arriving at Withdean one evening in November 2007 thinking I was a few minutes late for a FFA meeting I'd asked Martin to arrange, to discuss what we still had to do now that Hazel Blears had given us the final go-ahead. When I got there I found that Martin and Richard Hebberd, the chief operating officer, were in the middle of a heated exchange with the fans about the capacity of the proposed bar. Richard was quoting – you've guessed it – health and safety reasons why it could only hold around 130 people, and might have to be in the South Stand, the away fans' end.

I didn't like the mood of this meeting. Martin and Richard, whether they meant to or not, appeared to me to be talking down to these fans who had fought tooth and nail for the club. The attitude seemed to be that we were doing the fans a favour by giving them a bar, even though we'd promised it all along.

It was clear that the discussion had been going on for more than the five minutes I was supposedly late. I have rarely seen John Baine and Paul Samrah so angry and even the more mild-mannered members of the team were up in arms at the feeling that they were being patronised.

I said, "I don't know what's been said in this meeting, but here's the fact. We *will* have a bar in the stadium for our supporters, because they are special – and it *will* be along the lines of what we have already pledged to them. As chairman, you have my word." Richard then said, "You can't guarantee that" and quoted legislation about the area in square metres, to the decimal point, which each customer was allowed in a bar.

"Richard, don't start lecturing me," I said. "These people helped get the stadium. You will be in your shiny new job because of them. They will have a bar. And in the best and most sensible place, not tucked away in some corner. We will not short-change them."

In the end, the fans got most of what they wanted, although perhaps a sanitised version of it. John and Roy Chuter would have been involved in the choice of ales but, after I stood down, it was never likely to be turned into a real supporters' den, something a bit more down and dirty. That got lost somewhere along the way.

So it's not perfect – it is a semi-supporters' bar, with just a nod to the former chairman in the clever silvered portrait by Mike Payne, and the pop-art painting the fans gave me, which I donated. But John's poems *Goldstone Ghosts* and *Knighthood* are nicely prominent, and it's quite obvious that people like going in there before and after matches judging by the queues to get in. It's jammed on a match-day, with away fans mingling together with ours, and I frequently join them. It's exactly what I'd hoped would happen in our community stadium.

But before we could begin at Falmer, we had to say farewell to Withdean. It had attracted its fair share of criticism, especially from those – and that means everyone – who were soaked in its open seating, but the Albion had more success there in 12 years in terms of trophies and promotions than we had experienced in the previous 98. Of course, modesty forbids me to mention that the chairman for most of those 12 years might have been a factor!

And we left Withdean with our fourth promotion and third league title, as Gus Poyet's men picked up the League One trophy after the last Withdean match, a somewhat anti-climactic 3-2 defeat by Huddersfield Town.

I remember being asked by a reporter after that game for my reflections on the long stay at our so-called temporary home and my hopes for the future. I replied, "At Falmer, the Seagulls can really fly. At Withdean, we were just hovering with intent."

But no one should ever forget the role played by Withdean in our history. Without it our club would have died. Never mind how we would have managed if our exile in Kent had continued, we would have been expelled from the Football League if we hadn't returned to Brighton within three years. Of course, 12 years was much longer than we ever expected. And there is no doubt in my mind that we would never have been given permission to play there by the council if they had known we would be there that long. There would have been so much opposition.

We made the most of Withdean and it developed its own character, reflecting the idiosyncrasies of the club at that time – the ponchos, the Rocket Man, Palookaville, the nature reserve, the local resident who had the cheek to keep complaining about our presence even though we were already there when he moved in!

In most clubs, with directors and supporters it's a case of ne'er the twain shall meet. At Withdean, the twain not only met but bumped into each other, used the same toilets, walked to their seats along the same path and peered across the same running track to watch the game in the distance.

We had to develop a resilience, a hardiness. Fans developed their own match-day rituals, adopted favourite local pubs, learned to check the weather forecast carefully before setting off. They grew to respect the disciplines, got used to using public transport or the park-and-rides, buying tickets in advance. The fact that they showed they wouldn't park in the local streets if they were asked not to, helped us get the permission for Falmer. In that way Withdean was a blue-print, a 12-year-long dress rehearsal for the Amex, and the club learned a lot too, about ticketing, about transport policy and other procedures.

And there were wonderful memories. Bobby Zamora's great strikes, Michel Kuipers' penalty save against Manchester City, those important headed goals from Danny Cullip against Chesterfield, Lee Steele against Bristol City, Adam Virgo against Swindon. And serving champagne to the crowd against Ipswich.

So this stop-gap stadium became a wonderful part of our history. But now the Withdean residents would have to pick up their own litter and it was time for us to look forward.

First, though, there was one more unmissable piece of nostalgia – the revival of Paul Hodson and Dave Blake's play *Brighton 'Til I Die*, which was billed as 110 years of Albion's history in 110 minutes, a hilarious but also emotional trip through our club's story. First performed at the Gardner Arts Centre in 2001, when I also saw it, it was updated for the stadium opening in 2011 and staged on two nights at Brighton's Theatre Royal, one of the oldest and most prestig-ious theatres in the country. Paul Hodson had also co-compiled the well-received books *Build A Bonfire* and *We Want Falmer* with Steve North, one of the performers. The books chronicled the battles against Bill Archer and David Bellotti and for Falmer, and the theatrical shows were dedicated to the Falmer For All team.

We were invited to the second show, on Thursday July 28, just two days before the official opening of the Amex. I took Kerry and my best friend Geoff Watts and his partner Cheryl and we were given exclusive use of the Laurence Olivier bar. So after sipping free champagne among the ghosts of Vivien Leigh and Sir Larry himself before the bell rang for the first act, we made our way along the corridor to the Royal Box. When we emerged there was a thunderous wave of applause, and I waved back, suitably royally. Geoff loved it and waved too, while Kerry, who never seeks attention, was hugely embarrassed.

The old theatre was packed to the rafters, with a full house of almost 1,000 people, the atmosphere was of jubilant celebration and the show was fantastic. One of the highlights was Mark Brailsford, the creator of *The Treason Show* at Brighton's Komedia, performing *Seagulls Over The Rainbow* accompanied by solo banjo. The cast took four or five curtain calls and on the final one, after they had taken their bows to the audience, they all turned diagonally to their right, looked up, and bowed to me!

It was already an evening that would live with me, and was made even more indelible by the rapturous reception given to me – even from the stage. The audience raised the roof by a couple of inches. People who worked at the theatre told me that they were dumbfounded; apparently those hallowed portals had never heard cheering like it.

As the stadium reality got closer, everywhere I went people wanted to thank me. People were always coming up to me in the street for a chat anyway, but this was different, it happened more often and people were much more emotional. They said they were so grateful for the stadium and wanted to share their feelings about it with me. It carried on into that first friendly game at the Amex and has continued ever since.

The day of the official opening itself, two days later against Tottenham, was a glorious sunny summer day. I fought my way down through the crowds from the University of Brighton car park, where directors park, to the main West Stand reception to pick up a ticket for a member of my family. As I came out again I saw Norman and we hugged and had a long chat, interrupted at regular intervals by people who wanted their pictures taken with Fatboy Slim and me.

There was a celebration lunch being held in a big marquee on the university playing field near Falmer Station. Hundreds of fans were coming up the walkway, wanting to get to the stadium as early as possible, arriving from the station or from the city on foot, all of them travelling in the opposite direction from the one we were going in.

The lunch was due to start in 10 minutes when my niece Michele's husband, Nasser, began trying to shepherd me down to the marquee. I got talking to a group of young guys who could only have been about 10 when we had played the last game at the Goldstone, but they had been there that day, as they were telling me. It was lovely hearing their stories about how one of them had taken a bit of turf and it was still in his mum's back garden. Nasser was hovering, saying, "Come on, Dick, we've got to get down to the lunch."

But it took half an hour because I was inundated with fans who wanted to shake my hand, have their picture taken with me and tell me that they were so overjoyed that this day had finally arrived. There was a mood of euphoria.

The marquee was packed, just as Dick's Bar and the concourses were. The whole event was just right, with special presentations and moving speeches by Tony Bloom and Martin. Then we had to go back up to the stadium, with the tide this time, for the pre-match ceremonies.

Various Albion people went out on the pitch to be presented to the crowd, including former players and managers, and Tony, Martin, Derek Chapman and I were to go out last, to the centre circle. Tony and I were supposed to go out first, with the two teams lined up behind us ready to walk out. Typical of me, I started talking to someone – Brad Friedel, the Spurs goalkeeper, as I recall – so Tony ended up going out on his own with his little boy while I lagged behind.

But eventually I walked out in my new suit that Kerry had got me – I don't like wearing suits, but she had forced me to get this light grey Hugo Boss number – looking rather different from the other three, who were in dark suits and ties. It looked like *Reservoir Dogs* with me as Nice Guy Eddie.

My feelings right then were not what I had expected. The hard work had been getting the stadium, and now it was here – yet come the moment it was almost as if, yes it had been absolutely worth it, but I couldn't get worked up about it. We had done it and I was thrilled but it was almost too much to take in. Why didn't I feel more than I did?

Perhaps it was the distance from that centre circle to the crowd. We were the people who the spectators were cheering, but from my own perspective I was in a bubble. It was only when I left the pitch and went up to my seat in the directors' box in the huge West Stand, stood at the back surrounded by other fans, and could look out all around the arena at the sea of blue and white that I was able to join the emotion of the crowd. It welled up in me, an overwhelming sudden realisation, "We did it. We actually did it. After everything we've faced, I've got us through to this day."

It was 20,000 people united in a unique moment in time. Nobody there had felt that joy before. There was no other emotion being felt in the stadium. And then it really got to me and there was a tear or two.

Everyone around me felt the same, that this stadium had been part of their lives for as long as they could remember, before one brick had been put on another. And every fan had played a part. That made this place unique.

Harry Redknapp, the Tottenham manager, came and sat right behind me in the directors' box for the first half and said to me, "Well done, Dick. You must be a proud man today. You got there and all of football was on your side," before adding, "Who are your best players?"

I said, "Harry, we've got one who's exceptional. Defensive midfielder, No.26. Young, small guy, you'll recognise him. He's the nearest thing I've seen in English football to Claude Makelele."

After about 10 minutes, Harry leaned forward and said, "I see what you mean. Great vision and touch, and reads it so well – is he one of yours, come up through the youth system?"

'No, come on Harry,' I replied. 'You know players, I've given you a clue already, Makelele, Chelsea . . . his name's Liam Bridcutt, we signed him after they let him go.'

# ONE KNIGHT STAND?

Harry cupped his chin in his hand, "Yeah, now I remember, Bridcutt. Chelsea youth player. Blimey, you got a bargain there."

Harry and I were right, of course. Liam has been the best defensive midfielder in the Championship for the last two seasons and has made his full international debut for Scotland. I can't believe he won't play in the Premier League one day, hopefully with Brighton. And he told me some time ago that he'd modelled his game on Makelele, having watched him in training and been helped by Claude during their time together at Stamford Bridge.

The match was a training run-out, which Tottenham won 3-2, but afterwards the fans didn't want to leave. They wanted to relish the experience to the last drop, to enjoy the bars and the feeling of actually being at home again – and what a home – after 14 years of living rough.

And outside, I still couldn't walk 10 yards without fans wanting to talk, to get an autograph or a picture.It was clear the fans were not going to forget my role, not our fans, not after everything we had been through together. They knew that to get us home had taken all my determination and bloody-mindedness, not to mention a won't-give-up mentality, brains, and a bit of money. And an ability to lead people.

The people I led became an army, an irresistible force that overcame apathy, opposition, bureaucracy, frustration and a whole host of other obstacles that were put in our way. What makes that stadium unique is that it already had a history before a ball was kicked: the unprecedented struggle to actually get it built. A unity, a bond that was forged because of that struggle. A show of community strength. We were striving to reach a peak, and we made it.

We had written an incredible story, and all the people at that game, whether they were Albion fans, VIPs or even Spurs supporters, knew that story. The battle for the stadium has become folklore in English football. The Amex is a concrete example of what football fans can do when they rise up against mismanagement or worse. And it proved that fans will cross tribal boundaries and put aside traditional rivalries to help each other.

The stadium is a magnet for fans of all the other clubs who come to the Amex, many of whom played their own small part in securing planning permission. I've lost count of the number of times I've heard away fans say that to me in Dick's Bar. "We just wanted to come and see your stadium. We wrote letters and we signed petitions so we wanted to come and see what it was like now that you've got it." And most of them agree that it looks as stunning as we had always said it would, curving into the natural folds of the downland landscape.

We have a custom at the Amex of announcing the match attendance during the game, including the number of away fans who've come. Every time it's much more than their club's normal travelling army and, with one notable exception, always gets a huge round of applause. So, Brighton fans, why not for once break the habit of a lifetime and thank our so-called deadly rivals, the Crystal Palace fans, as well – they also helped the stadium campaign, remember?

We were proved right about a few things. I remember Mark Pougatch questioning why we needed a large stadium and suggesting that Withdean was big enough for us just before the 2004 play-off final. I'd like to know how he thinks we would have fitted our 26,000 average gates in 2012/13 in there. Or whether he'd like to interview our 23,000 season ticket-holders, who would have filled Withdean three times over. I knew that those fans were out there, waiting to return.

In the book *We Want Falmer*, Paul Hayward wondered what effect the whole struggle had done to me inside – having to pick myself up and carry on after every blow. But I always felt that I was not going to be beaten. I honestly never felt I would be broken by it.

My determination over the stadium was forged in my battle with Archer. The battle for Falmer was needlessly protracted and, in a fair world, the ridiculous hoops we had to jump through would never have been put in our way. With good people around me we got through every one. And I was never going to be beaten by red tape on something so important after I'd faced down Archer.

Our club would have died – no doubt about it. Nothing was ever going to faze me after I'd seen him off, although it took me long enough. We'd been through the darkest days – claiming the club back from people who would destroy it, hearing the Goldstone being dismantled around us, being one game and one goal from going out of the league, being sent away to Gillingham. I'd already faced the most ludicrous set of odds against me that any chairman can have faced. And I came through it.

No wonder this book is called *Mad Man*. No doubt some people thought I was crazy to take on what I did, but maybe that was what was called for. I was fighting madness with madness, blind stupidity with blind faith. And determination, or you could call it arrogance. I always thought we could outsmart them. And I always believed we had right on our side.

I've been asked whether I would go through it all again now that I know how much effort it was going to take. If somebody had come up to me after that last game at the Goldstone and told me, "It's going to take you 14 years to play another game in your own stadium," I'd have said, "I'm in the advertising business. We sell fantasies to people, achievable dreams. But that's ludicrous, unbelievable – much too far-fetched. It's not possible for it to take 14 years."

But if they'd then said, "But I'm blessed with the power of foresight. And I can tell you that it *will* take 14 years. And you'll face one battle after another to get you and the club to that promised land, that field of dreams. Now what are you going to do about it?"

I'd have said, "I'll make sure I win, then."

# DON'T GO CHANGING . . .

The Doncaster game at our glorious new home, of course, was everything we had all hoped it would be and more. I had referred to the 1997 game as 'desperate drama' but the 2011 version was pure theatre, as Albion went behind only to snatch victory with two late goals from new signing Will Buckley on his debut in front of a rapturous capacity crowd.

We'd come a long way from being a "millennium city without a millennium stadium," when the arguments for and against raged back and forth at Force 10 on the local emotional Richter scale.

The Amex was truly up and running, and under Gus Poyet the team went to the top of the table in September, as well as eliminating Premier League Sunderland from the League Cup before going out of the competition to Liverpool in front of another full house. (Late author's note: the defeat of Sunderland obviously did Gus's future job prospects no harm at all.)

In the end, the team fell just short of the 2012 play-offs, but the average attendances of just over 20,000 justified the installation of seating on the upper east side of the ground, which increased the capacity still further. The result was that the Albion attracted the highest average attendances outside the Premier League, 26,236, for the 2012/13 season – I always knew the crowds were there – when Gus Poyet's team reached the play-off semi-finals, only to suffer the crushing blow of losing at home to Crystal Palace.

In May 2013, during the build-up to the play-off second leg against Palace, I answered some questions posed by *Argus* readers. One asked how I had seen the club change since I stepped down.

I said, "When I was chairman I set the strategy and standards for the road to recovery, so seeing my vision for the club become reality, with the help of a tremendous bunch of people, was all part of the plan.

"As chairman of Albion in the Community, I am also proud of the way AITC has developed into one of English football's leading community schemes, again because of the hard work of good people, helping to improve other people's lives.

"But perhaps it's getting near time to call it a day on my 17 years' service to the club. Time to just sit back and watch Albion play, home and away. I've got a book to finish, my memoirs. Should be interesting."

But another reader asked if the Albion would lose its soul if the team won promotion to the Premier League. My answer was, "I hope not. I believe it's important for the club to remember where it has come from in a short space of time. Uniquely, our wonderful stadium had a unique story before a ball was kicked, because of the battle that was fought by the fans to win it. The soul of the club is founded in that culture and spirit."

Was I expecting too much by believing that that spirit would endure and that the club would remain true to those values? I think, perhaps, that I was.

Two months later I stepped down as chairman of Albion in the Community. According to *The Argus*, it was "amid concerns about the club's growing corporate image" and with "reservations about the direction the club is heading in".

Alan Sanders and Steve Ford had left AITC and I felt that the club had forgotten why that word 'community' was on the outside of the stadium after the words 'American Express.'

In answer to questions from my old sparring partner Andy Naylor, I said, "We keep hearing the club has to change and that the brand is all-important. But you have to understand what the brand is all about."

My point was: To change, and yet stay true to oneself. Of course the Albion should evolve into a Premier League outfit – where do you think I was aiming for? – but because of the club's history, most of the fans out there are not consumers, they have a personal and emotional commitment to the club which transcends any commercial relationship.

"You have to be careful that you don't lose your identity," I added. "With the Albion, that means keeping the right balance between community and corporate. The way they want to take AITC now is to be more like a corporate arm of the club. That is why this is the time for me to stand down."

It was in the same month, July 2013, that the University of Brighton conferred on me an honorary Masters of Arts degree, "in recognition of [my] major contribution to harnessing the power of sport for community benefit," in their graduation ceremony at the Brighton Dome. I sat alongside Lord John Mogg, chairman of the university's board of governors, and vice-chancellor Professor Julian Crampton on the top platform in my mortar board and gown in front of a packed audience of some 2,000 students and their families and listened to a tribute lovingly prepared by Peter Squires.

When I received my scroll, cries of "Seagulls, Seagulls" echoed around the auditorium, thereby laying to rest the concerns of Julian's predecessor, Sir David Watson, all those years earlier about our neighbourly incompatibility. I addressed the assembly, and in referring to AITC's role in helping the disadvantaged, concluded by saying: "This award is for all the highly dedicated staff who have ensured that Albion in the Community not only feels part of our city, but makes it beat faster."

It was a splendid affair with lunch afterwards at the Royal Pavilion and I got on famously with all the profs and especially Lord Mogg, who is also chairman of Ofgem and who enjoyed having his picture taken with him and me playing keepy uppy with a football – although I'm afraid I wasn't able to do anything about keeping down energy prices.

I must be doing something right, though, because just before this book went to press I was informed by Councillor Jason Kitcat, leader of Brighton & Hove Coulncil, that they are proposing to make me an honorary Freeman of the City at a ceremony in December 2013. Contrary to widespread belief, apparently this does not give me the privilege of running my sheep through the city. But wait a minute, remember I'm not a bad negotiator . . .

By then, the club had also parted company with Gus Poyet in the wake of the play-off defeat by Palace, suspending the manager who had transformed our style of play. He was the first manager since Steve Gritt that I had not appointed, but I grew to have a good relationship with him and felt the matter had not been handled as I would have done so.

"With Gus and the club, 'It started out with a kiss, how did it end up like this?' I've told Tony that I think it was unfortunate the club made the decision to publicly suspend the man that brought us the best football we have seen in years.

"The turmoil created has been damaging, both to the club and Gus, and I'm not sure it needed to happen like that. The club should have dealt with it in house. But at the end of the day, Tony is running the show now and he makes the decisions."

I felt it was sad for our club. The relationship between the manager and the chairman is the most important in any club, and I should know – I had to build that relationship a few times. With Gus that relationship seemed to change when the new chief executive, Paul Barber, arrived. Barber and Poyet may have had their differences, perhaps going back to their Tottenham days, but the buck stops with the chairman, and maybe Tony learned something from the whole unfortunate episode.

A casualty of the Poyet departure was Charlie Oatway, such a loyal club servant as player, AITC worker and coach, who was also suspended. He was in the middle of his testimonial year, and had promised to donate half of the proceeds to AITC – typical of the man, with a match against Liverpool to come.

I said, "That would probably have attracted a crowd of around 20,000 and AITC would have received something like £60,000 from that, which highlights Charlie's very generous offer, and that match has now been cancelled."

Charlie's suspension was still in the air. It had been over six weeks. "To deal with a true servant of the club in that way is absolutely wrong.

"They need to resolve the Charlie issue now and resolve it positively for him." No findings were ever made against him, but it was resolved with a parting 'by mutual consent'.

I received plenty of messages, both indirectly on messageboards and directly via letter or email. Some made direct reference to my parting comments, for example "Nail on head"; others were more general in their appreciation of my efforts for their club, our club.

They came from fans, club employees past and present, and even from former players. A couple even suggested a knighthood!

One summed it up rather nicely. "Thanks Dick. You and your bunch of trusted and true football fans at great personal expense saved the Albion, and fought a brilliant and ultimately victorious fight against the many enemies of football, to get the Albion to a beautiful new stadium. Your place in the club's future is assured forever."

Another simply said, "Thanks and good luck. You will be sorely missed." But I wasn't going away, just stepping down. Wherever the Albion were playing, I'd be there.

I'd watched them play at three different home grounds, four if Gillingham counts as a 'home'. I'd experienced unbelievable loyalty when fans like Barry Hemblade never gave up on us and bought season tickets for Gillingham even though work commitments usually stopped him going. I'd seen the Albion at almost a hundred different away grounds and I'd watched them in all weathers. I'd stood on the terraces, sat in directors' boxes, been locked out and had to go home and listen to them on the radio.

Was I going to pass up the chance to sit back and watch them play in the stadium that I and all our other fans had fought so long and hard to see become reality? Not a chance.

Sir Dave Richards, former chairman of the Football Foundation, visited the Amex in April 2013 and summed up my journey from its genesis. "Dick Knight came to see me. He wanted to build this stadium, his dream for Brighton, and we gave him the grant to get started. It was a fairly substantial one, but Dick was very persuasive and I'm delighted to be able to come and see the end result, it's fantastic."

Now, finally, I could go back to being a fan. Like all the others – John Baine, Paul Samrah, Tim Carder, Liz Costa, Sarah Watts, Ed Bassford, Roz South, Bill and Jan Swallow and all the FFA team and many more – I could forget about public inquiries, petitions, and publicity stunts and concentrate on fouls, free kicks and football. Instead of venting our frustrations with Nimbys, council officials and MPs, our targets would be referees and opponents who dive looking for penalties.

And there's another kind of football I'll be watching. The games my grand-children are playing in. Remember Max, who bawled when we scored in that first game at Withdean? He's now 15 and scoring goals for his Varsity team in Philadelphia, two years younger than the other players. His brother Louis, 13, is an out-an-out goal poacher, and if he took every chance he gets, he would notch up about 100 goals a season. In fact, last year he got three. (Only joking, Lou.) Their sister Daisy, 11, is trying to learn "soccer" but she keeps getting the giggles. Mum Amanda and dad John usually join in – the giggles, that is.

Over here, in Arsenal territory actually, Stoke Newington, grandson Sam, also 15 and even more handsome than me, is also doing a pretty passable imitation of Trevor Brooking's silky skills, while Natty, 11, runs like the wind for his school and club teams and is the Will Buckley of Hackney Marshes. Finally Emma, who survived that terrible illness when she was a baby, is really showing the boys up and is now captain of Arsenal under-13 girls' team. That's right, Arsenal. They played in a Premier League club tournament at Anfield and afterwards Em said to me, "You'll never guess who won it, granddad." It was Stoke City. Apparently they kept lumping long balls up to these tall girls up front.

In the summer of 2013, Emma's team represented England in a mini-inter-national tournament in Barcelona. They beat Spain, but lost the next game. However, someone watching was impressed. The great Johann Cruyff, no less, told Emma she was the most talented midfielder in the tournament. I don't think she realises why we're so proud of her. Mind you, while mum Jane takes it all in with her natural *sang-froid*, dad David still screams loudly at his kids during games, just like he used to at Withdean at Dean Hammond.

But in my view going back to being a fan should not mean becoming a passive observer, an outsider.

Most football fans raise their voices to jeer, chant and cheer, but otherwise, as I have said, their voices have not been historically listened to by those in charge of football clubs. Certainly that was the case at Brighton before I took over. But the voices of our fans have been heard in Town Halls, at CEDR and on the hustings, and in our boardroom. I hope they will continue to be heard by my successors.

Brighton & Hove Albion is a unique club where the fans played a unique role in making sure it has a future. Every club, but this club above all, must listen to its fans. Without them, what is the point of a football club? And without our fans, would there even be a Brighton & Hove Albion?

Which is why I want the fans to have my shares, so that their voices will always be heard at AGMs and elsewhere. So that future boards of directors can continue to take the club forward, keeping alive the traditions of the fans' voices being heard – which is actually what enabled our club to survive.

Directors should always be indebted to the fans – not the other way round. That is a tradition that this club, above all others, must maintain.

# OBSERVATIONS OF A FOOTBALL CHAIRMAN

## BETTER COACHES = BETTER PLAYERS. IF ONLY WE'D THOUGHT OF THAT

We've got a particular problem in this country regarding England not winning a major international tournament in the past five decades. There's huge media attention on the manager, of course, but if you stand back, that's not the reason we haven't won anything since 1966. The real reason is that it's all about our players' technique. That's down to the coaching, and the quality of it, therefore it's long-term and not an overnight solution, but much more should have been done about this basic need by now.

If you look at the most successful countries in Europe – Spain, Italy and Germany – the number of qualified coaches with the top UEFA badges (the B, A and Pro Licences) far exceeds the number in this country. Germany has over 35,000 UEFA coaches, in Italy it's over 30,000, Spain over 25,000. In England it's closer to 3,000. Whereas in those countries UEFA coaches are clearly at grassroots level – in Spain one for every 17 people playing the game – in England it's one UEFA-qualified coach for every 812 people playing the game. Therein lies the problem.

England has a promising bunch of young players at the moment and because they've been playing with foreign players, they've had some exposure to foreign technique. But under-21 and under-20 tournament results reveal that we are seriously adrift. Fundamentally, young English players are not getting the sort of quality coaching from a very early age that they should be, so that it's ingrained in them to be able to bring the ball under control easily with a touch of either foot, be aware of what's around them, and pass it quickly.

Some people say it's not the first touch that counts, it's the last, which is an interesting point of view if you're having sex. But in football if the first touch is no good, then you are likely to lose the ball and are therefore not able to make a telling last touch.

The unbelievable media hype is another problem. Take the 2006 World Cup in Germany, which I attended. England went there with the highest of hopes because the Lampards, the Gerrards, the Beckhams and so on were told that they were the 'Golden Generation'. They were a decent squad of players but they went there virtually expecting to win it. With the hype and then of course the WAGS getting more media attention than the players, everyone was in totally the wrong frame of mind to go into a tournament like that. We were never really in with a chance.

Eriksson, McClaren, then Capello have all been blamed for England failures, while Roy Hodgson carries our dreams to Brazil having qualified England for the 2014 World Cup. But whoever is the England manager, if he's got a squad of 25 really top-quality players, all tuned in to the same playing philosophy – as Spain have – he's got a chance of making a decent team. If he's only got three or four, he's got no chance.

How do we alter that? I think there's got to be a change in the squad structure of club football, and it has to start with the Premier League. Their clubs should have a minimum quota of English players in a match-day squad of 18. Six is not an unreasonable number in my opinion, with three playing sometime in the game. That will mean all the top clubs are developing English players properly because they know they have got to produce them and play them.

Any Premier League game is played at a higher tempo than a match in the other senior leagues in the world. So in fact, the technique required is of a higher standard. No wonder English players are missing out, especially as their transfer fees are normally higher than for overseas players. It's easier and cheaper to bring in a foreign player, who is usually more talented.

If the English national game is to thrive, the FA's expensive coaching centre, St. George's Park, won't suffice alone. A centre for the elite is fine, but it doesn't address the issue of regularly producing a wide seam of quality young players across the country. I believe Premier League clubs themselves should ensure that a lot more planning and money goes into the development of top coaches, as well as young players.

The Elite Player Performance Plan, introduced by the Premier League in 2011 and reluctantly accepted by Football League clubs against the threat of losing their youth scheme funding from the top tier, is more geared to predatory Premier League clubs snapping up all the best youngsters from smaller teams. And maximum compensation is now less than one 10th of the sum I was able to win at the Gareth Barry tribunal. There is no mention – or emphasis on – producing more top coaches, which a Premier League English player quota system would demand.

Otherwise that league will become merely a showcase for overseas stars, while the English game at grassroots level is moribund. The Premier League should be the dynamic for change, setting an example, inspiring coaches with the message that, as in all forms of learning, the quality of football education depends entirely on the quality of the teachers.

# WHY TRANSFER WINDOWS SHOULD BE SHUT – PERMANENTLY

I am against the present system of transfer windows. I think we should go back to the old system of having an open transfer period through the season up to a late March deadline date.

The January transfer window is especially artificial. Clubs desperate to avoid relegation or to improve their chances of promotion are forced to concentrate their transfer activity into such a small time period that it should really be called the 'final week of January panic sale' transfer window. In reality most business does not start getting done until then, with clubs unwilling to let players go until they have secured their own targets.

Even in the last minutes before the window shuts, clubs are desperate to get deals done, which is great for Sky TV, ticking the clock down. I remember my own nerve-shredding sale of Dean Hammond one January 31 evening, but many a club and player have been thwarted by last-minute hitches – medical records not arriving, international clearance delays – scuppering fingers-crossed deals.

In the retail world, the January sales are all about getting good quality merchandise, but cheaper. In football, the opposite applies – the January transfer window is a licence to treble prices for goods of doubtful value. What club is going to let a good player go in mid-season?

The same is true of the summer window too. Arsenal overspent in 2011 because they needed to reinforce quickly before the window closed. And Real Madrid took advantage of Arsenal's urgent need to make a marquee signing before the end of the August 2013 window by bumping up the price for Mezut Özil.

The way the loan system works now is a reaction to the transfer window system. Clubs effectively sign players by taking them on loan with a view to a permanent signing when the window opens. And to my mind there is no doubt that the sheer volume of loans is a direct result of the restricted buying periods.

Certainly transfer windows should not apply to the Football League. They were originally brought in to establish stability in the Premier League, preventing the rich clubs from snapping up all the best players prior to the March deadline.

Now, inexorably, the super rich are doing that more and more – in the transfer windows – and that rarely involves a Football League club.

Transfer windows are a godsend to agents – it's feeding frenzy time, because they can earn enough money to last the rest of the year. Prices are forced up and that takes more money out of football and into their pockets. If there was an open transfer market, deals would be done in a logical way according to true market values, and squad strengthening would take place naturally during the season according to a team's needs.

This is a meaningful issue for new FA chairman Greg Dyke to get his teeth into now – rather than the vainglorious attempt to improve the England team's fortunes, which as I have just argued is all down to the quality of coaching and will take years to rectify. I've done football business with Greg and know he's straightforward, honest and tells it like it is.

If he is up for it, shaking Sepp Blatter and FIFA out of their complacency would be doing world football a great service.

## FOOTBALL AND TELEVISION – THE FUTURE

On the talkSPORT *From the Boardroom* programme I did in July 2000 I gave my take on how the global game would be influenced more and more in the future by television. I had been very close to Rupert Murdoch's organisation in the '80s when Sky TV was launched – my ad agency handled *The Times* newspaper account and did development work for News International – and I knew that live football on traditional (terrestrial) TV was not only limited but extremely cheap to the broadcasters.

It was obvious to me that paying significantly increased sums to the rights-holders (ie the FA, the leagues and the clubs) to allow more live football was the fastest way subscription satellite TV could grow in the UK – while still being far less costly for Sky than competing head-on against the core BBC and ITV strengths of comedy, drama and entertainment. And that was the development strategy the satellite station embarked on.

By the start of the noughties, we had already seen how Sky's millions were shaping and driving the Premier League but I forecast that was only the start. Aware that Murdoch planned to further expand his broadcasting empire across Europe, Asia and the USA, I said that global satellite TV was the perfect means of bringing the game live to both developed and undeveloped football nations, such as China and North America.

I predicted that one day there would be a World Club Championship where Manchester United wouldn't be playing Manchester City (this was before they became rich), but Shanghai City, the LA Soccer Dream Team, and other new super clubs in major cities, created by the global TV market, to go up against established giants like Real Madrid, Juventus and Boca Juniors.

Maybe I was a little premature as far as new worldwide super clubs are concerned, but alongside the relentless TV-fuelled growth of the UEFA Champions League, I was hardly surprised by a *Guardian* front-page story (June 15 2013) headlined: "Murdoch plans global contest for football's top clubs." The article stated that Murdoch's global broadcasting company is exploring an ambitious plan to create a summer footballing competition from 2015 featuring Europe's top clubs "with matches to be played in cities from Los Angeles to Shanghai". Matches would be aired on Sky and by Murdoch's other broadcasters worldwide in Italy, Germany, Asia and the USA …

As I said on talkSPORT in 2000, "That's where television and football are headed and it's a long way from Brighton & Hove Albion." But it didn't mean we shouldn't be aware of it.

## ANOTHER KIND OF SUPPORTER

Not every football fan is born to be a campaigner. But that doesn't mean they love their club any the less. They show their dedication in other ways – usually by giving as much financial support as they can possibly afford.

I'm not just talking about local companies who sponsor matches, players' kit, the match ball, put ads in the programme and around the pitch, although to my everlasting gratitude we had plenty of those from the time I took over, doing their bit to help the Albion. I never wanted to sponsor corners, throw-ins, even added time, as some clubs do, because I never wanted to appear that desperate in the cause we were fighting for.

I'm talking about individuals. People who came forward when we returned to Brighton, to buy every bit of club hospitality, home and away, that they could (virtually no one splashed out on hospitality at Gillingham, because they kept all the proceeds).

We were squeezing as many tables as 'elf 'n' safety' would allow into the limited Portakabin hospitality area at Withdean, and one group of supporters seemed naturally to come together. Some of them knew each other, some were strangers, they had different kinds of jobs, but they all wanted to have a good time watching the Albion. Martin Perry called this disparate group who were going on one big table 'the odds and sods', and the name has stuck ever since. They even have their own Seagulls shirts, proudly displaying their 'Odds'n'Sods' moniker, which they wear at matches.

These guys were 100 per cent genuine Albion fans, but unlikely ever to man the barricades. Because my great friend, Geoff Watts, was one of them, I got to know, and grow very fond of, them all, and there are some real characters in the group.

Larger-than-life Steve Darby is the most jovial person I've ever met, with a heart of gold and a cheeky quip for everyone he bumps into.

Once, when they were at an away match at Swindon, Steve was chatting to Willie Carson after the game, then followed him out of the hospitality lounge to return soon after with a bulging black bin bag tied at the top, telling Willie to "be still and stop complaining" and that he'd let him out soon. Only Steve could get away with that in front of all those Swindon supporters. After Willie came back to the boardroom and told me what had happened, I decided to pop down to the lounge to restore some Brighton-chairmanly order to the proceedings, only to make a complete fool of myself when, after chatting to the fans, I went to make a dignified, statesman-like exit, opened the door and walked straight into a broom cupboard. Cue hilarity from the Odds'n'Sods, showing true respect for their chairman.

They are a great bunch of guys, united in their love of the club. They have their own chairman, Terry Boyle, who tries to restore order but Geoff – stubborn as a mule – Steve, Bob Martin, Dave Bryant, Steve Bristow, Simon Kay, Richard Heath, Paul Brogden, Geoff's son Matthew, Dave's son David, and the rest, have some pretty lively debates over who played well or badly, and over who owes what for the drinks.

And I should make special mention of another member of the group. Since I stood down as chairman of the club, Phil Bath has been on at me constantly to write my memoirs, to make sure I put on the record everything that happened, so that future generations understand and that the story is not lost forever.

Thanks for your persistence, Phil. As you read these pages, I hope you feel that it was worth it.

# EXPRESSION OF INTEREST

If you're interested in owning some of my shares in Brighton & Hove Albion – the shares that saved the club – let me know how many you think you might like to buy. Don't worry, you're not committing yourself to anything at this stage!

Send this form to me at (c/o Vision Sports Publishing, 19-23 High Street, Kingston upon Thames, Surrey, KT1 1LL) along with the 'Invitation' token that you'll need to cut from the inside front cover flap of this book. And at the same time, tell me some of your own story as an Albion fan.

I'll be in touch.

Name: ......................................................................................................

Address: ...................................................................................................

...................................................................................................

E-mail: ....................................................................................................

Indication of how many shares you would like to buy.

Each share is valued at £1: ...........................................................................

A brief synopsis of your Albion-supporting history
(continue overleaf if required):

......................................................................................................

......................................................................................................

......................................................................................................

......................................................................................................

......................................................................................................

......................................................................................................

......................................................................................................